LAW AND ORGANIZATION IN WORLD SOCIETY

LAW AND ORGANIZATION

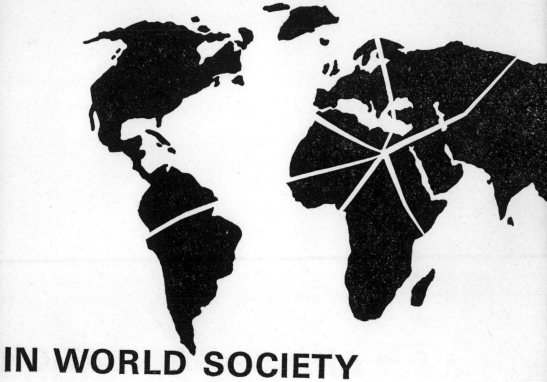

IN WORLD SOCIETY

KENNETH S. CARLSTON

University of Illinois Press, Urbana, 1962

After an extended reading of a fairly considerable body of literature in the social sciences, the author has reached the conviction that some common unifying themes must be found in them as a basis for their further growth. The splitting up of social science into a number of separate disciplines, each with its own terminology and each with a horizon beyond which few of its scholars penetrate, has its own virtue and necessity. The mastering of the extraordinarily vast body of data found in the social aspects of our complex, intricate culture would not otherwise be possible. It has enabled investigation to be empirically based and to develop ever new insights. It has brought forth highly respected and valuable contributions. Yet the flow of a massive river into a network of channels in its delta dissipates its energy and clogs its channels, as the force of the current no longer can carry its sediment. So it may be with the social sciences. There is a need for patterns of unification among them, as well as for continued individual growth.

To see the need is also to see the possibility; to see the possibility is eventually to create the reality. Interdisciplinary exploration has been attempted in the social sciences. A great deal of it has not been fruitful. It must be remembered, however, that at times more can be learned from an experiment which fails than from one that succeeds. For example, scholars in one discipline can most successfully adventure in other disciplines as a means of enriching their own. But to place a scholar from one discipline into an intellectual venture in another discipline is often to subject him to frustration.

There are phases of every discipline which can benefit from findings in others. Scholars may be exploring a problem in one which is duplicated in different terms in another. Scholars from a number of disciplines are at times investigating different aspects of the same problem.

The writer found the concept of the organization to be most fruitful for exploring the nature and province of law from the standpoint of the disciplines of sociology, psychology, including social and group psychology, anthropology, public administration, and business management. In his *Law and Structures of Social Action* (1956), he attempted to synthesize the results of his investigation as they bore on a number of aspects of law and legal theory. With its completion, the author saw the need to carry his study forward to a greater degree of conceptualization, organization, and synthesis. New perceptions and knowledge were needed; they were needed in the form of a statement of theory. How was a breakthrough to be achieved?

One of the common difficulties of intellectual ventures into broad syntheses and new methodologies is that they read well as prescriptions for action, but may be never or only poorly carried forth in action. Even though the failure may at times be a magnificent one, it still remains a failure.[1] It seemed imperative, therefore, that the author's next attempt to make a forward step should squarely place itself in the world of reality and set before itself a concrete problem in human affairs. Such a problem would be a starting point for a statement of theory, a means for its testing, and a basis for its application.

At the same time, the theory itself was yet to be stated. Only the necessity of the task of its formulation was seen at this stage. Any statement of theory must be comprehensive and detailed in its own terms. It must have its own standpoint and its own resultant content. As Professor R. S. Lynd said: "The controlling factor in

---

[1]See F. S. C. Northrop, "Underhill Moore's Legal Science: Its Nature and Significance," 59 *Yale L. Jour.* 196 (1950).

any science is the way it views and states its problems. Once stated, a problem yields no further insights than are allowed by the constricting frame of its original formulation."[2]

The impact of nationalization on concession agreements was chosen as the specific or concrete problem of study because nationalization, an act of a highly national character, was here confronted with the concession agreement, an instrument of a profoundly international character. Nationalization in its international impact tapped problems of organizational behavior and conflict which promised new bases and insights for stating and testing theory. The topic had the drama and the unique configurations of the geological structure and accompanying conditions which in nature produce the geyser. It was of the same explosive character on the surface and it was produced by social forces as deep seated and massive as the physical forces which create the geyser. Its impact on the world society presented a number of facets which demanded exploration. Professor Julius Stone has said that: "One problem discriminatingly chosen and explored in sufficient detail on a broad enough canvass, might yield results concerning the operation of the norms of international law which would cast light far beyond the problem."[3] Burckhardt has remarked that: "A single happily chosen source can to a degree replace a boundless number (unendlich Viele) of them, since through a simple function of his mind (the inquirer) finds and experiences the general in the singular."[4]

The scholar in international law would ordinarily confine his exploration of the nature of concession agreements to their legal nature, that is to say, to the ways in which they have been categorized for the purposes of legal doctrine.[5] Chapter II, however, embodies a factual inquiry into the character and function of concession agreements in the national and international economies, respectively. The inquiry brings to the surface a number of important points which might otherwise have been overlooked. The

---

[2] Quoted in G. Niemeyer, Law Without Force, 18 (1941).

[3] J. Stone, "Problems Confronting Sociological Enquiries Concerning International Law," Académie de Droit International, 89 Recueil des Cours 66, 146 (1956, pt. 1).

[4] Quoted in ibid., 146.

[5] T. T. F. Huang, "Some International and Legal Aspects of the Suez Canal Question," 51 Am. J. Int. Law 277 (1957).

typical pattern in a free enterprise state of the relation of the individual to the land, that of ownership, is found to be wanting for purposes of the exploitation of mineral resources in an industrially organized society. Since minerals are economic resources scattered in random patterns throughout the world, yet used in coordinated patterns as demanded by national economies, the international role of the concession agreement, and the international character of the joint corporate and state enterprise which it constitutes, are brought to the fore.

Chapter III carries forward the study of mineral economics in the world economy and reveals the mineral interdependency of industrialized and underdeveloped nations. It points to the importance of an international approach to the solution of some of the national problems of underdeveloped nations which rely on the export of minerals and other basic commodities to international markets as a means for achieving national welfare. It is seen that the failure of the international economy to provide a stable environment for such national growth is one of the causes of nationalization.

Chapter IV reveals that nationalization, as resorted to by underdeveloped nations, is a product of national social structures of a fairly consistent pattern. These states might well be termed "veneer" states, for they present to the world a veneer of development into viable, modern societies, although a larger part of their people live in an earlier stage of cultural development. The stress created by the unstable and imperfect integration and adaptation of these states, notably, their failure to provide adequate means for value realization by a large part of their population, is found to be a principal cause of resort to nationalization.

Chapters V and VI, together with the first eight propositions of Chapter VII, represent a statement of a theory of law and organization in the world society. It is set forth in a series of interdependent principles and propositions (see principle 8.a. of Chapter VI), which are to be read as an entirety and as consistent with one another. They embody a search for structure in the world society, for the values which influence action therein, for the types of social action and social structures which are required to bring order to the world society, and for the province and function of law therein.

The words of Dean Pound in 1923 concern the demands to be made on the international law jurist of the future:

Among the new philosophies of action or those which succeed to them the jurist of the immediate future, thinking of a great task of social engineering, as it were, whereby the conflicting or overlapping interests and claims and demands of the peoples of this crowded world may be secured or satisfied so far as may be with a minimum of friction and a minimum of waste, must find the basis of a new philosophical theory of international law. We shall not ask him for a juristic romance built upon the cosmological romance of some closed metaphysical system. But we may demand of him a legal philosophy that shall take account of the social psychology, the economics, the sociology as well as the law and politics of today, that shall enable international law to take in what it requires from without, that shall give us a functional critique of international law in terms of social ends, not an analytical critique in terms of itself, and above all that shall conceive of the legal order as a process and not as a condition.[6]

Dean Pound's ideal image is one shared here. It was the starting point of this venture, though its goal may still be eluded. Chapter VI endeavors to find the province and role or function of law in the world society. While the relevance of the findings made in these chapters to nationalization is from time to time indicated, they necessarily constitute an independent intellectual enterprise. They are intended to provide a background in which new insights into political and legal problems in the international arena might be found.

The ninth and tenth propositions of Chapter VII examine the impact of nationalization upon concession agreements with foreign investors from the legal standpoint. The analysis of the problem is, as far as possible, brought within the framework of theory set forth in Chapters V and VI and the first eight propositions of Chapter VII. It represents an attempt both to state the relevant law and to indicate a methodology for the solution of the problem. The first four chapters and the last two propositions of Chapter VII illustrate the functional manner in which international legal questions should be investigated and stated. Chapter VIII is a statement in the most universal terms of the theory of law expressed in the text.

An investigation of the meaning of the term, "nationalization," will be made. Nationalization has been used as an instrument for restructuring, in a substantial degree, the national economies

---

[6]R. Pound, "Philosophical Theory and International Law," 1 *Bibliotheca Visseriana* 73, 89 (1923).

of many states, ranging from relatively conservative, industrialized states, such as Great Britain and France, to industrially under-developed states, such as Burma and India, and finally to states fully dedicated to Communism, such as Russia and China. It has been described by Foighel as "one means among many towards the solution of economic-political problems in countries differing widely as regards geographical position, form of government, and ideological basis of the individual governments." The essential characteristic of nationalization, including the subtle and indirect measures of "creeping nationalization," is that it marks a step whereby the government of a state enters into, and assumes direct control and authority over, a substantial portion of the economic life of the state by displacing the control over private property by its owners.

The study as a whole represents the author's conviction that the investigation of problems in international law is just begun when the statement and analysis is made of the legal doctrine in accordance with the shared methodology of positivism. The rule which the international legal scholar reaches from his search of the legal materials cannot be viewed in isolation from its appropriateness as a functional rule toward reaching desired goals in the international order and as an embodiment of cultural values and ethical principles. The practice of states in their relations with one another, as evidence of rules of law, must be evaluated from the standpoint of the suitability of the rules thus indicated for promoting the viability of the international order and the opportunity of its actors to realize important values by participation in that order. This demands an intensive investigation of the underlying social, economic, and political aspects of the international legal problem under investigation. To fail to do so is to deny to law and the legal process the opportunity to perform in full measure their proper function.

Poincaré has said that every generalization is a hypothesis which should as soon as possible be submitted to verification.[7] Even if it should not be verified, we are still one step nearer in our search for ultimate truth. So it is with the "hard case" in law, such as nationalization. As has often been said, it may lead to bad law. On the other hand, it can also be availed of, similarly to the experiment which renders sterile a hypothesis, to push forward our

---

[7] J. H. Poincaré, *The Foundations of Science*, 150-152 (1913).

knowledge of the law and to state its doctrines with greater truth and relation to reality. It is the lawyer's fate, no less than that of any man, to search continually for the truth. For if, in the words of Plato, law is "the leading string, golden and holy," which binds a society together, then the pattern of its golden skeins reveals the structure of the society itself. As it is the scientist's faith that there is an ultimate symmetry, order, and truth in nature, so it is the lawyer's faith that the body of law will express the full image of the society which it unites.

It may well be that the image of the international society as a society of separate and independent nations, an image still held by the systems of public and private international law, no longer adequately reflects the true nature of that society. Yet we who are tossed about in the churning revolutionary forces of our time find it difficult to see the pattern of those forces and to create a new image which will encompass them and give them order. Perhaps a historical perspective will bring some measure of order and understanding. The technology of agriculture, transportation, communication, and war of the Middle Ages meant that order under law could be achieved in the highly localized patterns of the man-lord relationships of feudalism. But when man learned to coordinate his action through organization, when the countryside was transformed into a burgeoning industrial society and the sea became the scene of a new technology of transport and war, the order of feudalism ceased to be appropriate and was supplanted by the integrating force of the nation-state.

Today a political and legal order channeled through the nation-state finds it increasingly difficult to provide law as a "leading string, golden and holy" for the international order which is becoming so central to our lives. A system of public and private international law cast in the image of a society of nation-states finds it increasingly difficult to support the life of an expanding international society. States, as focal points in the growth of customary public international law, proliferate in number. Whereas the principal actors of the nineteenth century were relatively few states sharing essentially a common culture and type of social structure, today our political world is fragmentizing into an extraordinary number of states, which in turn reflect the widest variations in culture, political maturity, and economic and social development. In this context, we find many states assuming governmental control over much, if not substantially all, of their economic life. Yet this economic life no longer functions in isolation behind state borders, but is profoundly a part of an international system of action. Thus we find the thrust of increasingly dispersed political sovereignty moving into our international economy. Stated otherwise, the centripetal economic forces of the world are increasingly in conflict with its centrifugal political forces.

To bring order through law to the world society, as so constituted, the positivist view of public international law still postulates the nation-state to be subject to no law other than that based on the consent or practice of states generally. Yet consensus of state practice will become increasingly difficult to identify as states proliferate in number and move apart in ideology. Private international law, as a means for the resolution of private controversy in the world society, has no content other than that of technique—at times seemingly a *mystique*—for the selection of some one of the systems of law of the several states as a basis for decision. For a world society which with increasing desperation seeks to protect its order under law, the existing assumptions of public and private international law become more akin to feudal law at the emergence of industrial society. The nation-state is today faced with Bracton's command to the medieval sovereign: "Let the king, then, attribute to the law what the law attributes to him, namely, dominion and power, for there is no king where the will and not the law has dominion."[8] The nation-state today, proclaiming a sovereign supremacy of its will over law, discovers that there can be no effective exercise of sovereignty in the national weal when the separate wills of all, and not the law over all, have dominion.

To find the place and function of law in the provision of order in the world society is the ultimate concern of this study. In the words of Michelangelo, here are found the author's "bright things of heaven."

> With so much servitude, with so much anguish,
> And with false concepts periling my soul,
> Sculpt I must, here on earth, bright things of heaven.

KENNETH S. CARLSTON

Urbana, Illinois
September, 1961

---

[8]H. de Bracton, 2, *De Legibus et Consuetudinibus Angliae*, 33, fol. 5b.

ACKNOWLEDGMENT

Portions of the text appeared previously in the *Northwestern University Law Review*, the *American Journal of International Law*, and the *Proceedings of the American Society of International Law*. Permission to print the same is gratefully acknowledged. The author is indebted to Professor Wesley L. Gould of Purdue University, Indiana, who read the manuscript with care and gave many helpful suggestions.

CONTENTS

INTRODUCTION:
NATIONALIZATION

Nationalization of concession agreements with foreign investors is both the starting point and the terminal point of this intellectual venture. It is the concrete, behavioral, factual level from which begins an exploration into a theory of world society. It provides the means for testing and applying theory.

This exploration has two levels of approach. First, there are the statements of general theory set forth in Chapters V, VI, and in the first eight propositions of Chapter VII. These statements are of considerable breadth and scope. They were inductively arrived at from a consideration of relevant knowledge in the social sciences and jurisprudence. Second, there are the statements concerning the specific problem of the termination by states of concession agreements with aliens as a consequence of nationalization measures. These are designed to assist in creating and validating general theory and to indicate how a complex problem in international law should be explored functionally, as well as from the standpoint of legal doctrine. The first four chapters provide a definitional and factual background for the second level of approach. They enable an understanding and evaluation of the legal problem to be reached from the social, economic, and political standpoints. The last two propositions of Chapter VII delineate the answer to the legal problem and demonstrate how an international legal problem may be handled when a value approach is used conjointly with positivist international law methodology. From time to time, reference to the underlying legal problem of nationalization of concession agreements is made in the statement of general theory in Chapters V and VI. Thus, there is an interweaving of the levels of general theory and applied theory.

The methodology used seemed imperative, if any significant breakthrough were to be achieved. The manipulation of symbolic knowledge may produce useful creative ideas in certain areas of the physical sciences. The social sciences, law, and jurisprudence have, however, not yet reached that level of maturity and sophistication. They employ induction and conjecture to create knowledge no less than does nuclear physics today. The subject matter or knowledge upon which their theory building operates is, however, of a profoundly different character. They are largely constrained to build theory in what might be termed the middle range of knowledge. A considerable part of the knowledge upon which theory in the social sciences builds is quite concrete. For example, the typical behaviorist works with narrow sequences of action and few actors to reduce his variables to manageable proportions and to reach results of a highly empirical character. By and large, however, the information upon which theory is built is of a broader and more inconclusive character, but it is, nevertheless, information which enables a fairly satisfactory degree of plausibility or validity to be reached as a consequence of induction and conjecture.[1]

This chapter makes as clear as possible the meaning of the concept of nationalization and its impact upon concession agreements as a matter of legal analysis.

Above everything else, nationalization is to be understood to

---

[1]See G. Polya, 1, *Mathematics and Plausible Reasoning* (1954): "Strictly speaking, all our knowledge outside mathematics and demonstrative logic (which is, in fact, a branch of mathematics) consists of conjectures. There are, of course, conjectures and conjectures. . . . We secure our mathematical knowledge by *demonstrative reasoning*, but we support our conjectures by *plausible reasoning*. A mathematical proof is demonstrative reasoning, but the inductive evidence of the physicist, the circumstantial evidence of the lawyer, the documentary evidence of the historian, and the statistical evidence of the economist belong to plausible reasoning."

fall in the sphere of property. An act of nationalization affects property relations in two successive phases. First, it brings to an end those legal relations upon which the private direction and control of the use of a category of property rested. Second, it substitutes in their place a new aggregation of legal relations establishing a new institutional framework of direction and control of such property which is located in the government of the state. With the enactment of the law of nationalization, it is typically postulated that the carrying out of such law within the territory of the state is merely a matter of executive detail and judicial enforcement. When the legislative act is so viewed, there are no troubling problems of clashes with other social systems, state or international, or their relevant systems of law.

The neat, exact pattern of nationalization set forth in the preceding paragraph is seldom, if ever, found. Nationalization is an act of a profoundly national character, which also almost always has international repercussions. It is substantially impossible to restrict a nationalization so that its consequences will be exclusively confined to persons who are nationals residing within the state, whose expropriated property was exclusively theirs under the law of the state and was at all times located entirely within the territory of the state. The commingling of numerous nationalities within the borders of any one state, the international dispersion of credit and equity interests, the movement of goods in international trade, the coordination of international trade through the international contract and corporation, the intangible character of numerous property interests, among other things, render it difficult for one state to accomplish the nationalization of any considerable body of property without affecting the interests of other states and their nationals. Few large-scale or general nationalizations have taken place without their consequences becoming of concern to other states and the regulation thereof becoming the subject matter of diplomatic negotiations and a concern of international law.

The formulation of a precise definition of nationalization is a difficult task, as the discussions in 1952 of the Institut de Droit International reveal.[2] The definition of nationalization tentatively adopted by the Institut was as follows: "Nationalization is the transfer to the State, by a legislative act and in the public interest,

---

[2] *44 Annuaire de l'Institut de Droit International* 279 *et seq.* (1952, pt. 2).

of property or private rights of a designated character, with a view to their exploitation or control by the State, or to their direction to a new objective by the State."[3]

It must be admitted that nationalization has been used in too widespread a variety of situations to have a clearly defined content. A brief definition is that nationalization includes measures transferring a defined category of property to the state for the purpose of direct control by it in the exercise of a public purpose.

Two principal distinguishing features of nationalization are that it is widespread in its application to property and that it reflects strong political or economic motivations. Foighel[4] says that "nationalization may be defined as the compulsory transfer to the state of private property dictated by economic motives and having as its purpose the continued and essentially unaltered exploitation of the particular property."

G. M. White classifies nationalization measures as political in nature, exemplified by nationalization in the Eastern European states during the period 1945-50, or as nationalistic in nature, in which foreign capital is eliminated by a state in order to achieve greater autonomy. The Suez nationalization was characterized as motivated by financial and political considerations.[5]

Nationalization, in the view of Fawcett,[6] comprehends the transfer to the state of private property in the carrying out of national economic policy. It may be effectuated by either confiscation or expropriation. He distinguishes between expropriation and confiscation of property by the state on the basis that the former involves the payment of compensation while the latter does not. He further points out that "the state may interfere with or restrict the use and disposal of private property by managerial direction; currency and payments control; import and export restrictions; control of the use of raw materials by licenses or quotas; and other forms of *dirigisme*, which have been called 'creeping nationalization.'"

In the view of some, nationalization involves the assumption by

---

[3]*Ibid.*, 283, translation by author.

[4]I. Foighel, *Nationalization: A Study in the Protection of Alien Property in International Law*, 19 (1957).

[5]G. M. White, *Nationalization of Foreign Property*, 19-27 (1961).

[6]J. E. S. Fawcett, "Some Foreign Effects of Nationalization of Property," 27 *British Yearbook of International Law* 355-356 (1950).

the state of control over property to such an extent that the state itself may be said to have assumed new properties or characteristics.[7] In this sense, nationalization is said to be no longer merely the step by which a substantial degree of property of a productive character moves from the private to the public sphere of control. It is not viewed as part of the traditional historical pattern of expropriation or confiscation in the exercise of a public purpose. It is instead seen as a reflection of a new and unique view of property and an instrument for bringing about the social and economic transformation of states. When its exercise possesses such an ideological foundation and subject matter, it is thought to be a supreme executive act of the sovereign not subject to any judicial control.[8]

Whether "nationalization" is employed to indicate a special meaning of the terms "expropriation" or "confiscation," or whether it is instead viewed as a wholly distinct and unique concept, it is inherently concerned with the physical resources of a country and bringing about a transfer of their control from the private to the public sphere. A state may nationalize immovables or movables, but never persons. Nationalization does not as such enter the sphere of contract. Contracts may be indirectly affected, terminated, or frustrated by nationalization, but the performance of contracting parties is not as such directed to new social objectives by an act of nationalization.

The property law of a state is found in a system of legal relations concerning the patterns of use and control of its physical resources. Property law reflects the values cherished by the national society and the policies pursued by its political and other institutions, as embodied in the use of its physical facilities.

As will be examined in greater detail, the values of persons sub-

---

[7] Compare *Webster's New International Dictionary* (2nd ed., 1957): "Property: 1. That which is proper to anything; a peculiar and characteristic quality of a thing. . . . 3. Possessions irrespective of their ownership; wealth. . . ."

[8] K. Katzarov, "The Validity of the Act of Nationalisation in International Law," 22 *Modern L. Rev.* 639 (1959) and *Théorie de la Nationalisation* (1960). S. Friedman, *Expropriation in International Law*, 5-6, 12 (1953), distinguishes between individual and general expropriation, the former being directed to identified persons and property and the latter to property generally. In his view, the latter category, general expropriation, includes nationalization, which is segmental in character and does not transform the existing economic and social structure, and socialization, which involves the partial or total exclusion of private capital from the society.

ject to the legal authority of the state, as well as persons not so subject, are profoundly affected by an act of nationalization. For some citizens, the change in property relations will mean a violent departure by the perceived image of the state from its desired image and hence will create a strong sense of injury and frustration. For other citizens, it will conversely mean that the actual image of the state is by the act of nationalization made to conform to its desired or ideal image. For foreign investors, it will mean that a social and political system, with which they are not identified as members, has thrust them from further and beneficial participation in its economic system of action, with resultant injury. From the standpoint of the structure of world society, it means a further compartmentalization or fragmentation of that society. It is more than a play on words to say that nationalization displaces the status of internationalization.

Nationalization is in many sectors of underdeveloped nations viewed as a requisite means to freedom from external control of important phases of its internal economy. It is thought to be an essential step in reaching the stage of development of an industrially organized state with an ability to provide for the welfare of its citizens. In the view of many of the subjects of underdeveloped nations, their governments and the international society have failed to provide them with significant progress toward economic growth and widely shared participation in the benefits of such growth. They are prone to accept the Communist ideology of a complete social, economic, and political revolution, the expropriation of private property, and the establishment of authoritarian governmental control over all phases of the economy, as a means to such progress. For such nations, nationalization will be regarded as a necessary means to the creation of the socialist order.

The term "contract" imports the coordinated action of two or more persons. It is a product of consent, rather than of custom or habit on the one hand, or of authority on the other. Elsewhere the author has said: "Negotiation is that process by which two or more parties arrive at a consensus for the coordination of their activities. . . . Contract or agreement is the end-product of the process of negotiation. It establishes new, complementary, interacting relationships between the parties involved. Such relationships may be relatively short-lived or they may be of lengthy duration. While they exist, the activities of the parties in question are directed to a common end."[9]

Contract reflects particular or individual patterns of coordinated action in an enemy, whereas property reflects general or universal patterns of action with reference to the physical resources of an economy.

If we speak of the nationalization of a state contract or concession, we are in fact speaking of the unilateral termination of contract by one of the parties, even though such a termination may be formally proclaimed as incident to a nationalization of property.[10] When an act of nationalization leaves the domain of property and purports to enter the sphere of contract, so as to extinguish or terminate the promised performance on the part of the nationalizing state under a contract with a foreign national, it brings the contractual relations between the parties to an end. It cannot substitute new *consensual* relations in their place. The act of nationalization will operate upon the alien, if he be subject to the jurisdiction of the state, to the degree that the act requires obedience to its commands. It may require the resident alien to respect the new institutional *property* arrangements so established, but it does not require him to enter into or perform some other *agreed* complementary patterns of activity in lieu of those established under the terminated contract.

Properly speaking, the only respect in which nationalization may be said to impinge upon a concession agreement is in the motivation for its termination. It may well be that in order to effectuate a substantial restructuring of the property system of a state, a termination of a concession agreement, which has temporarily disposed of the use of state property and placed it with the concessionaire, may be necessary.

Friedman, in his study of *Expropriation in International Law,* vigorously supports the legal power of a state to nationalize property, and goes so far as to say that "the expropriation may apply to all movable and immovable property rights, with the exception of contractual right." He regards the "exclusion of contracts from the field of expropriation . . . to be complete," but this is said in

---

[9]K. S. Carlston, *Law and Structures of Social Action,* 117 (1956).

[10]Harvard Law School, *Convention on the International Responsibility of States for Injuries to Aliens, Preliminary Draft with Explanatory Notes,* May 1, 1959, art. 10, explanatory note, 65, distinguishes and excludes contracts or concessions from the concept of property.

a context in which unilateral breaches by states of concession agreements are said to be excluded from the sphere of international claims.[11] Professor de La Pradelle, as Reporteur at the 1950 meeting of the Institut de Droit International, affirmed that: "Nationalization, as a unilateral act of sovereignty, must respect engagements validly entered into, whether by treaty or by contract."[12]

The doctrinal discussion of the nature, validity, and consequences of nationalization in international law has, among other things, centered about the issues of (1) whether it is to be wholly assimilated with prior takings of foreign private property by states and the rules of international law resulting therefrom, or (2) whether per contra it is a wholly new and discrete phenomenon having a separate and distinct status in law. Discussion has been directed to the questions of whether there is any duty whatever to pay compensation, whether there is duty to pay at least partial compensation on the basis of ability to pay, or whether there is a duty to pay prompt, adequate, and effective compensation to alien property owners. Professor Wortley lists thirty writers supporting the existence of a duty to pay full compensation, saying the list is not exhaustive, as against seven writers denying the existence of a duty to compensate, at least in the absence of a treaty.[13]

The juridical characterization or classification of a particular case determines the character of the norms applicable thereto. To the degree that the nationalizing state can find means to distinguish nationalization from classic state practice and international law concerning expropriation, which requires prompt, adequate, and effective compensation, it will move into an area of freedom from the traditional legal norms imposing obligations to other states injured by an act of nationalization.

Insofar as the task of the jurist of international law is concerned, in any problem of this magnitude he must concern himself with its factual aspects and ramifications, the values and perceptions of the actors involved, the nature of its social, economic, and political setting, and the function and ends which the relevant rules of law should serve. If he confines himself to purely abstract discussion of

---

[11]Friedman, Expropriation, 220, 156-157.
[12]43 Annuaire de l'Institut de Droit International 68 (1950, pt. 1). No final decision was taken by the Institut on this matter, action being postponed to a later date. 44 ibid. 324 (1952, pt. 2).
[13]B. A. Wortley, Expropriation in Public International Law, 34-35 (1959).

the law, he will remove the law which he sets forth from the world of reality and justice. Classic positivism would confine the international jurist to the examination of the practice of states to find the rule of law without reference to such considerations as these. Yet the scholar and the judge in a *national* legal system do not in fact ignore such considerations. Their relevance in public and private international law today will be a principal topic of inquiry in the final chapters of this book.

THE NATURE AND ROLE OF
CONCESSION AGREEMENTS
IN WORLD SOCIETY

In a recent study of the Suez Canal nationalization, an inquiry was made into the nature of concession agreements. The author indicated that the subject matter of concessions fell into two principal categories, public utilities and the exploitation of natural resources. The author emphasized the discretionary character of a concession by a state, stating that, if the element of discretion were lacking, the grant was not a concession.[1] The discretionary character of a concession has also been indicated in an international arbitral award.[2]

---

[1]Huang, "Some International and Legal Aspects of the Suez Canal Question," 277, 292. Concession agreements have been noted in the fields of manufacturing, transportation, and banking, as well as the extractive industries and public utilities. T. Guldberg, "International Concessions, a Problem of International Economic Law," 15 *Acta Scandinavica Juris Gentium* 47, 56-59 (1944) and 25 *Acta Scandinavica Juris Gentium* 18 (1955).

[2]*Germany v. Reparations Commission*, Award of Sept. 3, 1924, United Nations, 1, *Reports of International Arbitral Awards*, 429, 478-479. The arbitrator reviewed German, Austro-Hungarian, Hungarian, and French law with respect to the exploitation of mineral resources and noted that grants of rights to exploit ranged from those determined strictly according to statutory regulation to those, as in French law, where the grant was discretionary. Citation was made of article 5 of the French law of 1810 that "mines may be

Another recent study stated that an economic concession "is a contract between a public authority and the concessionaire. . . . Whatever be its form, a concession always involves a more or less complicated system of reciprocal rights and duties between the concessionaire on the one hand and the state on the other. This relationship is one of mixed public and private law."[3]

A concession agreement in the international sphere reflects one aspect of the process of foreign investment. It is an instrument of coordination whereby a state and a foreign investor establish a complementary system of relationships in the conduct of an enterprise for a limited period. It includes the grant by the state to the concessionaire of the privilege of access to and use of property or resources owned by the state. Its essential character is that of coordination, its juridical basis is that of consent, and the grant of protected privilege by the state is but an incident of the co-ordinated activity contemplated by the agreement. It may more appropriately be termed an international economic development contract.[4]

It seems to be generally conceded that one of the accepted elements in the definition of a concession agreement is that it involves an agreement by a state to grant a privilege to conduct an enterprise of some sort for a defined period. This agreement may be made pursuant to constitutional or legislative authority, but such is the nature of the enterprise which is desired to be established that it becomes essential to function through contract as well as through general rules of law. The legislative process can lay down general rules of behavior, but consent or agreement on the part of an individual can never be established by legislative fiat.

The soil in which a concession agreement typically finds its roots is one in which the state has for disposal rights or privileges, for

---

exploited only by means of an act of concession deliberated in the Council of State."

It may also be noted at this point that ownership by the state of the mineral resources of the subsoil appears to have been first established in France by the law of July 28, 1791.

[3]D. P. O'Connell, *The Law of State Succession*, 107 (1956). Others empha-size the aspect that a concession involves a grant from the state to an individual of part of its domain or normal sphere of activity. P. Develle, *La Concession en Droit International Public* (1936).

[4]A term first suggested by J. N. Hyde, "Permanent Sovereignty over Natural Wealth and Resources," 50 *Am. J. Int. Law* 854, 862 (1956).

example, access to its mineral resources or the development and exploitation of a public work or utility. Concessions have been granted in other fields as well, such as manufacturing and banking. A state could, of course, dispose of its mineral rights by simply conferring their ownership upon individuals, leaving it to self-interest, in the workings of a private enterprise economy, to bring about the requisite degree of use and development of the rights in question for the benefit of the national economy generally. However, such is the importance to the state of the particular right or privilege of economic development with which a concession agreement is concerned, that reliance solely upon the interest of ownership to insure adequate exploitation of the economic resource does not suffice. It becomes necessary to formulate the legal rights and obligations of the party empowered to develop such resource, as well as the rights and obligations of the state itself, and to place these in the sphere of an enforceable contract. These rights and obligations must be functionally defined so as to accomplish the objectives of the mutual enterprise in which the state and private party are interested. It is for this reason that the so-called discretionary quality of the concession agreement emerges. It falls in the area of discretion simply because this is the only way in which it is possible to formulate and coordinate the objectives of the two parties and to impose upon each enforceable obligations so that their common ends will be reached.

The right or privilege in respect of which the concession is made is, as noted above, one which is at the disposal or within the domain of the state. Thus a concession agreement for the development of mineral resources imports that those resources are already at the disposition of the state and the effect of the act of concession is to extend to private persons the protected privilege of their exploitation. It may parenthetically be noted that to "nationalize" such an arrangement is merely to revoke, and thereby breach, the concession agreement. The property involved is at all times that of the state, and it would appear that no "nationalization" of property would be necessary to wrest it from private hands and place its control in the hands of the state. All that is necessary is the termination of private control of the property granted by the concession.

The concession agreement insures that the mineral resources of a state shall be worked. Such an agreement does not leave the concessionaire in the position of a private owner of land, who is generally accorded the privilege to determine in his own discretion whether to develop and use it. Unless a concession is actively used after a fixed period of time, it will usually revert to the state or be opened to competitive bidding for its use by others. The flexibility of the concession-leasing system enables obligations of use and development to be placed upon the concessionaire so as to insure that the maximum utilization of available mineral resources will be made. The President's Material Policy Commission reached the conclusion that "for mineral deposits with no surface manifestation, a concession-leasing system will produce a higher rate of discovery."[5]

The significance and importance of a mineral base in the national economy as a necessary condition for industrialization is not usually appreciated. A nation may possess considerable national wealth, yet be inherently incapable of achieving any substantial degree of industrialization. The principality of Kuwait, with a small population and vast petroleum resources, has a very considerable national wealth. Yet it lacks many important elements for industrialization.

A nation which has achieved a high degree of industrialization is one which possesses, first of all, assured and continuing access to large supplies of raw materials and basic commodities, including foods, timber, metals and other minerals, and adequate water resources. Central to its development is the possession of substantial iron ore deposits and reasonably accessible supplies of coal. In the second place, an industrial nation must possess a technique of production whereby its power or energy resources may be employed to convert a continuous flow of raw materials into usable goods. Finally, an industrial nation must possess social, political, and economic institutions which enable its people to make the best possible use of its foundations of power.

---

[5]President's Material Policy Commission, 1, *Resources for Freedom*, 31 (1952), hereinafter cited as *Policy Comm. Rep.*:

"A concession-leasing system can provide for exclusive exploration rights over areas large enough to make advanced techniques of exploration practicable. It can also provide for exploitation rights, in the event of discovery, extensive enough to be an effective inducement. A location system is not readily adaptable to such arrangements.

"A concession-leasing system can be used with great flexibility. If it covers metallic minerals, it could enable a private company to obtain, along with an exploration concession, the right of first opportunity to lease on generous terms a fair portion of the public land embodying any ore discovered. This is essentially what is now done under the leasing laws in the case of petroleum."

An industrial nation is one which has learned the organizational way of life and has found it possible to multiply the energy of its human resources by organized activity and by the vast mechanical power available in machines. It is one which has achieved a high degree of scientific knowledge and a widespread ability to employ it. A machine civilization is one which is pre-eminently dependent upon adequate supplies of iron ore and all the alloying and other auxiliary minerals necessary for completion of manufactured products. The possession of alloying and other auxiliary minerals, without iron ore, can never make a state a great industrial power. The terrifying significance of the depletion of mineral resources in the United States is little realized. As the United States moves to Canada and South America for iron ore supplies to support the functioning of its industrial machines and as it increasingly relies on imports of other essential minerals, the functioning of its industrial machine becomes increasingly vulnerable.

The Middle East includes vast regions where the only substantial national resource is petroleum. To the extent that any Middle Eastern state possessing oil reserves is lacking in the other basic requirements for a diversified industrial development, its future must lie in its participation in the international economy of the West. Its petroleum represents energy, but that energy becomes meaningful only as it becomes associated in the productive capacity of the industrial nations of Western Europe and the Western Hemisphere; the Soviet is not available for this purpose, since it is a net exporter of petroleum.

Some Latin American nations, such as Argentina, Brazil, and Uruguay, have become considerably industrialized as a result of a mechanized agriculture which supplies food and other commodities for manufacturing states in the Western Hemisphere. Other Latin American states possess important resources of alloying and other minerals, but are lacking in either iron ore or agricultural resources. Their potentials for industrialization are accordingly slight. Brazil, Venezuela, and possibly Peru possess important iron ore resources, but transportation difficulties and lack of adequate coking coal impose severe handicaps upon its use within the nation, and render its export a necessity for a considerable time.[6]

---

[6]W. Voskuil, *Minerals in World Industry,* 311, 313 (1955) and "The Strategic Position of Iron Ore in the Economy of the Atlantic Basin Nations," *Illinois Engineer,* Nov., 1956, 3.

For many nations, the development of their local mineral resources and the export of such minerals represent the only important means for increase in their national wealth. As will be noted, this need for foreign markets is supplied by the correlative need of nations of the West to import a very considerable amount of their mineral requirements.[7]

The experience of history has demonstrated that the initial assumption of the English common law that the owner of the surface owned the subsoil as well was not one to generate the greatest possible use of the mineral resources of a state. Not even this fundamental principle of the common law was absolute. In England, gold and silver mines were crown property and did not pass by royal grant. The crown had the exclusive right to work mines containing other metals as well as gold and silver, if the extraction of such other metals interfered with the exploitation of the gold and silver. The sovereign, of course, owned all minerals in public lands

---

[7]The role of minerals development and expansion of mineral exports in the growth of underdeveloped countries was pointed out by the President's Material Policy Commission in 1952:

"Minerals development and expanded production for export offer great opportunities to the less developed countries. The yield to the source country in government revenues and foreign exchange earnings is usually a substantial percentage of the value of mineral output and can provide the financial basis for a domestic development program. Public loans from industrial nations or international agencies are frequently available, in connection with minerals development programs, for the expansion of auxiliary facilities —railroads, roads, port development, electric power, and the like—which will increase the general productivity of the country. Mineral production, moreover, requires the development of technical skills on the part of local employees of foreign companies that are thereafter readily useable in other types of industrial development.

"If financed from abroad, minerals development diverts a relatively small portion of local capital and manpower away from other domestic activities and therefore interferes very little with other development programs in industry and agriculture.

"Venezuela is a particularly striking example of this process. The government's foreign exchange earnings from oil amount to about 500 million dollars annually, providing over 90 per cent of the country's exchange earnings, and 60 per cent of government revenue is derived from oil. Yet only 5 per cent of the labor is employed by the oil industry. Venezuela has the means to finance a broad program of general economic development and has already undertaken major steps in improving agriculture, health, education, communication, transport facilities, and other services. Productivity is on the rise in Venezuela, providing the basis for increased domestic savings and rapid economic growth. Since the oil industry can look forward confidently to a very large expansion, and since there is now the additional prospect of substantial royalties from iron ore, the potentialities of general economic development in Venezuela seem most promising." 1 *Policy Comm. Rep.* 61.

and river beds. It is significant that, by the Petroleum Production Act of 1934, the "property in petroleum existing in its natural condition in Great Britain" was vested in the crown, who was endowed with "the exclusive right of searching and boring for and getting such petroleum." The exploitation of this petroleum was directed to proceed through the grant of licenses.[8]

The rule that the owner of the surface owned the subsoil thereunder, which was fundamental to English common law, also became the law of the United States. Thus all land now owned by persons in the United States, even though it may have been originally owned by the United States government, includes the ownership of both the surface rights and the rights to minerals in the subsoil. The United States, however, still remains the owner of great areas of public land, as do most of the states. The latter, however, own only about one-tenth of the amount of land owned by the federal government.

For many years mineral rights in federal lands could be acquired under what was known as a location system of mining law. The Mining Law of 1872, based primarily on the mining experience and customary law resulting from the California Gold Rush of 1848, adopted the principle of extending ownership of the mineral lands to those who found them and performed a certain amount of development work thereon.[9]

The assumption that the mineral resources of the federal public lands should be transferred to unqualified ownership proved in practice to be an unsatisfactory method of development and became widely questioned. This was particularly true in what were then termed "the public utilities minerals" of oil and coal. From 1900 to 1910 several million acres of oil and coal lands and also some lands containing phosphate deposits were withdrawn from location by executive authority. The validity of such executive withdrawals of mining lands was sustained by the Supreme Court by 1915.[10] In 1910, however, the authority of the executive to withdraw public lands of the United States and Alaska from location and private ownership, except for lands containing "minerals other than coal, oil, gas and phosphates," was specifically granted by Congress.[11]

---

[8]24, 25 Geo. 5, c. 36.
[9]Rev. Stat. sec. 2319 (1875), 30 U.S.C. secs. 22-42 (1940).
[10]United States v. Midwest Oil Co., 236 U.S. 459 (1915).
[11]36 Stat. 847 (1910), 43 U.S.C. secs. 141, 142 (1952).

The unwithdrawn lands were to remain open for location under the traditional system of 1872. The lands to which the Mining Law of 1872 did not apply were in 1912 narrowed to those containing "metalliferous minerals."[12]

The above statutory arrangements left open the question of the method of disposition to be followed with respect to the withdrawn lands. This question was answered by the mineral leasing acts of 1920.[13] The mineral leasing acts made leasing the sole method of private development of oil and gas, coal, phosphate, sodium, potassium, and oil shale in the public lands. The 1920 acts thereby cut off any further location of these major nonmetals under the Mining Law of 1872.

The resulting pattern for the development of mineral resources owned by the federal government is a complicated one. The location system of private ownership still prevails, except for those minerals covered by the mineral leasing acts. These acts recognize that there is, first of all, an interest of a prospector in exploration which is distinct from that of a mining interest, and that grants for exploration purposes must be large enough to encourage exploration and permit the economic use of advanced exploration techniques. Thus, for coal, potassium, and sodium, two-year exclusive prospecting permits for 2,560-acre tracts may be obtained and converted into a production lease if a discovery on the lands in question is made. In most cases, however, when production of leasable minerals is desired, competitive leases are granted in units of only 640 acres.[14]

A variety of systems of mineral resources ownership prevails in Canada. They may be owned by private persons, by the Dominion, or by the provinces.[15] Elsewhere in the world, the interest of the state in its mineral resources is made manifest in the relevant law. The President's Mineral Policy Commission described the situation as follows:

---

[12]37 Stat. 497 (1912), 43 U.S.C. sec. 142 (1940).

[13]41 Stat. 437 (1920).

[14]See 43 C.F.R. secs. 192.40, 192.81 (1953); 30 U.S.C. secs. 201, 241, 261, 262, 271 (1940).

[15]"A Comparative Study of Laws Affecting the Production and Development of Oil and Gas in the Americas," paper delivered by W. D. Masterson, Jr., Inter-American Bar Assoc., April, 1956.

In almost all foreign countries minerals can be extracted only after obtaining government permission. In countries where the subsoil is owned by the state, the government concedes the privilege of working government property. In other countries, although the owner of the surface enjoys some rights in the subsoil, the privilege of mining or drilling depends upon contractual permission from the state as well as an agreement with the surface owner. The investor has "title," therefore, only to a privilege granted by the state under general law. Typically his rights will be defined in a concession contract negotiated with the country's government.

Even if the concession itself is governed by general law, the chances of developing it will often depend upon specific arrangements with the authorities as to terms and conditions of investments in transportation, housing, the erection of townsites, and other facilities necessary to make modern and efficient operation feasible where no facilities existed before. Thus, the assurance of a fair chance for profitable operation depends initially upon the terms of a concession and other agreements bargained for with officials of the source country.[16]

In a number of Latin American states, ownership by the state of the subsoil and its exploitation and development through concessions is specifically provided for in the basic constitution. Under the Brazilian Constitution of 1934, the federal government was recognized to possess legislative authority over mineral deposits and mines to the exclusion of the owner of the surface. Under Article 152 of the Constitution of 1946, mines and other subsoil wealth were regarded as property distinct from that of the surface for the purpose of industrial development or use. By Article 153, the utilization of mineral resources was expressly made dependent on federal authorization or concession. The Cuban Constitution in Article 88 provides that: "The subsoil pertains to the Nation which can grant concessions, for its exploitation as established by law." Article 96 of the Constitution of the Dominican Republic provides that: "Mineral deposits belong to the state and can be exploited by private persons only by virtue of concessions or contracts granted under conditions determined by law."[17]

Many other Latin American states recognize by constitutional or legislative provision the ownership by the state of the subsoil

---

[16]1 *Policy Comm. Rep.* 64.

[17]A. J. Peaslee, 1, *Constitutions of Nations*, 238, 626, 766 (2nd ed., 1956), hereinafter cited as Peaslee.

and provide for its exploitation through grant or concession.[18] In Venezuela, the Mining Statutes of 1783 recognized ownership by the crown of deposits of minerals. The Law of Mines of 1944 provides for the grant of concessions for the exploration for and development of certain mineral resources. The Petroleum Mineral Law of 1943 is also based on ownership by the state of the subsoil and provides for the grant of concessions for the exploration, exploitation, transportation, and refining of petroleum. An exploration concession gives the grantee the exclusive right to explore a specified area approximately 10,000 hectares for three years, with the right to sell up to one-half of the plot for exploitation, the remainder to revert to the nation. The exploitation concession, however, extends for forty years and is granted on the basis of sealed bids for specified plots.[19]

The above-described system of law, in which ownership of minerals found in the subsoil is attributed to the state, was known in early Spanish law as the Regalía (royalty) system. This dominial concept or system, in which the state is the owner of minerals, became the typical system in Latin American law. Under what is termed the true Regalía theory "the State has the power to regulate the uses of mines in the form of concessions or grants, regulates the exploitation in its relations with the public order, provides for the conservation of the soil and mine safety, and, receives as the sovereign, a portion of the product obtained from the exploitation."[20] It should of course be appreciated that this system is not the only system of law relating to minerals in Latin America.[21]

Under Islamic law, the ownership of the minerals in the subsoil lies in the Muslim community. The grant of a concession contract

---

[18]Argentina Const., Art. 40, 1 Peaslee 56; Bolivia Const., Art. 108, 1 Peaslee 194; Law 1551 of April 30, 1953, Mining Code of 1953 (Costa Rica); Law of Feb. 5, 1937, General Mining Law (as amended) (Ecuador); Guatemala Const., Art. 33, 2 Peaslee 124; Honduras Const., Art. 152, 2 Peaslee 175; Mexico Const., Art. 27, 2 Peaslee 667; Nicaragua Const., Art. 242, 3 Peaslee 35; Panama Const., Art. 208, 3 Peaslee 100; Peru Const., Art. 37, 3 Peaslee 138.

[19]"Observations on Law in the Americas Relating to Hard Minerals," paper delivered by R. W. Johns, Conference on Natural Resources, Inter-American Bar Assoc., April 18, 1956; 5 *Policy Comm. Rep.* 104.

[20]N. J. Campbell, Jr., "Principles of Mineral Ownership in the Civil Law and the Common Law Systems," 31 *Tulane L. Rev.* 303, 305-310 (1957).

[21]*Ibid.*, 305-310.

for mineral exploitation is made by the sovereign in the interest of the community and in the capacity of custodian or guardian of such interest.[22]

It accordingly becomes clear that any system of national law must promote and render secure the exploration, location, and use within the national economy of the mineral resources available within the borders of the state. In all countries noted above, the sovereign interest in the mineral resources is recognized, at least to some degree. The system of sovereign ownership of the subsoil is the predominant pattern. It seems to be the prevalent pattern in the civil law countries. In the United States laws relating to the development of mineral resources of the federal public lands, the leasing system has superseded the earlier system of location and private ownership, insofar as the fuel and fertilizer minerals are concerned.

Thus, the national interest, in promoting to the maximum extent the use of the mineral resources of the state, has brought about a form of law in which the development of such mineral resources by private persons characteristically takes place under a system of concession, leasing, license, or other equivalent arrangement with the state. Such a system enables the maximum flexibility of arrangements for the exploitation of mineral resources and insures a sufficient retention of sovereign control, so that the state is at all times assured that its mineral resources are being adequately developed in the interest of the national economy and that the state is receiving the maximum return for their value.

The resulting regime is one in which typically the ownership of the subsoil appertains to the state, and the concession agreement is formulated sometimes in the context of a rather comprehensive set of regulations, as in Venezuela, or at other times, a rather complete statement or body of law which is to apply to the joint enterprise of the sovereign and the concessionaire. The latter situation is found in a number of the Middle Eastern governments, with the

---

[22]*Nail al-Awtar*, vol. 4, 147-148 (Cairo, 1938). As one investigates the different schools of Muslim law, variances appear as to the degree to which sovereign ownership exists. There is generally a consensus that for the disposition of mines in the public domain a sovereign concession is necessary, but under the Malikite school all mines, including those in private lands, are regarded to be in the public domain, whereas under the Shafi'ite school only those below the surface of lands which are not private are so regarded. L. Milliot, *Introduction a l'Étude du Droit Musulman*, 585-586 (1953).

personal sovereign acting partially in his capacity of legislator, within the limits of Islamic law generally, partially as executive, and partially in his contractual capacity.

It is important to realize that, as a result of the fundamental requirements of national law in the use of the mineral resources of a state, states possessing mineral resources have quite consistently established a system of private rights whereby persons developing such resources enjoy a direct and personal legal relation with the sovereign and are the recipients of sovereign commitments of a different and broader character from those of a simple land owner.

When it was said above that an owner might perhaps possess a greater degree of absolute rights with respect to the property under his legal control than a concessionaire, his greater power as compared with the concessionaire primarily lies in his freedom to determine the extent to which his property shall be used. Except for that fact, both are subject to the duty to pay taxes and to comply with all regulatory and other legal requirements of the state.

When private persons are said to be the holders of concession agreements or other similar legal interests, the fact must be held in mind that only rarely are such persons individuals but are instead almost uniformly the corporate person and enterprise. Typically the foreign holder of a concession agreement is a corporation. The reasons for the corporate character of the foreign national party to a concession agreement in the sphere of foreign investment were well described in a recent United Nations study:

The operations of such industries frequently have to be carried out on a large scale. The considerable amounts of capital required and the economic advantages of integrating the primary production with various types of processing or with marketing abroad are handicaps to production financed by local capital in underdeveloped countries. Frequently, the foreign enterprises are very large in relation to the entire economy of the countries in question and have to provide basic utilities, such as transportation, communications and electric power, as well as facilities for the housing of workers. Such a range of activities tends to give the enterprises a quasi-public character.[23]

The impersonal corporate organization or enterprise, functionally directed to its specific corporate ends of exploiting and distributing

---

[23]United Nations, *The International Flow of Private Capital, 1946-52*, 44-45, U.N. Doc. E/2531 ST/ECA/22, 1954.

minerals in a world market economy, insulated by its impersonal corporate character from the political pressures of producing nations for the highest possible price for their mineral resources and of the consuming nations for the lowest possible price, provides a means for achieving a workable compromise of the conflicting demands of producing and consuming nations. The advantage of the private corporation, as against the state enterprise or public corporation, as a means of effecting interstate linkages in the economic sphere, is that the former is able to express its essential idea in a pure or unmixed form to a degree that is not possible for the latter. The end of the private corporation is the production and distribution of goods in the most efficient manner as a means for the maximization of profits. The state corporation or trading agency is, however, a captive of the state and its policy making, and is used for political as well as economic ends. Whether the state in which the minerals are located or a foreign state employs the instrument of a state corporation or agency to develop and sell such minerals in the world markets, the instrument is the captive of the state. It becomes used for the political and particularistic ends of the controlling state. Only in a subordinate way is it used in an objective manner as an instrument in the world economy. (For a further discussion of this point, see Chapter V, proposition 4.)

Insofar as the respective bargaining powers of the state and the concessionaire to arrive at a fair agreement are concerned, it must be said that, if anything, the preponderant advantage lies with the state. Practically speaking, there is little pressure of the classic imperialist character that the state of the foreign investor can today impose upon the host state. The clamor of competitors for valuable concession rights in itself insures that the host state will have full bargaining power. After the concession agreement is entered into with the foreign investor, the host state has ample means of pressure to insure that it shall be fairly treated. As a matter of fact, in most concession contracts there is a "living law" that the parties will negotiate in good faith to resolve their disputes.

An international economic consultant recently said that: "An international oil company must cope with competing demands among producing countries, and with the conflicting demands of producing and consuming countries. Withal, it must accurately forecast probable demand around the world; it must plan its long-run investment commitments and short-run production schedules. From these precarious operations, it must expect the earnings that are at once a return on past investment and an incentive to continued exploration, development and market expansion."[24]

Whatever may have been the character of earlier corporate ventures in the international scene, today's world-wide corporate enterprises whose stock is publicly held and who are subject to the control of enlightened management, become a peculiarly appropriate instrument for resolving the conflicting demands of producing and consuming nations. The alternative possibility of state control as a public corporation or agency means that their policy would be slanted in the interest of the controlling party, whether it be the producing or the consuming state. Their appropriateness as a means of effective reasonable compromise of the interests of producing and consuming nations is enhanced when they become subject to the antitrust laws of the United States or other anti-restrictive measures and thereby are prevented from participating in any cartel.

An examination of concession agreements relating to the production of oil in the Middle East reveals the comprehensive character of a modern concession agreement. Such an agreement becomes the fundamental or constitutive law of the joint enterprise of the government and the concessionaire. It embodies a statement of the rights, duties, powers, and privileges of the parties with respect to the joint enterprise and defines their respective spheres of action. It is an instrument of coordination. Typically, it sets forth the complementary functions of the parties in the conduct of the joint enterprise, the bases upon which the gains shall be shared, the manner in which differences shall be resolved, the law governing the agreement, and the term of the joint enterprise.

An examination of the contents of the agreements reveals that the term "concession" or "concession agreement" is an unhappy and misleading symbol for, or designation of, the instrument. It is true that in entering into the agreement the state is exercising the sovereign power of disposing a part of its patrimony. It is also true that the state agrees that the foreign investor shall have certain advantages and privileges. But these facts are not enough

---

[24]W. J. Levy, "Issues in International Oil Policy," 35 *Foreign Affairs* 454, 457 (1957).

to justify the appellation of the agreement as a "concession." The previous examination of the role of the concession agreement in the development and use of mineral resources demonstrates that the concession agreement is more than a mere sovereign grant. It is the constitutive or organic instrument for an organization of international economic relations embracing many states with diverse interests, as well as the nationals of such states and their property. It becomes the means whereby much of the world's mineral resources are exploited and internationally distributed. Its continued functioning becomes a basic expectation of producing, consuming, and investing nations, as well as a foundation of Western defense arrangements. A vast part of international transportation and communication is devoted to the distribution of the mineral resources produced under concession agreements and to the delivery of commodities and manufactures purchased on world markets by the nations involved from the proceeds of such joint enterprises.

A typical concession agreement first of all defines the area to which it is applicable, as does any agreement relating to the use of real property. This done, the agreement usually proceeds to set forth the necessary legal relations whereby the conduct of the respective parties is to be coordinated to the achievement of the agreed common ends.

By way of illustration, in part I of the Iranian Consortium Agreement of September 19, 1954, there is set forth a statement of the purposes of the parties in entering into the agreement. It is said that the government of Iran and the National Iranian Oil Company desired to increase the exploitation of Iranian oil with a view to achieving benefits for the Iranian nation, but additional capital, management, and technical skills were required to accomplish this end to a substantial degree. The agreement refers to the complementary capital, management, and skills which the international oil companies were in a position to supply. It is then stated that the parties are agreed that the oil companies should undertake the operation and management of the oil properties which were the subject of the agreement and that an equitable sharing of the profits from the operation of the enterprise should be made. The agreement at this point concludes with the significant statement that:

. . . each of the Parties has willingly entered into the negotiations leading up to this Agreement and such negotiations have been amicably carried out with the object of assuring to the Government of Iran and the National Iranian Oil Company, on the one hand, a substantial export market for Iranian oil and a means of increasing the material benefits to and prosperity of the Iranian people, and to the companies, on the other hand, the degree of security and the prospect of reasonable rewards necessary to justify the commitment of their resources and facilities to the reactivation of the Iranian oil industry.[25]

A concession agreement will indicate the duties of the concessionaire company in exploring and producing oil, its obligations in the matter of payments to the government, and all other appropriate duties.

In the Iranian Consortium Agreement, provision is made for two separate operating companies to be established. Article 4 contains a functional definition of the character of each company and a statement of the rights and powers which each shall have in order to carry out such functions. The agreement then specifies the obligations of each company to Iran in detail and the supervision by Iran to which each shall be subject. It sets forth the rights of the operating companies with respect to both the capital assets and the land which are under their control. The functions allocated to the National Iranian Oil Company in the so-called field of nonbasic operations are described, including the provision of housing estates, maintenance of roads, supply of medical and health services, operation of food supply systems, and the furnishing of transport, water, and electricity supplies, and other public services.

A broad grant of powers to the concessionaire may be made in a clause whereby it has the right to use all means and facilities it may deem necessary or advisable in order to exercise the rights granted under the contract. Such a general clause may be supplemented by a specification in detail of the rights and privileges of the company with respect to roads, transportation, communication, and storage facilities, camps, buildings, wharves, and terminal facilities, and the like.

By various provisions, a petroleum concession agreement will in effect recognize the right of the government to impose taxes on the net income of the company in such an amount as will bring the payments to the government up to a stipulated per cent of

---

[25]Hearings Before the Antitrust Subcommittee (Subcommittee 5) of the House Committee on the Judiciary, 84th Cong., 1st Sess., ser. 3, pt. 2, 1565 (1955). Platt's Oilgram, Oct. 5, 1954 (spec. supp.).

the company's net income, after deduction therefrom of the amount of the various stipulated payments to be made to the government. This is a highly significant aspect of concession agreements in the petroleum field, for governments are assured not only of fixed payments but, in addition, a very substantial revenue from the profits of the operations, representing a determination by the parties of distributive justice in the enterprise.

The company usually recognizes the obligation to employ citizens of the state in which it is operating and to do so as far as practicable. The Iranian Consortium Agreement sets forth the duty of the company to train and educate local personnel.

The agreements recognize the principle of the peaceful settlement of disputes through the process of arbitration and include detailed provisions for establishing the necessary arbitral machinery.

Often some statement is made recognizing the principle of the insularization of the company from the politics of the country and abstention from any political action. It is sometimes provided, with emphasis, that the concessionaire shall have no rights whatever to engage in, or interfere with, administrative or political affairs. In the Iranian Consortium Agreement the companies agreed "to be always mindful in the conduct of their operations, of the rights and interests of Iran."

The agreements contemplate a long-term period of operation. The Iranian Consortium Agreement was to extend for a minimum period of twenty-five years, subject to additional extension.

It is accordingly seen that the modern concession agreement establishes a system of legal relations between a government and a corporation under which the action of each is coordinated to the end of assuring the exploration and development of the particular mineral resources of the state. It defines the obligations and powers of the corporation whereby these purposes are to be accomplished. It recognizes a number of important principles, including insularization of the corporation from the politics of the country in which it operates, peaceful settlement of disputes through arbitration, and fairness in the sharing of the benefits of the joint operation of the government and the corporation.

The principle of arbitration deserves further comments. It embodies a recognition by the state that it shall not sit in judgment of disputes involving its own acts but shall rather join with the corporation in the establishment of an independent judicial body, to wit, an arbitration tribunal, to which such disputes shall be referred for final and binding decision. Herein the state implicitly waives any requirement of the exhaustion of local remedies. This waiver is, as we shall see in Chapter VII, consistent with the reasoning of a number of international arbitral awards recognizing the principle that a state should not sit in judgment on its own acts in matters involving contracts with aliens.

It should also be realized that resort to arbitration under concession agreements is extremely rare. It is the almost universal practice of the parties to resolve their disputes through negotiation and by recourse to the terms of the agreements themselves as a criterion for the solution of their differences. It may well be said to be a living law of the joint enterprise that negotiation shall in the first instance be employed and diligently pursued in good faith as a means for the solution of differences.

In article 46 of the Iranian Consortium Agreement a significant and important step was taken toward defining the law governing the agreement: "In view of the diverse nationalities of the parties to this Agreement, it shall be governed by and interpreted and applied in accordance with principles of law common to Iran and the several nations in which the other parties to this Agreement are incorporated, and in the absence of such common principles, then by and in accordance with principles of law recognized by civilized nations in general, including such of those principles as may have been applied by international tribunals."[26]

The Security Council in the fall of 1956 thrashed out in debate a set of six principles, which it stated any settlement of the Suez question must meet. In so doing, it laid down a set of basic tests which it is believed any enduring concession arrangement must meet.[27]

The first principle, that of "free and open transit through the Canal without discrimination," has its counterpart in the free and open distribution upon the world markets of the products of the concession.

The second and third principles, that "the sovereignty of Egypt

---

[26]*Ibid.* See also A. Farmanfarma, "The Oil Agreement Between Iran and the International Oil Consortium: The Law Controlling," 34 *Texas L. Rev.* 259 (1955).

[27]United Nations, Security Council, *Official Records,* 11th year, Oct. 13, 1956; *ibid.,* U.N. Doc. S/3675, supp. for Oct., Nov., and Dec., 1956.

should be respected" and that "the operation of the Canal should be insulated from the politics of any country," have their counterparts in the purely economic and impersonal character of the modern business corporation which is the recipient of the concession, in the carefully defined functions allocated by the agreement to the concessionaire and the state, and in the requirements of noninterference by each party in the sphere of action of the other, to which allusion has already been made.

The fourth principle, that "the manner of fixing tolls and charges should be decided by agreement between Egypt and the user," has its counterpart in the practice of concessionaires that the products are freely distributed in world markets at prices freely and competitively determined. Insofar as the concessionaire is concerned, its efforts are consistently directed toward a maximization of profits under given conditions of world markets.

The fifth principle, that "a fair proportion of the dues should be allotted to development," has its counterpart in the steady, and even rapid, development of mineral resources by concessionaires under an expanding world economy.

The sixth principle, that of impartial arbitration of disputes, has its counterpart in substantially all concession agreements of provision for the arbitration of disputes.

It was said in the opening paragraphs of this study that as one explores the meaning of a concession agreement in terms of purpose, function, and institutional context, it assumes in law a different and more vivid hue. Originally perceived as an act of an omnipotent sovereign graciously conceding rights and interests to some person, the concession agreement should instead be viewed as a means for the coordination of public and private interests in the development of both the national and international economies. Vital in the development of the mineral resources of a state, it is equally essential in the functioning of the international economy.

NATIONALIZATION AND THE INTERNATIONAL COMMODITY PROBLEM

III

The economic consequences of the scattered distribution of mineral resources and of the circumstances that such resources are often found in underdeveloped countries are commented on as follows in a United Nations study:

The location of extractive industries depends on the geographical distribution of natural resources of different kinds. The operations of such industries frequently have to be carried out on a large scale. The considerable amounts of capital required and the economic advantages of integrating the primary production with various types of processing or with marketing abroad are handicaps to production financed by local capital in underdeveloped countries. Frequently, the foreign enterprises are very large in relation to the entire economy of the countries in question and have to provide basic utilities, such as transportation, communications and electric power, as well as facilities for the housing of workers. Such a range of activities tends to give the enterprises a quasi-public character.[1]

It has also been pointed out that the needs of underdeveloped governments for power, transportation, and other basic services, and for increases in

[1]United Nations, *The International Flow of Private Capital, 1946-52,* 44-45, U.N. Doc. E/2531 ST/ECA/22, 1954.

agricultural activity, have little attraction for foreign investment. To the extent that such countries are able to attract foreign capital into materials development, they will find it possible to free their own funds for other uses contributing to their economic development.[2]

Although Canada is increasingly becoming an important world power, it recognizes that it has not yet attained the full potential development available to it from its own resources. Accordingly, the recent remarks of the Royal Commission on Canada's Economic Prospects become most significant for underdeveloped countries in general:

Quite apart from the dollar value of Canada's capital requirement is the question of the quality and character of that capital. Capital is not a simple or uniform product; it embraces a number of complex properties both quantitative and qualitative in nature. Of the utmost significance in this context is the fact that many investment projects undertaken in a modern industrial economy require large pools of venture capital concentrated in the hands of a single or of a very few enterprises. . . .

No less important than the availability of adequate pools of venture capital is the extensive industrial experience and market connections which must be associated with that capital before a large investment undertaking can go ahead. This embraces such diverse requirements as an advanced technology, specialized entrepreneurial and managerial skills and, in many cases, an assured export market for a large part of the output. . . .

In effect, then, what Canada has required, especially in the course of her recent economic development, is a "package" of substantial capital technology, skills and markets. It is this kind of capital package which nonresidents have helped to provide, thereby performing vital tasks which Canadians alone could do either less efficiently or not at all. Outside capital has brought with it the management, the technical skills, and "know-how" and, in some cases, the assurance of markets so vital to the rapid growth of Canada. An example of this is the very considerable development of the Iron Ore Company in the Quebec-Labrador area, made possible because associated with Canadians in the venture was a group of American steel companies which were in a position to contribute not only a considerable part of the capital and technical knowledge needed but also to provide a market for the ore to be produced. It may be assumed that many new projects for developing resources in the future will only be possible under similar conditions.[3]

---

[2] 1 *Policy Comm. Rep.* 61.

[3] Royal Commission on Canada's Economic Prospects, *Preliminary Report*, 86-87.

The complementary relationships of the economies of Canada and the United States are described in a recent study, which is most perceptive and thorough. It was said that:

Canada to a large extent has been exchanging raw and semi-finished produces derived from her forest, mineral and agricultural resources, against capital goods, fuels, industrial materials and farm products mainly of a semi-tropical variety. . . .

Primarily because of its size, its high level of productivity, and its natural endowment of resources, the United States has essentially been a closed economy. Canada, on the other hand, has continued to be one of the most open economies in the world. . . .

U.S. exports have also been highly diversified among a wide variety of manufactures and primary products whereas Canadian exports have been heavily concentrated on primary forest, agricultural and non-ferrous metal products. To a very large extent, U.S. imports consists of raw and partly fabricated products whereas a substantial share of Canadian imports consists of manufactured goods. . . .

Examination of the main export commodity classifications indicates that the largest *relative* increases in the next two decades are expected to occur in metal and mineral products, while the relative importance of forest products, agricultural produce, nickel, and sundry manufacturers is expected to shrink considerably.[4]

The last-quoted sentence above points to another important aspect of the symbiotic relationships established in the world economic society. This is the interdependence of materials-consuming and fuel-consuming industrial nations and their supplier countries. The facts of this interdependence were graphically described by Professor Voskuil:

"From Maine to California and from the Canadian border to Texas" no longer expressed the concept of a nation. To get the necessary ingredients of our country's industrial diet we went to the Straits Settlement for tin; to Brazil and Africa for indispensable manganese; to Ceylon and Madagascar for graphite; to Africa, Asia, and the islands of the South Pacific for chromium, and to the Guianas for bauxite. These are only a few examples which illustrate the wide geographical extent of the raw-material boundaries of our own nation.

What is true of the raw-material boundaries of the United States also holds for the industrial nations of Western Europe. Western Europe is deficient in or lacks resources of copper, chromite, lead, manganese, molybdenum, tungsten, nickel, platinum, tin and phosphate. The European industrial centers must seek their supplies from Africa, Asia, Aus-

---

[4] G. L. Reuber, *The Growth and the Changing Composition of Trade Between Canada and the United States,* 37, 38-39, 44 (1960).

tralia, and South America. Possibly the Soviet Union, with the confines of its exact area, is the most nearly self-contained industrial power.[5]

A brief description of the position of the United States with respect to certain basic minerals will make evident the interdependence of the economies of the United States and underdeveloped nations and a number of other nations.

The United States imports the majority of its bauxite requirements for the manufacture of aluminum, mostly from South America and the West Indies. In 1953, its percentage of self-sufficiency for bauxite was 26 per cent, having declined from 32 per cent in 1932.[6]

Manganese is another metal of prime importance for which the United States is almost completely dependent on foreign supplies. There is no substitute for manganese in steel making. It is also essential for dry cells and certain chemicals. The domestic United States production was less than 10 per cent of its consumption in 1953. The demand for this metal rises in direct proportion with the increase in steel production, and hence new sources of ores are constantly required. The significance of this dependence on foreign supplies was pointed out by a United States governmental agency: "The fact that the United States is more than 90 per cent dependent upon foreign sources in underdeveloped areas, some with strong nationalistic ambitions, presents a set of problems involving foreign taxation, restrictions on trade and the industrial demands of countries other than the United States."[7]

Since 1940 a large part of United States' supply of lead has been imported, principally from Canada, followed by Peru, Australia, Bolivia, Southwest Africa, and Yugoslavia. In 1955 and 1956 the United States consumed 1,213,000 and 1,209,000 tons of lead, respectively, and imported a net amount of 449,000 and 446,000 tons for each such year. Net imports represented 39.5 per cent of consumption in 1956 and an average of 38.5 per cent for the period 1951-55.[8]

The United States consumes 50 per cent and Europe 40 per cent of the world's tungsten production. Its production, however,

---

[5]W. Voskuil, *Minerals in World Industry*, 305 (1955).

[6]U.S. Dept. of Interior, Bureau of Mines, *Mineral Facts and Problems*, Bulletin 556, 26-27 (1956).

[7]*Ibid.*, 493-495, 508.

[8]P. W. Bidwell, *Raw Materials: A Study of American Policy*, 64, 69 (1958).

is distributed among Asia (54 per cent), North America (14 per cent), South America (14 per cent), Europe (13 per cent), and others (5 per cent).[9]

The United States is also a copper importing nation. In 1956 it produced over 1,574,000 tons of copper and imported 596,000 tons. Domestic mine production contributed 57.6 per cent of the total supply. Chile is the greatest single source of imports.[10]

Some unofficial figures on United States production of important minerals as a percentage of its domestic requirements show a range from 2.1 per cent for platinum to 76 per cent for iron ore and 76.1 per cent for copper, as set forth more fully below:[11]

Platinum	2.1	Mercury	43.7
Mica	6.7	Zinc	44.3
Manganese ore	14.1	Gypsum crude	70.4
Bauxite	21.6	Iron ore	76.0
Fluorspar	39.4	Copper	76.1
Lead	43.6		

Since the end of World War II, the United States has become the world's largest single importer of industrial raw materials, importing in 1956 over $5 billion of supplies. The mineral requirements of the United States are rising much more rapidly than other primary products and, with the size of the growth of the economy, are likely to continue to do so. Western Europe's mineral resources are largely limited to coal, iron, lead, and zinc.[12]

Over the long term, the United States and Western Europe are becoming increasingly dependent on imports of minerals for energy use as well as fabrication. Comparing 1955-57 with a base period of 1927-29, the gross imports on petroleum increased in the United States by 526 per cent and in Western Europe by 1,500 per cent. In 1955-57, net imports of petroleum were 12 per cent of consumption in the United States and 91 per cent of consumption in Western Europe. The gross imports of aluminum rose by 776 and 1,148 per cent, respectively, in the two regions. Copper imports increased by 252 per cent and zinc imports increased by 393 per cent in the United States and in 1955-57 constituted 12 and 48 per cent of

---

[9]Bureau of Mines, *Mineral Facts and Problems*, 932.

[10]Bidwell, *Raw Materials*, 103-108.

[11]J. H. Lind, "Strategic Materials We Must Depend upon from Outside Sources," 103 *Magazine of Wall Street* 237 (1958).

[12]United Nations, *World Economic Survey, 1958*, U.N. Doc. E/3244 ST/ECA/60, 79.

the total United States consumption, respectively. For Western Europe, the rate of increase for such metals was 183 and 82 per cent, respectively, and the rates of imports to total consumption was 95 and 63 per cent, respectively, in 1955-57.[13]

The importance of the underdeveloped countries as a source of a very considerable part of the mineral requirements of the industrialized countries is evident from a few salient figures. Africa has become a major source of nonferrous metals and has assumed a steadily larger share of world production of copper, zinc, and tin.[14] If 1927-29 is taken as the base period, it appears that by 1955-57 world bauxite production was 950 per cent of the base period production, of which Latin American production was 600 per cent; world copper production was 168 per cent, of which Latin America contributed 34 and Africa 42 per cent; world zinc production was 165 per cent, of which Latin America contributed 32 per cent and Africa 17 per cent; world lead production was 111 per cent, of which Latin America contributed 25 per cent and Oceania 19 per cent; while world tin production fell to 97 per cent, of which Southern and Southeastern Asia contributed 62 per cent, Latin America 17 per cent, and Africa 15 per cent.[15]

The supply of minerals by underdeveloped nations to the industrialized states is carried out partly by integrated international corporations which process the mineral ores or petroleum to usable form, but notably through the international commodity markets. The transfer of minerals from producer to consumer is in the phase of international economics termed the international commodity markets. The character of these markets and the problems they present to underdeveloped nations in their adaptation to the world society will now be discussed.

The position of producer countries engaged in the production and export of minerals is considerably more favorable than is that of producers and exporters of other primary commodities. The growth of world petroleum production outstripped the expansion in world manufacturing production. The increase in world trade of ores and nonferrous metals compares reasonably well with growth in world manufacturing output.[16] The growth in the internal

---

[13]*Ibid.*, 26.
[14]*Ibid.*, 31.
[15]*Ibid.*, 30.
[16]*Ibid.*, 18.

economies of individual countries producing primary products is in large measure a reflection of the expansion of their foreign exports. While the purchasing power in 1955-57 of exports of food and tobacco, for example, was only 102 per cent of their purchasing power in 1928 and of textile fibers only 123 per cent, the purchasing power of petroleum exports was 1,200 per cent and of ores and nonferrous metals 296 per cent of their 1928 purchasing power.[17] If the external purchasing power of underdeveloped countries of 1928 is compared with that of 1955-57, excluding from this the impact of petroleum exports, the increase of such external purchasing power was only two-fifths of the advance in world manufacturing activity.[18] Most nonferrous metals have not been as unstable in price as other primary products in the postwar years. The fluctuations in their trade have considerably lessened.[19]

If the situation of primary producing countries is viewed as a whole, their exports to industrial nations have grown more slowly than the total output or income of the latter. There has been an increasing gap between the total demand for primary products and the general rate of economic growth of industrial countries. Among the causes of the lag in demand for primary products in developed countries are the shift toward industries with a low input of primary products per unit of output, the drive toward economy in the use of primary products, and the increase in the use of synthetic substitutes. The imports of most primary producing countries have greatly exceeded the increases in their exports. As a consequence, with the exception of the petroleum exporting countries, their trade balances have been constantly subject to increasing pressures.[20]

Since the industrial countries provide the bulk of the market for primary products, the heart of the international commodity problem lies in the relationship between industrial and primary producing countries. Those relationships become a central facet of the problem of the underdeveloped nations. The aspirations of those nations to achieve an accelerated pace of economic growth are met with the obdurate fact of their dependency on the market provided by industrial countries. In view of the underlying fact

[17] *Ibid.*, 53, 55.
[18] *Ibid.*, 19.
[19] *Ibid.*, 39.
[20] *Ibid.*, 7, 57, 66.

that the export supply of primary products grows faster than import demand at constant prices, if export earnings from such products are to keep pace with the rate of economic growth in developed countries, then trade in primary products must grow even faster than the rate of economic growth in developed countries. Moreover, the much greater increase in population growth in underdeveloped countries as compared with the industrial countries means that, if only to equalize the per capita rate of income growth between the two, the absolute rate of income growth of the underdeveloped countries would have to be about 20 per cent greater.[21] Merely to maintain present consumption standards for their growing population would require an investment of 5 to 8 per cent of their income.[22]

In addition to the lag in growth of demand for primary products, the source countries of such products have had to meet highly unstable international markets. In 1956, for example, the price of copper fell within six months from 46 cents to 36 cents a pound, and did not begin to rise until it was below 30 cents. A recent study of the fluctuation of copper prices in international trade led to the conclusion that "the behavior of prices in the postwar years, particularly in 1953-56, seemed to indicate the absence of a world price for this metal."[23]

The drop in prices of primary products and the loss of export earnings by underdeveloped countries from mid-1957 to mid-1958, coupled with a slight rise in import prices, meant a loss in import capacity equivalent to about six years' lending by the International Bank for Reconstruction and Development at 1956-57 rates. For primary commodities as a whole, their price instability has exceeded their instability in volume. Viewing the situation from the standpoint of individual countries, their dependence upon the export of one, or at most, two or three, primary commodities, has meant that their export earnings have shown wide, short-term fluctuations. The budgeting of an orderly program for growth and development is thus confronted with the most extraordinary difficulties.[24]

There has been one alleviating circumstance in the comparative

[21]*Ibid.*, 7, 10-11, 57, 66.
[22]U.S. Senate Committee on Foreign Relations, *Worldwide and Domestic Economic Problems and Their Impact on the Foreign Policy of the United States*, 86th Cong., 1st Sess., Aug., 1959, 14.
[23]Bidwell, *Raw Materials*, 112.
[24]United Nations, *World Economic Survey, 1958*, 6-7, 41, 59.

increase of the outflow of capital into primary producing countries. In large measure as the result of official loans and grants, the flow of capital into such countries has increased over 1928, even though relative to export earnings the inflow of private capital was less. However, neither the size nor the direction of the flow of capital movements was such as to offset the gap in trade balances of most primary producing countries.[25]

A partial explanation of the failure of the process of foreign investment to provide stable and satisfactory economic relations between industrial and underdeveloped nations lies in the character of such investment. The private foreign investment of the United States has principally been in petroleum and manufactures and to a lesser extent for other minerals and ores, as against other primary commodities. The United States direct foreign investments in 1958 totaled $27,075 million, of which $9,681 million was in petroleum, $8,485 million was in manufactures, and $2,856 in mining.[26] On an area basis, the direct investment abroad for the United States in 1956 consisted of (1) $1,396 million for petroleum, of which $328 million went to Canada, $432 million to Latin America, and $407 million to Western Europe; (2) $184 million for mining and smelting, of which $74 million was spent in Canada and $70 million in Latin America; and $738 million for manufacturing, of which $148 million was spent in Latin America and $194 million in Western Europe. The United Kingdom invested heavily in Commonwealth countries and principally in oils, railways, and financial institutions. France invested heavily in its overseas territories, in insurance companies, banks, chemicals, and heavy metallurgical and oil companies. The West German Federal Republic invested in Canada, Brazil, Argentina, and in underdeveloped countries in the fields of iron and steel, chemical, pharmaceutical, and electrotechnical industries.[27]

Thus neither the volume nor the direction of the outflow of direct private foreign investment provides an answer to the international commodity problem. The problem cannot be met by the individual primary producing countries because it is inter-

---

[25]*Ibid.*, 58.

[26]S. Pizer and F. Cutler, "Capital Flow to Foreign Countries Slackens," U.S. Dept. of Commerce, *Survey of Current Business*, Aug., 1959, 25.

[27]United Nations, *Economic Development of Underdeveloped Countries, the International Flow of Private Capital*, 1957, U.N. Doc. E/3128.

national, rather than national, in scope. The area of maneuverability of a primary producing country seeking to diversify and increase its exports and industrialize its economy is small. Its working base is provided largely by its export earnings, and these are becoming constantly smaller in comparison with the economic growth of their principal customers, the industrial countries. Its export earnings are determined in private, competitive international markets and are subject to most considerable fluctuations. If an attempt be made to take advantage of a favorable market position through restrictionist measures, such steps only stimulate countervailing activities and growth of competition elsewhere which erode that advantage. Attempts to stimulate market demand are largely ineffective. To move toward industrialization is only to increase the pressures on limited supplies of foreign exchange. Again, the early stages of industrial development call for the purchase of capital equipment without first having the opportunity to put it to work to increase earnings.

A primary producing country seeking to enlarge its economic base encounters conflicting pressures in measures toward increasing self-sufficiency and opposition to price increase on the part of industrial countries. The latter fail to see the mutual or dual aspect of the problem. For example, an industrial nation tends to look at foreign aid as a separate problem and a burden instead of one flowing from a mutual interest in promoting stable and growing international markets, with resultant stable economies and governments. In fact, the industrial country shares with a primary producing country an interest in stable market prices, but it tends to act only when prices go up, not down.

Thus underdeveloped nations are inevitably pressed toward unilateral solutions of their unsatisfactory linkage with the international economy, such as nationalization. Yet unilateral approaches must inevitably fail, for the problem is in fact a joint or international one demanding an international approach. Until industrialized states act *politically* to solve, or at least alleviate, the problems for underdeveloped nations engendered by the failure of the international commodity markets to perform in a stable and satisfactory manner, we are likely to see nationalization increase rather than decrease as an international phenomenon. As will be demonstrated in Chapter VI, unless they take the necessary *political* measures to bring about an international system in which all states can derive benefit from their participation, a growth of law in the world society is not likely to eventuate.

Any coordinated solution of the international commodity problem must come from international, rather than national, measures. The international approach to the problem is limited to joint study, exploration, and such other specific measures as can be arrived at through consensus and agreement. The resulting situation has been described as follows:

International policy, in a context of sovereign nations and conflicting national interests, is in essence a policy arrived at among nations rather than above nations. There is therefore a strong tendency to gravitate to the compromise solution which offers the largest common denominator. In the process of incessant search for common ground, what is seriously objectional tends to be weeded out, but the final product often suffers from dilution and lack of vigour. The postwar international commodity arrangements are not immune from this process of international policy formation.[28]

The mineral interdependency of industrialized and underdeveloped nations discussed above is but part of the total pattern of economic interdependency of states. Occasion will now be taken to describe briefly some salient aspects of world trade.

While it is probable that from 1938 to 1955 there was a somewhat smaller rate of growth in world trade than in world production, this fact does not necessarily point to a diminishing importance to the world of the international economy. For one thing, the United States bulks enormously in world production but it has one of the lowest ratios of imports to total national output. The increase in production since 1938 has been most marked in those countries where trade is low in relation to their output. If we look at world trade simply on a volume basis, the total volume of world trade in 1955 was about 50 per cent higher than it was in 1948, and it exceeded the 1938 level by about the same proportion. In a group of thirty representative countries, including underdeveloped as well as industrial countries, twenty showed a rising ratio of imports to national income from 1937 to 1954 and ten showed a declining ratio. Most of the underdeveloped countries, as well as a substantial group of Western European countries, showed higher import ratios in 1954 than in 1937. Moreover, looking at the postwar period alone, most of the industrial countries, including the United States,

---

[28]United Nations, *World Economic Survey, 1958*, 129.

have shown increases in their import ratios.[29] By 1958-59, the total volume of the free world imports had reached over $100 billion.[30] World trade has steadily grown in volume over the long run and for many countries has become increasingly important in relation to their total national output.

Another important change in world trade patterns is in its regional compartmentalization. Before World War II, over 90 per cent of world trade had centered in five groups of countries, the tropics, the United States, other regions of recent settlement in the temperate belts, continental Europe, and noncontinental Europe.[31] In 1953, about three-fifths of world exports consisted of exchanges within three main trading areas, the dollar area, the European Payments Union area, and the centrally planned economies. Somewhat less than one-fifth of world trade consisted of the trade of these three areas with one another.[32]

In 1958, the United States had total investments abroad of $59,155 million, of which direct private investments were $27,075 million, of which petroleum accounted for $9,681 million, mining for $2,-856 million, and manufactures for $8,485 million. The foreign-owned, long-term assets in the United States in 1958 were $15.2 billion.[33] It is estimated that by 1966 the total United States investment abroad will be about $75 billion.[34]

Though the growing interdependency of the world is often mentioned as one of the factors to promote the growth of a stable international order and system of international law, the above data reveal that, if such a situation of interdependency is to lead to such an order and law, it must provide satisfaction for the parties involved. Only when the international order is prized as a means for reaching valued goals by most of the states who are actors in that order will there be a constant growth of an international law dedicated to the development of that order.

---

[29]United Nations, *World Economic Survey, 1955*, U.N. Doc. E/2864 ST/ECA/38, 50, 53.

[30]*Economic Report of the President*, 1959, 86th Cong., 2nd Sess., H.R. Doc. 286, chap. 2.

[31]League of Nations, *The Network of World Trade* (Publications, II, Economic and Financial, 1942, II, A3), 7-10.

[32]United Nations, *World Economic Survey, 1958*, 71.

[33]Pizer and Cutler, "Capital Flow."

[34]C. E. Silberman and L. A. Mayer, "The Migration of U.S. Capital," 57 *Fortune* 125 (Jan., 1958).

NATIONALIZATION AS A PRODUCT OF INADEQUATE INTEGRATION AND ADAPTATION

IV

The individual, as an actor in any social system, shows many faces to many persons in the groups in which he participates. He continually adapts himself to a shifting environment, as he moves from the family to the work group, the church, and other social institutions. His culture embodies a host of roles for conduct, which he must from time to time appropriately perform.

• As the individual performs his particular role in the group in which he is placed, the supreme importance of values in social action emerges.•Unless participation in a social system reflects preferred conduct by the participants, the system will disintegrate. "Man is . . . a value-seeking, value-affirming and value-building animal."[1] Individuals do not successfully coalesce into a social system until they share a common system of values in the goals which they pursue and the modes and gratifications incident to the attainment of such goals. They must learn to perform culturally established patterns of interaction toward reaching goals. They

---

[1] O. Tead, *The Importance of Administration in International Action*, Carnegie Endowment for International Peace, International Conciliation, no. 407, Jan., 1945, 7.

must learn to perform various roles, including occupational roles. They must develop methods and procedures which bring about integration in a group. They must adapt themselves to the environment in which they function. Finally, they must learn how to maintain the social system against external pressures and internal deviant performances.[2]

Before proceeding further, a number of terms must be defined. A social system has been defined to comprise, but not necessarily to be limited to, (1) a process of interaction between two or more actors (2) oriented toward a situation (including other actors who are objects of cathexis or gratification, either as goals to be pursued or means for the accomplishment of goals), (3) characterized by "interdependent and, in part, concerted action in which the concert is a function of collective goal orientation or common values, and of a consensus of normative and cognitive expectations."[3] The phrase "oriented toward a situation," as used in the preceding definition, implies the concept of "situation," that is, the external world to which an actor is oriented and in which he acts, and further implies the concept of "orientation," that is, the set of cognitions, cathexes (gratifications), plans, and relevant standards which relate an actor to a situation.[4] The term "common values," as used in the preceding definition, means a sharing of values by one person with another in the sense that "either he wants the group in which he and the other belong to achieve a certain group goal which the other also wants, or . . . he intrinsically values conformity with the requirements laid down by the other."[5] System, as an analytical concept, refers to a set of related phenomena, of which some interrelationships or interactions vary independently, but within definable limits.

The term "value" is to be distinguished from the term "goal." The latter implies an anticipated and desired state of affairs or object, which may be envisaged to lie in the physical or social environment, or both, and for the attainment of which action is

---

[2]T. Parsons and E. A. Shils, *Toward a General Theory of Action,* 23-26, 54-55 (1951); T. Parsons, R. F. Bales, and E. A. Shils, *Working Papers in the Theory of Action,* chaps. 3, 4 (1953); T. Parsons and N. J. Smelser, *Economy and Society: A Study in the Integration of Economic and Social Theory,* 16-19, 46-51 (1956).

[3]Parsons and Shils, *Toward a General Theory,* 55.

[4]*Ibid.,* 56.

[5]*Ibid.,* 55.

to be directed. "Values appear as the *criteria* against which goals are chosen, and as the *implications* which these goals have in the situation."[6] A value is "a conception, explicit, or implicit, distinctive of an individual or characteristic of a group, of the desirable which influences the selection from available modes, means, and ends of actions."[7] Values are implicit in goals and reflect the degree or standard of preference accorded goals by an actor.

Interaction of the group requires that its members share the values embodied in its goals and the perspectives from which its action is viewed and evaluated. Group participation may be brought about by fear and force, but this can only occur if the group can devote enough energy to control and repress the dissidents and at the same time provide satisfactions for the other members, sufficient to hold the group together. Here lies a problem of profound importance to all societies as they have moved from the traditional patterns of cooperation in the ancient groups of the family and the tribe to the modern corporate organization and the state—the problem of the use of power against the use of value realization as a means of holding a group together.

The world society functions largely through, and as a part of, the action of national societies. The fact that a national society is highly dependent on the functioning of the world society, the fact that the members of a nation may realize their desired values to a considerable extent through the interdependency of peoples, does not necessarily lead to the consequence that the members of the national society will lose their identification with the nation and their orientation to its value system, and instead become internationally oriented. A large degree of commitment by a national society to the world society does not necessarily mean the emergence of a high degree of preference for the functioning of the world society. Indeed, in some circumstances, it will lead to the appearance of a nationalism marked by an intense desire to escape from what is regarded as captivity by the international system. The law of that system, as found in international law, which is a product of Western civilization, will not necessarily be regarded as their law. (See Chapter VI, proposition 8.g.)

---

[6] Quoted from an unpublished memorandum "Summary of Discussions of the Cornell Value Study Group" (June 11, 1949), *ibid.*, 429.

[7] C. Kluckhohn and others, "Values and Value-Orientations in the Theory of Action," *ibid.*, 395.

Africa today witnesses a situation in which the African native still largely considers himself to be only a member of his family and his tribe, subject to the authority of his tribal chief, and does not identify himself with any other social system. Yet in increasing numbers he is a participant in a corporate and wage economy and is living in towns and compounds in the burgeoning mineral and industrial development of the African continent. The social systems of the modern corporation and industrial state are alien to many African natives. Even freedom, independence, and nationalism have meaning for such Africans only as freedom from white domination. Nationalism is not for them an expression of membership in a people or a nation, but is simply a vindication of their racial identity. The boundaries of African political entities are a product of great European power and power rivalry compromise and do not represent the slow, historical maturing and emergence of a people into a nation. When European nations divided Africa in the latter nineteenth century, they ignored tribal boundaries, split tribes apart, and grouped traditional enemies in the same territory. Northern Rhodesia has no common people, only the Bemba, Rosi, Nsenga, and numerous other tribes. Nyasaland possesses no common culture, sense of national identity, or language. Nigeria is an amalgam of the Muslim north and many tribal groups. The Ashanti of the north would like to separate from Ghana. For most emerging African states, the primary value for some time to come will not be nationalism but racial ascendancy. Nationalism is only a means to the end of white supremacy. The drive for racial ascendancy by at least some of the new African leaders may very well result in racial aggression through the instrumentality of the forces of the state. The African racial leader, vested with political power and authority, may obliterate racial boundaries through force. Racial rivalry characterized by the brutal use of force has been seen in the Congo and elsewhere. Authority in the new African state will be exerted from a remote central government and will tend, initially at least, to be based more on fear, prejudice, and hatred than on a shared consensus of values, attitudes, and perspectives of a constructive nature. Indeed, events in the Congo in 1960 suggest that some African states may be, sociologically speaking, "nonstates" in their failure to exhibit common acceptance of authority in a going social system characterized by integration, self-maintenance, adaptation, and goal gratification.

The primary distinguishing feature of the corporate life of an industrially organized state is the substitution of universal values of loyalty to, and indentification with, the corporate organization and the state, in place of the particularistic values of the family and tribe. Until such a universal value system is created in a state, authority cannot successfully emerge as a means of coordinating its action toward reaching its desired goals and controlling departures from approved and expected performance of norms.

The value system of a group is a product of its history. The problems and pressures it has encountered and overcome, the nature of its relationships with other groups, and the vicissitudes of its physical environment determine the character of the institutions and attitudes of a people. The manner in which the members of a society have come to perceive and express themselves as a result of their history determines how they encounter the present and anticipate the future. It may well be said that a social system, as well as an individual, has its own unique personality structure. It is in this vein that an examination of the actors, values, attitudes, and institutionalized modes of performance of certain typical patterns of integration and adaptation in underdeveloped nations shall be undertaken.

The foregoing remarks are a necessary background for the subject matter of this chapter. The following pages constitute the formulation of a hypothesis and its testing or demonstration of validity. It is to be observed that nationalization or large-scale expropriation, as an international phenomenon or a phenomenon having international repercussions, has appeared in certain Latin American and Middle Eastern underdeveloped countries. This suggests that there may be a correlation between a type, or variations of a type, of national society in underdeveloped nations and the resort to nationalization. Investigation will be made, therefore, of patterns of integration and adaptation in the social systems of these nations. Their historical background, social structures, economies, and adaptation to the world society will be briefly described. When that investigation is completed, nationalization may perhaps be seen to be simply a symptom of the existence of the unstable veneer state, as defined in the Foreword. The investigation shall begin with some typical patterns of Latin American society.

Although the independence of most Latin American states was established in the early part of the nineteenth century and only a short time subsequent to the independence of the United States, the two regions were then and still remain vastly different in social structure and degree of cultural homogeneity. The independence of the Latin American states found their peoples typically composed of a Spanish or Creole élite, comprising a relatively small percentage of the population, a laboring class of agricultural and mining workers, mostly Indians, Ladinos, or mestizos, and town workers, largely in the service trades. Whereas during the colonial period and thereafter the United States steadily liquidated the native Indian through war and used the reservation system for segregating the survivors from participation in the stream of national life, the Latin American colonies and ensuing states at least permitted the Indian to survive. Indeed, the Catholic ethic of conversion of the Indian to the service of God, and his dedication to mining and tilling the wealth of the Indies under a mercantilist philosophy, demanded his survival. When the native Indian population was encountered in numbers into the millions, with many centered in large cities, the policy of obliteration and segregation pursued by the United States toward its native tribes was hardly feasible for Latin America, even if it were ethically acceptable. However, Latin America developed a system of segregation of the Indian from the national society. To the degree that the Indian entered the social system, he was accorded a status in which he was malnourished, illiterate, without adequate shelter and clothing, and separated from the élite by a social distance which ranged from attitudes of utter indifference to recognition as subhuman.

The attitude of the conquering Spanish élite toward the agricultural worker in the colonial period persisted after independence was achieved and even to the present day. The landowner exploited both the land and its workers for the profit of his family. He turned the energies of society toward the production of export commodities which would yield the greatest monetary profit for family advantage. The land was not worked in such a manner as to reflect community responsibility, by devoting at least some of it to the provision of a rounded and adequate diet for the worker. Foodstuffs were imported rather than grown by small independent farmers. The land was mostly owned and worked in large estates or *latifundia*. The worker was, and is, typically deprived of the calories sufficient to provide ordinary energy and other food elements sufficient to prevent protein starvation and malnutrition. It is reported that in one Latin American state 60 per cent of the males have yaws, 50 per cent of the people have malaria, 90 to 95 per cent are illiterate, and 83 per cent of those who enter school do not pass beyond the second grade. Three-fourths of the Latin American states have populations of which more than 50 per cent are illiterate.[8]

The élite have historically looked to Europe, rather than the United States, for the education of their children and for travel, recreation, literature, and the arts, although these patterns are now changing. There was an assimilation and perpetuation of the European culture among the élite. Otherwise, there was only the most superficial mass culture, which lacked an indigenous base in view of the degree of illiteracy and the destruction of the native arts among the Indians. There was almost no social mobility upward for the agricultural worker and the industrial proletariat.

The landowning class lived in the town and its members dominated the government service, the professions, the army, and the priesthood. Industrialization meant the further growth of the towns, the emergence of an urban industrial proletariat, and the continuance of the cleavage between urban and rural social groups. Transportation flowed along lines from the rural hinterland to the town, rather than through an interregional network. While it is most difficult to characterize Latin America as a whole, because of the wide range of its economies and cultures, it has been said that the typical technological configuration of Latin America represents "a thin top veneer of industrial art, a substantial layer of European pre-industrial technology, and a bottom layer of pre-Columbian Indian technology."[9]

The composition of the élite is considerably unstable. Landowning families and their peasant clients tend to coalesce into informal alliances of patrons and clients which become individual centers of power and influence but which disappear and reappear in new blocs. Thus there is a repeated circulation in the membership of the élite, as blocs of power and wealth succeed one another. The peasant, held to the land by immemorial ties and social structures, as well as by debt, is simply shifted from one power bloc to another. His patron, even though he may only recently have reached wealth

[8]S. G. Hanson, *Economic Development in Latin America*, 29 (1951).
[9]S. Tax, "Economic and Ethnology," in *Heritage of Conquest*, 43 (1952).

and position, assumes many of the ideal patterns and attitudes of nineteenth-century aristocratic landed gentry.

The metropolitan upper class is composed of absentee landlords, upper level government officials and functionaries, industrial entrepreneurs, and successful lawyers, doctors, and members of other professions. It is this class which has the highest degree of influence in framing government policies, though in the industrial sectors it is increasingly compelled to accede to trade-union demands for social legislation. The metropolitan middle class consists mostly of first-generation professionals and white-collar workers. To the degree that it has an ideology, it is largely one of emulation of the upper class.

The bottom layer of the industrial proletariat, the *favella* of Brazil, the *descamisados* or shirtless ones of Argentina, and their counterparts elsewhere, live in makeshift shacks in rural slums, which are tightly packed reproductions of the patterns of rural life. These have at best only a slightly greater supply of light, heat, and running water than the rural environment. The industrial proletariat expresses its demands typically through trade unions and demagogic leaders. To the extent that its members are transplanted from the agricultural hinterland, Lewis' studies indicate that they bring their local attitudes with them. As a group, they represent a potent political force.

The agricultural villages may partake either of the traditional native form of closed or corporate primitive community, or of the open community, which has in fact changed its static orientation to the land and has entered the modern world. The open community has, however, lost its unifying core of traditional beliefs and practices. The welfare of the individual actor or the nuclear family is placed before that of the open community. The open community is weakly integrated and heterogeneous, with an ever-changing membership.

The closed or corporate Indian community represents a highly stable adaptation of its members to its way of life. Only dimly, if at all, do its members look beyond its boundaries. Their patterns of conduct are adjustive and permissive. The Ladino or mestizo member of the open community is oriented toward a larger universe than that of the local community. He regards himself to be a member of his nation and, in a comparatively ignorant way, he is aware of the world. Whereas the Indian typically adjusts himself to his community, the Ladino or mestizo strives to control his environment. The Ladino reflects domineering attitudes toward those under him and exhibits strong aggressive, competitive, and factional motivations. Feuds between families or cliques are frequent. His moods are unstable and swing from depression to exhilaration. Feelings of insecurity, inadequacy, and frustration seek expression in aggressive behavior patterns and attitudes. The shift from membership in the closed Indian community to the open one often produces the *trastorno,* an individual of extreme physico-mental disorientation or derangement.

The society as a whole may be said to be atomistic rather than homogeneous and unified, and reflects a wide sharing of values. Any progress resulting in benefit to only some of the members of the society produces reactions of envy rather than a perception of a forward step leading to common benefit. The notion of the bargain or transaction as a source of mutual benefit is lacking; the common assumption is rather that one side is bound to lose in a process of exchange. There is no widespread and long-sustained experience in cooperation and mutual trust. The social distance between groups, the dictatorial performance of authoritative roles, the rivalry of all actors to realize private benefit from an environment of meager resources, poor technology, paucity of management and other skills create a situation which is unfavorable for the growth and acceptance of the processes of agreement reaching, on the one hand, and effective decision making and acceptance of authority, on the other hand, so necessary to the organized society.

The emphasis on egoistic or family values instead of community values in the use of land meant that the land was diverted to the production of primary commodities for the international markets and the monetary rewards to be realized from them. Instead of production for family self-maintenance, there was an agricultural economy largely centered in one or two export crops. Industry to a considerable extent took the form of extractive industries for the export markets. The typical pattern of the underdeveloped country accordingly emerged. While not all agriculture was as crudely exploitative of the human resources as we have indicated, there was substantially no manifestation of that complex of research and employment of the findings of research, skilled use of mechanization, fertilization, rotation of crops, and growth of a rural economy which is a necessary basis for the viable system of relationships between land, labor, and capital characteristic of the more developed nations.

The historical preference of the élite for land investment was reinforced by inflationary patterns. The family value of security in the élite, from whom savings principally come, has meant that the chief interest in long-term investment, other than land, was in the accumulation of overseas holdings. The utilities, financial institutions, mining, and petroleum were typically left to development by the foreign investor. Since the élite were the center of political power, taxation of the land was relatively light. Export and import levies were a major source of tax revenue. Although the incidence of export levies was believed to fall on the foreigner, the competitive result was often the stimulation of other centers of mineral production, such as Africa, and the development of synthetic substitutes where possible. Import levies were typically imposed on mass consumption goods instead of luxury items consumed by the élite. Rural and urban land taxes remained relatively unimportant in the taxation system. In 1946 only 2 per cent of the taxes of Brazil were derived from rural and urban land, while sales and consumption taxes aggregated 45 per cent of the national revenue.[10]

The accumulation of capital through savings was a product principally of the upper classes, business firms, and government enterprises. The savings accumulated by a relatively small group in the upper income brackets of Brazil were estimated in 1948 to be 10 per cent or more of the national income.[11] Net domestic savings available for investment for Latin America as a whole probably represented 8 to 9 per cent of the gross domestic product for the 1950-57 period.[12] Chronic inflation in many countries discouraged savings and the channeling of investment in productive enterprise.

The Latin American investor turned to manufacturing or trade only in conditions where there were high profits per unit rather than high volume at low unit profits. Industrialization has been on a high cost basis. Stockholders and management, on the one hand, and labor, on the other, viewed government as a source of privilege

---

[10]Hanson, *Economic Development,* 467.
[11]*Ibid.,* 189.
[12]U.S. Senate Committee on Foreign Relations, Subcommittee on American Republics affairs, *Problems of Latin American Economic Development,* 86th Cong., 2nd Sess., Committee Print 6, Feb., 11, 1960, 68.

rather than as an institution devoted to the national welfare. The extension of a sheltered position to the landowning class was matched by tariff protection and governmental aid to business and by extensive labor and social legislation for trade union and labor groups. The stimulation of industrial development was viewed in a context in which there was an unfortunately high dependency on the international commodity markets. Freedom from such a dependency assumed such a high priority value that small-scale, high cost industrial development by local entrepreneurs accordingly became a tolerable governmental policy. Industrialization brought into being new monopolists and continued the class divisions.

The pattern was thus set for the process of foreign investment. The high risks incident to mining and petroleum exploration and development, the heavy long-term investments and technological requirements of these fields, as well as the heavy capital requirements and lack of immediate high yield in the public utility field, meant that these areas became dominated by foreign capital as local capital ignored them. For the reasons stated in Chapter II, the concession agreement became a typical means for establishing a foreign investment.

Foreign investment occurred in a local situation characterized by people who were keenly dissatisfied with their relative progress in the march of nations. They were denied a standard of living of even a minimum subsistence level, as compared to the economies of North American and Western European countries. It accordingly became easy for the Latin American peasant and worker to identify foreign investment with colonialism and imperialism. The foreign-owned segments of the economies of Latin America consequently became the focus of nationalistic pressures, discriminatory legislation, and enforcement of legislation.

It may be true that the early experience of Latin America with foreign investment was not always such that the foreign investor's standards and techniques were to be admired. Often he descended to the morals of the local market place, which were low indeed. But the true image of one century is not that of the next, any more than the "robber baron" of the nineteenth century is typical of twentieth-century management and capitalism in the welfare state of the free world. The image of the past, however, still persists and molds the present, even though its content is now lacking in reality.

The average net capital inflow into Latin America during the period 1950-58 was about $780 million annually. Over two-thirds of the inflow was in the form of direct private investment and meant that technical and managerial skills were imported, as well as capital. During this period the book value of United States' direct private investment in Latin America rose from $4.7 billion to over $8.7 billion. To this figure add a net inflow of nearly half a billion dollars from other countries, mostly European.[13] While in the past century and the early part of this century the foreign business enterprise tended to assume the practices and standards of the local market place in treatment of labor and quest of governmental preference, today it is frequently the victim of a higher standard of enforcement of social and other legislation than that applied to local entrepreneurs. In addition, the foreign-managed enterprise has introduced locally the enlightened standards of labor treatment, job training and promotion and the like, characteristic of the democratic free enterprise state.

The local cleavage in classes and value orientations and the local investment patterns, which brought the foreign-controlled sectors of the economy into being, created local tensions which only too readily found their outlet in identifying foreign control as a new form of the old colonial patterns. The standards of performance of the foreign entrepreneur in comparison with the local businessmen, the contributions of foreign enterprise to higher wage levels, training of labor and adherence to government welfare legislation, the assumption by the foreign investor of risks, heavy capital outlay, and delayed returns, from which local entrepreneurs shrank, were overlooked. The foreign contribution was not identified as participation in the essential life of the community, but was viewed in the false image of foreign exploitation created by local politicos.

The contours of the international system of economic relationships between Latin America and the world now appear. The Latin American élite possessed a value system which resulted in an institutional framework placing the country at the periphery of the international system. Its dependency on the international commodity markets was in considerable measure a dependency of its own creation, more precisely, of the historical and cultural forces. Instead of viewing its participation in the international economy

---

[13]*Ibid.*, 37, 71.

as an assumption by the latter of responsibilities and tasks which the local national economies were unable or unwilling to undertake, it reacted with animosity, and with, at times, violent political measures against what it deemed to be economic domination by the United States, Great Britain, and Western European states.

A sense of process was lacking, that is, a coherent, organized idea of ends and means of cultural growth. Political leadership ignored the need to lay the foundations for a rounded, vigorous economy and social structure, to develop a system of public education, to send promising young men abroad to learn of sciences and industrial management, and to establish a rational system of land tenure and use. Imperfect and distorted local social structures were not recognized. Instead, the Latin American perceived himself to be "closed in" by the politicos and generals, on the one hand, who formed an iron hand of authoritative control which persisted through all political revolutions, and the Yankee and British imperialists, on the other hand. It seemed that only a political, social, and economic revolution could open the closed circle.

The first phase of the Mexican Revolution of 1910-20 was primarily an agrarian movement toward the abolition of the *latifundia* system of large landed estates. The 1917 constitution laid the foundation for a program of agrarian reform, which, to a considerable degree, ended in an excessive fractionalization of land ownership and harmful land practices. The dominance of foreign ownership of Mexican natural resources was also a matter of profound concern to the revolution. The constitution excluded the owner of the surface from rights to the subsoil and, in article 27, vested in the nation direct ownership of petroleum and solid, liquid, or gaseous hydrocarbons. Expropriation was authorized on the basis of fiscal values. Ownership of land and the right to exploit natural resources were limited to Mexicans and to foreigners who would agree not to seek diplomatic protection from their governments.

After a 1921 decision of the Supreme Court of Mexico had recognized petroleum rights acquired prior to 1917 which had in fact been exercised by the holders, the government in 1928 began issuing confirmatory concessions for an unlimited period of time to these same holders. The assumption by the oil companies of a concessionary status did not, however, remove the imbedded image of their presence as a manifestation of foreign imperialism. The next ten years witnessed the emergence of a strong political force in organized labor and a growing sense of nationalism. A labor dispute beginning in 1936 led to tensions which ended on March 18, 1938, in the expropriation by governmental decree of the interests of seventeen oil companies.

The current crisis in Cuba furnishes another case study in the clash of human values which emerge when a state, as a latecomer to the industrialization process, establishes its linkages with the international society. The social pressures have reached an intensity where they appear to be creating a social and economic revolution, as well as a political revolution. Although an appraisal of the present Cuban political scene is not within the province of this study, a summary of the forces which brought it into being is essential to an understanding of the phenomenon of nationalization as a product of the historical pattern of Latin American participation in the world society.

Cuba was a typical counterpart of the Latin-American economy described above. It had become a part of the world society to the degree that in 1954 25 per cent of its national income came from the production and manufacture of sugar. Sugar and its by-products constituted 86 per cent of the value of Cuban exports during 1946-54.[14] Diversification in agriculture had taken place to a considerable degree after the depression of the 'thirties; however, the later world boom in sugar demand again distorted its economy as it returned to sugar production. Productivity per man was low. Although more than 80 per cent of farm power in 1947 was provided by oxen,[15] mechanization to reduce costs would throw labor upon an economy unprepared to absorb it. Cuba seemed doomed to remain a marginal producer in the world markets and dependent for much of its export on a legislative preference accorded sugar imports in the United States market.

The cleavage between the urban and rural economies is in part indicated by the fact that the illiteracy rate in the urban area is 11.6 per cent and in the rural 41.7 per cent, reaching a high of 49.7 per cent in Oriente province, where the Castro revolution began. In the province, 31 per cent of those over six years of age had received no formal education, 29.4 per cent had not gone beyond three years of elementary schooling, and only 11 per cent had

---

[14]U.S. Dept. of Commerce, *Investment in Cuba*, 6-7 (1956).
[15]Hanson, *Economic Development*, 117.

gone beyond elementary school.[16] While Cuba's standard of living is generally one of the highest in Latin America, its per capita income in 1950-54 averaged 312 pesos (the Cuban peso was then equated as equal to the United States dollar). The State of Mississippi's lowest income figure was $638.[17] More than 75 per cent of rural dwellings are huts and more than two-thirds have earthen floors. The urban dweller in Cuba has low housing standards in comparison with those of industrially advanced countries, but, in 1953, 87 per cent of urban dwellings had electric lights, compared to 9.1 per cent in the rural areas, and 54.6 per cent of urban dwellings had inside piping for water, compared to 2.3 per cent in rural dwellings. Eighty-five per cent of the rural areas received their water supply from rivers, wells, or springs. Ninety-five per cent of urban dwellings had some form of toilet facility, one-third of which were privies, but in rural dwellings 54.1 per cent had no toilet facilities and over 90 per cent had no bath facilities.[18]

Over twenty-five years ago, Cuba started a program of agricultural reform pursuant to a program outlined in 1934. If political leadership in Cuba had adhered to this program, many of its present ills would never have developed. The program recommended the withdrawal of poorly suited lands from sugar production for production of foodstuffs in the diversification of agriculture. It advised that farming provide an adequate diet for the farm family on a basis of self-sufficiency, that a class of independent farmers be established, that agricultural research, extension, and educational activities be encouraged, cooperative marketing and financing institutes be promoted, and that gainful use of the sugar workers be made during the off season.

Although the gross private capital formation in Cuba in 1954 was 13.4 per cent of the gross national product, as against a high of 16.2 per cent in 1952, only a small part of the Cuban domestic income and savings was invested in new and expanded industrial and agricultural enterprises. There is little interest in local purchase of securities, beyond a limited market for government and mortgage lands. Cuban investment is principally made abroad. As late as 1939, foreign banks held 83 per cent of all deposits, but by 1955 Cuban banks had grown to a position where they held 60 per cent of all

---

[16]U.S. Dept. of Commerce, *Investment in Cuba*, 181.
[17]*Ibid.*, 184.
[18]*Ibid.*, 187.

deposits. Government credit institutions provide medium- and long-term credits for agricultural and industrial enterprises.[19]

The international market for sugar has failed to provide a sound basis for orderly production and planning by individual producers or for stable governmental revenues upon which needed national policies can be carried out. Sugar was 22.5 cents c. & f. New York in early 1920 but fell to 3.625 cents before the end of the year. In 1929 it reached 1.471 cents c. & f. New York and fell to a low of 0.59 of a cent in 1932.[20] World War II and the Korean crisis pushed sugar to new highs only to be succeeded, upon the cessation of conflict, with a rapid fall in demand and prices, an inability to market crops, and consequent restriction in production.

The above discussion portrays in broad strokes the salient aspects of the Latin American social, economic, and political structure. Mexico and Cuba were the subjects of more detailed case studies. Mexico represents a situation in which the social, economic, and political change (which it is believed much of Latin America must experience) has proceeded to a point where a new equilibrium has been found and relative stability achieved. Cuba represents a situation in which a military revolution has taken place and a new basis of political power is in the process of establishing itself.[21]

Some of the salient features of the national societies under examination may now be indicated. There is no particular hierarchy of importance implied in the order of this listing. Examination will then be made of national societies in the Middle East in which nationalization has occurred and comparison of such societies will be made with those in Middle America. From these data, it may be possible to discern fairly typical conditions of national societies which are likely to produce profound and rapid change in their centers of authority and power, in the structuring of their classes,

---

[19]*Ibid.*, 12, 124, 125.

[20]Hanson, *Economic Development*, 107.

[21]In addition to the above citations, the preceding discussion is based on the following sources listed in the bibliography: books by P. C. M. Teichert, J. Walter Thompson Co., J. F. Rippy, A. O. Hirschman, L. W. Shannon, O. Lewis, M. J. Levy, Jr., S. Tax (particularly the following studies therein: S. Tax, "Economy and Ethnology," J. de la Fuente, "Ethnic and Communal Relations," F. Cámara, "Religious and Political Organization," J. Gillin, "Ethos and Cultural Aspects of Personality"), R. N. Adams and others; and articles by C. Wagley and M. Harris, E. R. Wolf, W. C. Sayres, and R. L. Beals.

and in the recognition of values of different groups. Nationalization thus becomes a characteristic symptom of a current malaise in a number of undeveloped nations.

1. They are societies characterized by a landowning élite whose members are primarily in the government, the army, and the church, by a submerged group of agricultural workers, and by an industrial proletariat, in which no substantial integration of the different classes and groups has taken place. They are characterized by extreme social distance between classes, though there may be formal equality before the law and often no antiracial sentiments, as such.

2. They are societies in which the values of the élite are realized to a considerable extent, but in which the values of the agricultural worker and the urban proletariat are only minimally recognized.

3. They are societies whose traditional values and social structures are rapidly changing, but whose centers of authority or power in the economic and political spheres remain largely unchanged.

4. They are societies characterized by excessive proliferation of personnel in the government and the army and by use of office for the realization of individual or family values instead of public values. The resulting situation is usually described as "corruption" by other societies possessing a more universal value system.

5. They are societies in which there was a failure of leadership to promote a viable basis for the organization and use of its resources in a wide spectrum of activities, including the use of land, the development of mineral resources, the growth of a well-rounded industry, the establishment of public utilities for the provision of electrical energy and communication, the building of transportation facilities, such as railroads, and the creation of an adequate banking system. In all of these instances there was a resort to the world society for the provision of foodstuffs and other primary commodities, manufactures, and capital investment for aiding the neglected sectors of the economy. In addition, the societies were characterized by a failure to provide for such basic needs of their people as an adequate diet, health, and education.

6. They are societies in which the failure to create a shared sense of progress toward goals desired by increasingly larger sectors of the population brought about by a very unstable equilibrium of social forces and increasing reliance on the military to maintain traditional

centers of authority or power. Many are at the point where the dominant élite class will resist innovation and modernization simply on the ground that it may be the final force which will topple their shaky control of authority. In their view, physical improvement in the conditions of the lower classes is equated with subversion of the authority structure.

7. They are societies with a history of colonialism and foreign development of economic resources. Although the new patterns of international economic relationships are not at all characteristic of those of the past, the political leaders in the societies make use of ancient identifications and resentments to divert to foreign scapegoats blame for domestic failures in the discharge of public responsibilities.

8. They are societies in which the explosive forces of nationalism are now coupled with mounting pressures of long-denied demands of submerged groups. The masses of unabsorbed labor and labor working at a marginal level of existence in the cities, together with agricultural workers in rural areas, show an increasing awareness of their submerged position. They comprise a political force which can readily be utilized by the opportunist, the demagogue, the Communist, or the charismatic leader. The direction which such a force might take, once it is unleashed, is highly conjectural.

9. The configuration of the value system and resultant social structure, as indicated above, is one which is most subject to manipulation by a leader who creates the image of the evil and exploitative foreigner as the source responsible for the social tensions of the local arena and advocates the expulsion of the foreigner from the economy as a means for opening the doors to national progress toward desired goals.

Any conclusion that the above description of the salient elements of typical underdeveloped nations in Middle America represents a somewhat universal pattern in underdeveloped nations should first be tested by turning to another national society of totally different racial components and a region in which a high degree of international tension has manifested itself. For this purpose a brief description will be made of Iran as a latecomer in the movement toward the industrial state, although its past reflects an advanced stage of civilization when Western Europe was, by contrast, a strikingly "underdeveloped" area. Such a description will be made on the basis of the above nine propositions.

1. The country is divided into the landowning élite and the impoverished and undernourished agricultural workers. At a lower level of the élite are the wealthy merchants and bankers of the bazaar. The rest of the bazaar includes the shopkeepers and the artisans. The bazaar is both a geographical and economic entity; it is the industrial center, exchange, and shopping center.

The counterpart of the Indian in Latin America is found in the unassimilated nomadic tribes of the north, notably the 800,000 Kurds. There are no caste distinctions and there is equality before the law.

2. The landowner lives in Teheran and rarely visits the rural village in which his tenants live, which he is regarded to own and for which he acts as patron. Typically the landlord receives 80 per cent of the produce and the tenant 20 per cent, but the latter is diminished by usurious loans made at times of individual economic catastrophe. About four-fifths of the population are agricultural workers, living in primitive villages, working with primitive tools, and ridden with disease and malnourishment. The lot of the artisan is little, if any, better, as he lives in urban slums at or below subsistence level. About 85 per cent of the people are illiterate. There is no public health service. There is a high infant mortality rate, but reliable mortality data are lacking. Lack of sanitation is a characteristic condition. The typical dwelling is made of adobe or mud and the average family of five may live in one room.

3. Iran is undergoing the process of change characteristic of the Middle East, with the emergence of a modest middle class and proletariat of the cities and a growing political awareness and demand for basic political, social, and economic change. Iran's traditional authority structure remains virtually unchanged, however, for the grant of the vote to the peasant clients of the landowners means in fact the effective disfranchisement of the educated middle class.

4. The government administration is said to be greatly overstaffed, inefficient, dedicated to routine, and characterized by a high degree of corruption.

5. The primary source of public revenue is from taxation of the petroleum industry and there is as yet no industrial or other base to take its place when it is exhausted or loses its competitive strength to the looming North African production from the Sahara.

6. The continued delay in agricultural reform, industrial prog-

ress, and provision of basic public services has brought about a very unstable political situation, the eventual outcome of which still remains highly unpredictable.

7. Iran has long been the scene of conquest. It was and remains a fearful neighbor of the Soviet, whose military occupation of the north is still a vivid memory. The British and Russian occupation of World War II helped to create strong feelings of xenophobia and foreign responsibility for domestic shortcomings.

8. Iran is the scene of a growing nationalism, characteristic of the Middle East, and the emergence of demands by depressed groups whose satisfaction cannot be long denied, if the existing authority structure is to remain. Yet to concede such demands may trigger unknown and violent changes prejudicing the authority of the dominant class.

9. The emergence of Dr. Mohammed Mossadeq as a national leader and the oil nationalization of 1951 were products of the forces described above. The static quality of national leadership and the failure to make needed reforms led to increased violence in political activity. On the left, the Tudeh, or Communist-oriented party, became an increasingly powerful force. On the right, a fanatical religious movement emerged under the leadership of Mullah Kashani. The economy of the country sharply fell after expenditures by foreign occupation troops ceased and catastrophic crop failures occurred in 1948 and 1949. Famine appeared and unemployment grew. Tax collections fell to such a low level that salaries of public officials were in arrears. A Kurdish rebellion occurred in 1950. Soviet political pressures increased, coupled with the continued growth of the Tudeh and an attempted assassination of the Shah by a Tudeh follower on February 4, 1949.

An attempt by the Shah to establish reform measures, as a means of obtaining Western financial aid, ended in a disappointing United States offer of a $25 million loan from the Export-Import Bank and a token foreign-aid appropriation of $500,000 by the United States in 1950. In September, 1950, the Imperial Anti-Corruption Commission made a long report listing honest and essential government employees, honest and superfluous officials, and corrupt officials, which created a violent stir.

The typical conditions appeared for a move against foreign interests, which were found in the oil concession held by the Anglo-Iranian Oil Company. In the winter of 1950-51 Dr. Mossadeq's

National Front demanded the nationalization of the oil industry. The prime minister, General Razmara, opposed this move, but he was assassinated on March 7, 1951, by a member of a fanatical religious group, the Islamic brotherhood, Fadayan Islam. On March 15 the Majlis unanimously voted in favor of an oil nationalization law, which was confirmed by the Senate on March 20, 1951.[22]

As one considers the pattern of the underdeveloped nation indicated above, its universality becomes more and more apparent. Thus Egypt, prior to the army-led revolution of Naguib and Nasser, was characterized by the typical pattern we have seen of the urban concentration of the élite, the centralization of political and economic control in the wealthy landowning and the emerging capitalist classes, the impoverished fellahin or peasants living in primitive squalor, the noisome proletariat of the cities, the governmental indifference toward public needs and political corruption, the failure to create any sense of progress toward desired goals with, instead, a feeling of continued regression, a history of foreign conquest and occupation and the presence of a substantial foreign interest, and finally the appearance of a strong sense of nationalism, a principal aspect of which was xenophobia manifested toward the British.

Egypt had been ruled by the foreigner for over twenty-five centuries when it attained autonomy in the nineteenth century and the status of a sovereign and independent nation in the twentieth century. Political control largely centered in the typical élite of landlords, industrialists, financiers, traders, and exporters. A small middle class of shopkeepers, officials, and intellectuals interposed itself between the élite and the mass of agricultural workers in the rural areas and industrial workers and unemployed in the cities. The submerged industrial proletariat became the highly volatile group known as the "Street," which political leaders employed as a weapon of violent force.

One-third of the land was held by one-twentieth of the landowners. Cotton accounted for four-fifths of Egypt's exports. A static quantity of land had to support a growing population and growing demands of all classes upon its production. The growing

[22]S. K. Ghosh, "The Anglo-Iranian Oil Dispute," chap. 4 (doctoral thesis, Urbana, Ill., 1956); W. S. Haas, *Iran* (1946); G. Lenczowski, *The Middle East in World Affairs*, chap. 5 (2nd ed., 1956); D. N. Wilber, *Iran: Past and Present* (1955).

intelligentsia found their primary place of employment in the government and, as such, became the victims of a patronage system.

The Muslim brotherhood and the Wafd, the principal political forces, were united in hatred of the British. The Wafd, however, was dominated by the landowner class and used anti-British sentiments as a means for protection of the particularistic values of their group. The bankruptcy of the leadership by the élite, in the military catastrophe of the war of 1948-49 against Israel, eventually brought about an army-led revolution, the abdication of King Farouk, and the premiership of General Naguib. The army represents a separate social group of great influence and importance. Antiforeign ideology persisted and remained a central factor in government policy even after the British were substantially excluded from the national system.

On November 14, 1954, Nasser assumed control of the government, following a seizure of power from Naguib by a group of young army officers. Nasser's subsequent anti-Western policies threatening the access of the West to the Mediterranean basin and the Middle East, together with a rather inept process of setting off the United States and Russia in bargaining against each other as to the amount of assistance each would offer for the building of the Aswan Dam, led Secretary of State Dulles to withdraw the financial offer of the United States. This was a project upon which Nasser had, to a considerable degree, staked the prestige of his regime. The consequence—a risk which Dulles had presumably assumed as a "calculated risk"—was the nationalization on July 26 of the Universal Suez Maritime Canal Company.[23]

Russia, at the time of its revolution of 1917 and the resultant expropriation of private property, enacted the above typical pattern. For many centuries, the land of the "Russ" was the scene of nomadic invasion and attack from Asia, culminating in the fall of Kiev by Mongol attack in 1240 and the ensuing occupation of Russia by the Golden Horde until 1480. The national structure which eventually emerged was a highly authoritarian, autocratic,

---

[23]E. B. Haas and A. S. Whiting, *Dynamics of International Relations,* chap. 15 (1956). Egypt is characterized by these authors as representing a typical situation of control by an oligarchical élite. See also C. C. Issawi, *Egypt: An Economic and Social Analysis* (1947); H. A. R. Gibb, *Modern Trends in Islam* (1947); and Royal Institute of International Affairs, *The Middle East: A Political and Economic Survey* (1958).

central government with authority held by a few hands, a landowning élite, to which was added a growing group of industrial and financial leaders, a vast submerged class of agricultural workers living at primitive levels, and an industrial proletariat in the cities. In Lenin's view, Russia was a prime victim of Western economic imperialism, especially in view of the French investments related to the Entente. The Marxist philosophy called for the revolution of the proletariat at the peak of development of monopoly capitalism. In Russia, it in fact took place in a society which was characterized by a great cleavage between the élite and the agricultural and industrial workers, but which was nevertheless a predominantly agricultural, instead of industrial, society. The seizure of power by the Bolsheviks and their allies in November, 1917, was made possible by the centering of authority in a relatively few hands under the tsars and the delayed development of a middle class. The transfer of the control of power to another minority group was thus relatively easy.

The configurations of the societies, social structures, and values of these underdeveloped nations exhibit in varying degrees the universal characteristics noted above.

The tensions engendered by the national patterns described above are perhaps of an explosive nature in the countries of Nicaragua, El Salvador, Honduras, and the Dominican Republic in Middle America and the Caribbean area, and in Peru in South America. In Peru, an open conflict between the Indian majority and the white élite at times appears to be close to the breaking point. Iran has by no means solved the tensions which created the 1954 break with the West. There is a most uneasy equilibrium in the Middle East.

In each underdeveloped nation there is, of course, a unique situation. As its social structure, value system, history, government, and economy are investigated in depth, it will be seen that there are groups among the élite which are aware of the need for change and groups among other classes willing to accept orderly, instead of revolutionary, progress—provided that there is progress.

The situation of the typical underdeveloped nation having an unstable adaptation to the world society is not one to be solved solely by the standardized patterns of foreign aid which have developed in the free world. This problem will be considered at greater length in Chapter VI.

THE INTERNATIONAL
SYSTEM: A STRUCTURAL
VIEW OF WORLD SOCIETY

This and the following chapter, together with the first eight propositions of Chapter VII, represent the statement of a body of theory of law and organization in world society. The search for structure in the world society means a search for repetitive and institutionalized patterns of action so clustered and so coordinated that we can say that organizations have emerged. It means that the principal types of organizations which are actors in the world society must be identified. When the actors are identified, it is then necessary to determine the degree to which their interaction possesses structure or order, the processes which establish structure or order, and the influences which determine the characteristics of such structure or order. The resulting international system will be defined in terms of its principal actors, the degree to which and the manner in which their action is coordinated by authority, on the one hand, and agreement, on the other, and the factors influencing the integration and viability of the totality of the patterns of action or processes of interaction taking place.

As the essentially analytical task of the remainder of this volume is begun, the elusiveness of the available terms becomes apparent. Words should provide precision and accuracy in the development of knowledge, as well as a means for communication. When the scientist or scholar tries to push forward the boundaries of knowledge, whether of man or of nature, the new image of the world which comes to him can only with difficulty be expressed in the current vocabulary. It is inherently the plight of the discoverer of strange and new regions that words fail him. Others can never know the fullness of the new vision which has come before his eyes and the full meaning and beauty which he has seen.

When the discoverer resorts to existing terms for the purpose of expressing and communicating new meanings and insights, the terms become laden with a multiplicity of meanings until creative thought and communication are enveloped by deeper and deeper fogs of confusion. "Power," for example, may mean energy, the ability to create energy, or the ability to influence the behavior of others through dominance in a desired manner. The latter meaning is a more familiar one in the social sciences, as distinguished from the natural sciences. The use of "authority" is preferred here to indicate the ability to influence others through commands or directions, which are accepted for purposes of conduct without reasoned persuasion of the rationality of their content, and "power" to indicate dominance as a means for establishing authority.

Then, too, words are emotive. "System" is a cold, neutral term. "Society" perhaps has some warmth. "Community" definitely creates an impression of warm, interpersonal relations of a close and cohesive character. "World community" is a more dramatic and appealing term than "international system," yet, as will be seen in the discussion of the first proposition below, there is in fact no more of a world community than there is an international system, in the more precise use of the terms community and system. Yet the term system is not without some basis when we look at world society as a process. It shall be found in this study that certain variables in world society can be described to possess regularities of behavior. The description of such a system will be made in a set of interdependent principles and propositions.

1. *The international system consists of the aggregate of the systems of action in which interaction takes place without regard to state boundaries for the attainment of the goals and the realization*

of the values of the persons and organizations acting in the world society.

One of the difficulties in communication is the absence of a term in the storehouse of terminology to create an adequate image of structure in the world society. The above definition of the term international system implies that there is no universal system of action extending to the limits of this terrestrial globe and embracing all its population. It implies, among other things, that social action viewed in a world environment does not yet reflect that degree of integration or cohesion, that degree of predictability of the interaction of actors as exhibiting common responses to the typical variables with which they are confronted, and that degree of sharing of goals and values which would justify its characterization as a social system.

Whether the term "social system," "society," or "community" is used to indicate the totality of the established patterns of interaction taking place in the world today, each term imports a meaning which is not in fact present in such totality. The above proposition states that there is no such international system, only an aggregate of systems. This is not to say that the elements of a social system in the international action with which we are concerned may not be emerging. Shared goals and concerted action or interaction toward the attainment of those goals are beginning to appear. This is notably true in regional patterns of interaction toward common goals. There may even be a modicum of empirical truth in the proposition that there is the beginning of a single international system. The proposition which is asserted, however, and which is believed to be the most accurate and comprehensive description of the situation, is that interaction among states and other actors in the world society has not as yet assumed the pattern of a single system.

The term "world society" was used, among other things, to refer to the patterns of action in the international scene. However, the peoples of the world do not constitute a true society. They do not interact with one another with a sense of realization of unity, belonging together, and sharing a common culture and institutional framework, so as to justify the appellation of the term "society." The term "world community" has also been used by writers to identify the same situation, but the peoples of the world do not yet exhibit that degree of intimacy, realization of group solidarity, loyalty to the group, a sense of belongingness, and consciousness of kind typically associated with the term "community."

Thus a term is used which is as neutral and as close to reality as possible, namely, the term "international system."

When *the* international system, or, more precisely, the international *social* system, does in fact emerge, it will be unique as against other and lesser systems of a regional or even global character. When the ultimate international social system of world scope appears, in which such lesser systems will act as subsystems and will be coordinated in the authority structure of the superior system, then the exercise of leadership in the international social system will for the first time involve a social system directed *exclusively* to goal gratification, integration, and maintenance of the system itself, and will *not* include the element of adaptation to its social base. The international social system will, of course, still have to adapt to its physical environment but, insofar as human environment is concerned, its leaders and members will not view such environment as something external to the system to which appropriate linkages must be found. Groups within the international system will still clamor for a recognition of their particular values. There will still be discrete organizations and many "we-they" identifications. But there will also be a comprehensive world-wide identification of "we" without an opposing "they" in a single dichotomy. The ultimate in unity of social action in the international sphere will have at last been reached.

While the international social system does not possess, in terms of empirical fact, the character of a single and discrete social system, the aggregate of the systems of action in which interaction takes place without regard to state boundaries embraces so much of the life of all peoples that it demands recognition and conceptualization as a social fact. The term international system identifies such a stream of action flowing through the life of all states. The commitment by states and other international actors to participation in the international system is now of such magnitude that the failure of such action to achieve the appropriate degree of organization is a cause of enormous stress in world society.

It may be noted that the pre-World War I system of interstate relations possessed a number of regulative features directed to maintain the characteristics of the system. The decentralization of power into a number of states, the consequent balance-of-power system, the role of Great Britain as a principal actor directed to the maintenance of the system, the ability of great powers to use force to sanction departures from the rules of international law, as in the Venezuelan pacific blockade of 1902, the function of gold as a regulator of international exchange and flow of investment and trade, worked together to create a fairly consistent, self-regulating international system.

The present system of interstate relations cannot be so neatly described. It has typically been called a bipolar power system, but such a symbol is a crude identification of its complexity. Stresses in the Soviet-led system of Communist states are now emerging, and their intensity will increase as Soviet leadership and authority encounters increasingly diverse national values and goals in other states of the bloc. On the other hand, patterns of integration are emerging in Western Europe. Both the Soviet sphere and the Atlantic community face a problem of adjustment to the modernizing states.

The transformation of the international system as it is now structured into a single and cohesive international social system will demand many things, not the least of which will be a shared sense of identification with the system by all peoples as they participate in it and the development of attitudes of compassion and understanding among all peoples.

The child is born as pure self and all his perceptions and actions are related to that self. As he interacts with his mother, his family, and with successively larger groups, he gradually becomes aware of the existence of the latter as realities. The growth of the perception or recognition of other actors and groups and the ability to adjust or adapt himself to progressively larger groups is an index of his maturity. We are mature as we can empathize first with our family, then our community and nation, and, finally, the world society.

The typical pattern of the individual maturing in the modern world is far from this ideal norm. As he moves into the performance of his roles in the various organizations of modern society, he becomes an alienated actor. He retains his personal identity, but he finds that another self, an alienated self, perhaps an organizational self, is doing many things and consuming much of his time and energy. There is little sense of personal responsibility or, in appropriate situations, of guilt for the actions of this alienated self. Those with whom he interacts become things or symbols instead of human personalities. They are things to be manipulated or even destroyed, as the organizational self demands.

The international system is at the periphery of action and perception of most individuals. We symbolize other actors therein in standardized forms. We impersonalize our relationships with them until we can tolerate or even welcome the killing of other actors. To bring the individual to perceive that the international system, though structured largely in organizations, is in fact composed of sentient individuals, who are products of their respective cultures and the value systems of such cultures, and to bring him to identify himself with the international system, is to travel a road of great distance and many turnings.

In using the concepts of self and alienated personality, it was not intended to assert universal propositions characteristic of all individuals. For example, the fragmented, nonintegrated personality does not fit into the above proposition. It is simply affirmed that adaptation of the individual can, with a considerable degree of generality or validity, be characterized in the concepts indicated, and these are fruitful concepts for viewing and describing action in the international arena.

2. *An individual will participate in the international system usually as the performer of a role, which will typically be an organization or occupational role.*

It is not the isolated individual but the industrial worker, the executive, the official, the voter, the soldier, or performer of some other organizational or occupational role who is typically the actor in international situations and the participant in the international system. States, corporate organizations, trade unions, military organizations, and other organized groups are more readily and more customarily identified as actors in the international society than individuals. Behavior is being described here in terms of the individual. Consequently, the ensuing discussion is begun with the proposition that the individuals who are most frequently involved in international situations are principally the performers of some organizational or occupational role, holders of some authoritative office in government or industry, government functionaries, or corporate employees.

Most individuals never leave their home country and, when

they do, it is most frequently as travelers. The tourist is the performer of a role. As such, he does not enter into the culture and life of the various national societies; he merely observes it in his travels. If the individual is employed abroad by his government or a firm, his interactions with others are principally in the performance of some organizational role. The individual as an artist or writer may at times considerably affect the character of values and consequent action within the international system, but, if so, it is still in the performance of his role as artist or writer. It may be said that the individual as the owner and manager of a small firm is a most significant aspect of the export and import markets, but, again, it is only in his performance of the role of trader.

When such a broad arena of action as that of the international system is reached, one is almost always concerned with some aspect of organized action. Organizations and not individuals may justifiably be characterized as the principal actors in the international system. When this is done, however, one must be extraordinarily careful in dealing with these abstractions and must at all times be clear as to the external and internal forces affecting decision making within the organizations and the consequent direction of their action.

It may incidentally be observed that participation by the foreigner in the life of the national society does not usually result in his immersion in the national culture. He may learn the language, read the local press, and converse with the citizenry, but, employed in a foreign office of his government or a branch of one of its corporations and working with his colleagues therein, living with his family transported abroad with him, and participating socially in an enclave drawn from his nation, his foreign acculturation is slight.

2.a. *An individual will be influenced by, and will influence, action in the international system by the perceptions, cognitions, and values which he derives from his membership in his culture.*

An individual is many things in many settings. He is an organism, an actor, a role performer, a member of a group, a tribe, a society, a nation, and a culture. He becomes meaningful in life and life becomes meaningful for him as a consequence of the totality of his knowledge of the world and himself. He may be the performer of a role, but the underlying fact remains that he is a sentient being, possessing a unique personality and value system. Yet his action, the way he manifests himself objectively and adapts to his environment, is a product of his experience or his immersion in his culture, as well as his personality. His experience, as a participant in his culture and its various subcultures and groups, determines his perceptions, cognitions, and values.

If the individual is to be a significant concept for the purposes of building a theory of action in the world society, he must be seen as a product of his culture.

3. *Order and structure in the international system will be found in the internal and external relations of organizations participating in it and not in the interactions of individuals as discrete personalities. The latter, in the extensiveness and intensity of their adherence to values, will act as a conditioning factor upon action in the international system.*

The study of the international system was approached with the initial proposition that order and structure was to be found in it only in the degree that major separate systems of action could be found in the world society and interaction took place between them. It was then hypothesized that individuals participated in it primarily in the performance of organizational or occupational roles. At this point, a description of action in the international system will be made which defines its principal actors and their modes of action.

It is asserted that organizations and not systems are the principal actors in the international system because organizations constitute the final state in the development of a social system. They are social systems in which action is consciously coordinated through authority to reach valued goals. They are the characteristic form of action in modern society. A social system may operate on the basis that each member of the system has learned (internalized) the responses expected of him in typical situations in the operation of the system, that is to say, its members learn and perform roles. An organization is unique in that the form of its action is characteristically the product of the exercise of authority. A search is made for order and structure in the internal and external relations of organizations because only in these comprehensive structures of human behavior can useful statements conveniently be made concerning the nature and operation of the international system. The value of the dignity and worth of the individual may influence the way in which the mass killing of Negroes by the South African police is evaluated but the principal actor in the situation is perceived to be the state of South Africa. Organizations instead of individuals are typically selected to be the entities to which personality, motivation, and responsibility are ascribed as meaning is given to international situations.

In the second sentence of this principle, it was said that individuals as such, in the extensiveness and intensity of their attachment to values, will act as a conditioning factor upon action in the international system. This is a fact of profound importance in the analysis of the international system. Whatever concepts of social action may be created, whatever analysis be made of social behavior in the international scene, the influence of values upon behavior is a fundamental starting point.

The demonstration and development of this phase of the above principle involves such widespread and important implications that it will be necessary to make them the topic of separate principles and propositions below. Certain observations must, however, initially be made. All individual action, of course, springs from such basic drives as hunger, sex, aggression, and heat and cold avoidance. An individual acts because he must satisfy needs. He may find his satisfaction in the activity itself or in the effect of the action. In any event, the character of his action is determined by the value or preference which he accords to the particular action chosen, as against other competing values inhering in other possible courses of action.

As individuals coalesce into groups and groups become structured into organizations, action is stimulated primarily by the effect which it produces and the contentment following its effect rather than by the satisfaction found in the action itself. Action becomes instrumental toward reaching goals desired by the members of the group. As attachment to values extends throughout the membership of a group and as the group is engaged in action directed toward the attainment of such goals, integration and solidarity will increase. If the group is hindered or frustrated in the realization of its values, tensions and a tendency toward disintegration will appear.

The prediction of social action is fundamentally a matter of the analysis of the values of the actors. If action is viewed in terms of the realization of values of the members of a group, the amount of group energy it will use, the direction it will take, and the control it will accept can be anticipated. Similarly in intergroup relations, the stability of the systems of interaction between members of different groups is a product of the sharing of values by the respective groups and the degree to which such systems of interaction yield realization of shared values.

It is now possible to set forth several definitional steps in developing the concept of the organization.

Action may, in philosophical terms, be viewed to embody (1) idea, (2) substance, form, or reality, and (3) reflection. The same point of view may be expressed, in behavorial terms, in the statement that action has its (1) creative or exploratory phase, (2) performance phase, and (3) control phase, or the phase in which past action is appraised with a view to its possible regulation. The three phases, however, take place in the individual in a continuum and not in neatly divided compartments.

An individual explores his environment and creates in his imagination various possible situations or relationships by which he may adapt himself to his environment, thereby defining his expectations. He decides upon action or performance, thereby committing himself to the attainment of specific goals and the realization of the values embodied therein, performs the activity thus determined, and appraises the goal gratification or contentment following his action. All of this is done with a view to the control of his future action and communicating to his exploratory phase of action information upon the basis of which he shall act out his next cycle of behavior.

The three principal phases of behavior become institutionalized in the organization in decision makers and role performers. An organization is that form of a social system in which authority is used in leadership, administration, and control to attain goals valued by its members and to effect self-maintenance, integration, and adaptation. The meaning of each of these terms will now be considered.

A social system is a process of interaction between two or more actors who perceive themselves to be in an identifiable or typical situation and are oriented to, or concerned with, that situation.

A goal represents an anticipated state of affairs for the attainment of which action is to be directed.

A value represents a preference. It indicates that which is desirable in action.

Authority coordinates or directs action through command which is accepted and carried out without reasoned persuasion of the rationality of the content of the command or direction. Authority is to be distinguished from the forces which create it, such as legitimacy and power.

Leadership, administration, and control will be fully defined at later points in this and the following chapter. Briefly, leadership creates the ideas for action. Administration reduces those ideas to substance, determines goals in terms of concrete action, and directs physical action to the attainment of such goals. Control reflects upon, appraises, and evaluates action in order to decide whether prior patterns of action shall be adhered to, reshaped, or replaced.

An organization, in order to come into being and to persist, must insure that membership and participation provide a surplus of satisfactions or realizations of values over the psychic and physical costs of such membership. Its system of action must be directed to the gratification of desired goals. The organization must insure that its integrity and its existence is maintained, notwithstanding internal and external pressures and changes. It must exhibit integration or cohesion. It must adapt successfully to its external environment. In its adaptation, it is vitally concerned with relating its system of action to the values of its social base, including its participants or possible participants.

4. *Actors in the international system typically may be regarded to be organizations but are not limited to states. They include universal, regional, and other actors.*

The use of the term "international organization" to denote a certain formal grouping of states adopts a meaning for "organization" which may be quite different from that which has been attributed to it. It was said that organization was distinguished from group by the exercise of authority in its system of action. An international organization may have little substantive authority in the behavioral sense. It may possess a degree of formal authority. Whether it will be able to exercise such a formal authority will largely depend upon its relation to the values of its members in a particular situation.

A universal actor is an association or international organization of states which has no territorial limitation on its membership but is instead at least nominally open to membership by states from any part of the globe. A regional actor is an association or international organization of states which is territorially limited.

An association of states, such as the North Atlantic Treaty Organization (NATO) or the European Common Market, is limited both functionally and territorially in its range of goals and interests. On the other hand, the Organization of American States (OAS) claims a very wide range of goals and interests, but is still regionally limited. A regional actor is thus an international organization whose membership consists of two or more states but which is territorially limited in its operation.

There are also individual actors which are organizations of members determined on a global or regional scope, but which have particularized goals and interests and are limited to membership by persons or corporations of a private instead of a public character. Examples are an international trade union, international association of manufacturers, or international association of learned societies, or the like. There will be little occasion in this study to refer to the last-named groups as actors in the international system. Their operation is principally directed either to the protection or realization of their particular values by influencing the action of other actors, that is, as pressure groups, or to the performance of action which provides its own satisfaction or cathectic effect, as in learned societies.

The most significant actor is, of course, the state. Other actors are international corporations and state trading agencies. From the standpoint of the observation of behavior in the international arena, cognizance must be taken of the international corporation, which is a private corporation, that is, an economic organization, whose operations extend over two or more countries. The inclusion of international corporations as actors in the international system may be regarded as novel and even confusing. The scholar of international relations may well say that there is enough difficulty establishing methods of predicting action when study is limited to the action of states and international organizations of states. Yet international corporations have grown in number and size to a point that they cannot be overlooked, even though they are subject to the laws of each state in which they are located.

International business today is increasingly taking place within an internationally structured organizational form. The international corporation seeks its capital in the currently most advantageous capital market, places its plants in the preferable country from the standpoint of costs, exchange, tariffs, taxes, transportation, and the like, and searches for markets on the basis of regions, continents, and even the world.[1]

According to a study of the Federal Trade Commission, among 215 large manufacturing companies with assets of over $50 million, 187, or 87 per cent, had some foreign investments. Out of the 1,000 large manufacturing companies investigated, 517, or 53 per cent, had some foreign investment.[2] An Office of Business Economics study, which included petroleum with manufactures, listed 245 companies with foreign investment; 131 of these were companies with assets of over $50 million.[3] Thirteen companies in the extractive field held foreign investments of over $25 million, and twenty-one others held investments of at least $25 million in food, paper, chemicals, machinery, automotive, electric, and other manufactures.[4] Of the total United States investments in foreign manufacturing, 298 companies held 89 per cent. Twenty-seven companies, with individual foreign investments of over $25 million, held 51 per cent of the total investment. By comparison, 261 manufacturing companies, with assets in 1949 of over $50 million, had only 44 per cent of the total United States corporate-held assets.[5] In the petroleum field, 69 per cent of United States companies with assets of over $50 million have foreign investments outside the United States and Canada. Of twenty-six companies holding foreign investments in the field of mining and smelting, sixteen were companies with total assets of over $50 million.[6]

The foregoing concentration of foreign investment in large firms is a part of the process of industrial concentration in the United

---

[1]J. J. Beauvois, "Internationalism: A New Concept for U.S. Business," 2 *California Management Review* 28 (Winter, 1960).

[2]E. R. Barlow and I. T. Wender, *Foreign Investment and Taxation*, 68-69 (1955), based on Federal Trade Commission, *A List of 1,000 Large Manufacturing Companies, Their Subsidiaries and Affiliates, 1948* (1951).

[3]Barlow and Wender, *Foreign Investment*, 69, based on U.S. Dept. of Commerce, Office of Business Economics, *Foreign Investments of the United States* (1953).

[4]*Ibid.*, appendix B-3, 415.

[5]*Ibid.*, 48.

[6]*Ibid.*, 40, 26.

States. Some 500 corporations own two-thirds of the industry of the United States.[7] Forty-six per cent of total corporate manufacturing assets are held by 113 manufacturing corporations, each of whose total assets exceed $100 million.[8] The largest 273 corporations hold 46.3 per cent of all corporate assets.[9]

Soviet Russia and its Eastern European satellites, together with the Peoples Republic of China, are steadily moving into the international economic sphere through trade, loans, and grants. The state trading agency represents the counterpart of the international corporation in the free world. It participates in the international market primarily for the accomplishment of the ends of the Communist state and only incidentally those of the free-world economic organizations, whose products it sells or raw materials it buys in the international market. It may in time assume a size and importance equaling or exceeding that of the great international corporations of the free world. Its performance in the international markets will not be directed solely to an impersonal, functional adjustment to those markets. Its buying and selling will be calculated to promote the political as well as the economic interests of the Communist bloc of states. Indeed, the political interests of the bloc will take priority over the purely economic one of realizing the maximum profit through maximum efficiency. These bodies will introduce types of action that will be highly irrational and erratic from the standpoint of the international corporations and states of the free world, but will be quite rational from the standpoint of achieving Communist global supremacy of authority.

Thus the exercise of authority within the Soviet trading agency is to be viewed simply as another step in the hierarchical exercise of authority within the Soviet state by the Communist party, utilizing its capture of the government of the Soviet primarily for the ends of the party and only in a subordinate manner for the ends of the Russian nation.

The international corporation of the free world, by way of contrast, has an orientation only toward its market. Its decision mak-

---

[7] A. A. Berle, Jr., *Power Without Property*, 18 (1959).

[8] Federal Trade Commission, *Report on the Concentration of Productive Facilities, 1947, Total Manufacturing and 26 Selected Industries* (1949).

[9] M. A. Adelman, "The Measurement of Industrial Concentration," 33 *Review of Economies and Statistics* 269, 276 (1951).

ing takes place in a framework of serving the public to which it sells and achieving the greatest efficiency in the use of its resources. Although management so exercised will maximize profits, the earning of profits will be a result of, and not the primary criterion for, decision making.

The international corporation of today is only remotely descended from the imperialistic East India Company. The management of today's international enterprise in the free world adjusts its operation to the culture of each country in which it finds itself. The goals of management are economic and not political. The corporation absorbs the shocks and pressures which each state thrusts upon it and acts as an impersonal mechanism for coordinating action in the international system for the benefit of its individual members in each state in which it operates. Subjected to the competitive forces of the international market and increasingly denied resort to cartel practices by the growth of legislation controlling restrictive business practices in many states, its profits are moderate in the light of the risks assumed. There is no other mechanism for handling interstate relations in the economic sphere which can so uniquely confine its action to the performance of its function and arrive at an equitable and acceptable distribution of benefits.

5. *The traditional model of the international system as composed of interacting states, each state being a pure and exclusive system of action comprehending a sovereign government and people in a defined territory, is misleading and incorrect. Each state is within its territory the axis or meeting place of both the national and international systems of action.*

This proposition represents a piercing of the corporate veil of the state. To use another analogy, it represents the use of the physics of particles instead of atoms. While from its own standpoint each state may regard the functioning of the international system within its borders to be merely a subsystem of its own system of action, from the standpoint of the international system some aspects of the national system become subsystems. Yet the classic territorial image of the state, as comprising government and people within a defined territory, together with a freedom of action called sovereignty, still remains with us.

The global view of action is typically of interaction between

states so identified. However, when one moves from a static model
of the state as comprising government, governed, territory, and
sovereignty, to a model based on social process or action essentially
characterized by the exercise of a type of authority known as
governmental, the entire character of one's perceptions changes.
The state is not a pure and exclusive system with authority confined to its own borders. The phases in which the internal structure
of the state becomes linked with other states must be discerned,
and it will be seen that each state is an amalgam of its own authority structure, as well as that of other states.

6. *Action in the international system will be the product of
authority as it is exercised within and over organizations.*

Authority, in this study, imports no notion of law, legitimacy,
power, coercion, or the like, although each of these may support
or create authority. Authority is held to appear in the relations of
individuals when commands or directions of an actor are regularly
followed by action of others in conformity with such commands
without reasoned explanation or persuasion of the rationality of
their content. Authority is thus distinguished from the forces which
create and maintain it. It may arise simply out of respect for the
wisdom of the person making the command, it may arise out of a
recognition and acceptance of the legitimacy of his command in
the making of organizational decisions, or it may arise out of fear
of the application of force or sanction. All such considerations
are relevant to the prediction of the appearance of authority, but
do not carry the central idea of authority itself.

Authority as a means for coordinating action is typically to be
found in the internal functioning of the organization as a form
of social structure. It is within the corporate organization and the
state that the exercise of authority overwhelmingly appears. A
state or a corporate organization may achieve sufficient dominance
or power or by other means exercise authority outside the sphere
of action of its members and in the sphere of its external relations.
However, for the most part authority appears as a means for
coordinating action within an organization, including the state.

Whether authority be exercised internally or externally by decision makers in an organization, it is almost tautological to say that
authority will be a means for coordinating action in the international system only in the degree that organizations can make it

so. By definition, an organization of the maturely developed character which this study employs for purposes of conceptualization and analysis uses authority primarily to direct and coordinate action within it.

7. *Authority may be exercised by one actor over another in the international system through dominance or "power," that is, its ability to employ its human and physical resources in such a manner as to render disadvantageous a decision not to accept its commands.*

The separation of the concept of authority from the forces which create and support it makes it possible to limit sharply the concept of power as a determinant of the relations of organizations, including states. The elusiveness of the concept of power becomes apparent when, as defined in a recent text on international relations, power became "the ability to influence the behavior of others in accordance with one's own ends." In such a context the determinants and instrumentalities of power range from "wealth, resources, manpower, arms," to "ideals," "esteem," "propaganda," and "the granting of good will."[10]

"The ability to influence others in accordance with one's own ends" is a valid and central concept in any of the sciences concerned with the study of human behavior. To call the ability to influence others without reasoned persuasion "authority," as we have done, and to equate "power" with dominance or the ability to manipulate human and physical resources, including force, in such a manner as to render disadvantageous a failure to accept a claimed authority, attributes meanings to "authority" and "power" which are likely to receive interdisciplinary acceptance and understanding and at the same time provide a means for more precise analysis.

Power is a word of many meanings. Authority often refers to a claim by one actor that another shall act in a stated manner, which the latter is expected to accept because it is made by one legitimately occupying a post of command in an organization. Admittedly, the alternative meaning used in this study is not free from terminological difficulties. As noted above, the meanings attributed to these terms represent an attempt to adopt a termi-

---

[10]A. F. K. Organski, *World Politics*, 96-99 (1958).

nology which might more successfully achieve interdisciplinary communication as well as accuracy of analysis. The political scientist is perhaps more likely to equate authority with formal legitimacy and law. In the present system of discourse, however, law may import a command which is formally legitimate within its sphere but which for its realization in action might very well require those formally subject to the operation of the law to be subjected to power, if the command is to be obeyed. The prediction of the exercise of federal authority in the southeastern states in eliminating the segregation of Negroes involves a weighing of the extensiveness and intensity of attachment to values by both the white and Negro groups, on the one hand, and the effectiveness of resort to force, on the other. In such a context, power, as a symbol for the ability to use dominance or force to create authority, is distinguished from the formal legitimacy of law as another means to create authority.

Egypt used its internal monopoly of force, in an act of nationalization, to establish a new regime for the Suez Canal in which internationalized control of canal operation disappeared. This use of internal force so impaired the free international character of the canal, as revealed in the continued use of force to exclude Israeli commerce, as to constitute a threat to any state which may take action deemed by Egypt to be inimical to its vital interests. Thus Egypt's authority over the use of the canal was established by its internal law, its internal monopoly of force, and an inability by actors in the international system to change such exercise of authority, even though it may have been in violation of international law and disruptive of the international system.

The United States, for example, may attempt to use its antitrust laws to affect the behavior of organizations created by and subject to the law of Switzerland, engaged in manufacturing watchmaking machinery, to remove barriers created by such organizations to the export of such machinery to the United States. Such an attempt to exercise authority through the employment of law would create strong reaction by the Swiss corporations and doubtless the Swiss public. They would view it as an interference with the realization of desired values within their national domain. They may, nevertheless, accept it as an authoritative command in Switzerland simply by virtue of the ability of the United States government to exclude Swiss watchmakers from a valuable market as a power sanction for the United States decision. The formal legitimacy of the United States' exercise of jurisdiction over Swiss organizations importing watches into the United States is largely irrelevant in the prediction of whether the authority of the United States will in fact appear in Switzerland by virtue of making such a command.

In short, the prediction of the appearance of authority is aided by considering separately the empirical data relating to power, as above defined, from the other determinants of authority.

8. *The exercise of authority through power is precarious.*

While most persons would subscribe to the abstract truth of the above principle without further demonstration, the principles and propositions upon which it rests will reveal the factors affecting the correlation between the use of power in a social system and the viability of that system. These will be stated first from the standpoint of the ways in which resort to power for determining the action of a system leads to instability, loss of energy, and disintegration. In the succeeding principle, such statements will be restated so as to express affirmatively the conditions in which authority becomes stabilized in a social system in order to permit the maximum release of energy for the attainment of desired goals.

Principles 8 and 9 are ultimately concerned with the establishment or accomplishment of policy through authority. The first refers to those situations in the relations of actors in the international system in which policy is unilaterally effectuated by power. All such situations necessarily imply a system of action which is held together only by an extreme reliance on power, including force. The second principle defines the conditions of a social system which will enable it to tap effectively the potential energy which it has and to use that energy affirmatively to attain desired goals, with only a minimal reliance upon power as a sanction. The two principles together comprise an attempt to state the inherent limitations upon power as an instrument for authority and the conditions in which power assumes its proper role in a social system. The term "proper" in the preceding statement refers to that combination of conditions in which the use of power as an instrument of coercion is minimized and as an instrument enabling the realization of shared values is maximized.

8.a. *The exercise of authority through power tends to impair the rationality of action from the standpoint of appropriateness of means to end.*

Authority in a system of action will arise and be maintained, among other things, by the appropriateness of the content of the command of an actor in a group as a means for the achievement of a valued group goal. The very meaning of authority has been said to lie in the fact that its exercise is uncritically accepted as a determinant of action, but unless commands in the exercise of authority bear at least a minimum rationality appropriate to the attainment of or progress toward a goal, an authority system will not long endure unless sanctioned by power. The reliance upon power in such circumstances shields the exercise of authority from reality. When commands are supported by power, they need not possess that degree of potentiality for reasoned explanation to elicit action which commands supported by a minimum of force must possess. When the ability to call upon force to sanction a claim of authority is absent, irrational claims of authority are likely to encounter such resistance as to frustrate their realization in performance.

8.b. *The exercise of authority through power creates a situation in which action of the social system can be directed to the attainment of goals valued by the actor claiming authority, instead of goals valued by the members of the social system generally.*

It is elementary that authority need not resort to power for its support when its directs action toward desired group goals. It is equally elementary that resort to power is required when authority is claimed over action not so directed. A claim of authority based on power will more likely be made to attain goals valued by the actor making the claim than the actor to whom the claim is directed.

In the interplay between authority, power, and values to which the above principle points, we find the ultimate conditioning forces upon the emergence of structure in the international system. As authority enables the realization of shared values, not only do stability and structure emerge but the conditions for the further growth of authority and structure are established. As authority supported by power denies the realization of shared values, such structures of social action as authority may establish become precarious. The relation of the exercise of authority to the realization of widely shared values in a social system may be termed "value rationality." Authority bears less value rationality as it is claimed over action embodying increasingly diminishing value importance to the actor.

Comparative power positions of actors change. Unless their value orientations also change, so that a status imposed by force yesterday is welcomed today, any system of action based on power relations is inherently precarious and unstable. Thus the degree to which values are shared by actors in the international system becomes the key element for its stability.

This may be restated as a principle of social mechanics. *Authority must be supported by power to the degree that the ideal image of authority, in which its exercise is viewed in patterns enabling the maximum realization of shared values, departs from the actual image of authority, in which it is in fact exercised and values realized.*

The successful exercise of authority supported primarily by power in the international system may be predicted by weighing (1) the degree of power possessed by the actor claiming authority and the actor over whom it is claimed, including their respective skills in the use of power, (2) the likelihood of resistance to the claimed authority as measured by the degree to which it impairs the foundations of power in the actor over whom it is claimed or frustrates the attainment of goals to which it attaches the highest value, and (3) the likelihood of resort to the use of power by the actor exercising authority as measured by the advantages to be realized from establishing authority without it.

The value attachments of the actors are the crucial factors in predicting resistance to claimed authority or resort to power. When authority influences action of an actor in a direction which fails to realize, or frustrates the realization of, his desired values, the intensity of his attachment to the values concerned will determine the intensity of his opposition to authority. If the value attachment of the actor claiming authority should in the circumstances be relatively low, he may well desist when he encounters determined opposition.

The tendency of those exercising authority through power to give priority to their own values, rather than to those of the members of the social system generally, is evidenced in the characteristic structure of the underdeveloped countries described in Chapter

IV. In those countries, a restricted élite controls and uses authority and power for the realization of their particularistic values, ignoring those of the agricultural worker and the industrial worker. In the Soviet, the perceptions, cognitions, and values of members of the Communist party, as party members rather than as Russians, considerably influence the exercise of their authority in the Russian state and in other states which have become captives of the party system. Their ability to exercise authority rests on the power which they command and use in the respective national societies subject to their control.

8.c. *As authority rests on power, instead of a consistent pattern of shared value realization, tensions will mount.*

The use of power to support a claim of authority identifies the likelihood of resistance to the use of power. It points to the instability or lack of equilibrium of the situation, the probability of it exploding into conflict, instead of the patterns of interaction demanded by authority, for tension is a symptom or product of a situation of conflict. Tension in the international system will typically arise when power is used to create authority in situations where it will frustrate the realization of values firmly held by the actor who is subjected to it.

8.d. *As authority increasingly resorts to power to maintain itself in the face of decreasing goal gratification by the members of a social system, the perverted use of power will eventually destroy the system itself.*

The principle stated is an elementary one in the mechanics of social action and was brilliantly set forth in historical terms by Brooks Adams in *The Theory of Social Revolutions,* published in 1913. Its classic examples are the French revolution of the eighteenth century and the Russian revolution of the twentieth century. Later demonstrations of this early principle are found in the Hungarian revolution of 1956 and the recent Cuban revolution, which ended in the Castro regime. As the available energy of the social system is diverted from a widespread realization of values of its members to those of a restricted élite and the resultant resistance is held in check only by an increasing use of power to support authority, the social system will eventually lose value rationality to such a degree that integration will cease and the system will disintegrate. The pathological condition of *anomie,* in which norms cease to exist, may supervene. Usually, however, the submerged groups will find leaders who will use the power of such groups to establish a new authority structure resting on a different and more widely shared value basis.

The Hungarian revolution of 1956 is not only illustrative of the above principle but it brings into light another principle of profound importance in the international system. The denial of the opportunity to satisfy adequately such basic needs as food, shelter, clothing, religion, and recreation, and to realize such basic human values as respect, dignity, wealth, and enlightenment, led to the revolution of 1956. So much of the energy of the Hungarian social system was used for the preservation of its authority structure, and the relatively little energy that remained was used so ineffectually for the attainment of valued goals of the members of the system, that disintegration became inevitable. However, Soviet intervention introduced a new element of force directed to the maintenance of the system. Power to support authority which was internally lacking was externally introduced into the system. The result was a reshaping of value priorities of the members of the system in which the value of survival supplanted all others. The system accordingly found a new equilibrium based on the external application of force to support it. Herein lies the ultimate meaning of war in international relations prior to the atomic age.

9. *Authority becomes stabilized in a social system in such a manner as to permit the maximum release of energy when:*

9.a. *There is a consistent pattern of rationality in the relation of means to end in the system of action.*

When authority was equated with the ability to elicit action without reasoned persuasion, it was essential to emphasize that this did not imply that authority could be exercised successfully apart from the rationality of the relationship of means to end in the action commanded. It was said that a claim of authority must possess a potentiality of rational demonstration. Moreover, unless actors claiming authority can demonstrate that their past exercise of authority has had a reasonable success in the economic use of resources to realize desired goals, their ability to influence action through command or direction will soon disappear in the absence of other supporting elements, such as power. The degree to which the means employed to reach goals represent an appropriate, efficient, and economical use of resources, in which risk is minimized, may be termed "mechanical rationality."

9.b.   *There is a consistent pattern of rationality in the exercise of authority to achieve goals valued by the subjects of authority from the standpoint of (1) the immediacy with which value priorities in the system are recognized, (2) the degree to which the resources of the system are allocated to the realization of values on the basis of their priority, and (3) the degree to which goals embodying these values are consistently attained.*

The above statement represents a type of rationality quite different from the logical demonstration of economy in the use of resources, once a decision has been made to commit them to the attainment of a specific end or goal. It refers to value rationality, that is, rationality within the domain of value. As unrealized values or preferences impinge upon the consciousness of members of a social system, it becomes essential that the action of the social system be directed to the realization of such values. A pattern of use of the resources of the system, human and physical, which consistently ignores pressing demands for action to attain valued goals, becomes irrational from the standpoint of the value orientations of the members of the system.

This type of rationality is of far greater importance in social action than is the mechanical rationality of which we were speaking in the preceding section. The viability of a social system is a product of the degree to which it enables its members to realize values. Those exercising authority in a social system must be ever sensitive to the values of its members and of its social base. In the organization called the state, the political institutions determine the goals to the attainment of which the action of the members of the state shall be directed, and in so doing, evaluate these goals from the standpoint of the demands or values of the members. It is their responsibility to ensure that its human and physical resources are used to attain these goals. In so doing, they must also give consideration to the needs and values of its social base, that is, other social systems with which it is linked and upon which it relies for its maintenance.

A social system reflects value rationality in the degree that it (1) immediately recognizes the value priorities and changes therein of its members or participants, (2) allocates action in the system to the attainment of goals in accordance with the priority or intensity of attachment of such members or participants to such goals, and (3) consistently attains the goals embodying these values.

9.c. *Authority is used in effective performance of leadership.*

Leadership in a social system represents the function of exercising foresight and oversight. Leadership occupies that post in which the totality of the system of action comes into perspective and is overseen. It foresees the important external and internal variables which will affect the system of action and plans action with a view to meeting and handling their impact. Leadership directs administration to carry out these plans and plans further action in the light of any failure by administration in its assigned tasks. The perspective of leadership is the future. It appraises the future and calls upon the present to plan to meet possible future demands.

Leadership is sensitive to the values of the members of the social system and of its external social base. It determines, on the basis of its inquiry into the values of those whom it must lead and those with whom the members of the system must interact, the goals of the system and the value priorities among the goals from the standpoint of committing the action of the system to their attainment. Leadership is not only concerned with insuring the realization of the values of the members of the system; it is also concerned with defining the relations of the system with other systems. It searches for ways in which its system can provide a means for participation by members of other systems with a view to a realization of their values and endeavors to harmonize the interacting systems. No system of action in the international system can function independent of all others, as has been seen. Its endowment with human and physical resources and its geographical relation to this environment means that leadership must be as aware of the variables in the social base of the international system as it is of those in its own system of action. The political, economic, military, and cultural implications of its geographical situation are a vital concern of leadership within a state. A prime function and concern of leadership, then, is adaptation of the system to its external environment.

In a world of change in human values, perceptions, attitudes, cultural growth, industrial development, and movement toward nationalistic organization and social and economic revolution, it is imperative that action coordinated through authority should reflect leadership of the highest order. Yet merely to state the desirable in action is not to assure that it will be achieved. Authority as such is merely a relationship. To speak of authority is to give no indication of the content of human behavior. Whether the exercise of authority will reflect leadership in the last analysis will depend upon whether the subjects of authority will accept a particular type or pattern of leadership. Those who tend to assume authority in a democratically organized society are those who typify the admired virtues of the national society at that particular moment, who call for action toward goals which embody values of the current highest priority, and who communicate an image most closely approximating the society's existing ideal image of authority.

The character of leadership in a democratically organized state can rise to heights in times of crisis and fall to mediocrity when change is slow. When the people perceive an imminent threat, they may respond with magnificent energy to the call of a great leader. The real crisis for a democracy is in those periods of its history when change is gradual. It is at these times that leadership must foresee the threat, awaken the society to it, and bring the society to take action to meet it. Otherwise, the gradual movement of forces reaches the point where they are uncontrollable. Suddenly, through inaction, the situation has become irreversible. The eventual toppling of the structure is the work of termites instead of storm. Leadership must communicate to society the reality of the distant as well as the imminent threat and inspire action to meet both.

Leadership in a social system, moreover, is not to be considered as being exercised solely within its political or economic institutions. There is also the leadership of the scholar. It is the scholar, whether he is a philosopher or a physical or social scientist, who through creative thought discovers new perceptions of the order in which man lives. Remote as they initially may be from the decisions of man and his action brought about by decisions, the discoveries of the scholar eventually are disseminated to the actors in the social system and influence their decisions and action. When it is realized that four-fifths of the body of science is said to have been discovered by persons who are still living, when it is understood that man's probings in space are only one consequence of the vast expansion of knowledge made in the past several decades, we may then somewhat appreciate the extraordinary changes which will be thrust upon us in the coming years of the twentieth century. When we compare the laggardness in the growth of the social sciences with the rapid growth of the physical sciences, we have at least one factor conducive to the political, economic, and social instability of the day. Energy used ineffectively through ignorance will do little to solve the massive problems of today.

Leadership acts in "macro-time," that is, in the long perspective of time, and not in "micro-time," the immediate present or short-run time. It is concerned with the important internal and external variables which will affect the social system in macro-time. In the control of internal variables, leadership is concerned with those changes in values, attitudes, and perceptions which affect the goals to which action will be attracted and influence the degree of integration within the system. In the control of external variables, leadership in a state is concerned with the preservation of its foundations of power, with the development of its external authority by all possible means—means not limited to power as we have defined it—and with establishing and preserving externally those conditions in which the society can best achieve its goals.

Leadership must relate the organization to the culture in which it functions. The organization's values and standards must be consistent with those of the culture. Its action must be subjected to normative evaluation under the ethical system of the culture. Leadership which is wholly organization-oriented will lose contact with cultural reality and cultural change and thereby steadily weaken the viability of the organization.

Leadership must search for and communicate ways in which participants and possible participants in its social base can realize their values by their participation in the action of the organization. As it relates its action to a social base which it calculatedly endeavors to develop, it finds the most enduring and powerful basis of viability. The Marshall Plan was an extraordinary application of this principle. Foreign aid could become another such application, if it could surmount the inadequate perspectives, such as national defense, from which it is viewed.

The development of the social base of an organization opens a new dimension to its prosperity and growth. A new factor is added to the creation of energy by the interaction of the organization and its social base as the latter expands in strength. The resultant growth of energy enables a wider realization of values by the members of both the organization and its social base. A more enduring lodging place for the organization is thereby created.

While creativity is an essential element in each phase of action in organization, at no place does its importance loom as large as it does in leadership. For leadership must coalesce all the present and future variables with which it is confronted into an all-embracing idea of action. This idea must express an order in which the system of action appropriately reflects or embodies the values of its participants and is adapted to the character of its environment, as such values and environment change over time. The perception and statement of the nature of such an order, which is the task of leadership, demands creative imagination and insight coupled with a realistic pragmatism.

9.d. *Authority is used in the effective performance of administration.*

Administration finds its perspective for decision making in the present. It acts in micro-time. Its task is to establish the decisions of leadership in the world of reality. Administrators or executives are those who effectuate the decisions of leadership by their direction, management, or coordination of the human and physical resources of the social system. Administration accepts the definitions of goals and the decisions of the degree of commitment of action to the attainment of goals made, in the exercise of leadership and it also effectuates such decisions in action.

The execution of leadership decisions by administration involves (1) redefinition of a given goal in terms of lesser goals more directly related to concrete human behavior, (2) determination of the manner and extent to which the human and physical resources of the system allocated by leadership for reaching a given goal shall be employed toward reaching such lesser goals and taking into account the important variables likely to affect the planned performance, (3) decision to carry out the foregoing in action, (4) verification whether the action thus commanded has reached such lesser goals, and (5) further performance of the above steps in the degree that such lesser goals have not been reached.

It will be observed that steps (1) and (2) above involve an exercise of the leadership function for the sphere of administration and that step (4) discharges the function of control within the sphere of administration. This phenomenon of the duplication of leadership, administration, and control *within each of the three phases of organization action* is a seldom appreciated point.[11]

For example, while leadership plans for the future, it must also act and make decisions in the present. It must communicate its decisions to persons who can make them effective in the world of action. It must state its decisions in terms which are capable of realization in the world of action. It must know whether its commands to administration are understood and performed. If there is a departure by administrative action from the commands of leadership, the latter must know the reasons for such a departure. If administration encounters important change in the external environment in which it operates, leadership must know the nature of such change in order to perform effectively its planning function. To relay such information is in part the function of control. Control in turn is not only concerned with verification and appraisal procedures for the benefit of leadership and administration; it must also verify and weigh or appraise its own action in its own sphere.

In other words, the exercise of leadership, administration, and control requires that each in its sphere must create, perform, and control its own unique type of action.

9.e. *Authority is used in the effective performance of control.*

Control, it has been said, is the appraisal and regulative phase of action. It is that aspect of action in which the individual (1) reflects upon specific past action, (2) verifies whether the action had in fact carried out the decision to act to which the individual had committed himself, and (3) appraises past action from the standpoint of (a) economy of effort or efficiency of the means selected as against alternative available means and (b) goal gratification, that is, weighing of contentment following the attainment of the goal from the standpoint of whether it justifies further commitment to the goal as against the values embodied in competing

---

[11]Professor Thomas H. Haynes of the Department of Philosophy, Lehigh University, first called my attention to the above phenomenon of reduplication of structure in the components of an organization.

goals. It is also that aspect of action in which the individual reflects upon the design of the totality of his past action and, as a consequence, reshapes his values and value priorities so that he commits himself to a different design of action.

In the organization, three levels or aspects of control are perceived. There is, first, that type of control to verify whether or not specific authoritative decisions or rules for behavior were performed and, if not, the respects in which there was a departure of behavior from command or rule. This leads to regulation designed to restore behavior to its desired pattern. There is, second, that type of control to resolve interpersonal conflict arising in an organization, typically as a consequence of behavior departing from specific commands or expected standards or norms of behavior. There is, third, that type of control concerned with appraising the adequacy of the total design of the action of the organization, as a means for realizing the values of the participants and reflecting the relevant goals, values, and standards of the society and culture in which the organization finds itself. This last phase of control refers directly to the leadership function and provides it with information which is essential for the effective performance of its task.

Thus control is not to be perceived as operating in an unchanging system. It is not to be viewed as having the sole function of mechanically regulating deviant behavior and thereby restoring equilibrium to the system. Control has a creative function as it regulates conduct. Control is exercised to appraise and evaluate a deviation in conduct and to decide whether some other alternative mode of action might be more appropriate than the previous institutionalized or established action, which was the standard for determining the deviance. Appraisal and regulation are not to be confined to deviant action; they are to be applied to the entire action of the social system in the light of experience, cultural standards, and cultural change.

9.f. *The social system has defined authoritative roles and attributed to them formal and substantive or social legitimacy.*

A social system has reached a considerable degree of structure when its patterns of interaction become characterized by authority relationships instead of the relationships of complementary, institutionalized roles. Indeed, it is at this crucial point that a social system becomes an organization. When a norm for conduct emerges

within a social system to the effect that the commands or directions of a person occupying a certain role should be followed without reasoned persuasion in typical, identifiable situations, it may
be said that an authoritative role has appeared.

When the patterns of interaction of an actor and those with
whom he interacts become so fixed as to establish a set of expectations of conduct for those involved and when, in addition, the
actor is perceived to occupy a position or post in a social system,
he is said to possess a role. More briefly stated, a role is "a way
of behaving associated with a defined position in a social system."[12]

Roles may, among other things, be characterized by the fact
that an actor will be able to exercise authority in certain types of
situations, that is to say, in certain typical situations the commands
or directions of an actor will be followed without reasoned persuasion. When an actor possesses such authority and, in addition,
there is recognized to be an *obligation* to carry out his decisions
in such typical situations, the actor may be said to occupy an
authoritative role. The typical situations in which such exercise
of authority may be predicted to be successful may be termed his
area of authority. Political or legal terms expressing the same notion in their particular system of discourse are authority, responsibility, jurisdiction, area of discretion, and the like.

When action in a social system will respond to stimuli of this
character, the direction which its system of action may take becomes enormously flexible. Instead of habit, custom, and tradition
to determine the course of action, now action will quickly respond
to meet new demands and threats from without and new demands
and threats from within the system. Herein lies the great strength
of the organizational way of action that has come to permeate
modern society. Flexibility of action by a social system is a source
of maximizing satisfactions among its members and thereby promoting stability and integration.

The structural rules of a social system define its authoritative
roles or offices, the manner in which they are to be filled and va-
cated, the area of authority within which decisions or commands
may be made by the occupant of the role, and the persons who
will be expected to carry out such commands. A structural rule

---

[12]P. Selznick, *Leadership in Administration: A Sociological Interpretation,* 82
(1957); Parsons and Shils, *Toward a General Theory of Action,* 23.

is postulated to reflect observable and predictable behavior, and, as such, to concern authority as it in fact exists. It is concerned with identifying the actual patterns of action of a social system bearing on the occupancy and performance of its authoritative roles. It is not concerned with identifying the repositories of authority in accordance with some formal statement of the constitutive or founding act of a social system, such as the political act creating the constitution of a state.

Legitimacy in its formal sense refers to the formal inscription of the rules which represent, or are intended to represent, the structural rules of a social system. Such a formal inscription may take place in a symbolic and constitutive act which will itself tend to establish the substantive or social legitimacy of the rules so affirmed. Substantive or social legitimacy refers to that aspect of influence over the behavior of others, or support of the exercise of authority, which arises from the fact that the performance of a command is motivated by the belief in the rightness of, or by the acceptance of, the whole pattern of the structural rules of a social system and the right of the occupants of authoritative roles, as defined by the structural rules, to issue commands. Substantive or social legitimacy exists when the subjects of an authority structure feel that it ought to exist, that it is right that it should exist, or that it has consistently demonstrated mechanical and value rationality. For example, those who assumed the roles of legitimate authority following the death of Stalin in 1953 were confronted with the task of establishing substantive or social legitimacy when they issued their appeal against "disorder and panic."

9.g. *Power is used as a sanction to support law in the control of deviant behavior, when deviance arises out of action which is a product of the effective performance of the functions of leadership and administration.*

Law and deviant behavior, as used above, import that all of the conditions previously set forth are reasonably satisfied. In order that law may provide the utmost of which it is capable in the functioning of an organization, the organization must exhibit mechanical and value rationality in leadership and administration and must embody substantive or social legitimacy. It is at this point that law can provide its function of control in such a manner as to enable the most harmonious functioning of the organization.

The concept of law and its relation to the political function in the provision of order in a social system will be the topic of inquiry of the next chapter. At this point, it is necessary to say that the element of constraint or force in a politically organized society should operate in a context in which force is used only to preserve those valued norms for behavior identifiable as legal norms, which have emerged in a social system characterized by wise, energetic leadership and administration. When such a situation exists, inconsistent behavior is justifiably called deviant behavior. When it is not, the problem of control which will develop is the handling of many principled dissidents instead of a relatively few deviants. Such a problem of social control will not be solved solely by the application of force in the name of law. It demands the inculcation of other motivations than fear. It demands the provision of a changed environment and the direction of the action of the organization to the realization of a new system of values, among other things.

Ultimately the meaning of the term "deviant behavior" and the problem of its control through law finds its answer in perceptions and cognitions of action from the temporal standpoint. The function of leadership is to insure that the present is directed to meet the demands of the future. Law, on the other hand, requires that social action be faithful to those prior patterns of action which have come to embody ideal and valued forms of action. Law can in its sphere no more ignore the future than leadership can the past. Law reflects upon past action with a view to the control of future action.

When leadership and its servant, administration, perform their respective functions in a social system and perform them well, then power or force as a sanction for law will be at its minimum.

10. *The transformation of the present international system into a unified organizational structure requires that it shall develop into a social system characterized by a conscious coordination of action to attain valued goals through authority manifested in leadership, administration, and control.*

Principle 9 brought to the fore those elements which, when they appear in a social system, transform it into the developed organization in which social action is today typically structured. The present principle provides a working definition of the organizational structure of social action.

The organization is that form of a social system in which structure emerges in the dimensions of authority and of time. The structure of an organization is not only to be perceived in its pattern of authoritative roles and the manner in which the occupants of such roles influence action throughout the social system; it is also to be perceived in the exercise of authority by decisions concerned with macro-time as well as with micro-time. When the exercise of authority in a social system becomes concerned with the persistence of the system over a long period of time and makes decisions which establish the system as a relatively permanent group, then an organization has come into being. To accomplish permanence, authority must coordinate action in the system to attain goals, valued by its members and others who participate in the system, by decisions which manifest leadership (macro-time), administration (micro-time), and control (both macro-time and micro-time). To rephrase the classical formulation of the branches of government, leadership is primarily found in the legislative branch, administration in the executive branch, and control in the judicial branch. Yet officials throughout all branches of the state find themselves concerned with questions of leadership, administration, and control in their respective spheres. Similarly in the economic organization, there is an institutionalization of leadership, administration, and control in the board of directors, managers, supervisors, and other officials, yet the occupants of all authoritative roles find themselves confronted with problems for decision in all three types of action.

The above principle is not intended to affirm either the desirability or undesirability of the eventual transformation of the present international system into an organizational structure of action embracing the peoples of the world. Only the requisite elements of such a structure are stated. The succeeding principles will indicate some of the fundamental principles applicable to bringing about such a change in the international system. There is one point, however, that should be made in reaching the decision of whether the problem of war and peace can be solved only by the establishment of a world organization. It is not the form of such a structuring of social action in the world which will solve the haunting, harrowing problem of war. The solution of the problem of war is a product of the solution of a great many underlying problems in social relationships, of which war and aggressive behavior are merely symptoms or objective manifestations. The magnitude of these problems is the true index of the magnitude of the solution of the problem of war.

The problem of creating a viable world organization cannot be cast solely in terms of creating a "reign of law." The existing conditions of interstate relations are largely supported by the power relations of the principal actors. To create a world organization or to create a reign of law, in which authority is based on consent instead of force, demands something more than consideration of questions of formal structure. It demands the most careful exploration of those ways in which ordered progress to a different kind of a world society can be achieved. Such a society will demand that all states become good neighbors to one another. It will require that they create an international system, the continued existence and development of which is valued by all participants. When such a system is established, the use of force will be reduced to its proper role, that is, the preservation of the system as a means for the realization of the important values of all actors therein, instead of the particularistic values of actors possessing a preponderance of power.

11. *The transformation of the international system from a system which is almost entirely lacking in centralized coordination of action through authority to an organizational structure in which authority is used to attain goals embodying globally shared values must give consideration to the following principles and propositions:*

11.a. *The growth of integration in the international system is not necessarily a function of the quantitative growth of participation therein, but is instead a product of the degree to which participation in the international system yields valued goal gratification.*

The quantitative growth of participation in the international system reflects mechanical interdependency or solidarity and has little relevance to the value which the actors will attach to their participation in the system. Whether participation in the international system will promote its integration depends upon the degree to which such participation brings about valued goal gratification.

A state will not attach importance to the value of subordinating its system of action to that of the international system merely as a consequence of its dependency or of the degree to which its system of action is a part of the international system. Such a value will emerge in the national society only as the benefits of its participation in the international system are satisfactorily shared by the members of the state.

These rather elementary propositions point to a widely held fallacy. There is considerable adherence to the view that international solidarity or integration will be a direct product of the degree of international interdependence or mechanical interdependence. It is assumed that as the world becomes more interdependent, it will become more international in outlook and more dedicated to the value of promoting the viability of the international system. The preceding chapter shows that there is no necessary correlation between the two.

An agricultural or pastoral national society may become considerably concerned with the production of one or two crops or one or two types of animals or meats for export. In such a situation, it might become considerably dependent upon the revenues therefrom to provide the foodstuffs and other materials necessary for national existence. The society would then become highly dependent upon its participation in the international system. Whether, however, such a society would attach importance to the economic interdependence of the world will depend, among other things, upon whether the international markets for its exports exhibit orderly price behavior and an ability to absorb increased production without decline or sharp fluctuations, and whether the benefits of its participation are extended throughout the national society instead of being seized by an élite for its exclusive enjoyment. If increased participation in the international system leaves essentially unimpaired the degree to which members of the national society attain goals and realize values, then there will be no change in the degree of its attachment to the value of participation in the international system. An industrial society may reach a point where foreign trade is steadily declining in relation to total national output and still be highly dependent on international markets for the import of critical raw materials. A decline in the relative monetary importance of foreign trade as compared with the monetary value of the national output of an industrial society reflects the fact that such a society vastly increases the value of the final product made from the original raw materials. The significance of the relative decline in value of raw material imports as against total output is somewhat lessened when this fact is considered. Moreover, as shown above, an industrial society is typically one in which there is increasing reliance on mineral imports as its own mineral resources become depleted. It is also a society in which the lack of important or critical mineral resources, including energy minerals such as petroleum, together with alloys and auxiliary metals, becomes of increasing national importance as the society grows in size and power.

The relative amount of petroleum imported into Western European countries as compared with the total national output of these countries is slight. But the need of such national societies for the energy, which such imports provide, is so critical that, for example, the absence of petroleum in the Suez crisis created a paralysis of production and transport.

On the other hand, an industrial society will find the erosion of national boundaries in the economic sphere and resultant dependency on the international system a means to increased national income. The movement by states to acceptance of the common market idea demonstrates this fact. Thus an industrial society may reach a point where growth can be achieved only by active encouragement of dependency on the international markets and participation in the international system. Whether, however, a national society will seek increased participation in the international system as a means for increased wealth or income will depend upon whether it is willing to assume the degree of dependency which such a step would entail. The values of self-sufficiency, protection of local manufacturers and agriculture, insularization from the vicissitudes of the international markets, and freedom from control by the exercise of power by other actors upon which it might become dependent, may cause it to decrease rather than increase its participation in the international system.

11.b. *Authority will be exercised by a universal or regional actor over the action of its members inversely to the universality of its membership and range of its goals or directly to the restriction of its claims of authority to coordinate and control the action of its members.*

11.b.1. *Whether a state will accept a claim to the exercise of authority by a universal or regional actor of which it is a member will depend upon the degree to which the totality of its systems of action, including its purely internal systems of action as well as its participation in the international system, results in the gratification of desired goals, promises increasing goal gratification for the future, and achieves internal integration of the national society, successful adaptation to its environment, and maintenance of the patterns of its social structure.*

An individual participating in the international system usually will not come to identify himself with anything more than his state or national system and will view the larger international system as alien and discrete. His values will not be perceived to be realized by the international system—though in fact they may be—but instead by the national or local groups of which he regards himself a member. The media of communication to which he is exposed, the interpretation of international situations by his political leaders and the press, the usually dissimilar cultural background, language, modes of dress, and behavior of the foreigners with whom he or his group, organization, or state interacts reinforce the notion of separateness and the persistence of a "we-they" identification. If the individual's system of values does not extend beyond that of his own welfare or that of his wife and children, his separation from the international system is still more remote.

The fact that an individual, in the performance of his roles in his national system, is at the same time a participant in the international system, will not by itself cause him to assign a value to the functioning of the international system. Whether he will do so will depend upon the degree to which his linkage with the international system is perceived to result in desired goal gratification.

Moving from the individual to the state, viewed as an organization of individuals, it may be said that a necessary foundation for the acceptance of the authority of a universal actor by a state is a predisposition among state members for such an authority. Such an attitude is a product of all those elements which together establish a viable social system, that is, goal gratification, integration, adaptation, and maintenance of the patterns of its social structure. In this context, the most significant group of individuals is perhaps that of the élite. While the massive pressures of the great body of individuals not found in the élite can by no means be ignored, as

Chapter IV demonstrates, it can fairly be said that the attitudes, perceptions, and values of the various groups found in the élite are most important in this connection. The degree to which they find important goals and values involved in participation in the international system will determine the character and amount of participation by the national society in the international system.

11.b.2. *As a universal or regional actor narrows its goals and relates their attainment to important values of its members, the likelihood of their acceptance of its authority will be enhanced.*

The society of nations today is characterized by the proliferation of states as actors therein and the increasing diversity of states in their national cultures, value systems, degree of integration, progress toward an industrially organized economic system and a viable political and legal system. The perceptions which the members of these states typically have of the international system and of other actors therein vary in the widest degree. The African or Asian state will characterize the industrially organized states of the West as imperialistic, when in fact imperialism as an international phenomenon now exists primarily behind the Iron Curtain. The Communist state will view the Western welfare state as embodying an image of a capitalist society which has long ago ceased to exist. In so doing, the Communist state ignores the disparity in consumption standards between its party and managerial élite and its own industrial proletariat and agricultural workers.

States differ in the degree to which they are latecomers to the industrial techniques and methods of organization and to the sharing of the values of the integrity of the individual and the responsibility of the individual in his roles as citizen, worker, and community member, which are so central to the viability of the modern state. They differ in the degree of sharing the benefits of their productive energies among their members. They differ in the matureness, discipline, dedication to public interest, knowledge, and skill of their leaders. All such differences in turn create considerable differences in the value orientations of states.

As a consequence of the foregoing considerations, if a universal or regional actor is to attain any appreciable authority in relation to its members, it must continually search for those goals to which they will be most attracted. As the heterogeneity of its membership increases, it will become increasingly difficult to state such goals.

The universal and regional actors which exhibit the greatest degree of authority and attraction are those which are concerned with the technological aspects of the operation of the international system. Insuring a satisfactory technical administration of international air travel and telecommunications, circulation of postal communications, and provision for health are goals of universal appeal. They embody no ideologies. An organization of an intermediary type, entailing common as well as conflicting values, is the European Economic Community. This body has attained a considerable degree of viability, since its goal of an enlarged common market for its member states is steadily increasing in value to the states, even though, in particular instances, interests of a specific member may conflict with the general interest. When a value is reached as profound as that of defense and survival involved in NATO and a regional grouping of states sharing to such a considerable degree a common culture, ideology, history, and tradition, as its members do, the regional actor emerging will possess substantial authority over its members. Yet the cohesiveness and authority of NATO fluctuates as its members vary their perceptions of the imminence of the threat of force posed by the Soviet. For a universal actor as inclusive as the United Nations, however, there are few important political issues upon which there is sufficient world concensus to establish a universal authority structure in the political sphere.

11.c. *Institutions and procedures must be found for the coordination, on a basis conducive to the growth of viability of the international system, of the increasing extension into the world society of the authority systems of individual actors.*

Individuals, as members of states, are increasingly finding the scene of their activities outside the territorial jurisdiction of their state and in that of another. They thereby become subject to the application of a number of systems of authority at the same time. If they are employees of an international corporation, they would be coincidentally subject to its authority, that of their home state, and that of the state of their foreign residence. If they should be members of such public organizations of their home state as governmental departments, armed forces, and the like, they will be required to accept the authority of such organizations, as well as the state's authority exercised over them in their capacity as citizens and the foreign state's authority, in their capacity as residents.

The juridical bases of the extraterritorial exercise of authority by states have been stated elsewhere by the author[13] and others.[14] The fact should now be emphasized that the state no longer assumes an attitude of *laissez faire* toward the expanded activities of the international corporation and the increased participation by its nationals in international trade. Relying on any and all bases of legal justification, the conduct of foreign business in foreign territories is considered to be a subject of national concern and control. The grasp of jurisdiction by states has become international in scope.[15]

The international corporation, although it is subject to the authority of the states in which it operates, as well as the state of its incorporation or in which its seat is found, has its own internal authority structure extending throughout its sphere of operations.

The resulting intermingling and interplay of diverse systems of authority in the international corporation means that conflicts over which authority system shall have supremacy will increasingly arise. Insofar as their resolution may be entrusted to public and private international law, a subject explored in the next chapter, it is becoming increasingly evident that the dichotomies hitherto evolved by these systems of law are of a crude character. Public international law established the dichotomy of the sovereign and private spheres. It extended immunity from the local jurisdiction to any state activity characterized as sovereign in nature. Consider the stresses created by such a dichotomy in a recent international episode in which the diplomatic officials of one state located in another were reported to have been instructed to murder a colleague. Or consider the strains created by the extension of immunity to commercial activities carried forward in the name of the sovereign. The dichotomy of public and private law which marks the cleavage between public and private international law becomes increasingly difficult to apply as the state moves into areas of activities traditionally considered to be private. What, for example, shall be the status of a contract between a state and an

---

[13]Carlston, *Law and Structures of Social Action*, 153-158, and "Antitrust Policy Abroad," 49 *Northwestern U. L. Rev.* 569, 574-580 (1954).

[14]K. Brewster, Jr., *Antitrust and American Business Abroad*, chap. 4 (1958); W. L. Fugate, *Foreign Commerce and the Antitrust Laws*, chaps. 2, 3 (1958).

[15]See, further, K. S. Carlston, "The Grasp of Jurisdiction," *Proceedings of the American Society of International Law* 170 (1959).

international corporation? Is it for all purposes and at all times within the domain of private law?

The traditional boundary lines of the public and private spheres tend to become diffuse as a result of changes in political and social organization. The jurist must accordingly define these lines with greater precision and sensitivity to the social needs and values involved. The jurist may deplore the confusion which any different conceptual approach may create. The legal systems, however, must eventually accommodate themselves to such fundamental changes. When law ceases to reflect the organic realities of the system in which it functions, it ceases to perform its function of binding that system together by adherence to its true image. Further consideration will be given to this question in the succeeding chapter.

11.d. *Institutions and procedures must be found for controlling or preventing the use by the state of its internal monopoly of force to support its exercise of authority in directions which destroy the foundations of a viable international system.*

There are grave implications for the international system of the state's internal monopoly of force. The state is held to possess the supreme coercive authority within its territorial jurisdiction, save only for its obligations under international law. Yet the international system can function only within the territorial borders of the states of the world. This simple fact is overlooked whenever we use such terms as supranational organizations and refer to the supremacy of international law. In its internal monopoly of force, the state has *de facto* supremacy.

It is conceded that states generally respect international law. In many circumstances, however, the content of international law as it applies to the facts of specific disputes cannot be demonstrated with clear finality. In others, the rules of international law do not restrict conduct by the imposition of duties but leave conduct which is likely to create conflict or tension in the area of privilege or permission. In any event, the obdurate fact remains that, as a consequence of the very substantial abnegation by states of the external use of force, international law is largely a law without force.[16] The state now has a pure monopoly of the internal use of force. It may by reliance on force establish domestic laws,

---

[16]Compare Niemeyer, *Law Without Force.*

which impair the foundations of a viable international system or do violence to the cultural values of the world. In such circumstances, other actors in the international system are largely limited to moral condemnation, though states may resort to measures of coercion short of force when their rights under international law are violated.

A social system which denies to law the sanction of force for its support and, moreover, allows a deviant actor to use force to render him invulnerable from social control, is one which is almost without parallel and is extraordinarily weak.

The implications of the above discourse are apparent when its propositions are applied to those widespread situations of maladjustment of national societies to the international system which were discussed in the previous chapter. These situations often lead to the enactment of local laws, such as nationalization, which may violate international duties owed other states and disrupt the functioning of the international system. Whatever may be the logic and necessity of the supremacy of international law from the standpoint of its organic relationship as part of the international system, whatever may be the solidity of evidence to demonstrate the supremacy of international law, the national society of the underdeveloped state feels that it cannot tolerate the recognition of any restrictive rule of international law in restructuring its internal system of action. It rejects the *mode* of its linkage with the international system. It cannot terminate the linkage itself when its industry or agriculture is dependent on foreign markets. The imperative fact remains that the state must continue to produce and sell abroad. By resort to nationalization, it terminates the mode of its linkage and excludes the foreigner from its national society.

A violent termination of foreign participation in the national economy does not necessarily come to grips with the real causes of the social tensions which brought about such a step. More than that, it may actually restrict the opportunity of the underdeveloped nation in question to make those advances toward economic growth which it hoped to achieve. The essential problem faced by the underdeveloped nation with which we are concerned is distributive justice in its own internal functioning. To deny justice to the foreigner by a violent expropriation of his property is not to solve the underlying internal maladjustments of the society. The foreigner made his investment on the basis of the current local conditions. When he entered the local society, he respected the cultural realities as they then existed. His skills and capital were contributed to the national system and enriched it in a measure not otherwise possible, if reliance for growth were limited to local capital. He was not a member or citizen of the state. The responsibility for local ills was not his. Injustice is only mounted on injustice when his property is expropriated without adequate compensation as a consequence of a failure of the domestic social system to achieve distributive justice in its functioning. To expel him from the national economy means that other actors in the international system will not be prone to make another contribution on similar terms. The national society will thus be thrust back upon its own resources as it seeks to achieve economic growth.

Leadership, as has been seen, should be concerned with the adaptation of the organization to its external social base as well as with its internal integration. To render insecure the lodging place of a state in the international system is not a wise exercise of leadership in a state.

A failure of leadership in a national society to achieve the degree of goal gratification, integration, and other conditions necessary for a viable system will not be cured by nationalization of property utilized in the international system. The national society may reflect the sentiments of xenophobia just described. The fact that it does so may be inexorably the product of its past history. This fact, however, has nothing to do with what is rationally sound for the society, either from the standpoint of the maximization of its income or of the effective realization of its values. To alleviate a symptom is not to effect a cure. The underlying causes lie in such common denominators in underdeveloped states as the we-they dichotomy of all groups, the proneness of the members of a group to exhibit hostility to out-groups, the tendency to place blame for disfunction upon external forces instead of internal factors, and the utilization of all these elements by national leaders to direct the internal forces of dissatisfaction and resentment of the members of a group externally toward the foreigner, to preserve the existing unstable internal social and authority structures.

The basic difficulty with the type of underdeveloped national society examined here is that the purely internal segments and the international segments of the society are organized on a basis to promote the interest and values of a governing élite rather than all parts of the society. Nationalization of foreign property may temporarily divert explosive internal pressures but will not change the inherently unstable social equilibrium. If anything, it may set forces in motion which will only heighten the violence of the eventual social revolution.

The substitution of government for private control may very well result in a wasteful oversupply of labor and supervisory personnel and wasteful and inefficient production. Since the sector of the economy which is under foreign ownership and control is the one which is most likely to be characterized by large-scale corporate organization, management and technological skills, and heavy capital investment, the substitution of government for private control will probably result in a lessening of competitive strength and net contribution to the economy. The goals of diversification of the economy and promotion of industrial growth are goals that should be approached in their own terms and not solely from the standpoint of expropriation of foreign capital. The imposition of effective and progressive taxation upon an élite which has long successfully evaded its social and public responsibilities, the utilization of their savings for national development instead of private gain in foreign banks and security holdings, and the promotion of education and public health measures are the type of measures which would, on the one hand, eliminate the local tensions resulting from a failure of the leaders of the society to insure a widespread degree of goal gratification and, on the other hand, would both provide national funds and encourage the further investment of foreign capital for industrial diversification of the economy.

When such a social foundation has been laid, respect will come from the underdeveloped nation for those rules of international law which reflect the enduring realities of that system. A failure to accord respect in the absence of such a foundation does not denigrate the rules, for the international system must respect the fundamental principles upon which any viable social system is based.

11.e. *In selecting procedures for promoting the growth of the international system, it must be realized that resort to agreement, rather than authority, is the principal means for coordinating systems of action in the international system.*

11.e.1. *An agreement is a means for coordinating the action of two or more actors by the internal exercise of authority within their respective systems of action in conformity with the patterns indicated in the agreement.*

No hierarchical structure of authority is implied in establishing the complementary patterns of action laid down in an agreement. An agreement, as an instrument for the coordination of action, means the acceptance by the actors involved of the principle of *pacta sunt servanda* and the consequent performance of the processes of interaction stipulated in the agreement brought about by the exercise of authority in the internal structures of such actors.

An agreement still remains the principal instrument for coordinating action in the international system. This is true in both the public sphere, in which the treaty or other international agreement is employed, and the private sphere, in which the contract and the transaction are the primary instruments of cooperation. It may be contended that agreement and coordination by resort to power are not inconsistent, in that a formal agreement, as well as a tacit understanding, may be produced by a state's resort to power. As a typical instrument of coordination, however, the agreement records not only the comparative power position of the signatories to the agreement but many other factors as well, including shared advantages and benefits flowing from the agreement.

Elsewhere the author has defined the process of negotiation and the establishment of the social relationship known as contract as follows:

Negotiation thus involves co-ordination through consensus rather than through leadership and authority. When negotiation succeeds in formulating the new hypothesis and that hypothesis is accepted by each party as a guide for conduct, the resulting co-ordination in the activity of each of the co-operating parties is made more effective in reaching their respective goals because the power potentials of each are united towards reaching the agreed new goals.

Negotiation is that process by which two or more parties arrive at a consensus for the co-ordination of their activities. It involves the joint search for a new hypothesis for such co-ordination, and the acceptance by each party of that hypothesis as a guide for conduct. The joint search is not only an exploration on the technical level to lay down the patterns of behaviour which shall characterise future interactions between the parties; it is also a process in which the value attachments of the parties are reshaped. Through discussion, education, and even through fatigue in the course of the negotiations themselves, the process of negotiation redefines the value systems of each party and thereby enables them to formulate complementary rather than conflicting patterns of behaviour and to devote their joint power or energy towards reaching a common goal.

Contract or agreement is the end-product of the process of negotiation. It establishes new, complementary, interacting relationships between the parties involved. Such relationships may be relatively short-lived or they may be of lengthy duration. While they exist, the activities of the parties in question are directed to a common end. That is to say, contract primarily deals with either the internal or external relationships of the organisation. It is the consensus concerning common ends and the means to such ends which characterises the concept of contract. Negotiation is the process by which that consensus is arrived at, while law seeks to ensure that the relationships thus envisaged shall remain a social fact and their breach appropriately repaired.

In the preceding discussion, we used the term "parties" to indicate those persons who were brought into a co-operating relationship through negotiation and contract. When one such person is that fictitious legal personality known as the corporation, however, care must be taken that this personification of the corporation does not mislead. In terms of human behaviour, the making of a contract by a corporate organisation is the making of an authoritative decision that certain members of the organisation shall engage in specified forms of behaviour. This decision is authoritative; first, in the sense that it is made by a person who has an office within the corporation of a kind which will enable his decision, evidenced in the established form and ceremony, to be reinforced by the appropriate governmental institution and, second, in the sense that such person within the organisation will, by virtue of his office, and his decision in the performance of his office, call forth the described behaviour on the part of the members in question of the organisation when the content of that decision is communicated to them. Obviously, we do not need to repeat all this whenever we refer to the making of a contract by a corporation any more than the mathematician needs to repeat a x a x a when he wishes to express the concept a^3. But we must always remember the content of our concepts when we use them, and not let fictions which we adopt for the sake of convenience become realities.[17]

The counterpart of diplomacy and treaty was described as follows:

The analogous process in the international scene is that of diplomacy and the analogous end-product the treaty.

The rule *pacta sunt servanda* is a rule of international law. Among the expectancies included in the office of a head of state is the expectancy

---

[17]See Carlston, *Law and Structures*, 117-118.

that a decision made by him in the performance of his office, expressed in the established form of a treaty and carried to completion by certain established ceremonies, will be communicated to the members of his State whose behaviour will be affected by the content of such decision and will be followed by their performance of the specified behaviour. This happens with a sufficient degree of uniformity to enable us to predict social behaviour on the basis thereof, and to say that it is a principle of international law that international agreements, duly made, are binding.[18]

11.e.2. *Universal and regional actors primarily represent an environment for negotiation and agreement-making processes rather than the making of authoritative decisions or commands.*

It should be realized at the outset that the present discussion refers to the use of authority to coordinate action toward the realization of desired goals. It refers to the transformation of the international system into a true organization, in which authority is exercised in authoritative roles or institutions. It is primarily speaking of the type of authority which is termed political. This is authority typified in the state by the legislature. It is a type of authority in which the bold contours of group action, as an embodiment of group values, are laid down by authoritative institutions.

There are few *structures* of social action in the international system in which the action of states is coordinated by authority. Situations of authority in the relations of states may appear from time to time. Such situations may persist as the power relations of the actors involved remain relatively constant. The emergence of structures of social action characterized by the exercise of authority at defined posts or in authoritative roles is infrequent. This aspect of the international system was discussed in principle 11.b. It will be recalled that the appearance of regularized patterns of authority in a universal or regional actor was postulated to rest on the degree to which it equated its claims of authority with the realization of important values of its members. This postulate may be restated in terms of the acceptance of the exercise of authority by the members of a universal or regional actor, as follows: *States functioning as members of a universal or regional actor will accept a claim of authority only when it enables, or does not materially impair, the realization of important values or, if it should do so, when it is supported by the exercise of power by other member states.*

---

[18]*Ibid.*, 122-123.

The legal capacity of the United Nations to make decisions binding its members to action without their consent is strictly circumscribed. The General Assembly can make only recommendations. The making of decisions by the Security Council is subject to the concurrence (veto) of the five permanent members. The Secretary-General is authoritative primarily for the secretariat. The United Nations is characteristically an instrument for deliberation and reaching understanding, consensus, and agreement among its members as a basis for action.

The success of the recommendation of the General Assembly in November, 1956, of a cease-fire and withdrawal of the forces of Great Britain, France, and Israel from Egypt was a product of the coincidence of values and power status by the states involved. Yet a recommendation by the General Assembly made in the same month that the Soviet withdrew its forces used to crush the Hungarian revolt failed, because the values of the Soviet impelled it to use its power to retain its *de facto* position of authority in Hungary.

It is said that the six-nation European Parliament acted legislatively for the first time on March 29, 1960, but the form which such action took was a modification of the Treaty of Paris of 1951 establishing the European Coal and Steel Community. The characterization of the action as partaking of legislation arose from the fact that it had the immediate force of law in the six member states without further implementation. The action in question was the final step in a most carefully circumscribed series of steps in the High Authority, the Council of Ministers, and the Court of Justice of the community.[19]

The High Authority of the community is its principal organ but its decisions are subject to a variety of checks. Some must be unanimous, others require concurrence of the Council of Ministers, and still others require either a two-thirds vote or a majority based on the productive capacity of the member states, which would require the concurrence of both France and West Germany. Centralized authority, therefore, is minimal and such coordinated action as the community may reach is still largely the product of agreement, although the legal form may be couched in terms of decisions.

---

[19]*The New York Times,* March 30, 1960, p. 7, col. 2.

12. *Fostering the development of a number of emerging factors or variables represents a further economical means of promoting integration in the international system.*

12.a. *Increase in the international dispersion of the members of various organizations, both public and private, as well as the members of the professions, will promote the integration of the international system.*

The extraterritorial extension of the state, the increase in number and size of international organizations, and the growth of international corporations, mean that the staffs of such organizations are increasingly discovering the world to be the scene of their activities. The state functionary located abroad, the international civil servant, the employee of the international corporation, the member of the professions who finds himself performing his services abroad—all of these may be said to be members of a new international élite possessing an international outlook and acting in the international arena.

The promotion of the circulation of such personnel in the international system, the development of educational institutions and procedures for training such personnel for roles in the international system, the processes of exchange of artists, scholars, scientists, and students, the formation of learned societies upon an international as well as a national basis will hasten the integration of the international system. It is from the growth of such an international élite that the perceptions and attitudes necessary for a viable international system will develop in the respective national societies.

12.b. *Increase in the number and membership of universal and regional actors and the expansion of the range of their activities to provide valued goals for their members will promote integration of the international system.*

The sheer proliferation of international organizations and comprehensiveness of the range of their interests and goals, both collectively and individually, mean that the state's exclusive control over its finance, tariff, defense, health, food, transportation, communication, and other basic concerns increasingly becomes subject to international coordination, even though the authority of such bodies may remain slight. The state is increasingly dependent upon the procedures of the international organizations to furnish it with information necessary for decision making and for providing it with environments in which it can arrive at needed procedures of coordination through agreement with other states, as well as personnel which can assist in the administration of international action.

The above facts represent the emergence in the international system of those conditions in which it will be possible to make use of evolutionary planning as a means for integration and the realization of values. This is a possibility of extraordinary importance. It means, among other things, that international organizations may have reached or may soon reach that degree of interdependency in which the establishment of each new organization directed toward a new goal so varies the functional relationships of existing organizations with one another as to make the changed pattern of relationships the basis for establishing still another organization, which will in turn create a new pattern of interrelationships that will promote further growth and integration of the international system.

The above principle demands that "increase in the number and membership of universal and regional actors" be accompanied by an "expansion in the range of their activities," if "integration of the international system" is to be promoted. The increase in the membership of the United Nations, occurring as a consequence of the emergence of the new states of Africa and Asia, means that all actors in the organization must view it in a new light. It is now an organization in which the largest single group or interest bloc is that of the modernizing states. Unless its changed character is recognized and accepted, its potentialities as an integrative instrument for the international system will not be achieved. Its action must be directed toward providing ways in which the modernizing state, whether African, Asian, or Latin American, may realize its values. It is no longer enough that the United Nations shall strive to preserve the peace in the conflict between the East and the West. Assistance in strengthening the political processes of the modernizing states and hastening their economic and social development must now become an additional prime concern of the United Nations.

International organization will grow and prosper as it finds ways for its members to reach their valued goals. The successive development of the Coal and Steel Community, the Common Market, and Euratom, with the same international court serving all three organizations, illustrates the manner in which international organization may achieve viable growth.

The implementation of the above principle requires an appreciation of the ways in which coordination of action may be achieved. Coordinated action may be established through agreement or through authority. Motivation to reach and adhere to agreement may arise in actors because the agreed patterns of action embody the lowest common denominator of goals embodying shared values among the actors. Alternatively, such a motivation may arise in a situation of compromise, that is, one in which the actors perceive that although they will have to undergo some deprivation of the realization of their particular values in adhering to the agreed patterns of action, the total value realization for each actor nevertheless will be enlarged through performance of the agreement.

The task of establishing a viable international organization, in which authority is exercised as a means of coordinating action to maximize value realization by the members of the organization, is one of establishing a set of conditions in which the members, as actors in the organization, will move fluidly through a sequence of situations in which they accept authority, at first minimally, with slight commitment of time, action, and resources, and low risk of value impairment, and thereafter, in successively larger commitments of time, action, and resources and higher risk of value impairment. Such a set of conditions involves planning a sequence of goals embodying a desired pattern of value realization. The ordering of the sequence of goals will involve an expansion of the area of authority of the organization only after there has been a substantial previous experience in a narrower use of authority to attain more limited goals and the actors have found gratification in the goal attainment thereby made possible. Such a splitting up of a long-term plan of action and resulting favorable experience in value realization in each phase will reduce the precariousness of a decision by each actor to commit itself to participate in the organization as compared with irrevocable commitment to a single long-term plan which would very seriously affect its total pattern of action to realize values and entail unacceptable risk of value deprivation. An international organization which so plans action for its members and brings about an initial acceptance of its program will be one in which supranational authority will most likely steadily grow.

12.c. *Increase in the importance of the value of good citizen-ship as displayed by states as actors in the international system will promote integration of the international system.*

Whether it is prized as a means of influence over and esteem by other states or whether it represents the independent growth of standards of conduct by states as actors in the international system, the value of the display of good citizenship as a determinant of an action in the international system is steadily increasing. The standards of conduct implicit in the notion of good citizenship are constantly being developed and defined.

The industrialized and other maturely developed states have shown an increasing concern for the promotion of the welfare of all states, notably the underdeveloped states. The work of the specialized agencies of the United Nations, the establishment of procedures of technical assistance, the extension of grants and loans to latecomers to the family of nations, the widespread concern over catastrophies in particular states and common contribution to their rehabilitation, the condemnation of action impairing human rights and instances of the brutal use of force by states over their subjects, and the institutionalization of an international court for the protection of human rights reveal the emergence of international standards of conduct which are a far cry from those of only half a century ago. It may be said that in one form or another, whether loans, grants, foreign aid, or the Marshall Plan, the international system has established modes of self-imposed taxation as a means of its integration and growth.

A value has also emerged in the abnegation of the use of force as an instrument to establish external authority. This standard has reached a rather curious stage of development. As a factor in the relations of East and West, it would seem that either group would resort to force if action were taken by the other threatening its survival or vital foundations of power. In international situations falling short of this point, threats of the use of power as a tactic in the relations of states still persist. This appears to be notably true for the Soviet, increasingly true for the People's Republic of China as its power waxes, and occasionally true in the West. Outside the sphere of bipolar power relations between the East and the West, however, and particularly in the relations of latecomers to the international system, threats of force still loom. The Middle East and Middle America bear witness to this fact.

13. *The transformation of the international system into a world organization will require the interdependent functioning of its actors to produce a widespread realization of commonly shared values and the occurrence of adaptive difficulties which only the centralized exercise of authority can adequately solve.*

This principle and its demonstration may be somewhat more conjectural than others. It is, however, believed to be sufficiently well founded to justify its insertion. Whether the necessary conditions for the establishment of a world organization will ever occur is certainly beyond the realm of prediction. The formulation of such conditions is, however, a matter of considerable certitude.

13.a. *The establishment of a world organization will require the emergence of at least a surface mass culture and system of shared values for the peoples of the world and their respective élites.*

The above statement is perhaps the most debatable of those asserted herein. It is true that history has recorded federal states of diverse cultural elements, of which Switzerland is a notable example, and that a federal world state of diverse national societies should be possible. It seems fairly clear, however, that the existence of at least a surface mass culture enormously facilitates integration and the establishment of authority in a social system. Common attitudes and perceptions, a common sharing of values and value priorities, and common patterns in the outward or surface design of living are all fairly necessary conditions for a viable social system which will be disposed to accept the exercise of authority not based primarily on power. Cases such as Switzerland are instances in which historical and geographical forces over the centuries have brought unique entities into being.

If the world organization is to be one in which the exercise of authority and the resort to power to sustain authority are kept within their proper province, it would seem to be essential that a mass surface culture and system of shared values among the peoples of the world and their respective élites shall at the minimum have developed. The first and essential step in this process is the creation of a sense of unity and common realization of shared goals and values among the élites of the various national societies. The élites of different national societies and, indeed, of different regions, will vary in their predisposition toward integration in some supranational organization. Their attitude will be a most important factor in attaining world organization.

Whether a world devoted to the common man will be a world of the uniform, standardized pattern of man is something over which there is relatively little control. Whether our evaluation of such a world as one of grim monotony will be that of our descendants living in such a world is at least open to question. Yet the inevitability of such a world sharing common perceptions, cognitions, and values seems clear if the international system is eventually to be transformed into a world organization.

The world may be said to share a common system of values when they are removed to the degree of abstraction represented by such terms as wealth, enlightenment, respect, and the like. The establishment of a shared value system, upon which an integrated social system must rest, demands that it possess a fairly common orientation toward values or shared priorities in values. It further demands that such values be embodied in specific human conduct, situations, and institutions, and that preferences among such concrete ways of behavior be widely shared.

Elsewhere the author has outlined the problems to be solved in the movement of a national society toward a democratically ordered state:

While the forms of political democracy have been introduced in most nations of the world, including Soviet Russia, each State has its own real structure of authority and distribution of power. Each State varies in the extent of its industrialisation, competitive patterns of behaviour, division of labour, mobility of the individual within the social structure, social distance between individuals, dynamism of change, and energy. The problem of changing the pattern of a particular culture is the most massive of all social problems. For as we move from autocracy to democracy in a social system, we create new stresses elsewhere in the system. The expansion in participation in decision-making in political institutions and economic organisations involves, among other things, changes in leadership, techniques in training in primary groups such as the home, in education, and in the media of communication. It involves the substitution of universalistic for particularistic values. It involves not only a transformation of the centralised and institutionalised controls of a society but also of all those indirect influences and standards which pattern conduct in a host of situations. Democracy, in short, is the product of a culture. An individual transplanted from one culture to another can in most instances be rather rapidly "enculturated" or assimilated in his new environment. A democratic order of society, however, is not a product of manipulation or of export, though conscious manipulation will indeed hasten the process of democratisation. A democratic society is a product of deeply grooved patterns of behaviour and a highly complex integration of institutions and value-systems developed through centuries of growth. Thus the democratisation of Germany, for example, involves changing authority patterns in the home, in the school and in the factory; the substitution of new national legends and myths; changing habits of submission and deference; creating a sense of the inviolability of the person from the child through adulthood (for example, the German child is apparently not immune from demonstrations of affections from strangers), it involves, in short, a shift in political power, leadership techniques in all forms of social action, and in the values pervading the myriad of situations involved in day-to-day life.[20]

When the problem of establishing true democratic patterns in such a developed state as Germany is compared with the establishment of a true parliamentary democracy in the emerging states of Africa or with the establishment of an integrated social system in states which are latecomers to the world society, the magnitude of the problem of establishing a world organization becomes apparent.

13.b. *The establishment of a world organization will require the interactive relationships of the actors in the international system to reach a substantial degree of homogeneity and integration.*

In the description of the international system, with which this chapter began, it was said that the configurations of systems of action in the world society could not properly be identified as a single, integrated system. The above statement is an affirmation of the fact that not until the actors in the international system, notably individuals as subjects of the states, identify themselves as members of the international system, and not until the systems of interaction of the actors in the international system have reached a pattern of widespread interdependency, cohesiveness, and shared value realization will that degree of integration appear which will enable it to be truly characterized as a separate and distinct social system. The attainment of such a situation seems essential if there is to be the widespread readiness to accept authority which is so central to the emergence of an organization of a democratic character.

---

[20]Carlston, *Law and Structures*, 187-188.

13.c. *The establishment of a world organization will require the international system to encounter situations of disfunction or inappropriate adaptation demanding the exercise of authority in order to reach valued goals.*

When the customary ways of adaptation of a social system become inappropriate means toward reaching desired goals or when the environment in which a social system has hitherto functioned changes materially new patterns of conduct must be found if goal gratification is to continue. Usually the successful coordination of conduct in such situations is a product of the exercise of authority by leaders. Such leaders occupy a position in the social system to which information is fed about the situation to which the system must adapt itself and from which decisions or commands can be communicated.

As long as institutionalized or stabilized patterns of interaction between different cultural groups or societies lead in a fairly consistent way toward desired goal gratification, there will be no drive toward cultural change. When, however, such patterns of interaction fail to accomplish the desired ends and instead lead to frustration and internal conflict, cultural change is stimulated. As the author stated elsewhere:

Whether inter-cultural contacts produce cultural readaptation and change is, accordingly, in part dependent upon the incentives to learning which such contacts produce. Stated more comprehensively, whether such contacts will produce change will depend upon the kind and relative number of the individuals engaged in such interaction, the conditions under which the interaction takes place, including the incentives to and opportunity for learning, that which is learned, and the results of the process within each group and in their subsequent relations.[21]

In the world of change in which the West immemorially has found itself and in the world of change in which the peoples of Asia and Africa now find themselves, the meaning of life is in action and struggle. It is not found in the blissful nirvana of repose and contemplation of more static societies. In such a world, traditional patterns or habits of conduct are constantly outmoded. It is creative action and the overcoming of disfunction which give meaning to life. This means that the organizational way of life must supplant that of custom. Similarly in the international system,

---

[21]*Ibid,* 95.

not until states as actors are faced with situations of disfunction preventing the realization of highly prized values, which can be resolved only by the exercise and acceptance of centralized authority, will they be ready to become members of a world organization. Yet not even the threat of atomic warfare, threatening the ultimate value of survival itself, appears to be such a situation of disfunction to create the needed stimulus. Perhaps it is because we have lost our individuality in our organizational roles; perhaps it is because we have succumbed to *anomie* instead of maturing as individuals to a point where we are prepared to recognize, accept, and try to meet the challenge.

13.d. *Integration of the international system demands the integrity, purity, and efficiency of its channels of communication.*

If any one factor in the analysis of action in a social system could be selected from all others as crucial, it would be the concept of value. The drives or impulses of hunger, sex, heat, and cold avoidance, aggression, anxiety, or fear furnish the ultimate sources of energy for action. The form and structure which action takes, however, is determined by values or preferences as they operate in a universe of individual personality, culture, institutions, organization, and social control.

Communication, however, may perhaps be a factor of equal importance with value. Communication is the first conditioning factor of action. Communication brings to the organism the information concerning itself and the situation from which its perceptions are derived and upon which it differentiates its responses. Communication brings to the organism its picture of the outside world and establishes its internal chemical balance. For the amoeba, communication brings to it perceptions of light and dark, heat and cold, freedom and resistance. Communication also brings to it the sensations of pleasure and discomfort, that is, the selective responses of attraction and withdrawal which represent the evaluative aspect of action. In man, the brain refines these fundamental aspects of thought and action to an extraordinary level of exactness, not only by virtue of the precision and complexity of its mechanism but also because its capacity to store experiences in memory makes it possible for the organism to appraise and control action. Communication provides the information for action, evaluation determines the direction or goal of action, decision determines the content of action, and control holds action to those central patterns which experience has determined to be essential if action is to be meaningful in its context.

Communication brings to an actor the information about the situation in which he finds himself, both as a matter of his external environment and his internal world of perceptions, cognitions, needs, or values. Communication provides an actor with the information with which his brain must perform its function of enabling adaptation. Communication tells the actor where he is. Memory enables the new observation to be fitted in with the past, to be given meaning, and thereby to provide the factual background upon which decisions must be based.

Freedom of knowledge and liberty of thought are more than liberal principles or dogma; they are the basic foundations of action. These principles have unfortunately entered the area of ideology. The rights to knowledge and liberty of thought are increasingly the captive of ideological and political considerations. Respect for them is, however, more than a matter of evaluation of the preferable or the good as against the undesirable or the bad. It is as basic to social action as fidelity to established principles is to successful action in the world of science. Without purity of communication, action cannot be faithful to the needs of an actor or successfully adaptive to its environment.

A politician who is unfaithful to truth in his communications will inflict or corrupt the social system in which he functions with far greater damage and havoc than one who is merely venal. There can be no intelligent action, there can be no action responsive to the values of the actors, and there can be no basis for the effective control of inappropriate action in a social system unless its channels of communication are pure and unless they record true and adequate information. The political system can tolerate graft far more readily than it can the fouling of its channels of communication.

The communication by the leaders of one state of false images of other states and their characterization as sources of menace and oppression is too often a means for the ascendancy by individuals to positions of authority and the use of power. Regularized distortion of fact may be pursued in the use of communication media of a state as a means for maintaining an internal authority structure and achieving influence over other states. The communication of such distorted images leads to maladjustive responses by the state itself, as well as other states, to international situations. The departure of the perceived images from reality not only leads to behavior which others will regard as inappropriate or even neurotic, but it also leads to behavior which casts great or intolerable stresses on the international system itself, notably behavior such as war. And when the states in question come to face reality itself, instead of its false image, as in the course of time they eventually must, it may well lead to crippling injury of the system.

For the international system, this means that the right to knowledge must become a human right of the highest order. It means that institutions and procedures should be established to condemn and correct the communication of false pictures of situations and false images of states as actors. It means that an institution comparable in dignity and impartiality to the International Court of Justice should be established to investigate important international situations when controversy ensues over the facts of events.

The growth of science and knowledge and the degree of experimentation in the arts are central aspects of the culture of the world society. Scientists and artists emerge in the national society and their products are in part a reflection of the society's design for living and the images of life held by its members. Once the scientist or the artist has spoken, however, his communication should be free and open to all peoples. The internationalization of science, knowledge, and the arts is a process so vital to the actions of each scientist, scholar, or artist that no national boundary, not even the Iron Curtain, can prevent its flow. It is a process which is inherently for the benefit of the world society instead of the exclusive advantage of the nation, since it so vitally affects the values of men and the energies of their societies.[22]

---

[22]The subject matter of Chapters V and VI and, to a lesser extent, of Chapter VII, represents further reflection upon the bibliographical sources in the behavioral sciences indicated in the author's *Law and Structures of Social Action.* It also embodies consideration of works by the following authors not cited elsewhere in text but included in the bibliography, and which have been published since the author's earlier study: H. H. Anderson, F. K. Beutel, K. Boulding, F. Cottrell, J. T. Dunlop, M. E. Dimock, R. Eells, J. B. Fordham, C. J. Friedrich, E. Fromm, M. Haire, S. H. Hoffmann, M. A. Kaplan, J. G. March and H. A. Simon, E. S. Mason, G. Myrdal, S. F. Nadel, F. S. C. Northrup, T. Parsons ("Suggestions for a Sociological Approach to a Theory of Organizations"), T. Parsons and N. J. Smelser, A. M. Rose, P. Selznick, M. I. Stein and S. J. Heinze, O. Tead *(Administration: Its Purpose and Performance),* R. S. Weiss, W. H. Whyte, Jr., Q. Wright, and R. Young (ed.). See also M. Weber, pages 130-132 and 328-329.

VI

LAW AND THE PROVISION OF ORDER IN THE INTERNATIONAL SYSTEM

1. The search for the roots and meaning of law in the international system, as elsewhere, is subject to universal principles derived from empirical observation of human behavior to which meaning and order is attributed in the light of all relevant knowledge of the culture.

Law, as a conceptualization of certain aspects of the relations of men, is thought to be man made and to share nothing of the notion of law in the physical or natural sciences as a statement of predictable behavior of phenomena. The attempt of the natural lawyer to attribute universal validity to certain fundamental principles of law, without subjecting them to the rigorous testing of the application of the scientific method, has not been treated kindly by most modern philosophers of law. The ensuing statements concerning law are not to be considered an attempt to create a new system of natural law. Instead it is asserted that a statement of the ultimate nature of law in the relations of men must be based on observed phenomena and the attribution of meaning and order must be the product of a search of all relevant domains of knowledge. He who would study the nature and province of law must seek to enlarge his perceptions and conceptualizations so that they become in the broadest possible sense a product of his culture. Only when he achieves such a perspective is his contribution likely to reach its maximum meaning, usefulness, and validity.

The exploration into the nature of law and its function in providing order to the international system will start at the very roots of the meaning of law, perhaps approaching law as a philosopher would. It will then move to a definition of law based on findings of the behavioral sciences and supported by empirical data. A basis will then have been laid for an examination of law in the international system, which will be sufficiently broad and true to test the validity and adequacy of existing assumptions concerning law and the legal process in that system.

2. *Law in social action is a statement of the patterns to which action must adhere in order to express its idea or ideal form.*

Action must faithfully reflect the typical form of some cultural idea if it is to be meaningful social action. Action which is random, scattered, or passes rapidly from a fleeting aspect of one idea to another momentary aspect of a different idea, without any governing idea, cannot be characterized as action for any useful purpose. The law of an action may in its most elementary sense be said to represent a consistent adherence to those typical patterns of conduct which embody a cultural idea.[1]

A fishing trip, for example, implies something more than a venture by a group of individuals to a body of water in search of recreation. It implies at the very minimum some association with fishing equipment and boats. If the trip be purely recreational, it may stop at that point, with the members of the fishing group finding their recreation in other forms in the cabin at the water's edge. If the trip be for subsistence, there will be a greater fidelity to the patterns of action which the culture calls fishing. In either event, there must be a minimal fidelity of action to an idea if it is to be meaningful.

Fundamental as this thought may be, there is, of course, considerably more to the meaning of law than this rather elementary principle. The phrase "patterns to which action *must adhere*" carries

---

[1]The above statement of law is a product of collaboration with Professor Thomas H. Haynes.

within it the full meaning of the concept of law as shall be developed here. For the term "must adhere" has the implication of "action which is constrained to adhere."

3. *Law is an entity of an ideal and valued norm of action coupled with regulatory behavior designed to restore to the ideal norm action deviating from it.*

When the culture establishes an ideal and valued norm of action, that norm then becomes the standard for, or the determinant of, the regulatory action of law which subjects deviant behavior to control.

The universality and inseparability of norm and deviance in which regulatory action takes place was brought out brilliantly by E. W. Sinnott in his *Biology of the Spirit.*[2] The search was made for a universal principle which would illuminate and render consistent biological behavior. Sinnott asserted his fundamental thesis or major premise to be:

That the insistent tendency among living things for bodily development to reach and maintain, as a norm or goal, an organized living system of a definite kind, and the equally persistent directiveness or goal-seeking that is the essential feature of behavior, and thus finally the basis of all mental activity, are *fundamentally the same thing*, merely two aspects of the basic regulatory character all living stuff displays. Regulation implies something to regulate *to*, a norm or goal. The goal in embryonic life may be regarded as the series of stages that lead to a mature and properly functioning individual; and the goal in psychic life as a purpose or series of purposes, simple and unconscious in primitive instinct, but rising in the mind of man to far higher levels. Mental activity is the most complex form and culmination of that universal regulatory behavior in life which we have been discussing.[3]

He then moved to the statement of his minor premise in the field of biology:

The goal of the organism, implanted first in the genetic constitution of the egg, unfolds itself in structure and activity as development progresses. In every cell of the body, so it seems, are to be found the same genes, derived from those first present in the egg. These cells gradually become different as growth proceeds, until the great diversity of structure present in tissues and organs of the mature individual is reached. This goal is not a static one, gained once for all, for genetic control does not cease when growth is ended but extends to the behavior of the

---

[2]E. W. Sinnott, *Biology of the Spirit,* 52-65 (1955).
[3]*Ibid.,* 52-53.

mature organism. At all levels the organism is held to a straight course by constant regulation, which brings it back whenever it deviates from the norm. The pattern of development and activity that works itself out in this way is not the result of a mere collection of independent genes, like beads on a string or marbles in a bag or separate chemical substances, but of a precisely integrated and continuing *relationship* between them. It has well been said that the organism is not an aggregate but an integrate. The nature of this relationship is the basic and still unsolved problem of biology.[4]

The reappearance of the regulatory adaptive mechanism in the brain is described as follows:

This emphasis on the regulatory character of mind may help make clear one of its fundamental functions. In all living things there are mechanisms that receive and react to stimulation. The more complex animals possess sense organs, which are sensitive to stimuli and transmit them to a central clearing-house, the brain. Another portion of the nervous system controls the reaction to this stimulus, muscular or otherwise. . . . Between stimulus and response in an organism, something very important occurs, an act of *regulation*. What the response will be depends on the norm or purpose set up in the living system, for the response will tend to maintain or restore that norm. How an animal reacts—even the tiniest and simplest of animals—depends on its inner state. A hungry one will respond to a food stimulus very differently from one that is fully fed, for a particular physiological goal has been attained in one but not in the other.[5]

Yet regulation in the organism and in the brain does not exhaust the meaning of life, for life is also creative:

In addition to the regulatory character that both [organism and mind] display, there is a further similarity between the development and the behavior of living things. Both produce novelties in nature. Both are creative.

An organism draws in random material from its environment and builds this into a living system which it maintains against the disruptive tendencies of the lifeless world. Life is inherently synthetic, and synthesis is an organizing process. It puts substances together to make the almost infinite number of organic compounds found in the bodies of animals and plants. During the course of evolution this synthetic process has steadily produced *new* compounds. . . .

In a similar fashion, psychical activity is creative. Even homeostasis, so evident in physiological processes, is not to be thought of as merely the maintenance of a static condition, for its norms change as development progresses. It is in behavior, however, that the constant change

---

[4]*Ibid.*, 57.
[5]*Ibid.*, 58-59.

in goals and the origin of new ones are most conspicuous. As Lillie puts it, "Psychical existence is in present time and carries with it a quality of novelty; the past is left behind, and there is an advance into the future. . . . The psychical is the source of initiative when action takes on a novel, unforeseen, or creative form, as in purposive activity or (in a broader sense) in natural creative action in general." Whitehead has expressed this idea in a famous line: "The psychical is a part of the creative advance into novelty."[6]

These statements reflect the ultimate roots of action. The creative idea of a goal as an end of action of the individual organism becomes the concern of leadership in the social system and the province of the political institutions of the state and the directors of the economic organization. The performance of action by the organism becomes the concern of administration in the state and management in the economic organization. The regulatory behavior of the organism becomes the concern of law and the legal process in the state, and of authoritative roles in the organization itself, coupled with resort by the organization to law and the legal process. As the culture develops ideal and valued norms of action, regulatory patterns of behavior appear designed to inhibit departures from these norms. When such regulatory behavior assumes the discrete form of the sanction of force applied pursuant to decisions made by occupants of authoritative roles termed judicial, then regulation or control reaches its full institutionalization in a social system.

The above remarks should not, however, be understood to affirm the intrinsic validity of the quoted remarks of Sinnott as a proposition in biological science. The remarks were introduced to illustrate in a vivid form the triad of (1) ideal form of action, (2) action which is deviant from this ideal, and (3) regulation, which appears in the concept of law. Biological science, in the above quotation, illuminates this notion of law. The notion in biological science of different levels of organization in organisms is another analogy which may be helpful. There may be different levels of integration in different types of national societies and international organizations, to which different rules or principles of organization will apply. In any event, law as regulation must be seen as part of a larger entity or whole. There must always be an ideal or culturally approved and valued form of action which becomes the standard for determining deviance and the stimulus to control. A demon-

---

[6]*Ibid.,* 60-61.

stration of this fact from the behavioral sciences point of view will be found in the first chapter of the author's *Law and Structures of Social Action* (1956). To say that law is found in behavioral norms within a group supported by regulatory or sanction mechanisms, without indicating the role of individual perception, cognition, and values in stimulating such behavior, is to be unduly restrictive in approach.

4. *The regulatory process of law identifies those institutionalized rules of behavior within a social system which embody shared values of the members of the system to the degree that control of deviation, designed to inhibit its further occurrence and to restore the equilibrium of the system, is essential for self-maintenance, goal gratification, integration, and adaptation.*

To identify law solely in those patterns or norms of behavior which are sanctioned by the imposition of force in a social system is to observe the outward manifestations of conduct apart from the inner perceptions and motivations of the actor which give meaning to action. To identify law with its institutionalization in the courts and to say that law is simply the predictable behavior of courts is to remove law still one step farther from its meaning in action. It is the value inherent in the norm that is identified as a legal norm and that brings into being the regulatory behavior we call law and the legal process.

When (1) a sequence of action in a typical situation encountered in the functioning of a social system becomes a repetitive and fixed pattern of action, and (2) an actor in such a situation has imbedded or "internalized" in his mind that such a pattern of action is expected to be performed by him, an *institutionalized* pattern of action may be said to have appeared. It may be termed a behavioral rule.

When behavioral rules embody shared values of such importance in the social system that interference with or departures from their performance create conflict and tension, it may be said that at such departure point the members of the system will regard such rules to indicate behavior which ought to be performed. The expectation of the performance of the rules is so emotionally reinforced by the values which they embody that the actors involved feel they have a *right* to their performance and, conversely, that their performance is *obligatory*.

Obligation is involved in the performance of a behavioral rule when the conduct embodied is perceived to be important to the attainment of goals whose gratification involves strongly held values. It is true that a necessary condition for the involvement of obligation is that the rule shall reflect mechanical rationality, that is, a rationality of appropriateness of means to end. The norm of conduct described in the rule must be viewed as essential to the expression of the idea of the action as developed by the culture. The departure from the norm thus becomes erratic, irrational behavior, which destroys the ideal image of appropriate action in the situation. Behavioral rules become rules of law when the values they embody are so critical to the social system that the rules not only reflect a standard for the determination of deviant behavior but they are also a stimulus to the diversion of some of the energy of the social system to the control of such deviance.

The foregoing may be summarized in terms of group theory by stating that, as norms for conduct emerge within a group, deviational conduct will also from time to time appear. No group exhibits a neat, invariable adherence to its rules for conduct. When rules for conduct have become so established in a group that it is expected that roles will be performed in consistence with their appropriate rules, unexpected conduct departing markedly from these rules is perceived to interfere with cooperation. The performer of a complementary role is no longer able to mesh his action successfully with that of the deviant actor.

The deviant behavior may reflect a desired innovation. If recognized as such and accepted, then no problem or conflict arises. If, however, it is perceived as behavior tending both to frustrate effective cooperation within the group and to reduce its efficiency in reaching a valued goal, the need for control is seen. Some group energy must be used to repress the deviant conduct and keep the group on its accustomed track to its desired goal. In the primitive group, a whole range of pressures may be applied, ranging from the informal and diffuse, such as loss of respect and prestige, ridicule and denial of reciprocity, to the formal, such as ritualistic purification and punishment, and finally to the institutionalized office of control, such as the police function of the military societies of the Plains tribes.

The regulatory phase of law, therefore, is found when repressive group action takes place in situations where there has been a departure from a valued behavioral rule of the group. Law as control imports a determination of deviant behavior, using a valued behavioral rule as the point of reference for such determination, and in addition, a determination that such deviance shall become the point of reference for the application of corrective measures.

The rules of law thus become those behavior rules of a social system which are so valued as to lead to the regulatory action of the legal process in the event of deviance. The regulatory process in primitive society is institutionalized in a variety of behavioral patterns, applying sanctions of differing degrees of constraint, ending, of course, in the application of force. In the state, it is institutionalized in the judicial organ.

The rules of law can be said to be an index or basis of prediction of the appearance of the regulatory action of the legal process. To fix upon the behavior of the judicial organ apart from its organic context or its post and function in the social system, however, is to create a partial and distorted image of law and the legal process. Law and the legal process are an entity. Law comprises those norms for conduct which embody valued expectations in the functioning of a social system, deviation from which leads to measures of control, which may or may not be institutionalized in a judicial organ but which are designed to prevent the further occurrence of such deviance and to repair the resultant injuries.

The operation of law and the legal process in the flow of events which constitute the action of a social system takes place *after* action directed toward goal attainment, *in* a situation of interpersonal conflict, and *at* a time perspective in which the experience of the past has a pre-eminent but not an exclusive influence in decision-making. The process of law comes into operation after trouble and conflict have occurred between actors in the system by virtue of their action in role performance. While the legal process interprets, applies, and even makes legal rules, it is always directed to the resolution of interpersonal conflict arising from action. It never comes into operation until *interpersonal conflict concerning past social action definable in terms of legal rules* takes place.

The role of the judicial organ in carrying out the legal process is to maintain a perspective of the entire domain of action of the social system, to stabilize action at that point in the system where the governing legal rule will reflect the best accommodation or composite of mechanical and value rationality in the light of the goal to which the action is directed, and to resolve interpersonal conflict, on the foregoing basis. The conflicting values of the parties are viewed against the background of the culture, in which decisions as to goals and as to action to reach those goals have already been made. Basic value conflicts of different groups of actors within the society will have largely been resolved through the exercise of leadership and administration. The full performance of the legal process requires that appropriate action be taken to eliminate the tension of interpersonal conflict, thereby promoting integration and restoring the equilibrium of the social system in question from its disturbed position occasioned by deviance. This involves, in a developed legal process, the issuance of commands of a reparational or restitutional character by a judicial organ, as well as the selection of the appropriate legal rule to apply to the conflict.

Law and the legal process do not characteristically reflect the creative aspects of action inherent in leadership and, to a lesser extent, administration. Law and the legal process reflect, consider, and evaluate past action, and require that future action shall adhere to those patterns which embody the ideal and valued image of action in situations which the culture has come to recognize as typical. Law and the legal process are concerned with insuring the appropriateness of means to end in action and demand that action shall reflect *mechanical* rationality. More important, they penetrate beneath the objective reality of mechanical rationality into the subjective realm of *value* rationality, and insist that action shall also reflect that fidelity to the realization of important and shared values of the social system which is necessary for self-maintenance, goal gratification, integration, and adaptation, including provision for the realization of significant values of other social systems to which the system must adapt itself. The legal process orders action in an authoritative way to restore the disturbed equilibrium of the system resulting from conflict and tension. It also influences the future course of action in the system by its continued clarification of required forms of action, as it affirms positive legal rules for action in situations of interpersonal conflict.

A social system does not reach that point of development at which its control mechanisms will become institutionalized in a judicial organ until its legal norms are a fairly comprehensive set, defining, for the most part, relatively narrow and concrete sequences of behavior. The conflict must be capable of being stated in competing legal norms demanding recognition in the decision-making process of the judicial organ. The situations of conflict which are allocated to the legal process for resolution accordingly present rather precisely defined problems of mechanical and value rationality. They will be situations which will generally receive an acceptable and desirable solution when they are turned over to the legal system and its analytical processes of advocacy and judicial decision, operating against a background of accumulated social experience represented by the written jurisprudence concerning legal norms.

5. *The provision of order in a social system is not the function of law and the legal process alone, but is also the function of leadership and administration, which will determine whether the system will survive and prosper as it encounters changes in its value system and environment.*

Any social system will reflect an order, state of affairs, design, or arrangement of its patterns of interaction. The full realization of order in a social system, however, imports that arrangement or coordination of action which is a product of a sensitive, intelligent, and harmonious performance of the functions of leadership, administration, and control. It means that design of action in which the system achieves the maximum release of energy for the attainment of valued goals with the minimum of tension and conflict.

When leadership fails to recognize important emerging values in the system and fails to require administration to use the human and physical resources of the system to reach manageable or attainable goals which will embody these values, the resulting tension and conflict is so widespread that its control is beyond the proper province of law. And when the legal process selects *one* case of interpersonal conflict as a vehicle for the resolution of a deeply felt mass conflict, it will usually find that the legal rule then affirmed is so lacking in value rationality to many members of the social system that the rule can become authoritative only by resort to power.

It was the continued neglect by the political institutions of the southeastern states and the federal government to find an interrelated series of approaches, each manageable in its own sphere and all directed toward the eventual complete integration of the Negro in the social system, which led to the present episodes of violence in that region. The attempt of the legal process in the segregation cases to constitute a new order in such circumstances, while imperative to avoid irreparable disintegration, was nevertheless an assumption by the court of a role which was more appropriately that of the legislature. The disorder in Africa today is another and more violent demonstration of the principle that it is primarily the function of leadership and its servant, administration, to provide order in the social system of a state.

Leadership and administration call for action; law controls action. The primary function of leadership and administration is to bring order to, establish the properties of, a social system in order that it may respond to changes in its value system and be the master of changes in its environment. (The full meaning of this statement and of the concepts of leadership and administration was developed in postulate 9, Chapter V.) The primary function of law and the legal process is to stabilize and preserve the order thus established through decisions, applying the valued norms of behavior, which are the legal rules of the social system, to the resolution of interpersonal conflict in the system.

In addition to its responsibility for discerning changes in the value orientations of the members of the social system and directing action in the light thereof, leadership must also foresee changes in the physical environment and social base and adapt the system to these changes. For example, in the United States, it must foresee the erosion of the foundations of power as its mineral resources are depleted and plan for alternative means of meeting these needs. It must plan and decide upon policies with respect to countries which will supply such needed minerals. It must, for example, foresee the consequences of the ascendance to power of a People's Republic of China and plan policies with respect to Formosa and Southeast Asia in that light.

The organization of social action is subject to universal principles. It must be creative; it must not only continually mature and develop its existing patterns of action, but it must also innovate action in order to solve ever-changing problems of integration and adaptation. It must find ways of bringing to the world of reality creative ideas for action. Finally, it must control action so that it will be faithful to its central idea. Herein lie the ultimate meanings of leadership, administration, and law in social life.

Toynbee's notion of challenge and response may be usefully adopted at this point. The culture, in its massive, never to be fully governed, drift, constantly presents challenge to organization. Leadership, administration, and control must always work with imperfect knowledge to master cultural change. Leadership, in its long-run perspective, and administration, in its short-run perspective, can never fully divine the future. Action may not go according to plan. The environment is never as fixed as it is predicted to be. Life itself is often irrational.

6. *The character of the law and legal process of a social system is principally determined by the prior performance of the functions of leadership and administration.*

The character of the law of a social system and the degree of reliance upon power by its legal process to establish its law as authoritative are ultimately shaped by the character of its leadership and administration. Law must be creative within its sphere and from time to time extrapolate new legal rules from the body of the old, when the latter fails to provide a needed ideal norm of action. For the most part, however, the legal process is concerned with the application of the existing body of legal rules to conflict arising in action which is brought into being by leadership and administration. The domain of law is a residuum of rules developed in the social action of the past.

The recognition of values and the use of energy of the system to realize values are a product of leadership and administration. The valued patterns of action which the latter bring into being, as they operate within the conditioning factors of human values and culture, are those which become the valued behavioral rules known as legal rules and recognized by the legal process. The sphere of the process of law is *past* action creating interpersonal value conflict and exhibiting sufficient tension to require resolution for the continued functioning of the social system.

A tribal group living in the Amazon Valley or other environment characterized by the cultural traits of clearing the forests or brush by fire, tilling with primitive technique the burned-over land until its chemical elements are leached out by the elements, and then moving on, is one likely to emphasize the value of the nuclear family over any community values and to exhibit few characteristics of law or organization. A similar emphasis on the value of the nuclear family will appear in a social system characterized by an agricultural economy in a fixed environment, where the peasant lives at the margin of subsistence under an authority structure designed to exploit his production for the benefit of an élite from which he is socially separated. In the latter situation, the law operates primarily to maintain the stability of the existing authority structure of the system. The law will be disregarded whenever there is no fear of a sanction. Many members of the social system will not equate the law with public welfare. They will regard the official to be motivated by private instead of public advantage. The law will not be perceived to have any necessary bearing on the practical aspects of life.[7]

On the other hand, a tribal group living in a relatively fixed territory under established patterns of agriculture or animal husbandry, yielding more than a marginal level of subsistence but facing a hostile environment of war and the incursions of warriors from other tribal groups, will typically develop a rather substantial degree of organization, reflecting leadership, administration, and control through legal norms. Much of African tribal society and the Plains Indian society exhibit these features. Internal stability resulting from a widely diffused value realization, rigorous establishment of authority through power, or intermediates between these two poles, seem to be the invariable conditions for organization, whether in the tribal group or the modern state.

7. *The vitality of law, as a body of formal rules created by the operation of the legal process, is a reflection of the faithfulness of such rules to the life, values, and ethics of the culture in which the legal process functions.*

The operation of the legal process is always directed to the evaluation of past action, which has resulted in interpersonal conflict, in the light of competing legal norms. These norms are, as a precedent or rule for decision, in turn a product of even more remote past action. To the degree that the legal norms depart from the cultural reality of the present, law and the legal process become sterile. Each situation of interpersonal conflict arising within a society tests the vitality of its law and legal process. Un-

---

[7]E. C. Banfield, *The Moral Basis of a Backward Society,* notably chap. 5 (1958).

less the legal process finds that nice balance in decision making between adherence to the accumulated social experience represented by its written jurisprudence, on the one hand, and response to social change, on the other hand, it will fail to perform in full measure its function of social control.[8]

The legal process must constantly test the validity of its norms for conduct, refining and developing these in the light of cultural reality and cultural change. It must discard yesterday's truth which today's experience demonstrates to be false. It must state today's truth which has emerged as a product of social change. The law must faithfully reflect in the statement of its norms the reality of life beyond the courtroom doors. It must, above all else, be responsive to the values and ethics of the culture which are its function to unite and integrate. Unless valued norms for action in life somehow find their way to the body of the law, it can never attain its full measure of vitality.

The accomplishment of this end must take place in a methodology of decision making, in which the legal process essentially proceeds to expand and mold the law by the interpretation and extension of existing legal norms. The author has elsewhere expressed this point in the postulate that: "The resolution of . . . conflict through the exercise of the judicial function imports that the judicial organ has its sphere of action marked out by the rules of law entrusted to it for enforcement; only in applying such rules to cases of conflict may the Tribunal give recognition to . . . other factors in decision making."[9]

The body of the law is not static and the operation of the legal process is not merely one limited to the recognition of the rule of law which logically is appropriate to a particular situation of interpersonal conflict. The operation of the legal system is creative within its particular sphere of action. The court, for example, has the domain of the law for its province, but its function, in that province, is to search for that compromise or adjustment of values, as expressed in one of the competing legal norms for decision, in which future action by members of the society will find its most meaningful realization of values.

---

[8]See W. Friedmann, *Law in a Changing Society* (1959).
[9]K. S. Carlston, "International Administrative Law: A Venture in Legal Theory," 8 *Journal of Public Law* 329, 267 (1959).

8. *The conditions in which the international system functions deny it the opportunity to establish and control its own order as an independent system of social action and deny, in substantial measure, its actors the opportunity to realize their important values by their participation.*

8.a. *The perception of the international order through such rudimentary models as represented by the terms "family of nations," "international society," "world community," and the like, is an obstacle to realistic and effective decision making in the international system.*

Any statement of international order must, among other things, include the premise that such order is a product of decisions made in the performance of authoritative roles in its principal actors, identify such actors and the nature of such roles, take cognizance of the environment and conditions in which such decisions are made and resultant interactions of individuals take place, analyze the effect of such environment and conditions upon such decision making and interactions of individuals, and determine the degree of influence possessed by such decision makers upon the order of the international system.

Interaction in the world arena is customarily viewed as interaction between states. The acts which are seen to be the subject matter of such interaction are primarily political acts of state governments affecting the interests of other states. The law of nations or international law is the body of rules which legally bind states in their intercourse with one another. The trade of nations is viewed to be largely a matter of statistical tabulation in which columns of figures are set opposite the names of states. While international organizations are also recognized as entities or actors in the international scene, they do not dominate the stage. Those who loom large against the footlights are the great powers. The United States and the Soviet are those who, above all others, are the towering figures in the world drama of today.

Some such image as the above comes to mind whenever terms such as the family of nations, international society, world community, or the like, are used. It is rare that writers on international relations or international law pierce the corporate veil of the state.

It is questionable whether the approach to the study of international relations and international law should restrict itself to the study of the acts of states viewed primarily as the acts of governments as they fall in the sphere of politics, on the one hand, and law, on the other hand. Under such an approach, matters of trade and economics in the relations of states are relegated to the discipline of international economics. Matters of values, attitudes, and social institutions in the relations of states are relegated to the anthropologist, sociologist, psychologist, and historian.

The validity of the preoccupation of scholars with their respective disciplines is not questioned. The compartmentalization of knowledge in separate fields of study is a cultural necessity. However, the failure of the scholar of international law, and, to a lesser extent, the scholar of international relations, to develop for the purposes of their disciplines a model of international relations which will couple comprehensiveness and fidelity to the elements of the international order with simplicity, precision, and elegance of structure, is increasingly becoming a cultural catastrophe.

Semantics has certain central concepts which are useful at this point. A number of words or symbols to identify referents possessing a more or less common core of meaning are available. Some of the most frequently used symbols are "international society" and "world community." A rapidly growing body of knowledge constitutes the reference from which referents are drawn. This will provide a great deal of information about individuals as discrete personalities and as members of varied groups, about groups and organizations, about states and their relations, about international politics, international economics and international law, in short, about all the fields and aspects of knowledge that are germane to the rather loose and vague symbols which label world society.

Until a model of greater accuracy and clarity is available—one which more adequately covers the salient aspects of the categories of actors and types of decision making and action taking place in the international arena—the ordering of scholarly thought for analytical and predictive purposes will proceed in a most disorganized fashion. A fundamental principle in research is that one must know clearly the standpoint from which data are to be gathered, classified, organized, and interpreted. There must be a basic point of view, a model, or a set of interdependent principles and propositions from which one works or thinks. It is the writer's conviction that the structure or order of world society can now be arrived at, with a reasonable approximation of truth, only by the last-named means, that is, in a set of interdependent principles and propositions.

In such a situation, thinking does not take place with the ease implicit in the use of such rudimentary models as are expressed by, say, the "family of nations" or "world politics." Yet it is a kind of organization of knowledge and type of thinking to which the physical scientist has come. It is inevitable for the social scientist to follow his footsteps.

However the model, system, or scheme for portraying interaction in the international scene may be constructed, it is believed that its formulation must be faithful to the statement laid down in the first sentence after proposition 8.a., as well as take account of the propositions subsequently set forth. No startling intrinsic novelty for these is claimed; it is only hoped that as a body they may in some respects encompass a greater measure of the truth or indicate a more comprehensive and accurate model of the order of the world society than is now possessed.

The writer's fundamental assumptions, in arriving at such a model, are that (1) no action can be perceived apart from the cultural setting which gives it meaning; (2) of the types of action which are significant for describing, analyzing, and predicting social behavior, action in organizations seen in their cultural and physical environment is the most important and inclusive; (3) organizations manifest themselves, and are distinguished from other collectivities or groups, by the exercise and common acceptance of authority; (4) when order is sought for a given social scene of some magnitude, (a) search must be made for the organizations who are the principal actors and the authoritative decision makers in such organizations, (b) identification must be made of the value and other environmental conditions affecting their decision making, and (c) determination must be made of the human and physical resources which are subject to the exercise of their authority, as well as other means which they may possess for influencing the character of the order in which they act.

Yet the portrayal of the international system exclusively from such a standpoint would provide only a classification of data. It represents a necessary foundation for the conceptualization of the order of the international system. Data of the nature described above are distributed among the set of principles and propositions set forth in this and the preceding chapter for the reason that this study is not only interested in the data simply as information but also, and primarily, in providing a conceptual structuring of such data.

It will be observed that the following propositions and principles of this chapter are formulated somewhat on the basis of a dialectic of thesis and antithesis struggling to establish an eventual synthesis. Another way of viewing this ordering is as a statement of the movement of the international system to establish its own independent order against the pressure of countervailing forces. Such a formulation of theory was chosen, after rejecting an alternative approach on the basis of stating the data in terms of constant and independent variables found in the international system, for the reason that it seemed most faithfully to reflect the present position of the international system. We have reached the situation in which interaction in the international arena not only profoundly affects the internal order and viability of states but also in which the past has given a structure to the international system which is increasingly inappropriate for its functioning. As the character of our lives is being changed by massive forces in the international arena, the need to provide a rational order for these forces and for the international system becomes increasingly desperate.

8.b. *Decision making in the international system is predominantly made by those in authoritative roles who view situations of an international character in the light of their respective national cultures, value systems, and goals.*

In arriving at the bold contours of the order of the international system, perhaps the first fact which stands out from the rest is that decision makers are persons who hold office or exercise authority subject to state direction or control. States are the most encompassing of organizations and the final repository of authoritative roles for determining the directions of our lives. The state as the embodiment of law, in the sense of directives, legislation, and jurisprudence, pervades the action of its individual members. This is true whatever their sphere of action—whether public or private—and whatever their role—whether within the state, the private corporation, or the purely interpersonal and individual aspects of life. The ultimate goals and ordering of the human and physical resources of society are determined by the state.

The officials of the state in its legislative, executive, and judicial spheres may, in the phrase of Georges Scelle, perform a *dédoublement fonctionnel* (functional duplication),[10] in that they act as agents of both the national and international systems of actions. Ideally, it could be said that their decision making in each of these systems should be responsive to its particular needs and conditions. In fact, the goals and values of the states, the overriding organizations of which they are members, largely govern the performance of their roles. The state, rather than the international system, provides the controlling environment, perspective, and boundary for their decision making in the international system.

Decision makers in an organization must respond to its particular system of values and the perceptions by its members of their external environment. Decision making under organizational conditions will result in action which may be viewed as irrational in its cultural or empirical context, but which is nevertheless quite rational in its organizational context. Nuclear warfare is highly irrational as a way of life but is nevertheless quite rational when viewed from the standpoint of a particular actor who would employ the threat of its use for establishing a certain policy or for deterring others from disturbing its established patterns of authoritative control in the international system.

Decision making in universal and regional actors might at first be thought to reflect an international orientation. It is true that when any such actor is acting in a functional capacity, that is to say, when it is concerned with reaching a specific goal embodying shared values of its members, such as the World Health Organization or the Universal Postal Union, decision making is relatively uncontaminated by particularistic national values. However, when decision making enters those spheres which reflect the clashing national values of strong intensity which we call political issues, then the representatives of states which are members of such universal or regional actors primarily respond to the viewpoints and values of states which they respectively represent. They do not at such times possess an international perspective and orientation.

Decision making in international corporations is functionally directed to reach, as economically as possible in the light of the

---

[10]G. Scelle, *Droit International Public: Manuel Élémentaire* (1944).

global area in which the corporation operates, a particular corporate goal. The human and physical resources which constitute the corporation and the external resources upon which it may draw, through contract, purchase, or otherwise, are viewed internationally. Purchases, loans, sales, and the like are made in that particular national environment which will provide the most advantage to the corporation. Yet the directing personnel and the capital of such a corporation tend to be largely drawn from a single state. It is usually the law of such state which, as the place of its incorporation or its seat, is its governing law under the principles of private international law. Thus not even the international corporation provides a purely international outlook in decision making.

8.c. *The channels of communication relevant to or affecting decision making in the international system fail to communicate adequately the truth concerning international situations.*

To be effective, decision making must conform to reality. But what avenues are available in our search for reality and when do we stop our search, decide, and act? Even for the scholar of international relations, truth tends to be the captive of his particular national culture. He uses its language and particular body of scholarly resources, responds to the emotive content of its words, and reflects, perhaps less than others but nevertheless inevitably, its values. The state official, as executive or legislator, relies on national channels of communication. The citizen, whose values in a democratically organized society largely determine the content and priority of the national goals, is exposed to channels of communication of a considerably emotive and distorted content.

Facts may be universally valid, but the selection, ordering, emphasis, and evaluation of facts for purposes of communication is always a product of the communicator and the channel of communication in which he functions. The scholar and highly placed executive are exposed to the least impure channels of communication. The typical minor official, legislator, or citizen, however, acts with only a most rudimentary appreciation of the truth. In the open societies of the West, there are available at almost all levels of society means for communication which carry a far more faithful and complete version of the truth than those of the closed totalitarian societies of the East. Yet even in the West, truth, whether it be concerned with the history of the past or the events of the day, is considerably the captive of the national culture and the state.

8.d. *Decision making by states as actors in the international system can never accept, for all purposes, the value of promoting the integration and viability of the international system.*

Adaptation to its environment, particularly to its social environment or social base, is a function of all organizations, including the state. Decision makers in an economic organization acting within the state are generally aware that their organization will prosper in the measure that they find means to serve their social base of customers. They accept their social base as a given fact and devote themselves to its service for their private benefit. As they enlarge the measure of their service, by increasing provision of consumer satisfactions, so they grow and prosper. Manipulation of the relevant portions of its social base through such means as advertising may be a technique of the organization, but it is limited in its results and does not represent the central philosophy of decision making in a successful organization.

It may safely be said that members of states do not so view their participation in the international system, and decision making in states does not take place under such a philosophy. The fact of the state's dependency upon and participation in the international system may be appreciated, the circumstance that phases of its participation in the international system are beneficial may be recognized, but the value of promoting the integration and viability of the international system can never be accepted for all purposes. The world society presents a situation or independent variable of such magnitude and complexity and is the source of disadvantage to such a degree, including its menace as the repository of nuclear extinction, that it is not possible for it to be viewed as something friendly and productive of advantage as a whole. It tends to be regarded as alien, hostile, and refractory, not friendly, congenial, and malleable. It is something to be mastered and controlled, to the degree that mastery and control are possible. It is something to be utilized for national advantage. Humanity in other states is, or can quickly become, as impersonal as physical environment itself.

8.e. *Interaction between individuals in the international system for the attainment of valued goals, which by definition transcends state borders, tends to be viewed from the standpoint of the state in which it occurs instead of as a part of a discrete and independent social system.*

The very fact that all action must take place in space and that substantially all terrestrial space is subject to state authority and control means that interaction in the international system must necessarily take place in national societies territorially viewed. Interactions between individuals in the international system can never take place as a part of a discrete and independent social system which is free to achieve and perfect its own innate order. There is a clash between what may be regarded as the vertical systems of order of states and the horizontal system of order of the international system. The international system is often viewed from the perspective of the state in which it takes place, and a distorted emphasis is accordingly given to that phase of its totality which takes place within the territory of such state. For example, it is the national, rather than the international, impact of an act of nationalization which typically comes to the fore.

8.f. *The law and the legal process of the international system are those of the several states, subject only to the limitations of international law and treaties as they affect the intercourse of states in their public capacity and to the occasional exercise of jurisdiction by international tribunals.*

As set forth more fully in the next principle, the consequence is often to subject the international system to control by inappropriate laws and legal processes, as well as to other types of stresses.

When the view of the international system is enlarged from that of the political acts of states, or the acts of governments of states in their relations with one another, to the totality of interactions transcending state borders, it is realized that the international system finds its law primarily in the laws of the several states. Resolution of conflict in the international system, which is of such a character that the conflict can be stated in terms of the applicability of rules of law, generally takes place in the courts of the several states. Even in the public sphere, a situation of conflict, which diplomacy or international judicial settlement fails to resolve, remains, in its several territorial segments represented by the states in conflict, governed by the policies and laws of such states.

Private international law is part of the municipal law of a state, and it merely indicates the law of a state to be selected, for purposes of decision, in situations possessing a foreign element. Public international law and treaties find their primary impact upon decision making by state officials in situations involving intercourse with other states in their public capacity. The grand design of the law and legal process of the international system, therefore, accords primacy to the laws and legal processes of the several states. It is important to record this fact at this point, although its development will be the subject matter of principle 9 that follows.

8.g. *The proliferation of new states as actors in the international system, who view its order and international law as a product of an imperialist and colonial past, the actions of other established states whose participation in the international system has failed to realize important values, the actions of still other states who use their power as a means for establishing external authority to realize their important values, impair the integration of the international system and the establishment of an order which would provide equal opportunity and security for all actors to realize their important values by participation therein.*

The international system is no constant of a fixed character and the states which are actors are not abstract, interchangeable units. The international system is a composite of all the international action of its actors. States, as actors, possess diversity of culture and bases of power which are fascinating to the traveler and the anthropologist, but baffling to those who strive to discern the road to a stable, viable international order.

In one sense, tension and conflict in the international system are a product of varying rates of cultural growth and varying degrees of cultural maturity of states in the system. There are states which may appropriately be termed latecomers to the world society. They are recently emerged from a colonial status, possess the resultant configurations and social stratification, reflect a strong adherence to particularistic family or tribal values, exhibit a type of nationalism characterized by external hostility, usually have only the most unsatisfactory economic ties with the international system and a distorted and underdeveloped internal economic order, and are governed by untrained decision makers having stronger family or other particularistic loyalties and values than those of their state. Their view of the international system and their actions therein, political and otherwise, are a product of a unique combination of forces not found in more mature and viable national societies. Their view of the international system perhaps represents the peak of fear and suspicion, in comparison with that of other actors, and reflects itself at best in policies of withdrawal and neutralism, and at worst, in acts highly disruptive of any stable international order.

There are other states which have long been actors in the international system but still have failed to become industrially organized and democratically structured societies. They are states which have failed to reach a reasonably satisfactory adjustment of their national economies to the international system. Somehow means must be found, both within such states and in the international system, whereby their linkage with the international system will better satisfy their demand for material welfare and widespread participation in the enjoyment of its benefits. Until such means are found, they are not likely to be governed by the value of promoting the integration and viability of the international system.

There are, finally, states having a highly developed industrial system and degree of cultural maturity, whose participation in the international system is vital to their cultural vitality, economic welfare, and maintenance of their bases of power, but who still fail to accept the preservation and growth of the international system as a fixed and essential factor in their decision making. Such states, possessed of great power, use that power in a considerable measure to establish their authority externally over other actors in the international system in such a manner as will best enable them to realize their own individual values. The democratically organized states of the West now share an ideology in which there is a respect for the independence of other states so long as the bases of their power are not threatened with impairment or destruction by action of these states. There are, however, states whose very ideology envisions an extension of authority over other states by all means, including force, when force is a suitable, economical means. In such states, the Communist party, as a subsystem of each state, dominates, directs, and considerably coordinates on an international basis the respective national systems of action of the several states in the Communist bloc. In no state is there an unconditional acceptance of the proposition that there is a common

interest in establishing an international order which would provide equal opportunity and security for all to realize their important values of economic and cultural growth and similar values
of peaceful intercourse.

Yet a distorted picture would emerge, if the present discussion
were to end at this point. There are countervailing influences of
considerable importance. Proposition 12.c. of Chapter V noted the
emerging value that good citizenship shall be displayed by states
as actors in the international system. To this may be added the
fact that the emerging group of small, neutralist states, as well as
the peoples of all states, exert pressures of considerable effectiveness in the international system based on their common sharing
of the fear of nuclear war among the great powers. They demand
that the acts and policies of the great powers shall not too closely
approach "brinkmanship," or acts of a highly inflammatory or
menacing character. The smaller states, by their weight of numbers and unity of voices on this issue, act as an inhibiting influence
upon the tendency of the great powers to use their power to
"negotiate from strength," engage in "massive retaliation," or boast
of the pre-eminency of their missile power and power of their
armed forces as a means of establishing external authority.

8.h. *The possession, use, or threat of use of force by states in
a manner disruptive to the order of the international system and
threatening the destruction of its principal actors and sources of
energy is an integral part of the international system.*

8.h.1. *The possession of force with a view to its external use
has typically been a phase of the integration of national societies.*

The growth of cultures is characterized by a developing ethic
and an increasing number of social controls designed to inhibit
aggressive responses in the form of killing by members of the
cultures. Yet it has also been the overwhelming social experience
that when man learns to live in groups he also learns to kill in
groups. His attitudes toward members of his own group are not
necessarily those which he adopts toward other groups to which
he does not consider himself to belong. Accordingly, group goals
which can be efficiently attained by the killing of others are
adopted by the clan, the tribe, and the nation. It is simply a
matter of the value of the goal and the appropriateness of the
means. The group against which war is waged is viewed merely

as a hostile part of the physical environment, to be mastered by force for the profit of the warring group.

With war-making becoming a typical form of group relationships, other groups become the source of menace and their attack must always be guarded against. One's own group is not only a source of advantage in war-making; it is also essential for survival against attack. Although participation in the group and action directed toward group advantage may considerably conflict with individual values, the overriding value of the group as a vital means for survival prevails and produces integration and cooperation. As group integration develops, a culture of peaceful cooperation brings forth the ethic of condemnation of killing, first within the group and later as an absolute moral principle. Personality, as a product of culture, then shrinks at killing, regards it with abhorrence, and is enveloped by guilt when it is responsible for death. Yet man as an alienated personality in organizational action cannot only adapt himself to the role of the soldier in organized killing, but he can also even assume the role of torturer of his fellow citizen in a police state.

Organized killing reflects the rationality of the organizational view of life, when the culture may abhor murder. There is an organizational truth as well as a cultural truth. Whatever the values of the culture in which it operates may be, the organization will exist and function in a manner antithetical to those values whenever its members oppose them with sufficient strength. The organization always possesses its own value rationality for appraising and creating action. The state, as the ultimate organization of society, can create within its sphere of action organizations devoted to killing of others or torture of its own members, because it can always find members who will, as alienated personalities, adapt themselves to such roles.

The translation of cultural reality into the cryptic terms of Marxist dialectics by the leaders of Communist states places them at a point still farther removed from reality. Their organizational policy is stated in ritualistic terms, the meaning of which is readily significant only to actors in the organization. Life is never directly perceived and dealt with; it is perceived and dealt with in the symbolic terminology of Marxist ideology.

Thus the paradox emerges of the existence of the absolute moral condemnation of killing and the legal interdiction of killing within national societies, on the one hand, and the persistence of the military organization of the state, on the other hand. No state has emerged which does not devote part of its energy to the creation of an organization of force with a view to its possible external use, or at least use as a symbol of power. Few, if any, states have emerged which have not used, or have been subjected to the use of, force as a means to establish external authority. Without force as an element in the relations of states, it would be difficult for a state to surmount the stresses and tensions incident to the sacrifice of individual and group values which continued participation by its members in its system of action demands. Fear of the external environment makes internal compromises of values possible and acceptance of governmental authority tolerable.

8.h.2. *The use or threat of use of force to establish the external authority of states for the realization of important values is a constant in the relations of states.*

Those who determine the direction of the system of action of an organization will usually prefer to solve problems of its adaptation to its external social environment by bringing the relevant portion of the social base into the sphere of their authority. It is only then that refractory, unpredictable external action becomes manageable, predictable action directed to corporate advantage. Thus, a decision maker will prefer to bring about participation in an organization by the exercise of authority as against inducing participation by reasoned persuasion or through agreement. The corporate manager will prefer a merger to a contract, for the merger brings the seller of precarious supplies or the unwilling buyer of overflowing products irrevocably into the sphere of authority, in which command, instead of persuasion, elicits desired conduct. The supplier of products which are in short supply who is merged with a particular buyer is committed to the supply of that buyer's needs. When competition to sell is keen, it is comforting to have a former difficult customer a part of the seller's enterprise. Similarly, an exclusive dealing or sales contract over a number of years is preferable to the harsh realities of maintaining existence by a volume of separate sales transactions, each separately induced. Ultimately, of course, the organization must face reality in its adaptation to its social base at some stage. In the meantime, reliance on authority and routine will ease the task of the decision maker.

The executive in the state similarly is placed in an environment of decision making in which problems are typically solved by the exercise of authority. It is easier to command than to persuade. It is easier to identify and structure the solution of a problem of foreign relations by bringing it within the sphere of authority. When this cannot be accomplished, the executive in the state may flee from reality, postpone the hard task of finding a viable solution to the problem of external adaptation by the exercise of the leadership function, and instead cast the problem in routine, administrative terms to which a routine, administrative solution may be applied. The fact that the routine solution will someday collapse, as the ignored elements of the problem increase their pressure, is of no consequence. The occupancy of his office, and the possession of authority by his political party in the state, for the time being continues in effect. The values of the members of his state will still continue to be realized by the traditional, standardized patterns of administrative action, even though the prospective consequences of action arising from the explosive values embedded in the social base are ignored.

Those who direct an organization find that when a policy problem can be couched in terms of the value of survival, support for policy is more readily and massively forthcoming. Foreign military aid was provided by the United States to the French in Indo-China to the extent of nearly $3 billion. Perhaps a lesser sum spent in creating different attitudes among the populace toward their government through programs of land and economic reform might have led to a different political outcome. Yet it is to be doubted that members of the United States would have been willing to finance any such program. Only by viewing the problem in defense terms was massive, though unavailing, aid forthcoming.

8.h.3. *The internal legal monopoly of force by states and the formal legal interdiction on the external use of force by states, coupled with the failure of the international legal system to establish compulsory jurisdiction over states, prevent the establishment of a stable legal order providing security under law for the functioning of the international system.*

The circumstance that a state may subject that phase of the international system which is within its territorial jurisdiction to its control through law and that such an act is sanctioned by its internal legal monopoly of force does not necessarily make such an internal exercise of authority appropriate from the standpoint of the functioning of the international system or lawful from the standpoint of international law. The nationalization of the Universal Suez Maritime Canal Company of Egypt on July 26, 1956, brings out in bold relief the implications of the control by the sovereign over the international system within its territory.

The Suez Canal is the world's most vital artery in the commerce of nations, located at a point which may, for the sake of graphic simplicity, be characterized as the axis of three continents. The free flow of commerce through the canal is essential not only to the adjacent or neighboring continents of Europe, Asia, and Africa, but also to North and South America. The United States, France, and the United Kingdom stated that an institution so impressed with an international character was beyond the power of Egypt, under international law, to bring within its national control through the exercise of the power of nationalization.[11] Without at this time entering into the question of the correctness of their position as a matter of international law, subsequent events bore out the stress created by the subjection of the international system, as embodied in the Suez Canal, to national control.

The Suez Canal thereafter became an instrument to be used by the United Arab Republic to achieve its national policies. These policies include the exertion of power pressure upon Israel today. The wheel of time will inevitably bring other states to occupy the place of Israel tomorrow. There have been a steady series of international incidents, not limited to the scene of the canal itself, demonstrating the international tensions created by this situation.

The meaning and value of the Suez Canal is not the fact that it is a channel of water found in the territory of Egypt connecting the Mediterranean and the Red Sea. The meaning and value arise out of the fact that its use by the nations of the world makes it a "great international waterway."[12] The economic well being and military strength of many nations, in Asia as well as in Europe and the New World, is dependent upon the functioning of the canal.

The international character and function of the Suez Canal, in-

[11]Declaration of Aug. 2, 1956, U.S. Dept. of State, *The Suez Canal Problem,* July 26–Sept. 22, 1956, 34 (1956).
[12]Case of the S.S. "Wimbledon," P.C.I.J., ser. A, no. 1, Aug. 17, 1923, 25.

cluding the system of arrangements by which it was established, are recognized in a number of international conventions and decisions.[13]

When Egypt nationalized the organization operating the canal and prematurely terminated its contract with that company, taking over the operation of the canal as a national enterprise, the interests of all states, whether or not of a maritime character, were affected by these acts. Yet none possessed a remedy, save only diplomatic protest and negotiation. No compulsory jurisdiction over the dispute existed in the International Court of Justice, and, therefore, there was no means to test the legality of its act in an international forum. The issue of legality could only become the subject of debate by writers on international law. The use of force by the United Kingdom and France to vindicate their rights as members of the society of nations, and under its law, was formally condemned by the United Nations but substantively accomplished by power pressure, primarily of the United States and the Soviet, whose interests at the time happened to coincide on this issue.

Thus Egypt's internal legal monopoly of force prevailed. The international system failed to determine in an impartial manner by an international tribunal the lawfulness, under international law, of Egypt's acts.

International law developed as a system of law in a period when states were privileged to use force as a sanction against a violation of their rights. Admitting the crude and primitive character of such a system of law, what substitute system of guaranty of rights is now offered them? The General Assembly and the Security Council of the United Nations are primarily political organs. Disputes of a legal character, in general, have an opportunity of reaching the International Court of Justice, or some other international court on the basis of consent of the parties, only when the political or power interests of the states involved are minimal. To the degree

---

[13]*Convention Respecting the Free Navigation of the Suez Maritime Canal,* Constantinople, Oct. 29, 1888, G. Fr. de Martens, *Noveau Recueil Générale de Traités,* ser. 2, vol. 15, 557; *Treaty of Alliance Between the United Kingdom and Egypt,* Aug. 26, 1936, Great Britain, 1937, Treaty ser. 6; *Anglo-Egyptian Agreement Regarding the Suez Canal Base,* Oct. 19, 1954, U.S. Dept. of State, *The Suez Canal Problem;* Case of the S.S. "Wimbledon," P.C.I.J.; see doctrinal note, Case of the Suez Canal Company, Award of Emperor Napoleon of July 6, 1864, A. de La Pradelle and N. Politis, 2, *Recueil des Arbitrages Internationaux, 1856-1872,* 376 (1932).

that international law has developed as a law merely recognizing and permitting the exercise of sovereign *powers*, instead of a law of respected *rights* and *obligations* directed to the support of the international order, international law will fail to perform the necessary task of any legal system of defining and enforcing those norms of conduct required to preserve the structure and functioning of a social system.

8.h.4. *The state will seek to establish for itself the largest possible space of free movement and to maximize and stabilize that space by establishing authoritative, external relationships based on power, including the use or threat of use of force.*

Each state, as well as each organization in the state, is faced with adapting to its external environment. The failure of the international system to provide a stable and secure environment, in which there is an equality of opportunity of states to realize their important values by participation therein, has led many states to adopt a policy of self-sufficiency and maximum feasible isolation from the international system. When, however, a state turns inward in its system of action, it denies itself the opportunity to move more rapidly and in larger measure toward the realization of valued goals which participation in the international system provides.

In directing its action outward toward participation in the international system, the state then becomes subject to the same conditions influencing decision making that other organizations encounter as they adapt themselves to their environment or social base. The organization wishes to secure for itself the maximum advantage from its interactions with others, but it wishes to do so in a situation where it will have the largest possible space of free movement and the greatest possible security. When desired forms of external adaptation cannot be achieved by other means, the decision maker in the state turns to the use of power, including the use or threat of use of force, as a facile and reliable means for achieving these ends.

The term "space of free movement" means "totality of possible events or actions" available to an actor. As stated by Kurt Lewin:

If one approaches the description of a situation from the dynamic point of view (that is, from a point of view which should finally allow prediction), one has to understand the situation as a totality of possible events or actions. . . . One may speak here of the *space of free movement* and its boundaries. By movements, we have to understand not only bodily locomotions but, above all, social and mental "locomotions.". . . The space of free movement of a person or a social group can be represented as a topographical region encircled by other regions that are not accessible. Mainly two factors prohibit the accessibility of regions. One is the *lack of ability,* for instance, lack of skill or intelligence. The other is social *prohibition* or any kind of taboo which stands as a dynamic "barrier" between the person and his goal.[14]

The space of free movement is a salient element in the notion of the sovereignty of the state.

To establish a space of free movement for the realization of its goals *by extraterritorial action,* whether of its own members or members of other states, the state must define some pattern of interaction which will embody a preferred means for the realization of values shared by itself and those with whom it would interact. It may find it possible to arrive at a consensus that would take the form of an agreement. But the making of an agreement always demands the sharing of benefits. A price of some sort or another must be paid for the desired cooperation, and that cooperation is always subject to termination and the risk of breach with the passage of time. The external environment of the state becomes reasonably stable and effectively available for the realization of the values of its members only when it is subject to the exercise of authority. In influencing external action in desired channels, power is the readiest and most certain of means from the standpoint of the decision maker. When the values of actors strongly clash, power and force, instead of persuasion, are the only effective means to establish and maintain authority by one state over another as a means of value realization.

The above principle may be rephrased in broader terms, as follows: *Each state, as a composite of territorial and extraterritorial order, will strive to establish an authoritative direction and control over all the elements of that order, both human and physical, and will use all appropriate means, including power, to the end of realizing its important values.* Whether power or force will be used by one state against another will depend, on the one hand, upon the importance of the values whose realization are threatened by the action of the latter state and, on the other hand, by the

---

[14]K. Lewin, *Resolving Social Conflicts,* 5-6 (1948); see also N. R. F. Maier, *Principles of Human Relations,* 24ff. (1952).

traditional orientation of the state toward the use of force as an instrument of policy. The United States, for example, traditionally relies upon international law in its foreign policy and is not inclined to use force as an instrument for the expansion of its authority abroad. The Soviet, *per contra*, talks peace and wages a highly expansionist foreign policy. Whenever Western action threatens its expansionist aims, it finds no embarrassment or inconsistency in threatening rocket and nuclear war. The *extent* to which any one state will reflect the above principle in its foreign relations will be determined by the above two factors, subject, of course, to its comparative power position.

To the degree that a state becomes more law-minded and less inclined to rely upon force to establish its external authority, it will tend to lose its space of free movement. Other states will then exert their internal monopoly of force to its prejudice. They will move into the international system in a manner which will threaten or impair the state's external foundations of power. Cuba's foreign policy in Latin America, as it affects the position of the United States, and the Soviet's foreign policy, as it affects the free world, illustrate this principle.

It must also be realized, in this connection, that the readiness of a state, implying its people as well as its leaders, to use force to protect its important values, as expressed in state action, will enhance its space of free movement. Yugoslavia under Tito and Poland under Gomulka—even the Poland of today as compared with that of the early Gomulka period—bear witness of the varying abilities of peoples to resist cultural and economic subjection by an expansionist power.

This principle should be read in conjunction with principle 11.b., particularly 11.b.2. and 11.e.2. of Chapter V, and 8.i. of this chapter. These references relate to the nature and limits of authority of universal and regional actors over state action. For example the growing attraction of European states and Great Britain to the European Economic Community is primarily a consequence of the fact that it has provided an environment for rational agreement making in the economic relations of the member states. It is hardly a consequence of an acceptance of the authority of the policy-making organs of the community, as authority is defined here, as a means to achieve shared goals. Agreement, rather than authority, remains the prime coordinating instrument.

8.h.5. *The present-day patterns of the use or threat of use of force as a practice of states is a product of historical growth from which humanity can be freed only by a profound and widespread cultural revulsion.*

The historical development of ethical patterns in the modern organizational, industrialized state, possessing the power to wage nuclear warfare, represents a curious paradox. On the one hand, there has been a steady growth among its members of the ability to empathize. Class divisions, racial hostilities, and group animosities become less and less violent. As group demands demonstrate an ethical basis, recognition of their political validity is given with increasing readiness. No group is considered to be subhuman, as is so often the case in the veneer state. On the other hand, the identification of the individual with his state and the growth of the alienated personality of organizational man (8.h.1. above) seems to make it possible for the citizenry of the modern state, at its most sophisticated point of technological and cultural growth, to tolerate a prospective organized mass killing, maiming, and suffering by the tens of millions of persons and the substantial destruction of much of civilized society.

There is a dark spot in man of the modern state in his acceptance of the inevitability and validity of nuclear warfare, to say nothing of his acceptance of bacterial and chemical warfare. Not to be forgotten is his past resort to such modes of warfare as saturation aerial bombing of great population centers. His mass burning of families and babies was savage in its personal impact and lacked the deceptive practices of Dachau, whereby the unsuspecting victims were led to a death which was revealed to them only at the last moment.

Victors who at Nuremberg condemned with revulsion, as spokesmen of the cultural standards of their respective national societies and of civilization itself, the Nazi extermination of some six million Jews, now apparently accept the responsibility for nuclear warfare which will destroy or grievously wound whole national societies. Inasmuch as the decisions of leadership are bounded in their execution by the perceptions and values of those who are led, it seems that there can be no deliverance from the impasse to which history has led us, except by a profound and widespread cultural revulsion from, and abhorrence of, organized mass killing. Man must cut himself loose from the shelter of his alienated personality and return to the reality from which it shields him. It is not to assert a paper principle of natural law to say that there are some forms of interstate rivalry or that there are some forms of action which so violate our cultural experience and which are so irrational in their cultural context that they must cease to be tolerated and must be excluded from the world of reality.

The modern system of interstate relations and of international law established in and after the Peace of Westphalia of 1648 was one in which war was an instrument of interdynastic struggle. The principle was then recognized in warfare that the warring forces were distinct from the noncombatant civilian populations and that the latter were generally to be protected from mass destruction by force. Their destruction was indeed senseless when interstate conflict was a struggle for dynastic ascendancy and control over territories *and* their populations. This principle of warfare persisted until its foundations were drastically changed by the Napoleonic wars. Thereafter, war continued as a relation of states. It was a factor in the balance of power of the nineteenth century. In the words of St. Simon in 1814: "This is equivalent to engendering war and maintaining it constitutionally; for two groups of equal force are necessarily rivals, and there is no rivalry without war."[15] Blockade, as an instrument of war, expanded in its sphere of control until the principle of the inviolability of the noncombatant sphere as a limitation upon naval warfare was substantially obliterated in World War I. World War II produced not only saturation aerial bombing of civilian populations but also atomic bombs. The customary rule of international law, which treated war as an objective fact, was a product of an earlier time when warfare little touched civilian populations. War today is of a wholly different nature; nuclear warfare presents a content of mutual destruction.

We are at a point in history in which we are gripped by an apparently irreconcilable conflict between organizational rationality of force as a relation of states and the cultural irrationality of such a type of relationship under conditions of nuclear warfare. This is a dilemma from which leadership cannot free us until all peoples assert with a single voice that such a mode of warfare cannot be tolerated. Some profound shock is apparently necessary

---

[15]Quoted in Niemeyer, *Law Without Force,* 71.

to free us from the rejection of reality into which we have succumbed. Until revulsion and abhorrence of nuclear weapons can
take the place of the resigned acceptance of death that is the base
for nuclear warfare leadership, then the peoples of those states
which possess nuclear weapons, those which aspire to their possession, and those which are committed to a helpless neutralism
can only await the doom of blast, fallout, starvation, and want.

8.h.6. *Any legal prohibition of the use of force has not removed
the use of threat of use of force.*

The recognition of the use of force by states as an objective fact
in the international law of the nineteenth century, when resort to
war was not destructive of state populations, has now been superseded by the formal interdiction of resort to force under article
2 of the United Nations Charter, subject to the right of the exercise
of self-defense under article 51. The formal legal condemnation of
force does not, however, reflect the underlying political realities
of the use of force in the relations of states. The demonstration
of these realities is the function of other parts of proposition 8.h.

8.h.7. *The so-called nuclear stalemate is no assurance that
decisions to engage in nuclear war will not be made by the
possessor of nuclear weapons, because the use of such means of
force by states is a risk which cannot be precisely calculated and
may be a product of accident or of decision making in the domain
of organizational rationality.*

The actions of states in the use of force reflect no greater wisdom
than that possessed by the occupants of the relevant authoritative
offices. The blunders incident to the U-2 air espionage incident
prior to the break-up of the so-called summit meeting of May,
1960, illustrate that the occupants of the supreme offices of the
great powers are human and subject to human emotions and
frailties of judgment. The blame for such blunders should be
placed less on those who committed them than on the existence
of a system of action devoted to the use of force and all its accompanying paraphernalia. Decision making will always produce
its quota of accidents and actions exhibiting organizational rationality, if not cultural rationality. The armaments race, the episodes
of Greece, Korea, Indo-China, Suez, and Tibet, and the warnings
of resort to force made by a Dulles, a Stalin, a Khrushchev, and

other leaders in the postwar years are a witness to this fact. Such present-day issues as the status of Berlin and Formosa cannot be viewed apart from the use or threat of use of force, including nuclear weapons. The status of Tibet and the location of certain portions of the Indian northern frontier are products of the use of force. Whether or not the possible use of nuclear and other weapons be made the subject of veiled or outright threats by the representatives of states, their possession is not to be presumed to embody solely symbolic purposes and to have nothing to do with policy and its implementation.

8.i. *States, as such, are characteristically unsuitable for organization; that is, their action is primarily adaptable to coordination through consensus and agreement instead of authority. The establishment of authority by a universal or regional actor over states as members requires, among things, that (1) its goals embody commonly shared values of its members, (2) its members reflect a substantial degree of homogeneity in their respective cultures, and (3) force is available to and used by such universal or regional actor as a sanction for law.*

Participation by states in decision making in the United Nations, as the paramount universal actor in the international system, does not characteristically take place in a full acceptance of such organization of states as a paramount system of action for realizing shared values, but instead as a subordinate instrumentality for realizing each state's own values.

Decision making in any organizational structure must take place under conditions of value rationality. Action in an organization will be committed to the attainment of particular goals as a consequence of the values of the members of the organization. An organization must exhibit in its action an appropriateness of means to ends viewed from the standpoint of the degree to which it enables the realization of the values of its members. This has been termed the value rationality of action.

The motivation of each state as a participant in the decision-making process of the United Nations, however, is to foster its own advantage and the achievement of its own policies *through* the United Nations. For example, regard for the rationality of words as indicating commonly accepted referents and regard for the meaning of sentences and statements constructed with these words imposes a minimum degree of rationality of argument and decision making from the international standpoint in the United Nations environment, as opposed to particular national standpoints. Regard for the rationality of words, as compared with the reality of which they are symbols, however, often reaches an Alice-in-Wonderland irrationality on the part of Soviet representatives. Their dedication to the values of their state is so complete that regard for the purity of communication becomes slight indeed. Yet their position is only the extreme end of a series of positions of the various member states, each of which is motivated by national purposes in an international setting.

Accordingly, the principle may be laid down that *international organization can be established among states, with an acceptance of its authority by its members, only when the elements to be organized become manageable, that is, only when the states in question so value the goals of the organization that they will accept leadership, administration, and control to attain those goals.* When the organization performs essentially a valued staff function, such as the provision of a universal postal system or the regulation of telecommunications or safety on the high seas, its authority based on its expertise will be accepted. When it enters into such a political, value-charged question as that of the liberation of the states of Eastern Europe from Soviet domination, it will not.

Authority in a social system cannot become fully effective and organization cannot emerge until command possesses sanction. Law does not fully unfold in a society until deviant performance of its ideal and valued norms of behavior is subject to control through force. The King's peace in England was not established until the highways were made safe from robbers, and the King's law, as laid down in Parliament and the courts, was law respected by virtue of the king's power as well as right reason. The place of power or force as a sanction to support law was set forth in proposition 9.g. of Chapter V.

9. *The changing conditions in world society require a further maturing of the methodologies of private and public international law and the operation of the legal process in the international system.*

As presently constituted, law and the legal process in the international system are primarily directed to preserving the primacy of the state as an actor in the system and the primacy of the state's law and legal process within its territorial jurisdiction, together with the resulting decentralized structure of the international system.

9.a. *The control of the international system through law is primarily attained in the laws and legal processes of the several states.*

9.a.1. *Action in the international system, except to the extent that it is accorded immunity from local law under the principles of international law, takes place subject to municipal or state law.*

Rules of public and private international law are directly applied by state officials and judges in the performance of their roles. International situations of interstate conflict are capable of resolution by international courts only to the degree that states may consent to such resolution. International situations of interpersonal conflict are primarily resolved in national courts.

The substantive content of private and public international law, the influences determining such content, and the adequacy of their principles and methodologies to control action in the international system will be the subject matter of later principles and propositions. For the present, it is emphasized that it is not international law but municipal or state law which controls the greater part of action in the international system, and that it is not the international legal process but the national legal process which resolves the major part of conflict arising in the operation of the international system. Although action may possess an international character in that it transcends state boundaries, it is nevertheless segmentalized under the territorial sovereignty and authority of the several states in which it takes place. In each, it is subject to local law, with private international law a part thereof. In each, it is the local court which is the only means for resolving interpersonal conflict, unless the parties—whether individuals or individual and state—agree to arbitrate their dispute. Access to an international court is denied individuals unless, in general, they have exhausted their local remedies, with the result of a denial of justice. For this purpose, a most severe and restricted meaning of the term justice is adopted. Even then, if their claim is to be decided judicially, it must be espoused as an international claim by the state of which they are nationals, and the states concerned with the dispute must consent to its settlement or adjudication by an international court.

At the public level, to the degree that a state, in the exercise of its territorial sovereignty, has effective power to resolve an international dispute in a manner desired by it and its freedom so to do is valued, it will resist international adjudication of that dispute. Accordingly, Iran will resist international adjudication of the international dispute arising out of its nationalization of oil properties,[16] Egypt will resist international adjudication of the international dispute arising out of its nationalization of the corporation controlling the operation of the Suez Canal, and the United States will resist international adjudication of the international dispute arising out of its expropriation of the properties involved in the *Interhandel* case,[17] because each, in its internal monopoly of force implicit in the concept of territorial sovereignty, has the effective power to resolve that dispute according to its domestic law and in a manner responsive to its national values. Although the exercise of the state's domestic jurisdiction may in at least two of these cases have most considerable international repercussions and although in all three cases the dispute was clearly a matter for international adjudication, in each the local jurisdiction and the local law prevailed because the local sovereign had effective power to control the situation in a desired manner. True, the Anglo-Iranian oil dispute and the Suez Canal dispute received an eventual resolution by negotiation at the *private* level, in which state pressures were not without influence. True, international law was a strong factor in determining the final outcome of the disputes. The fact remains, however, that each of the disputes escaped decision by the international legal process.

Ad hoc international arbitration has also exhibited the same decline that international adjudication has shown. There have been only a few such international arbitrations in the postwar years. An examination of the volumes 1946-56 inclusive of the *Annual Digest and Reports of International Law Cases* and their successor publication of *International Law Reports* reveals only nine *ad hoc*

[16]Anglo-Iranian Oil Co. Case (Jurisdiction), Judgment of July 22, 1952, I.C.J. Reports 1952, 93.
[17]Interhandel Case, Judgment of March 21, 1959, I.C.J. Reports 1959, 6.

arbitrations between states, excluding the decisions of the conciliation commissions sitting under peace treaties with the Axis powers and three arbitrations between private corporations and Middle East sheikdoms. The contents of these volumes startlingly demonstrate the validity of the proposition that most judicial decisions of international law questions are made by state courts. A perusal of the pages of the section on judicial decisions of each issue of the *American Journal of International Law* would further substantiate this proposition.

9.a.2. *Private international law is a branch of municipal law primarily applied by state courts. Whatever form its methodology may assume under its several doctrinal formulations, it ultimately places an international situation of interpersonal conflict within the framework of some one national body of law for the purpose of decision making.*

This proposition is subsidiary proof of proposition 9.a. The nature of private international law and its adequacy as a means for the resolution of international situations of interpersonal conflict will be the subject matter of propositions 9.b. and 9.c. The demonstration of the second sentence of the above proposition will be made there.

The borderline between public and private international law is by no means a precise one. Professor's Wortley's study, "The Interaction of Public and Private International Law Today,"[18] is well named. International courts as well as state courts have occasion to consider questions of private international law. The dichotomy which the two fields of law present and the fact that private international law is a part of municipal or state law was most lucidly set forth in an often-quoted statement of the Permanent Court of International Justice:

Any contract which is not a contract between States in their capacity as subjects of international law is based on the municipal law of some country. The question as to which this law is forms the subject of that branch of law which is at the present day usually described as private international law or the doctrine of conflict of laws. The rules thereof may be common to several States and may even be established by international conventions or customs, and in the latter case may possess the

---

[18]B. A. Wortley, "The Interaction of Public and Private International Law Today," Académie de Droit International, 85 *Recueil des Cours* 245 (1954, pt. 1).

character of true international law governing the relations between States. But apart from this, it has to be considered that these rules form part of municipal law.[19]

9.a.3. *The orientation of a state official toward a rule of international law as a factor in his decision making will be to take action at the outer limits of rationality in the application of the rule when it conflicts with national policy and values.*

It is, of course, not contended that international law does not influence decision making by state officials. Officials of a state strongly committed to the preservation of the state-structured international system will always be mindful of legal considerations in their decision making.[20] Where strong policy considerations do not conflict, decisions will respect rules of international law. There are a number of aspects of the point of view of an official toward a rule of international law, compared with the view of a judicial organ, which must be borne in mind. Decision making of the judicial organ is centered upon the rule itself. The various criteria and forces affecting the judicial process come to bear in a methodology in which faithfulness to the law and the legal method is foremost. For the official, however, the rule of law is simply one element among others affecting his decision making. It is not the central element. It is placed at the periphery of the situation at hand. It marks the boundary of his action beyond which he may not trespass. At that point, moreover, the official does not determine the applicability of the rule of law with the nicety and accuracy of the court. Nor does he search for, examine, and weigh the evidence of law and consider the appropriateness of competing rules of law for the resolution of conflict and the provision of order in the same manner as in the court. When the rule conflicts with national policy or strongly held national values, the official will search for and adopt that legal justification for action which carries some plausibility and rationality, even though the likelihood of its adoption by an international court may be fairly conjectural. There is, however, a limit which his culture and his responsibility in the discharge of his official function will place upon his action. In the maturely developed states in the Western free world there

---

[19]Cases of Serbian and Brazilian Loans, P.C.I.J., ser. A, no. 20/21, 41 (1929).
[20]Compare P. E. Corbett, *Law in Diplomacy* (1959).

is basically a respect for law. When their application is fairly clear, rules of international law can to a considerable extent become the basis of prediction of official action.

The decisions of the official of a state which is a captive of the authoritarian and expansionist philosophy of the Communist party, however, will frequently reach and even pass the outer limits of rationality in respect for rules of international law. When party policy demands certain state action, the function of the official and the international law jurist is to find some verbal or formal legal justification for that action, however irrational may be the normal or established referents for the words employed or the meaning ordinarily attributed to the sentences constructed from them.

9.b. *The fundamental premise of private international law, from which its varying methodologies are derived, provides an inadequate basis for the operation of the legal process in international situations of interpersonal conflict.*

The title of Luigi Pirandello's play, *Six Characters in Search of an Author,* is suggestive of the history of private international law, except that the latter includes a considerably larger *dramatis personae* in the jurists who have searched for a basis for order in competing systems of municipal law. Here Justice Holmes's "inarticulate major premise" becomes highly articulate with a clamor of voices. Justice Cardozo said of private international law that: "I find logic to have been more remorseless here, more blind to final causes, than it has been in other fields. Very likely it has been too remorseless."[21] It is suggested that his difficulty with private international law is not its logic, as such, but its major premise and the results produced by a remorseless exercise of logic in the application of the premise. The history of private international law is a history of jurists in search of a perception or an image of order and law in the international system which would provide justice in the decision of disputes arising in international situations of a private character, that is, disputes in which the parties are not solely states. It is a search of jurists for a final hypothesis or *grundnorm* for a legal process to govern decision making in private conflict in international situations. The concern of the discipline of private international law is the just solution

---

[21]B. N. Cardozo, *Paradoxes of Legal Science,* 68 (1928).

of "a suit that contains a foreign element,"[22] a dispute "extending over several legal units,"[23] or "a case having contacts with more than one territory."[24] The search for a methodology which will provide justice in the decision of disputes arising in international situations is one, in the words of Professor Yntema, arising from a perception of the international legal order as:

decentralized among a plurality of sovereign or autonomous authorities, asserting jurisdiction each within a defined territory over activities that concern their respective subjects. As the pretensions of the corresponding local laws to control international or interstate commerce thus inevitably overlap, the legal order also involves integration of the diversity of laws of which it is composed. The mode in which this adjustment is or should be affected is the concern of conflicts law . . . the basic assumption of conflicts law [is] that the legal order implies unity in diversity, or in other words the appropriate recognition of special local interests and practices as expressed in local legislation, integrated in terms of a basic community of common standards in the choice of the applicable law, offers a more realistic basis for the necessary adaptation of law to the changing needs of the modern world. Historically, this conception has been most perfectly realized under federalism . . . on the background of a common legal culture. In contrast, basic differences in legal ideas and the prejudice inspired by nationalistic self-interest too frequently engender major difficulties in securing just and uniform solutions of conflicts of laws among independent national states. The absence of an effective international community of law necessarily impedes the development of a conflicts law in international situations.[25]

The discipline is based on the fundamental postulate that when a suit involves an international situation of interpersonal conflict, the search for a basis for decision is a search for the appropriate legal system or body of law, and not the appropriate rule for decision. It is a search which assumes that the appropriate *rule* for decision will be found when the appropriate legal *system* is determined. The methodology of private international law views a dispute, the facts of which arise in two or more states, as one which can be decided by a methodology of classification which stops with the law of a particular state.

Any judicial decision involves thinking on the basis of classifica-

---

[22]G. C. Cheshire, *Private International Law,* 3 (5th ed., 1957).

[23]C. M. Schmitthoff, *A Textbook of the English Conflict of Laws,* 7 (3rd ed., 1954).

[24]A. Nussbaum, *Principles of Private International Law,* 3 (1943).

[25]H. E. Yntema, "The Historic Bases of Private International Law," 2 *Am. J. Comp. Law* 297-299 (1953).

tion. The dispute must be classified in its appropriate category of law, for example contracts or torts, and to its appropriate rule of law and remedy. The decision is always stated in the classic model of reasoning by classification, that is, the syllogism. The appropriateness of the judicial decision in any one dispute is, among other things, a function of the degree to which the rule of law selected for application to the case reflects mechanical and value rationality in the light of the goals and values of the actors involved in the situation. Conflicts law assumes that such rationality will be reached when the facts of a dispute are related to some one national system of law. Conflicts law demands that the facts of a dispute be analyzed with a view to determining which, of a number of so-called competing or conflicting systems of laws, is the appropriate system for decision making.

The conflict of conflicts law, namely, a conflict between bodies of law instead of competing rules of law, is "inevitable" only in the sense that it is a logical consequence of the assumptions of the discipline. Whether those assumptions are rationally inevitable as deductions from the relevant empirical data, whether those assumptions exhaust all the assumptions which can rationally be drawn from such data, whether the fundamental hypothesis for decision making in international situations involving interpersonal conflict derived from those assumptions is the best method of social control in the circumstances, are issues all open to question. The truth of yesterday is often not the truth of today. It is but one of a successive number of steps in the growth of knowledge.

The conflict of conflicts law is a self-created conflict in the sense that any methodology of decision making demands choosing among alternatives, and the resolution of the conflict which their very existence engenders. To state a problem of decision making upon the basis that laws are in conflict and a choice must be made among them is perhaps the most crude and rudimentary form of statement of the nature of the legal process or legal reasoning which can be made. To state the problem of the judge in a system of municipal or national law upon the basis that rules of law are in conflict and inevitably a choice must be made is merely to restate the existence of his initial problem in different terms and to give no indication of the methodology for its solution.

The question the above discussion raises is whether the search for a basis of decision of an international situation of interpersonal conflict is validly viewed as a search for the appropriate local law or simply for the appropriate rule of law, for the way we look at a problem largely determines how we solve it. The physicist or the mathematician, for example, finds that his search for a solution of a problem is a search for a standpoint from which, after investigation, order and a hypothesis will emerge from disorder.

There is perhaps no field of law in which varying perceptions of a legal order have appeared in greater number than in private international law. The history of the discipline is a fascinating succession of images and hypotheses of the nature of law and the legal process as applicable to international situations of interpersonal conflict.

For Professor Yntema,[26] "the cardinal principle of conflicts law" is "the application of foreign law to foreign cases." The use of the symbol "foreign case" suggests a referent of a dispute which falls wholly within a foreign sphere, that is, the sphere of something other than the national sphere in which the speaker finds himself. In using such a term, the speaker may be said to identify himself as being within a local or closed environment looking outward at a suit which is alien or foreign. Of course, such a simplification of the rich, sophisticated, pragmatic outlook of Yntema is absurd. The term was lifted out of context to indicate how symbols subtly indicate the nature of an image embodied in the referent, as well as influence the course of reasoning in the mind of the recipient of the communication.

Cheshire's[27] term "suit with a foreign element" is a symbol which more closely indicates the complex nature of the referent which is considered significant for purposes of discourse and analysis. The dispute is not wholly foreign; it contains a "foreign element"; it is a composite of domestic elements on the one hand, and foreign elements on the other.

Nussbaum's term, "that part of private law which deals with foreign relations,"[28] was advisedly chosen by him as a symbol for a vague and shifting referent for the reason that "it embodies the actual indefiniteness in past and continuous literature" and "offers, therefore, a shelter to an immense variety of existing and contradictory opinions."

---

[26]*Ibid.*, 301.
[27]Cheshire, *Private International Law*, 3.
[28]Nussbaum, *Principles of Private International Law*, 3.

Schmitthoff's term, "disputes extending over several legal units,"[29] seems to be the most precise, comprehensive, and accurate indication of the referent so far reached in this discussion, yet the referent is still implicitly stated on the basis of the severality of the *laws* of different territorial jurisdictions which come into play when one encounters what is called an "international situation of interpersonal conflict"; whereas the term used here is not so limited and employs symbols, such as "international situation" and "interpersonal conflict," which point to the behavioristic approach characteristic of this study.

The one constant involved in the use of all the quoted terms is that private international law, under its prevailing philosophy, is concerned with the methodology of decision making when the administration of justice requires a choice to be made between two or more systems of law in resolving an international situation of interpersonal conflict. The question raised at the outset is whether the "administration of justice" in the international system must be confined to obeying the requirement of making such a choice or whether "justice" might not be found in obeying a different requirement. The assumption of private international law is that, once the appropriate system of law is found, it will yield the appropriate and just rule of law for the decision of international situations of interpersonal conflict. This assumption is denied.

In asserting that the fundamental hypothesis of private international law points to a basically inadequate methodology of dispute solving, it is not to be understood as denigrating the achievements of private international law. When a private dispute in the international sphere arises, the applicability of the various national cultures involved, as they bear on the expectations and values of the parties involved, is an essential factor in the decision-making process. The strength of private international law is found in the fact that it became oriented to this fundamental fact when it adopted the notion of laws in conflict as its central concept. Its weakness lies in the fact that it is too much the captive of its central concept. The world which is its function to control is now inadequately reflected in its model or image of laws in conflict. While it is conceded that private international law represents an accumulated body of knowledge which should not be jettisoned,

---

[29] Schmitthoff, *English Conflict of Laws,* 7.

it is suggested that there are international situations of interpersonal conflict which its methodology prevents handling with that maturity and wisdom which the legal process yields when the judge can examine and evaluate directly the competing rules of law, instead of systems of law, striving for recognition as the law of the case.

It is thought that this critique of private international law can best be developed if the history of its development, which brought it to its present structure, is explored.

The *jus gentium* of the Roman world reveals that it is possible to apply the legal process to the solution of controversy, arising in a context of different cultures and their legal systems, by reasoning on the basis of the appropriateness of rules of law, instead of systems of law. The Roman imperial government left largely untouched the customs and institutions of the conquered peoples and denied the foreigner protection under the classic *jus civile,* which existed solely for the Roman *quiris,* a member of the Roman *gens.* The foreigner eventually found his protection under the *jus gentium,* a body of rules of law created on a case-by-case basis through the decisions of the *praetor peregrinus,* whose office was established in 242 B.C. It was the function of the *praetor peregrinus* to advise rules for the decision of disputes involving foreigners. In doing so, the *praetor peregrinus* looked directly at the facts and the merits of the case before the *judex.* Such a case was as foreign to the *jus civile* as today a foreign case may be foreign to the forum court. He found it possible to decide the case on the basis of the appropriateness of a rule of law for human behavior. This rule was drawn from the facts of the situation and the requirements for the appropriate control of the situation, not from some sealed envelope bearing the label of foreign law.

The adoption of such a methodology of decision making for cases foreign to the *jus civile* did not take place simply because such disputes occurred under the imperial authority of Rome. The conferral of a common Roman citizenship throughout the empire in 212 A.D. brought into the Roman state those who were already within the province of the *jus gentium.* The Roman empire "was not congenial to the development of a conflicts law"[30] for the reason that its decision makers never adopted the initial hypothesis

---

[30]Yntema, "Bases of Private International Law," 301.

that cases arising outside the Roman *urbs* and *jus civile,* thereby possessing a foreign element, were to be decided by the application of some one of a number of legal systems deemed to be in conflict. The strength of the *jus gentium* arose from the circumstance that its development was fact-oriented and rule-oriented. Facts of human conduct were the basis for legal reasoning and judicial decision.

There was nothing inevitable about such a turn in legal history. The Roman legal process could have embarked upon the alternative road of preserving the autonomy of the *jus civile* and the considerable *de facto* autonomy of the systems of law of the provinces, subject to the commands of their governors and the *lex generalis* of the empire. A quasi-federal system might have then ensued. The *praetor peregrinus* could have refrained from piercing the corporate veil of the law of the province, as does modern conflicts law refrain from piercing the law of the foreign state before it selects such law. Such an initial point of view would then have made necessary for him a conflicts law methodology for handling disputes containing a foreign element. His failure to adopt a conflicts law methodology was not because there was *in existence* for the solution of disputes a common system of law throughout the empire for the common citizenry. This was the product centuries later of an initial hypothesis for regulating the society of the Roman world which looked to the particular *rule* of law instead of the general *system* of law as a means of establishing a unified system of justice in a world of diverse societies and cultures.[31]

The nomadic Germanic tribes, who had conquered Europe and overthrown the Roman empire, developed only a personal or tribal law. Their law was a product of a structuring of society on a basis of authority which had no relation to the spatial or territorial aspects of human behavior. The localization of law to territory was a product of the later feudal and state systems. The Frank, Burgundian, and the Goth, for example, each had his own personal or tribal law. Hence the remark of Bishop Agobardus: "It often happens that five men each under a different law, may be found walking or sitting together."

North of the Alps, the fixed, local law of the *feodum* became the law of a society organized on the basis of the holding of land and

---

[31] The foregoing should not be understood to imply that conflicts law was completely a stranger to the *corpus juris.* J. H. Beale, 3, *A Treatise on the Conflict of Laws,* 1882-85 (1935).

the supremacy of the lord over his vassals and over all matters occurring within his fief. South of the Alps, the powerful, prosperous,
independent, Italian city-states and their respective surrounding territories emerged as the structure of society. Law there became
embodied in a diversity of municipal laws. Although the city-states
considered Justinian's Code to be the common basis of law, each had
its own body of ordinances, or *statuta*, later generally known as its
statutes.[32]

When law became identified with territory, that is, the spatial
aspects of action instead of the totality of action in a situation,
including its spatial aspects, the solution of interpersonal conflict
on the basis of law determined by the place of action instead of the
nature of action became, as it logically would, the hypothesis for
conflict-solving legal procedures in the intercity arena. The post-
glossators or commentators on Roman law of the thirteenth century
adopted the hypothesis that all cases involved statutes, that all
statutes were real, personal, or of a mixed character, and that certain rules of construction could be adopted for their application
to a case containing facts occurring in the territories of two or more
city-states. These were that real statutes involved property or
immovables within the jurisdiction, that personal statutes involved
persons, that mixed statutes involved acts, such as the making
of a contract, performed in the territory of the enacting sovereign,
and that when the character of the statute in a case was determined,
the basis for its decision was reached.

The statutist approach reached its full elaboration in the French
jurists of the sixteenth century, with the thesis that every legal
relation could be classified under the statutist system. The basis of
classification was so abstract and vague, however, that predictability
of results was unattainable. Professor Beale quotes a plaintive
remark made in 1729 by a conscientious and revealingly frank
French jurist named Froland, which is not without contemporary
overtones:

I fully agree that the statute real is concerned with a thing, the statute
personal has to do with the person, and the statute mixed has to do with
both thing and person. . . . But with all these distinctions the difficulties
which I meet hundreds and hundreds of times do not seem yet removed;
and my mind, hesitating because it is not sufficiently informed, often

---

[32]See the brief summary of the emergence of the feudal system in Carlston,
Law and Structures, 45-46.

does not know what conclusion to reach. In my opinion it is not enough to know that the statute real has to do with a thing, that the statute personal has to do with the person, and that statute mixed has to do with both thing and person. There is another difficulty much more important to solve; that is to know when the statute does concern the thing or the person or both; and that, in my opinion, is the question most embarrassing and most difficult to explain; and it does not appear to me that the old writers who were contented with general definitions have given us very certain rules in this particular.[33]

In Italy, it was the decentralizing of the authority of Rome into the hands of the city-states, each with its own territory, which led to the identification of law with territory, which was the basis of the statutist theory. In France, it was the settling of the Burgundians in the territory which became known as Burgundy, the settling of the Normans in the territory which became known as Normandy, and, in general, the territorializing of the tribes and the emergence of the feudal system based on the holding of land, which led to the territorialization of the law. Whereas in Italy the conflict of the statutes of the cities gave rise to the statutist methodology, in France it was the conflict of the customs (or *coutumes,* the laws of the provinces) which led to the adoption of the statutist theory. A new flexibility was given to it by Dumoulin in advancing the doctrine of intent of the parties as an element controlling the determination of the proper law of a transaction. This was a development of enormous importance in providing security to commerce, which thereby became considerably freed from the subjection to a variety of local laws which was implicit in the rigorous application of statutist theory. Its interpretation, as embodied in the adage *les coutumes sont réelles,* strongly leaned toward an emphasis upon the statutes real or upon a territorial, instead of a personal, law.

In England, the common law courts decided only local English causes of action to which the common law was applied. The jurisdiction of the various courts of the land over foreign cases, that is, cases of foreigners and cases of English traders containing foreign elements, was indeed an intricately detailed matter. It may be crudely summarized by saying that the choice of law problems was long postponed by the decision of such cases under the law merchant.[34]

---

[33]Froland, *Memoires concernans la Nature et la Qualité des Status,* quoted in Beale, 3, *Conflict of Laws,* 1905-06.

[34]A. N. Sack, "Conflicts of Laws in the History of the English Law," *Law:*

The formulation of the foundations of modern private and public international law by the jurists of the Netherlands in the seventeenth century was part of a great historical design. Huber and Grotius are to be seen in a continuum of political theory and the history which created it, ranging from Marsilius of Padua to Jean Bodin of France. All such thinkers may be looked upon as creators of the great and daring hypotheses which become the points of crystallization of new political and legal orders. They offer an opening view of a new order, together with its explanation and justification. The culture is ready to flow, or indeed, is already flowing into the pattern they reveal. Then, as the centuries flow on and further cultural change demands the perception of a new order, other creators of hypotheses of social and political order emerge and proffer their images of such an order, some of which become the point of crystallization of cultural change.

The strength of organization has been found to lie in the flexibility of group action when it is directed by authority. This study examined the external relations of states as organizations and found that interaction between them is ordered in part by agreement as a means of value realization for two or more actors, by a partial acceptance of authority of universal or regional actors, by law, and by power or force.

Turn now to the organizational problem which the city-states of Italy faced in the thirteenth and early fourteenth century. They found that the claims of authority of the church no longer expressed a means for the realization of their values in the temporal sphere. Conflict between the governments of those territories and the church arose. At the close of the thirteenth century, the attempt of the papacy to maintain for its benefit a balance-of-power system among the city-states of Italy meant continual conflict and an order in which the third estate of trade and the professions could not effectively realize their values.

In the broader canvas of Europe, the papal claim to supremacy in temporal affairs created conflict as it affected the aspirations of the Capetians to establish authority in France and the Hapsburgs to establish authority in Germany. For Philip IV of France, the claims of Boniface VIII to superiority of authority meant an

---

A Century of Progress 1835-1935, 342 (1937); T. F. T. Plucknett, *A Concise History of the Common Law*, 222-233 (1929); Cheshire, *Private International Law*, 39-44.

inability to establish final authority within his realm. For Rudolf of Hapsburg, papal supremacy meant that his establishment of the authority of the house of Hapsburg and the remaking of the German monarchy was never recognized in an imperial coronation at Rome as head of the Holy Roman empire. For Ludwig of Bavaria, papal supremacy meant intervention by John XXII in Ludwig's struggle with Frederick for control of the empire and papal nonrecognition of his assumption of the crown of the empire.

In this setting, Marsilius of Padua lived, acted, observed, and wrote. Marsilius first lived in the milieu of the Italian city-states; he was born in Padua, where he spent his youth and early years of manhood. Paris became his home in 1311, near the close of the reign of Philip IV in 1314. The court of Ludwig of Bavaria became his refuge in 1326. Thereafter, he was directly involved with Ludwig's struggle with John XXII, including Ludwig's expedition to Italy in 1327, entry in Rome in 1328, deposing of John XXII as pope, and the naming of a new pope. His doctrine of papal subordination to the state was made manifest in the acts of Ludwig.

Marsilius saw the problems of the day as centered in the goal of establishing an order of peace and the sole exercise of power by the state within its territory. In his world of Western Europe, the papacy was a temporal as well as a spiritual power. Its manipulations of power in the sphere of politics, pursuant to its claim of superior authority over temporal matters within the state, were seen by Marsilius to destroy the order of peace in the state in which man could attain his highest self or being. Peace, as a matter of relations *between* states, was not his concern, except as its loss was a consequence of papal claims to a supremacy of authority.

Marsilius' conclusions were expressed in his *Defensor Pacis*, published in 1324. The state, in his view, was to be defined in the possession of supreme coercive power. Its end was the resolution of conflict in order that its subjects could live a sufficient or good life. The sole source of its legitimate exercise of power was the will or the consent of the people. The establishment of an order of peace demanded that the government must possess supreme coercive power. The concept of the unity of the state demanded that no part of the state, except the government, could have supreme coercive power. The church, therefore, should be a part of the state and should not possess supremacy, even within the spiritual sphere. These were the principal tenets of his thought. To summarize his position in one statement, he stood for the sovereign supremacy of the pagan state in its territory, in which the good was determined by the popular will.

The struggle of Philip IV with Boniface VIII and Ludwig of Bavaria with John XXII vastly weakened the papal claims to exercise of temporal power and set in motion forces which eventually established the sovereign supremacy of the modern state. The struggle between the crown, together with the nobility, and the third estate in France of the latter sixteenth century, the resurgence of religious troubles, and the exacerbation of difficulties of royal taxation and debts, led Jean Bodin, in *Les Six Livres de la Republique* (1576), to hypothesize sovereignty in terms of absolute and perpetual power or the ability to exercise the highest power over the subjects of the state, unrestrained by any other power, including positive law. There was the qualification, however, that the prince or apparent sovereign must respect divine law, the law of nature and law common to all nations, or the *jus gentium*.[35]

The process of the territorialization of law, discussed above, cannot be considered apart from the above historical forces. The conflict between the papacy and the city-states for supremacy or even coordinate power in the same territory led to Marsilius' hypothesis of the supremacy and unity of the state to the end of establishing the state as the sole territorial power. The conflicts between groups for power in France led to the hypothesis of Bodin of sovereignty within the territory of the state as a supreme, absolute power. The conflict of the provinces of the Netherlands to free themselves from claims of sovereign authority by Catholic

---

[35] A. Gewirth, *Marsilius of Padua: The Defender of Peace* (1957) is the only adequate study of Marsilius in English. It is in two volumes, the second of which contains an English translation of the *Defensor Pacis*. A brief summary of the political philosophy of Jean Bodin will be found in B. Reynolds, *Proponents of Limited Monarchy in Sixteenth Century France: Francis Hotman and Jean Bodin* (1931). An English abridgment and translation of Bodin's classic work is *Six Books of the Commonwealth*, abr. and trans. by M. J. Tooley (Oxford, n.d.). See A. Gardot, "Jean Bodin: Sa Place parmi les Fondateurs de Droit International," Académie de Droit International, 50 *Recueil des Cours* 545 (1934, pt. 4).

Spain and to achieve external security under law for their bur-geoning world trade led to Huber's hypothesis of the territoriality of laws and to Grotius' hypothesis that the law of nations could be proved a posteriori by the actions of states instead of a priori by deductions from a pre-established system of natural law, thereby making way for a positivist approach to public international law.

Marsilius' structure of theory ignored the problem of peace be-tween states and concerned itself only with peace as an order of the state. Its normative standard was the will of the people. Grotius laid the foundation for a law between states in their public capac-ity which was eventually to be a positivist law, with no normative standard other than state practice itself. Huber reaffirmed the territorial supremacy of the sovereign and placed the basis for interstate enforcement of rights in private law in the sphere of comity. (Huber's position in the history of private international law is, however, to be understood in the light of the present gen-eral discussion.)

Thus the structure of public and private international law, which was to govern the modern world of decentralized power in many states, emerged without any normative standard to subject it to evaluation, other than state action itself. The proviso of Jean Bodin that the prince was subject to divine law and the law of nature was obliterated with the nineteenth-century demolition of the authority of natural law, led by Bentham, Savigny, Austin, and others.

Political and legal theory thus laid the foundations for the in-ternal supremacy of state power, but created only the most minimal bases for an international legal order. Not until the Statute of the Permanent Court of International Justice incorporated the standard of general principles of law recognized by civilized na-tions as a basis for judicial decision did it become possible for an international court to evaluate interstate conduct by an inde-pendent, normative standard of law. This standard was not that of a system of natural law created a priori, but a system of basic principles of law created by common social experience in civilized nations. This source of law will be discussed in proposition 9.e.4.

Although the struggle by the Netherlands to free itself from claims by Catholic Spain to sovereign authority and to end its recurring wars with Spain did not end until the Peace of Westphalia, the Netherlands became a great world power by the seventeenth century. Three-fourths of all seagoing vessels bore the Dutch flag. The East India Company was founded in 1602. Its counterpart, the West India Company, was created in 1621. Dutch traders supplied from Lisbon the European demand for spices and overseas products. The trading class was the center of power in the state. Government and law were directed to promote and protect its interests.

A very considerable reception of Roman law took place in the seven provinces of the Netherlands, beginning as early as 1473. By the first part of the seventeenth century, Roman law had established itself in the inferior courts of the province of Holland and elsewhere in the Netherlands to a degree that the legal systems of the provinces generally resembled one another. The discussion of the problem of conflicts of laws among the provinces by the renowned Dutch jurists of the seventeenth century must be understood as taking place in a context of fairly homogeneous but separate systems of law of the provinces. It must, moreover, be understood as taking place against a background of extensive trade with the carrying of Dutch-Roman law by the great trading companies to many parts of the world.[36]

The order of a commercially organized state demanded a security of transactions wherever they might take place. At the same time, it demanded a local supremacy of the sovereign to create and enforce the law of the state. To achieve these two ends in a world of diverse legal orders of a number of states demanded at least some recognition of reciprocity among such legal orders, even though the *obligatory* intrusion of a multiplicity of diverse foreign legal order into the local law might not be tolerable.

The Netherlands of the sixteenth century presented a situation fairly comparable to that of the United States of the nineteenth century. The several provinces possessed their own laws but also

---

[36]Dutch-Roman Law is a term invented by Simon van Leeuwen (1625-82) to describe the system of law which obtained in the province of Holland from the middle of the fifteenth century to the early years of the nineteenth century. Holland was one of the seven provinces which declared their independence of the Kingdom of Spain in 1581 and formed the Republic of the United Netherlands, which later became the Kingdom of The Netherlands. The reception of Roman Law in the Netherlands and the development of a composite of Dutch and Roman law was not, however, confined to Holland. See R. W. Lee, *An Introduction to Roman-Dutch Law,* 2-17 (5th ed., 1953).

exhibited a fairly homogeneous cultural and legal order. Both the Netherlands and the United States were commercially organized states, in which the value of the security of transactions was a pre-eminent social value. The genius of the Dutch jurist Ulrich Huber (1636-94) developed a doctrine of conflicts which was highly appropriate to the requirements of each social order. It profoundly influenced the character of conflicts law of the United States and England, notably through the writings of Story, Dicey, and Beale.

Huber began the publication of a commentary on the Institutes of Justinian in 1678, the third edition of which, published in 1689, contained a chapter on the doctrine of the conflicts of laws, which became the subject of wide study and citation by later treatises on private international law. The 1689 edition was known as *Praelectiones Juris Romani et Hodierni* and the chapter in question was entitled "De Conflicta Legum Diversarum in Diversis Imperiis."[37] Later in the century the writings of Johannes Voet (1647-1713 or 1714) highly coincide with Huber's views on the territorial supremacy of the sovereign and on comity as the governing principle in the application of foreign laws.[38]

The classic statement of the territoriality of laws and the initial foundations of the doctrine of vested rights made by Huber was as follows:

All acts and transactions, as well in court as out, whether *mortis causa* or *inter vivos*, rightly accomplished according to the law of any particular place, are valid even though a different form of law prevails, by which they would be invalid if transacted there. And on the other hand, acts and transactions done in a certain place contrary to the laws of that place, since they are void from the beginning, can nowhere be valid; and this, not only with respect to men who have a domicil in the place of the contract, but even with respect to those who happen to be there at the time: with this exception, nevertheless; if the sovereign of another country would be affected with a serious inconvenience thereby he would not be expected to give use and effect to such acts or business, according to the limitation in the third axiom.[39]

---

[37]See E. M. Meijers, "L'Histoire des Principes Fondamentaux de Droit International Privé a Partir du Moyen Age," Académie de Droit International, 49 *Recueil des Cours* 547 at 654 (1934, pt. 3); D. J. Llewellyn Davies, "The Influence of Huber's *De Conflictu Legum* on English Private International Law," 18 *British Yearbook of International Law* 49 (1937); Lee, *An Introduction to Roman-Dutch Law*, 16.

[38]J. Voet, *Commentarius ad Pandectas* (1698 and 1704).

[39]Beale, 3, *Conflict of Laws*, 1903-04.

The axiom to which Huber referred was one of three maxims incorporating his methodology for the solution of conflicts problems. They were as follows:

I. The laws of any sovereignty have force *within the territory of that* country, and bind all subected to it; *but not beyond.* II. All are considered as subjects of a sovereign who are found within his territory, whether permanently or temporarily there. III. Sovereigns *out of comity* act so that the laws of each nation, brought into existence within its territory, may hold their force everywhere so far as they do not prejudice the power of another sovereign and his subjects.[40] (Italics supplied.)

Under Huber's methodology, the social fact of the territorial supremacy of the new nation-state was recognized. It became the basis for a guaranty of security of transactions, a value of enormous importance to a commercially organized society, under the vested rights principle. Yet uncomfortable repercussions to which a rigorously logical application of his premises might lead were safeguarded at two successive points. First, there was no binding obligation to apply foreign law; it was applied only "out of comity." Second, if the precise rule of law to which adherence to comity led should produce "a serious inconvenience" or "prejudice the power" of the local sovereign, the rule could be ignored.

The principle of the territoriality of laws implicit in the first and second maxims can be regarded as a restatement of the fundamental jural norm that the judge must apply the law of the land, that is, the law of the legal system in which he functions. Within this context, the norm expresses a rule for decision making in situations of interpersonal conflict, statable in terms of competing rules of law and competing values embodied in such rules. The internal basic norm for judicial action is, under conflicts law theory, made the exclusive norm for decision making in international situations of interpersonal conflicts. In such situations, the forum court looks for the appropriate foreign law as a basis for decision. When it has selected such law, it acts *as if* it were a court under a foreign system of law, to the degree that its local system of law will permit.[41] Only when it has selected a particular corpus of foreign law, does it look for the precise legal norm to apply to the case before it. And the search for that legal norm is not a search made

---

[40]*Ibid.*, 1903.
[41]See W. W. Cook, *The Logical and Legal Bases of the Conflict of Laws,* 20-21 (1942).

as the foreign judge would make it in the performance of his function under his system of law. In practice, the cause of action before the court is first classified according to the methodology of the local and not the foreign legal system. The search for the appropriate foreign law typically takes place only after the jural classification of the cause of action has been completed.[42]

The vested or acquired rights theory of conflicts of laws, derived from the quoted principle of Huber, became to a very considerable extent the basis of conflicts law in judicial decisions under English and American law. It is succinctly summarized by Cheshire: "A judge cannot directly recognize or sanction foreign laws nor can he directly enforce foreign judgements, for it is his own territorial law which must exclusively govern all cases that require his decision . . . what the judge does is to protect rights which have already been acquired by a suitor under a foreign law or a foreign judgement. Extra-territorial effect is thus given, not to the foreign law itself, but merely to the rights that it has created."[43]

The process of determining a vested right, however, simply phrases the problem of the legal classification of the cause of action in different terms for decision making in conflicts law. As Savigny correctly pointed out, a conflicts law methodology based on the fundamental norm of the protection of vested rights begs the question and involves circular reasoning.[44] When, out of the total chronology of facts involved in an international situation of interpersonal conflict, a right is perceived to be created and to vest or to become an acquired right, the determination of the proper territorial law to govern the situation is automatically made by the coincidence of the time and place of vesting or acquisition. Such a methodology has no formal relevance to any independent criterion for determining the appropriateness of the foreign law in the light of the total situation before the court. Yet this very lack of a statement of formal rules for the selection of a foreign law may be the source of strength of the vested rights theory as

---

[42]Cheshire, *Private International Law*, 44-49.

[43]*Ibid.*, 32.

[44]"This principle leads us into a complete circle; for we can only know what are vested rights if we know beforehand by what local law we are to decide as to their complete acquisition." F. C. von Savigny, *A Treatise on the Conflict of Laws*, 102-103, trans. by W. Guthrie (1869). This volume is the last in his *System des heutigen römischen Rechts* (1849).

tested in the crucible of the judicial process itself. By leaving the judge a free agent, it permits a pragmatic case-by-case approach, enabling the consideration of each case on its merits, that may lead to viability in results, if not in predictability, in decision making. At least this seems implicit in Cheshire's remarks that the English lawyer's approach to conflicts law problems is a highly pragmatic one: "There is no sacred principle which pervades all decisions, but when the circumstances indicate that the internal law of a foreign country will provide a solution more just, more convenient and more in accord with the expectations of the parties than the internal law of England, the English judge does not hesitate to give effect to the foreign rule."[45]

The notion of the "vesting" or "acquiring" of a right from a conflicts law viewpoint is a curious one from the standpoint of jurisprudence. The problem of vested or acquired rights from the standpoint of the retroactivity of laws and the protection of individual interests from governmental abuse of power, which is a concern of constitutional or administrative law, is not being discussed here. The notion of "vesting" or "acquiring" of rights implies that events transpire and that law operates upon those events so as to create rights, and that such rights are objective facts inhering in events which take place in a temporal-spatial reality. This reality has nothing to do with any subsequent operation of the legal process for the resolution of interpersonal conflict. This reality exists outside the judicial process. Rights "vest" before the case reaches the courtroom. In a more sophisticated form, the notion of vested or acquired rights may be said to embody expectations of the parties which in justice ought to be protected. The decision-making process should identify those criteria which determine when a "right" becomes a "vested right" or an "acquired right."

Law is no "brooding omnipresence" operating upon temporal-spatial reality as an independent reality. The expectations of the parties in any social situation are simply that the action in question will realize certain values through the attainment of the goals to which such action is directed. To the degree that such action is institutionalized, that is, reflects established patterns of actions, expectations exist that such institutionalized patterns of action

---

[45]Cheshire, *Private International Law*, 37.

will be forthcoming upon the occurrence of their fixed social cue. These are expectations which become the foundation of rights in the legal system. When a situation involves departures from valued institutionalized patterns of action, a problem in social and legal control arises. The content of the appropriate legal right *is not to be discerned by resort to the legal system as an entirety,* but rather by a factual analysis of the situation in which interpersonal conflict has occurred and by consideration of the appropriateness of the various legal norms which compete for recognition from the standpoint of mechanical and value rationality of the actors in the situation, including the cultural appropriateness of the rule that is finally fixed upon as the rule for decision.

Interpersonal conflict arising in a situation which is statable in terms of competing legal rights or privileges, creates a concern for legal rights. Even though a judicial decision may deny a remedy on the ground that the disputed action was privileged, this fact does not alter the circumstance that the original situation included elements of trouble or interpersonal conflict statable in terms of competing legal norms. The judicial approval of the situation before the court as one which occurred as it *ought* to have occurred, when a decision is made that the contested action was privileged action, merely means, in appraising judicial behavior in any future occurrence of a similar situation, that under the rule of *stare decisis* the court will again deny a remedy. The contested action is now privileged because it cannot be predicted that any person subsequently contesting such action in a comparable situation will have a right to a remedy.

The foregoing remarks concern remedial rights, or rights to invoke the operation of the legal process. In the course of judicial decision, a particular rule of law is selected for application to the situation of controversy because, among the various competing rules of law demanding recognition, *stare decisis* and justice requires its selection and application. This study is not at this point concerned with what is law, as a body of juristic knowledge, but rather with control of situations of conflict through the operation of the legal process.

The author has commented elsewhere on the hypothesis of the territorial nature of laws and the notion of territorial laws in conflict as the governing law for an international situation of interpersonal conflict:

It is submitted that the initial hypothesis upon which the system of conflict of laws was erected is incorrect. Law is not territorial; it is a product of human behaviour. The circumstances that in most situations it is just that the expectations of the parties in situations taking place in or predominantly connected with the territory of one State should be deemed to include the expectation that the law of that State would be applied thereto in case of conflict, does not necessarily lead to the conclusion that in *every* situation there *must* be some one and only one proper or governing law. When a court is confronted with an inter-State transaction, there is no reason why in the first instance it should not be able to apply such a rule of law as seems best in the light of the facts. Where the transaction is strongly localized in one of the several States, it may well decide to select the law of that State as the basis of decision. However, this result need not flow from the nature of things, from a major premise of universal application that there must be some one proper law governing every transaction. Rather, the inquiry of the court in an inter-State transaction should be: What decision will best serve the interests of security and stability in international transactions of this nature and carry out the expectations of the parties? In answering that question it should be free to turn to the law of any of the States with which the transaction is connected for guidance, or to make its own rule as did the *praetor peregrinus*. The answer to that question should be made in the spirit of free inquiry which is essential to the judicial method. In that spirit the court should be free to examine the law of any or all of the States with which the transaction is connected. It should not, however, be compelled *ipso facto* to apply any such law. Rather its approach should be that of the *praetor peregrinus*, seeking that rule which will best solve the dispute and adopting the foreign law only when it meets that test. The search for certainty and justice through the application of mechanical rules for the choice of law can never succeed, whether those rules be expressed in simple formulae or in a highly complex and detailed code of regulations. The moment that a court finds itself powerless to deal directly with the facts of a case and decide it on its merits . . . it ceases to be an intelligent instrument of social control.

The consequences of the system of private international law are that it has compartmentalised into the territories of the several States transactions which are international in scope, and to which a truly *jus gentium* or law merchant should be applied. It has cloaked with the conceptualism of territorial sovereignty and jurisdiction the interdependent life of world trade, communication and intercourse. It has treated international facts as if they were national and has perpetuated a national viewpoint where an international viewpoint is needed.[46]

---

[46]Carlston, *Law and Structures,* 158-159, generally at 149-161. The basis of the *grundnorm* of public and private international law that order and law are achieved through the territorial competence of states as law-making organs is suggested in the following remarks of Professor Dorsey: "When the function of states was to govern, they came into conflict with each other over

The methodology of private international law is derived from a nonempirical metaphysical absolute, that is, *some one law among laws in conflict ought to apply by the inherent nature, territorial or otherwise, of the situation truly conceived.* The notion that laws are in conflict, that the *law* of the forum is always in conflict with a foreign *law* in any situation viewed to possess an international character, that in the resulting struggle for primacy the *law* of one of these states must *yield* in favor of another, is fundamentally a false method of categorization of an international situation for purposes of decision.

The regulation and control of the situation itself on its merits should be the prime concern of the judge. And indeed it usually is. If it were not, private international law as a methodology would long ago have foundered. The difficulty is that its mechanical system of rules often hides the function of law in the regulation of the situation, and that the rules do not spring from the innate order of the situation itself, but instead from formulae which often have a mechanistic application.

It is insisted that the ideology of private international law, whether one adopts the notion of the territorial nature of law or any other basic norm for conceptualizing its rules, is that inevitably and finally an international case is always decided from a national perspective, that is, by a rule emanating from a body of law which is a product of a particular culture, type of society, stratification of social classes, configuration of group pressures, value system, and patterns of leadership and administration. All of these determine the character of the rules of law found in a national legal system. Whether the successive steps in the operation of a conflicts methodology—that is, (1) determination of jurisdiction, (2) classification of the cause of action, (3) selection

---

governing, and to establish order it was necessary for them to accept a principle for distributing governing competences among them, and to accept as binding the rules resulting from the application of this principle to various situations. Territorial sovereignty was the principle adopted by the states of Europe that formed the international community three hundred years ago. As I have pointed out above, traditional international law (except for the law of war) is comprised of delineating the right or obligation of territorially sovereign, independent states to govern over certain pieces of territory, or over certain persons, or with respect to particular territory, in the light of the natural law interpretation of the heritage of Western civilization, drawing heavily upon Roman law." G. L. Dorsey, "Chinese Recognition: Law and Policy in Perspective," 23 *U. Pitt. L. Rev.* 56-57 (1961).

of the *lex causae,* and (4) application of the *lex causae*[47]—will finally produce a *body* of law which will contain the appropriate *rule* of law for controlling the *particular internationl situation of interpersonal conflict* is always subject to risk. The principal element of this risk is found in the fact that whatever theory of private international law is adopted, it *always* conceals the contents of the rule of law which is finally applied as a basis for the decision of the case. One may perhaps make an analogy of this procedure to that gambling device of the search for the pea under the elusive shells manipulated by the gambler.

In any event, a rule of law which makes national sense may make international nonsense. As states multiply and move apart in their ideologies and value attachment to the international system, the likelihood diminishes that the selection of a national system of law as a basis for decision making will produce the appropriate rule of law for an international case of a private character. Even the exception of public policy, or *ordre public,* usually does not reject the rule for decision which is found by the application of principles of conflict of laws because such a rule is inappropriate from the international viewpoint.[48]

Professor Yntema put the present posture of conflicts law as follows: "How can the formal doctrine postulated by the modern theories, that the local law is supreme, explain the phenomenon of conflicts law, the precise purpose of which is to define the necessary exceptions to be made in the substantive rules of this very local law? Obviously, the reasons for these exceptions and not the formal doctrine, present the real issues."[49]

This historical study of conflict of laws will close with the so-called international school. The basic notion of the territoriality of law still underlies the methodology of this school, as it is found in the conflicts law of the Continent, and particularly Germany, even though its proponents decry the vested rights theory of Huber. In a work published in 1849,[50] Savigny postulated a conflict of laws methodology which would classify legal relationships to states or territories to which, by their peculiar nature, they inherently

---

[47]Cheshire, *Private International Law,* 45-46.
[48]See K. S. Carlston, "Nationalization: An Analytical Approach," 54 *Northwestern U. L. Rev.* 405, 416-418 (1959).
[49]Yntema, "Bases of Private International Law," 317.
[50]von Savigny, *A Treatise on the Conflict of Laws.*

belonged. In such a methodology, the international situation of interpersonal conflict would not be examined to determine whether its statute was real, personal, or mixed. Instead, it would be examined to determine the character of the legal relation which it involved. When this was determined, the methodology postulated a series of rules whereby such legal relation was to be allocated "according to its spatial contacts, to a certain territory, and thereby to a definite legal system."[51] However, the equality of treatment of all international situations of interpersonal conflict which Savigny hoped to reach still eludes attainment, for the methodology is still tied to some national system of law and not to a rule of law. The content of the rules of law increasingly varies from country to country, becomes less homogeneous, and provides less security for international commerce, as nationalistic, autarchic, and other local pressures mount.[52] The *de jure* international equality of application of conflicts law rules promised by the internationalist school fails to yield a *de facto* equality among diverse nations.

9.c. *The introduction into private international law of certain subordinate propositions would provide a substantial improvement in its methodology.*

Despite the vigor of the above attack upon the fundamental premise of private international law made in 9.b., it is not suggested that the system as it is now developed be rejected. There has been a steady progress of private international law toward the statement of principles for the selection of the applicable municipal law which would protect the important expectations of the parties. This achievement should not be cast aside; the administration of justice cannot be subjected to such a violent change. The continued adherence to the developing conflict of laws methodology is accordingly affirmed, subject to an important exception or new principle. A norm for decision making in conflict of laws cases arising in the international system follows:

When private international law would require the application of a municipal rule of law whereby participation in the international system as a means for the realization of shared values would be

---

[51]Nussbaum, *Principles of Private International Law*, 22.
[52]See W. Simons, "La Conception du Droit International Privé d'après la Doctrine et la Pratique en Allemagne," Académie du Droit International, 15 *Recueil des Cours* 437, 468 (1926, pt. 5).

impaired, the forum court shall then select, for the purposes of its decision, from the various systems of municipal law involved in the case, that particular rule of municipal law which would best promote a structuring of the international system as an effective means for the realization of commonly shared values by participants.

This proposal might be viewed as an extension of public policy, or *ordre public*, indicating additional circumstances in which a judge would be at liberty to look at, consider, and evaluate the contents of a foreign rule of law before he is compelled to apply it. The adoption of the proposal might mitigate some of the remorseless logic of the conflict of laws of which Judge Cardozo complained.[53] It is similar to a proposal raised some time ago by Professor Cavers.[54] He urged that in conflict of laws one should move from rules concerning the choice of law to a simple search for rules for decision in a particular case. He contended that judicial decision should be directed to a choice between competing rules for decision, as proffered by competing jurisdictions or systems of law, instead of stopping at the point of the choice of law, in the sense of law as the body of law of a state. He explained that: "The end-product of this process of analysis and evaluation would, of course, be the application to the case at bar of a rule of law, derived either from the municipal law of the forum or that of some foreign state if proof of the latter law were duly made. The choice of that law would not be the result of the automatic operation of a rule or principle of selection but of a search for a just decision in the principal case."[55]

The proposal would clarify the term "just," as used by Professor Cavers, and render it more precise. It would orient justice to the "overriding policy" of private international law to promote "the interests of international society."[56] It would demand that private international law, as a system of law, be directed to promoting a type of order in the international system whereby it would enable a maximum realization of values by participation therein. The adoption of the proposal would violate no rule of international

---

[53] Cardozo, *Paradoxes of Legal Science*, 68.
[54] D. F. Cavers, "A Critique of the Choice-of-Law Problem," 47 *Harv. L. Rev.* 173 (1933).
[55] *Ibid.*, 193.
[56] E. E. Cheatham and W. L. M. Reese, "Choice of the Applicable Law," 52 *Colum. L. Rev.* 959, 963 (1952).

law. It would instead provide a firmer foundation for the growth of international law.[57]

Writers on the conflict of laws today generally reflect a profound concern that decision making in this field should not be mechanical but should fully consider the policy aspects which the case at hand presents. There is, for example, an awareness that formal, abstract rules for the selection of the governing law in contract cases must be replaced by rules which will better enable the intent of the parties to be accomplished. There is a growing realization that cases arising in the international arena must consider the interests of individuals as actors in the international society. The proposal is quite consistent with the current trend of development of conflict of laws.

It may be mentioned that the methodology recently advanced by Professor Currie is a significant step toward the recognition of policy factors in situations regulated by private international law. He suggests, among other things, that the law of the forum should be applied when the forum state has an interest in the application of its law and policy, that its law should be so applied even when the foreign state has such an interest, and clearly so when the foreign state has no such interest. He affirms that the law of the foreign state should be applied only when such state has an interest in its application and the forum state has none.[58] His proposed methodology is related to conflicts law in a federal system. As a methodology for private international law, however, it would appear to represent a virtual abdication of such international character as that law may now possess, for it limits the recognition of issues of policy primarily to those of whatever individual state happened to become the situs of the forum court. There is no place for the recognition of the policy interest in promoting the strength of the international system as such.

---

[57]In addition to the citations concerning private international law above, see the books listed in the bibliography by: H. Battifol, A. K. Kuhn, and M. Wolff; and articles by A. A. Ehrenzweig, B. A. Wortley ("The Interaction of Public and Private International Law"), M. Gutzwiler, J. R. Stevenson, and A. Nussbaum ("Rise and Decline of the Law-of-Nations Doctrine in the Conflict of Laws").

[58]B. Currie, "On the Displacement of the Law of the Forum," 58 *Colum. L. Rev.* 964 (1958); B. Currie, "The Constitution and the Choice of Law; Governmental Interests and the Judicial Function," 26 *U. Chi. L. Rev.* 9 (1958). In the writer's view, a much more sophisticated approach to the applicability of the *lex fori* will be found in A. A. Ehrenzweig, "The Lex Fori—Basic Rule in the Conflict of Laws," 58 *Mich. L. Rev.* 637 (1960).

Another proposed methodology for private international law based on recognition of policy factors will be found in a study by Katzenbach, who affirms that each state should endeavor "to secure maximum effect for its policy in and with regard to the international or interstate community" and "to effectuate the compatible policies of all." He points out that in the sphere of political questions, such as nationalization, the concept of territorial supremacy does not furnish a satisfactory answer. "But the national interest is here more obscure, for what benefits the citizens of one state may do so at the expense of others. . . . Where what is sauce for the goose is something else for the gander, power to enforce locally through unilateral determination of appropriate policy is unlikely to prove a mutually satisfactory solution."[59]

The point has been made by Professor Rheinstein that if private international law is to develop into full maturity as a body of law, its broad doctrines will have to "be broken down to a very much larger number of narrower rules of more specific applications, until they are similar to the rules in all other fields of law."[60] Such a development still would not free private international law from its basically inadequate structure. Professor Ehrenzweig may have admitted too much when he said of this proposal "such a breakdown would achieve both too little and too much. Too little because it would lose sight of indispensable general principles, too much because it would dissolve the discipline of the conflict of laws in a necessarily unsuccessfully attempt at determining interspatial applicability for every rule of municipal and foreign law."[61]

While private international law is generally regarded to be a part of municipal law, its articulation with public international law is a matter of vital concern to the international system. In considering the events which are comprehended within an international situation of interpersonal conflict, it would seem that the legal significance of those events under the principles of public international law ought to be a matter of vital concern to private international law. If acts take place in violation of public international law, the forum court should be free to refuse to recognize such acts as a source of rights under the maxim *ex injuria jus non*

---

[59]N. de B. Katzenbach, "Conflicts on an Unruly Horse: Reciprocal Claims and Tolerances in Interstate and International Law," 65 *Yale L. J.* 1087, 1147 (1956).

[60]M. Rheinstein, book review, 28 *Ind. L. J.* 443, 449 (1953).

[61]A. A. Ehrenzweig, 1, *Conflict of Laws,* 16 (1959).

oritur.[62] But for the so-called act of state doctrine of Anglo-American private international law, the forum court would be free to establish the paramountcy of international law in attributing legal effect to foreign acts of state.[63] In its most restricted sphere, the act of state doctrine would deny to the forum court the power to inquire into the validity of a foreign legislative act taking effect in the territory of another state, at least insofar as concerns the constitutional validity of such act under the law of such state. This is quite understandable, as a matter of judicial policy, in reflecting a disinclination of the forum court to assume the role of judicial review on foreign state constitutional grounds over foreign legislative acts. To extend the doctrine further, so as to preclude any inquiry by the forum court into the validity of a foreign act of state under international law, is neither necessary nor desirable. For private international law to bar the forum court from making such an inquiry is to assert that such law should never concern itself with a matter which, indeed, should be for it a matter of primary concern, namely, insuring the subordination of the foreign sovereign to public international law. The executive of the forum would, of course, always be permitted—no, it would be his duty— to examine the validity, under international law, of a foreign act of state affecting the interest of his state. The forum court, however, under the act of state doctrine, finds its hands tied in any

---

[62]H. Lauterpacht, *Recognition in International Law*, 420 (1947); L. Oppenheim, 1, *International Law*, H. Lauterpacht, ed., 270 (8th ed., 1955); F. Morgenstern, "Recognition and Enforcement of Foreign Legislative, Administrative and Judicial Acts Which Are Contrary to International Law," 4 *Int. L. Q.* 326, 329 (1951); B. A. Wortley, "Expropriation in International Law," 33 *Grotius Society Transactions* 25, 30, 31 (1947); Wolff *v.* Oxholm, [1817] 6 M. & S. 92; *In re* Fried Krupp A/G, [1917] 2 Ch. 188; Confiscation of Property of Sudeten Germans Case, Dec. 7, 1948, *1948 Annual Digest and Reports of Public International Law Cases*, Case no. 12, 24-25 (1953); Anglo-Czechoslovak and Prague Credit Bank *v.* Janssen, [1943] V.L.R. 185; N. V. de Bataafche Petroleum Maatschappij and Ors. *v.* The War Damage Commission, Singapore Court of Appeal, April 13, 1956, 22 *Malayan L. J.* 155 (1956) and also 51 *Am. J. Int. Law* 802 (1957).
[63]F. A. Mann, "The Sacrosanctity of the Foreign Act of State" (pts. 1, 2), 59 *L. Q. Rev.* 42, 155 (1943); see also the valuable report of the Committee on International Law, Association of the Bar of the City of New York, "A Reconsideration of the Acts of the State Doctrine in United States Courts" (1959). Compare P. C. Jessup, *The Use of International Law*, 101 (1959); "a state may be held responsible for the decision of one of its courts which violates a treaty or international law. . .," citing E. M. Borchard, *Diplomatic Protection of Citizens Abroad*, 197 (1915).

attempt to apply the policy of the forum, as well as of states generally, to support in this regard the application of international law in the international society. That which ought to be the very question at issue, namely, whether the act of a foreign government is to be given legal effect in the forum when it is violative of international law, is ruled out simply on the ground that the foreign act of state is as such sacrosanct.

The act of state doctrine demonstrates the extent to which the application of the "remorseless logic" of private international law may operate to exclude public international law as a basis for decision making in important international situations of interpersonal conflict. The expropriation by a state of foreign property in its territory with inadequate compensation at the very least raises an issue of the lawfulness of its act under public international law. If the ownership of such property should come into question in the court of some state other than the expropriating state, it would seem that the question of the conflict of the foreign law with international law would be highly germane to the decision of the case. Dr. O'Connell comments on this situation as follows:

> The question has arisen in this form in the past twenty years in the courts of Holland, France, Italy, Japan and Great Britain. With very few exceptions these have applied their own internal conflict of law rules for the solution of the problem, and have regarded the international law rules as irrelevant. This is a fundamentally dualist technique employed in the process of the recognition of foreign law, which seems to be inconsistent with the trend towards abandonment of that technique in the solution of problems of the interaction of international law and internal law in other matters.[64]

9.d. *The rules of international law, as determined by classic positivist methodology, are confined to those which state officials value for the stabilization of interstate intercourse at the public level.*

The action of each of us reflects the microcosm of our physical and psychical beings and the macrocosm of our culture. Born with a complex neural system enabling an extraordinary degree of adaptation to our environment, we react consistently with our personality and on the basis of the internalization of the learning of our culture to satisfy our drives of hunger, aggression, fear, sex, and the like, or our needs for self-maintenance, self-actualization, safe-

---

[64]D. P. O'Connell, "The Relationship Between International Law and Municipal Law," 48 *Georgetown L. J.* 431, 485 (1960).

ty, love, and esteem. It is our culture which enables us to identify the elements of our physical world, give meaning to the surrounding environment of meteorological and geographical phenomena, flora and fauna, and shape the design of our living. Each society develops its own culture or its own "historically derived system of explicit and implicit designs for living" or its "historically created selective performances which channel men's reactions both to internal and external stimuli."[65] Each century adds to its accumulated body of learning, beliefs, symbols, and traditions which determine its daily course of life. Yesterday's hypothesis for action becomes today's reality and tomorrow's myth. At whatever cost of life and suffering, we eventually learn to adapt. Though we may cling desperately to an outmoded way of life, chastening reality will eventually beat its way to our perception and break our hold of ancient custom. One of the tasks of the scholar of history is to show when yesterday's solutions of problems cease to be appropriate for today's realities.

It was by no means a historical accident that Holland in the seventeenth century was the scene in which the foundations of modern public and private international law were largely laid. The world which Holland then encountered, as well as the other existing or emerging states of Western Europe, was a world of aggression and interdynastic rivalry. The paramount need of each was to secure that freedom from external dominance which would enable it to organize the human and physical resources within its borders to reach its goals. The term "sovereignty" became a symbol for that freedom. It attained an extraordinary influence as a symbol because its referent embodied a cultural fact of profound importance, namely, the fact that each national society, as a social system, must possess a space of free movement adequate to enable effective integration and adaptation. A dynamic, rapidly changing society demands a very considerable area of freedom for organizing action to achieve these ends.

A social system does not become an organization or a national society does not become an organized state until there is in each an exercise and acceptance of authority. Authoritative roles must

---

[65]G. P. Murdock, "The Common Denominator of Cultures," in *The Science of Man in the World Crisis*, R. Linton, ed., 123, 127ff. (1945); for quotations see C. Kluckhohn and W. H. Kelly, "The Concept of Culture," in *ibid.*, 78 at 84, 98.

emerge and be accepted. Formal and substantive legitimacy must define and reinforce the exercise of authority. The locus and character of authority must be defined and its accountability or responsibility made explicit. Sovereignty, as a symbol for authority in the social system called the democratic state, identifies the ultimate source of authority, that is, the public. It is the people whose values and demands ultimately determine the ways in which authority is exercised and the limits beyond which it cannot press. Sovereignty also points to the organ or organs of the government which are authoritative, as a matter of formal and substantive legitimacy. It defines who shall be regarded to exercise the supreme legislative authority, that is, who shall determine the *properties* of the social system, as they eventuate from the direction and allocation of the energy of its human and physical resources to the attainment of its goals.

These are enduring facts conditioning the creation of the state as an organizational structuring of a social system. In this respect, the hypothesis of the territorial supremacy of the sovereign state met the needs of the Western European state of the seventeenth and eighteenth centuries, as well as the state of the twentieth century. Compared with the seventeenth and eighteenth centuries, the postwar years are also a period of nascent and emerging states, witnessing a considerable external threat to the continued existence of all states. But the character of that threat and the character of the culture have since undergone profound change. It may be true that the power of the territorial sovereign was in fact no more limitless in the sixteenth century than it is in the twentieth. The fact that the hypothesis of the absolute supremacy of the sovereign power was unfounded, however, mattered much less in the days of the birth of the modern era than it matters today.

The seventeenth and eighteenth centuries in Western Europe found a world in which force, as a relation of states, was not carried to the point where its use meant the total destruction of the states themselves. In the dynastic struggle for power, war as an instrument of national policy found no logic in the destruction of conquered peoples. The acquisition of control of the riches they could produce was the very subject matter of war. Hence, war did not commit the total civilian population to the total destruction of others and of itself as well. Travel, commerce, and intercourse still persisted among the populations of the warring states. It remained for the French revolution and Napoleon to transform the character of land warfare, for England to transform the character of sea warfare, for the great powers of World War I and II to create the methodology of air warfare, and for nuclear warfare to threaten the total extinction of organized societies.

The Holland of Grotius (1583-1645) and Bynkershoek (1673-1743) in public international law, of Paul Voet (1619-77), his son Johannes Voet (1647-1713 or 1714) and Ulrich Huber (1636-94) in private international law, the England of Alberico Gentili (1552-1608) and Richard Zouche (1590-1660) in public international law, were states in which commerce and trade found a fairly secure internal and external protection. The Third Estate of commerce and the professions possessed substantial security under law within a state's boundaries and outside a state as well, as it carried to the overseas dominions the Dutch-Roman law and the English common law, respectively. Elsewhere, the law merchant and the growing reception in Western Europe of Roman law provided a firm legal foundation for commerce.

Thus the symbol of the territorial supremacy of the sovereign did not possess in the reality of life the referent of the absolute character which its use imports today. There was not, in fact, the subjection of commerce to the exercise of the legislative supremacy of the sovereign which exists today. Territorial sovereignty found its meaning essentially in freedom *from* external control or independence. The seventeenth-century personal sovereign, in his occupancy of his sovereign role, was not above the judgments of natural law and morals. His sphere of interest was politics. The market place was for the traders. Their profits and trade, however, were a valued source of power.

The positivism of Grotius and Zouche was positivism in a natural law setting. Their era was one in which a natural law philosophy and outlook were all pervasive. The immutable, universal truth of the law of nature, discoverable by natural or right reason, provided a unity or unbroken continuum in which the law of a people or nation *(jus gentium)* and the law between peoples or nations *(jus inter gentes)* became a unified whole. In Grotius' eyes, the law *between* peoples and the law *of* peoples was an unbroken whole in the *jus gentium*. Family law, property, ownership, and delict were all deemed to be a part of the *jus gentium*. Although the *jus gentium* was to be distinguished from municipal law emanating from a civil power,[66] it included the law of the relations between peoples simply as a part of the whole.[67]

Grotius did not envisage any separate and distinctive sphere or body of law in the sense of international law as it is viewed today. The term "international," from which the current term "international law" was derived, was created by Bentham.[68] The term "law of nations," which is the ~~typical~~ translation into English of the term *"jus gentium,"* has today a very concrete referent, namely, the concept implied by the current equivalent term "international law" as the law governing the relations of states. Bentham's term "international jurisprudence" meant law for "persons . . . considered as members of different states." For the earlier writers of the seventeenth century, the term *jus gentium* did not have the modern referent implied in the "law of nations," but rather the referent of that body of principles binding all peoples in their internal and external relations which was established by natural law and was discoverable by natural or right reason. Grotius rarely refers to the law between *populos,* ~~as in his prolegomena.~~ The term *jus gentium* was the one which he almost universally employed and today it can perhaps best be said to denote the law of peoples.[69]

---

[66]H. Grotius, *De Jure Belli ac Pacis Libri Tres,* 44 (trans. by F. W. Kelsey, 1925).

[67]H. Grotii, 1, *De Jure Belli ac Pacis Libri Tres,* prolegemena at 4 (1646).

[68]J. Bentham, *Principles of Morals and Legislation,* 326 (1823). The 1823 edition of this work, printed in 1780 and first published in 1789, is described "A New Edition, corrected by the Author." Bentham justifies his coining of the term "international" in the phrase "international jurisprudence" (not, it is to be noted, "international law") on the ground that the law of nations is "an appellation so uncharacteristic, that, were it not for the force of custom, it would seem rather to refer to international jurisprudence . . . that what is commonly called *droit des gens,* ought rather to be called *droit entre les gens."* For Bentham, the term "law" meant "nothing more nor less than the sum total of a number of individual laws taken together." These could be classified among Bentham's principal categories of jurisprudence, one of which concerned "the *political quality* of the persons whose conduct is the object of law." Such persons "may, on any given occasion, be considered either as members of the same state, or as members of different states: in the first case, the law may be referred to the head of *internal,* in the second case, to that of *international* jurisprudence."

[69]H. Grotii, 1, *De Jure Belli* (1646), 7; H. Grotius, *De Jure Belli* (1925), 44. The use in this translation of the modern term "law of nations" as a translation of the classic term *"jus gentium"* may have considerable usage and some philological justification in its support, even though it may create a faulty communication and a false referent for the modern casual reader. Less justifiable, however, is the introduction of such a modern term as "international law" in a context which does not require it, for example, Grotii, *De Jure Belli*

Zouche identified a distinct body of a "law which is observed in common between peoples or princes of different nations," which he called *jus inter gentes* or "law between nations," but it still remained a part of the *jus gentium*. The latter consisted of the law "which natural reason has established among all men" and which "is respected by all alike."[70]

Even for Bodin of the sixteenth century, the sovereign power vested in the prince was subject to the *lex divina*, the *lex naturae*, and the *lex gentium*.[71] Other writers of the period, such as Samuel Pufendorf (1632-94), Christian Wolff (1676-1756), and Emmerich de Vattel (1714-67) were far more strongly imbued with the natural law outlook.

Grotius challenged the church as the authoritative interpreter of natural law, as for example, in his assertion that the "law of nature . . . cannot be changed by God. Measureless as is the power of God, nevertheless it can be said that there are certain things over which that power does not extend . . . God, then, cannot cause that two times two shall not make four." The law of nature could be discovered a posteriori from secular proof, as well as a priori from the written word of God. To this end, the "testimony of philosophers, historians, poets, finally also of orators" could be adduced. Proof a posteriori was permissible, since "an affect that is universal demands a universal cause." Accordingly, the proof for the *jus gentium* was found in "unbroken custom," for the study of which "the illustrious writers of history are the greatest value to us."[72]

The secularization of law and of the proof of law by Grotius was the precursor of the denial of scholasticism by Thomas Hobbes

---

(1646), 196, compared with Grotius, *De Jure Belli* (1925), 295. Max Huber noted that the term "international" in English comes from the term "nation," which refers to a politically organized people or state. Thus "international" referred to the political and not the cultural relations of nations. The term "nation" in German had much more of an ethnical and cultural connotation. M. Huber, "Die Soziologischen Gründlagen des Völkerrechts," 2, *Internationalrechtliche Abhandlungen* (1928).

[70] R. Zouche, 1, *Juris et Judicii Fecialis sive Juris inter Gentes, et Questionum de Eodem Explicatio*, trans. by J. L. Brierly (1911), 1.

[71] J. L. Brierly, *The Basis of Obligation in International Law*, 21 (1958). This is the original English version of the course of lectures published under the title, *Le Fondement du Charactère Obligatoire du Droit International*, in Académie de Droit International, 23 *Recueil des Cours* 549 (1928, pt. 3).

[72] Grotius, *De Jure Belli* (1925), 23, 40, 42, 44.

(1588-1679) in his *Leviathan* (1642) and the denial of natural law itself by Bentham, Austin, and the positivists of the nineteenth century. Removed from its natural law foundation, the bases of legal obligation for the rules of international law became a baffling problem for international law scholars. The notion of the territorial supremacy of the sovereign created an irreconcilable logical conflict when it was confronted with the notion of the supremacy of international law. An international order composed of sovereign states under law was logically impossible. The solution of this conceptualistic problem long preoccupied international law jurists in their search for a basis for obligation in international law in a world of diverse and hypothetically supreme legal entities. There is, in the author's view, no better exploration of the differing views which have been advanced concerning the nature of law and obligation in the international order than Professor Brierly's masterly study on *The Basis of Obligation in International Law*.[73] None can surpass it for clarity, conciseness, and cogency of analysis, and it is an essential background for the present pages. Certain portions of the author's study, *Law and Structures of Social Action*, should also be consulted in this connection.[74]

Even today the methodology of international law followed by the International Court of Justice under article 38 of its statute exhibits a restricted view of the judicial function. Shabtai Rosenne, in his recent exhaustive study of the International Court of Justice, characterized the conception of its role, as revealed by the performance of its judicial task, as follows: "This discussion on the conception of the nature of the judicial task made manifest in the recent work of the Court may be briefly summarized as being: so far as possible to isolate, in the concrete case, the legal problem from the circumstances in which it had its immediate origin, *to consider that legal problem in an objective and even abstract way, and to reach its decision on the basis of that examination, to the exclusion of all political, moral or other extra-legal considerations*"[75] (italics supplied).

---

[73]Brierly, *The Basis of Obligation*, particularly 3-64. On the history of international law, the following additional references may be consulted: A. Nussbaum, *A Concise History of the Law of Nations* (2nd ed., 1954); J. Kosters, "Les Fondements du Droit des Gens," 4 *Bibliotheca Visseriana* 1 (1925); E. Nys, *Les Origines du Droit International* (1894).

[74]Carlston, *Law and Structures*, 53-62, 105-106, 120-122, 131-135.

[75]S. Rosenne, *The International Court of Justice*, 66 (1957).

His remarks reveal a persistence in international law of a view of the judicial function which has largely vanished in modern legal philosophy. There is an illuminating parallel of the above remarks in a review written in 1887 of Austin's *Lectures on Jurisprudence:* "Modern judges . . . are seldom moved by considerations of justice, equity, good conscience, common sense, or other such misleading notions."[76]

Thus the methodology of international law today finds itself at a juncture in which the international court typically takes only a most restricted view of the facts of a dispute, and it fails to inquire into all the facts upon which a vital "living law" norm might be based and to consider all those value and functional aspects of a legal norm which are today considered by legal theory to be an appropriate and necessary province and function of judicial inquiry and reason.

The assumption that the classic positivist methodology of international law will, if faithfully adhered to, find a norm of universal application which will always be a vital "living law" norm is questioned. Rosenne mentioned "the disruption of the homogeneity of the Court" as one of the factors indicative of "a general *malaise*" in the international legal process "not yet fully diagnosed."[77] He explored in this connection the changing patterns in membership of the International Court of Justice and their impact upon the adjudicative process. He tabulated membership in the court since 1922 on the basis of the representation of continents, of the principal legal systems of the world, and of the nationalities of judges. His findings are most suggestive. It appears that the court no longer has a predominantly European composition. Its membership consists of judges drawn from a wide variety of types of cultures. Its opinions consequently exhibit a wide variety of views as to the international law norms which shall be *valued* or selected for the purpose of decision making. Rosenne's conclusions in this connection are as follows:

These three tables disclose an interesting pattern of evolution. Most significant of all is the sharp decrease in the number of European judges. The Court is no longer predominantly European in composition as it was throughout the period before the Second World War. This partly reflects

---

[76]G. H. Smith, "The English Analytical Jurists," 21 *Am. L. Rev.* 270, 284 (1887).

[77]Rosenne, *International Court,* 71.

the shift of political power from Europe elsewhere, and partly is a result of the general under-representation of Europe in all United Nations organs as a consequence of the War and the later deadlock over the admission of new members. This process is matched by an increase in the representation of the American continent, now exactly double what it had been in 1921, and by a new factor, representation on the Court of the African continent. Somewhat paradoxically, there has nevertheless occurred a marked growth in the influence of the common law in the composition of the Court. This too, in 1956, is double what it had been in 1921. The common law representation, however, reflects the increasing independence of the common law countries—these judges coming from the United States, the United Kingdom, Canada and Pakistan. The two places held by Islamic law are also a notable feature. The representation of the West European heritage of Roman law has naturally dropped significantly, and it will be observed that a very important branch of legal culture, namely Germanic law, is completely unrepresented. On the other hand, the representation of Communist law is a new feature. Whereas previously the Court was essentially the reflection of European legal philosophy, it has become a catalyst for fundamentally different legal cultures. The Court is less homogeneous, from the point of view of the representation of legal systems, than ever before. But the tables show that this general pattern of evolution has been a steady one.

It is believed that all in all, this evolution may have had an adverse effect upon the ability of the Court to operate effectively, upon the willingness of States to submit disputes to the Court, and, possibly, upon their willingness to abide by its decisions. The introduction to the bench of several judges (not merely those representing Communist views) holding strong opinions either about the role of the Court and international law, or on the nature of modern international law, has undoubtedly made it more difficult for the Court to reach decisions, or, perhaps more accurately, to agree on the statement of reasons upon which a given decision was based. In any Court, especially an international Court of fifteen judges, there will be found differences of appreciation as to facts and to law which will lead to diminished majorities and vigorous dissents. However, it is possible, from the published opinions of the Court, to detect greater differences than this, and there are a number of separate and dissenting opinions which can only be satisfactorily understood on the basis of assumptions and postulates different from those traditionally expounded in the literature of the law. This is particularly evident in the stimulating and provocative opinions of Judge Alvarez who has zealously fostered, in the Court, his conceptions of the new international law. This undoubtedly has increased the unpredictability of litigation. While certainty as to the result of projected litigation can never exist, a government's ability to calculate its chances of success is certainly an important factor enabling it to reach its political decision of whether to litigate or not.[78]

---

[78]*Ibid.*, 138-141, quotation at 140-141.

So long as the methodology of international law permits consideration of no other fundamental sources for its rules than the practice of states, so long as the practice of states is equated with the practice of state officials in interstate intercourse at the public level, the corpus of international law will be confined to rules of practice valued by state officials in the performance of their roles. Their values in that connection will in part be shaped by their national cultures, perspectives, value systems, and character of adaptation of their state to the international system. The values which were shared by Europe in the nineteenth century, from whom the great positivist international jurists were drawn, are no longer shared in similar degree throughout the world. States as international actors are now many and varied. The international stage is suddenly crowded. No longer is there a common acceptance of the perspectives and values of Western European traditions and culture. Conflict between states now emerges because, among other things, states occupy different points in cultural time in a chronological present. Conflict between states now emerges because states exhibit the widest degree of commitment to the international system, ideologies, types of government, social structures, and cultures. In such a context, the valuation of legal norms in international situations of interstate and interpersonal conflict will exhibit the widest disparities.

The appearance on the international scene of the Communist bloc of states is a fact of profound importance of which international law theory, in its claim to universal authority and validity, must take account. While for Soviet legal theorists international law is a reality, their view of the nature of the historical and cultural realities which determine the structure and content of international law is quite different from that of legal scholars of the free world. The necessity of the utmost freedom of action for the Communist state, in discharging its assumed inevitable historical role in leading the struggle of the proletariat for the liquidation of capitalist society, has, for example, led to an extraordinary emphasis upon absolute national sovereignty. It is an established function of the Soviet international jurist to facilitate the accomplishment of the ends of the Soviet state, *as a Communist state,* in the international arena. For them, law must not only justify but must also advance the successful accomplishment of the class struggle and the action of the Soviet state therein. The

Soviet jurist is a far greater captive of Communist state policy than is the Soviet physical scientist.

In a perceptive summary of the Soviet view of international law, published in 1957, Professor Gould remarked that: "The freedom of the Soviet thinkers has existed within the framework composed of Marxian-Leninism-Stalinism and governmental policy. Within that framework there is much opportunity for the play of theoretical minds, for it is sometimes extremely difficult to juggle the three balls of Marxism, Soviet policy, and the rules of international law, especially since one of them is prone to unpredictable bounces."[79]

In the Soviet philosophy of law, the norms of international law produced as a consequence of interstate relations in the capitalist world are not viewed to possess validity for the socialist world, although specific rules may be valid even in the socialist world. Western international law as a whole, however, cannot be regarded to possess a valid base for the socialist sphere of action, at least insofar as it is traceable to law as a product of the capitalist ruling circles. To the degree that the norms of international law protect the integrity of the Communist state and assure respect from others for its independence and validity for its sovereign acts, international law has reality. To the extent that it hampers the extraterritorial exercise of Soviet authority and the territorial expansion of the Communist system, it loses reality.

The insistence upon the custom, or practice, of state officials in interstate relations as the source of law, except for treaty law based on consent, brings to mind the cautionary remarks of Sir Henry Sumner Maine on customary law, first expressed in 1861. Sir Henry said:

Now a barbarous society practicing a body of customs is exposed to some special dangers which may be absolutely fatal to its progress in civilization. The usages which a particular community is found to have adopted in its infancy and in its primitive seats are generally those which are on the whole best suited to promote its physical and moral well being; and, if they are retained in their integrity until new social wants have taught new practices, the upward march of society is almost certain. But unhappily there is a law of development which ever threatens to operate upon unwritten usage. . . . A process then commences which

---

[79]W. L. Gould, *An Introduction to International Law,* 88, see generally chaps. 2, 3 (1957). A well-chosen bibliography appears at page 86 of the text.

may be shortly described by saying that usage which is reasonable generates usage which is unreasonable.[80]

In his article on "Codification and Development of International Law," Sir Hersch Lauterpacht said:

For, once we approach at close quarters practically any branch of international law, we are driven, amidst some feeling of incredulity, to the conclusion that although there is as a rule a consensus of opinion on broad principle—even this may be an overestimate in some cases—there is no semblance of agreement in relation to specific rules and problems. . . . The fact, which is both disquieting and chastening, speaks for itself. There is, upon reflection, nothing astonishing about it. How could it be otherwise in a society in which judicial settlement is sporadic, in which there is no legislative activity in the accepted sense and in which custom is slow of growth and controversial in interpretation and application?[81]

"The central function to be performed in international law," said Julius Stone, "is the promotion of a better rate of development of a system of law lagging ever more seriously behind its essential tasks."[82]

In the author's study, *Law and Structures of Social Action*, it was proposed that the nature of international law should be defined more precisely in behavioral terms. It was stated that:

the law of nations [comprises] those institutionalised rules for behaviour which indicate the content or permissible limits of behaviour of a government agent in the performance of his role in situations, one or more constituent elements of which are characterised by the fact of their identification with another State, that is, by the fact that other actors involved therein are government agents or members of another State or that territory or property involved therein appertains to another State or its members. Described in terms of deviant behaviour, a violation of the law of nations occurs when the behaviour of a government agent in the performance of his role so far departs from the expectations developed through custom in the performance of his role in situations of the foregoing character as to lead to the reaction that his conduct is outside the proper limits of his role.

. . . .

Any system of law must relate to concrete sequences of individual behaviour involving interaction with other concrete sequences of individual behaviour, such concrete sequences of individual behaviour possess meaning only in their situational aspects, some situational aspects involve conduct and relationships cutting across State boundaries or

---

[80]H. S. Maine, *Ancient Law*, 7, 11 (1917).

[81]49 *Am. J. Int. Law* 16, 17-19 (1955).

[82]J. Stone, "On the Vocation of the International Law Commission," 57 *Colum. L. Rev.* 16, 29 (1957).

involving members of different States; the term international law may be applied to the content of the decisions made by the relevant officials of the government concerned in dealing with such conduct and relationships under the belief or conviction that they are bound by legal norms so to decide. The official in question may occupy any one of the widest variety of roles. He may be an official in the Foreign Office, an officer in the armed forces, a legislator, a judge, a police officer, or a customs official. As the required behaviour in the performance of his office falls through repetition into fixed patterns, his official behaviour becomes predictable in given types of situations. The institutionalisation of such behaviour will of course lead to other institutionalised responses on the part of other persons affected thereby. Treaties will be signed and ratified in accordance with established custom, the relevant officials of each State acting their traditional roles. A military aircraft of one State crossing the border of another without consent, a public vessel of war overstaying its permitted period in the harbour of a neutral in time of war, an alien thrown into jail without due process of law, each will lead to predictable responses on the part of various officials of the second State. Individuals such as pirates and contraband-runners will find their behaviour leading to institutionalised action on the part of officials whose role it is to act in such situations. Other individuals may refrain from being pirates or contraband-runners because of the predictable behaviour of such officials and their command of instruments of force.

International law thus conceived falls into a system of rules of conduct for State officials indicating, as does any system of law, that behaviour which is permissible, obligatory or prohibited in the given situation. In each type of situation in which such rules for behaviour have developed, those with whom the official interacts will expect that he will perform in accordance with the relevant rules. Sometimes those in whom such expectations will exist will be the officials of other States, sometimes they will be merely private individuals. If those expectations are frustrated by deviant behaviour, then such deviant behaviour will give rise to still other institutionalised responses on the part of yet other State officials. Whether such other responses will be in exercise of a legal "right" will depend on the facts of the particular situation. If an individual without any official capacity be primarily affected by such deviant behaviour, his "rights" can be enforced only through such "official" institutions and procedures as have developed for that purpose. If the person affected be an official of another State, his "rights" *in the performance of his role* can similarly be enforced through certain established "official" institutions and procedures. The description of the permissible, obligatory or prohibited official conduct in situations involving members of another State, and the indication of the official conduct to follow upon deviant official behaviour in such situations, constitute the science of international law. Thus, neither "individuals" or "States" are the subject of international law, for neither term points with sufficient precision to the persons whose behaviour in the performance of their role is governed by the rules of this system of law. . . .

Determining the subjects or persons affected by the rules of international law is quite a different matter from determining the subject matter of those rules. In ascertaining the content of the rules of international law we are concerned with the behaviour of a limited number of persons in limited situations, namely, the predictable behaviour of government officials in situations one or more constituent elements of which are characterised by their identification with another State. The persons affected by such official behaviour in such situations cannot, however, be so neatly categorised. They will vary widely in their roles. They will not necessarily be an official of another State. They may be an owner of a farm located at a river boundary, a smuggler, a traveller, a resident alien, a corporate officer or a member of the armed services overseas. Many persons other than government officials will find their conduct circumscribed and determined by the rules of international law. Though those rules may be limited in content, they will nevertheless affect the legal relations of many individuals.[83]

Stated as precisely as possible, international law consists of those rules which limit the sphere of action or prescribe the manner of performance of authoritative roles of a state in international situations, that is, situations in which decision making is perceived to be affected by the fact that other actors therein are the occupants of authoritative roles in, or members of, another state, or that territory or property involved appertains to another state or its members. The selection and characterization of such situations and the determination of the content of such rules are determined by the methodology called public international law. That methodology, in turn, is the art called the study of international law, developed in the great Western universities and in the foreign offices of states.

The wellspring for the rules of international law is found in the practice of state officials in the situations described above. Such officials, at the outset of the norm-creating process, determine the content of the norms by which they shall be governed. The perspective from which they view the creation of such norms is their post in handling problems arising out of interstate relations. The rules of international law which accordingly result are simply those rules which state officials *value* for the stabilization of interstate relations and the preservation of the decentralized structure of the international system, in which such system functions for the most part through the subsystems of the several states.

Once the fundamental fact is perceived that international law

---

[83]Carlston, *Law and Structures*, 128-129, 137, 143-145.

simply represents the rules which state officials value as a means for preserving the existing structure of the international system, it can be seen why international law is more concerned with identifying states as actors, defining the territorial boundaries of their sphere of authority, and stating the tolerable limits upon the manner of exercise of their authority, than it is concerned with promoting the integration and viability of the international system as a means for the realization of values by participants therein.

International law, to the degree that it represents the law of the international system, is in the law of peace a body of rules for the most part concerned with (1) identifying states as actors in the international system in the various situations in which conflict concerning such identification appears, such as, subjects of international law, recognition of states and governments, and state succession; (2) marking the territorial sphere in which states shall possess that freedom to exercise authority known as territorial jurisdiction; (3) defining the limits of the exercise of authority at the maritime frontier and upon the high seas; (4) regulating the limits of the exercise of authority by one state, as it prolongs or extends its system of action into the territory of another, and by the latter, as it may assert its authority over such prolongation or extension of, for example, rights and immunities of states and state officials, jurisdiction over nationals abroad, and jurisdiction over aliens and responsibility for the treatment of aliens; and (5) international agreements.

One part of international law is concerned with placing limits on the conduct of state officials (in the broadest sense of the term "officials") as such conduct affects the person and property of foreigners within the territorial jurisdiction of the state. This is known as the law of the responsibility of states. There is an international standard of justice applied by international law to such conduct, which holds that "the treatment of an alien, in order to constitute an international delinquency, should amount to an outrage, to bad faith, to neglect of duty, or to an insufficiency of governmental action so far short of international standards that every reasonable and impartial man would really recognize its insufficiency."[84] In other words, as the international system be-

---

[84]L. F. H. Neer and Pauline Neer (U.S.) *v.* United Mexican States, General Claims Commission, United States and Mexico, 1926, United Nations, 4, *Reports of International Arbitral Awards*, 60, 62.

comes a subsystem of each state and is thereby subjected to the exercise of its territorial sovereignty or authority, international law does not require that it be assured fair, just, or reasonable treatment.

Standards of fairness, justice, or reasonableness are the minimal standards of the legal systems of civilized states. Under international law, as viewed above, the alien is to be accorded protection only against "outrage," "bad faith," or treatment which "every reasonable and impartial man" would concede to be insufficient. This is indeed a pitiful basis for the security of persons and the protection of important expectations in the international system. It is remote from the cultural standards of law and the legal process of civilized nations. Yet it is quite understandably the basis for the adjustment of interstate relations and the resolution of conflict which state officials, as distinguished from individuals, would prefer. Each such official, in his own organizational environment in the state and as a captive of his national social system, seeks to secure the largest possible area of freedom and the minimum of restriction upon the exercise of his authority.

9.e. *Current methodology in international law includes sources of law in addition to the practice of states as postulated by positivism. International law theory should acknowledge this fact, and international law procedure should take further steps toward its orderly development.*

International law theory has not been immune from the developing perspectives of law, its place in the social order, and the nature of the social order, in the twentieth-century philosophy of law. Leon Duguit, writing at the beginning of the twentieth century, found that law arose from the fact of social solidarity. The fact that man lived, and could only live, in society was an inescapable datum from which all law arose and was conditioned. Law was purely objective and had as its function to preserve and promote social solidarity. International law arose from a widespread consciousness of bonds of solidarity uniting citizens of different states.[85] Kelsen's abstract, logical, monistic approach to law may

---

[85]For these various perspectives on international law, see the books included in the bibliography by H. Kelsen, H. B. Jacobini, W. Sauer, E. Sauer, Charles de Visscher, P. E. Corbett, J. L. Brierly, H. Lauterpacht, P. C. Jessup, C. W. Jenks, M. Huber, M. S. McDougal, and articles by J. C. Gidynski, W. Samore, R. Ago, D. Schindler, B. Landheer, J. Stone, and M. S. McDougal.

seem remote from the present context, but his emphasis upon the individual as the central point for focusing legal theory and custom as the *grundnorm* for law gave stimulating new perspectives. Alejandro Alvarez emphasized the political, social, and, above all, the psychological character of international law. In his view, it was based in social interdependence and its function was to further international solidarity. Wilhelm Sauer and Ernst Sauer each have a deep concern over the relation of international law to individual and cultural values. Robert Ago revealed a perceptive awareness of the limitations of a too exclusively positivist or sociological approach to international legal science. Charles de Visscher wrote a brilliant study of the interplay of the rules of international law and the political and social realities of the national and international orders. Percy Corbett adopted a similar approach in an earlier study. James L. Brierly was a jurist who was extraordinarily attuned to social and political realities and displayed a constantly constructive outlook as to the role and limits of law in the international arena. Sir Hersch Lauterpacht exhibited imaginative insights into international law and gave it new perspectives, as does Philip C. Jessup today. C. Wilfred Jenks combined expertise in international administration and law with a broad and humanitarian outlook. The sociological aspects of international law concerned such writers as Max Huber, Dietrich Schindler, B. Landheer, and Julius Stone. Myres McDougal strenuously insisted that the methodology of international law be related to human values and human dignity.

The nineteenth- and early twentieth-century ideal of the man of the law as Justice Holmes's black-letter man of the law books[86] may considerably persist as the mid–twentieth-century ideal of the international law jurist. It still possesses validity in that it is imperative in any legal system that the area of freedom of the judge be small, that is to say, his liberty to extend and develop the law should exhibit a high degree of fidelity to the existing body of jurisprudence. He must not, in his decision, unduly strain logical consistency with the past patterns of the law in order to recognize the changing social patterns and values of the day. Such a role is characteristically that of the legislature. Yet the judge does not

---

[86] O. W. Holmes, Jr., "The Path of the Law," 10 *Harv. L. Rev.* 457, 469 (1897): "For the rational study of the law the black-letter man may be the man of the present, but the man of the future is the man of statistics and the master of economics."

live in isolation from his culture. He is aware of its changing values and ways of life. Unless he reflects that awareness in his decisions, the law and the legal process will become sterile. Similarly, "international law . . . cannot be considered in isolation. Unless continually related to international politics it becomes unreal. Its sources and its sanctions are to be found in the conditions of international relations no less than in its own traditions and institutions. Like any system of law, international law is always in flux between the inertia of past customs and precedents, the pressures of present politics, and the attractions of the ideals of the future. To neglect any of these sources and sanctions is to study a dead system, not a living and growing international law."[87]

The international judge is, under the tenets of positivism, constrained to find his law in the body of custom known as the practice of states. If his decision making should be limited only to proof of the practice of states and he should be denied resort to such evidence of law as judicial decisions, opinions of writers, and other sources of law, such as general principles recognized by civilized nations, it would indeed often be difficult to select a norm for decision which would promote the integration of the international system as a means for realizing values by the participants therein. Should he attempt to create such a norm without fidelity to the proof of law made by counsel, he would be exposed to the charge that he has succumbed to "the almost irresistible tendency shown by arbitration to compromise and split the difference."[88] The judge's sphere of action is marked out by the body of the law. Only in applying rules of law to cases of conflict may he give recognition to issues of policy and values.[89] The clash between legal norms and values, which it is the function of the judge to resolve, has been described elsewhere by the author:

as . . . action affects strongly held values, friction and tension develop. . . . [The parties] perceive the same situation differently and hold differing views as to what action shall be appropriate. . . . Both . . . tend to skewer their perception of a situation of conflict, and the appropriate rule to govern it, in the light of their particular value system. As the

---

[87]Q. Wright, "The Teaching of International Law in the Post-War World," *Proceedings of the Eighth Conference of Teachers of International Law and Related Subjects,* 27 (1946).

[88]W. C. Dennis, "Compromise—The Great Defect of Arbitration," 11 *Colum. L. Rev.* 493, 494 (1911).

[89]See postulate 12 in Carlston, "International Administrative Law," 329, 367.

intensity of attachment by the actors to the values involved in the situation increases, their respective images of the situation and the appropriate rule to govern it become increasingly separated from one another. As the disparity of the views thus held increases, the likelihood of the dispute leaving the domain of law and entering that of politics is enhanced. Hence, the need for law is not only the greatest at that point where disintegration is most likely to occur, but it is here that the need is the greatest for a law applied by a judical organ which is both faithful to the law and aware of the needs and values of the parties. In reconciling the conflicting demands of the parties, the judicial organ must also fix upon those patterns of conduct in the situation which will enable its essential idea to be expressed and its ultimate goal to be achieved.[90]

The growth of a viable culture is stumbling, fumbling, and costly. The findings of the philosopher, who seeks ultimate reality, and of the scientist, who seeks ultimate empirical truth, are only slowly embodied in the social order. The birth of reality from a distant vision of truth is slow and painful in the progress of a people. Yet over the centuries we learn.

It is abundantly clear that progress in the methodology and enlargement of the basic assumptions of international law is necessary. Though it is possible to demonstrate on a logical basis that revolutionary reformation is the ultimate solution, it does not preclude the taking of lesser and more practical steps of growth. There are five steps which the international legal process can take today which would most considerably increase the effectiveness of international law and promote its growth. Each of them is feasible. Two of them are already accepted in the methodology of international law and merely require a wider acceptance or acknowledgment of their existence. The five proposed measures are stated below.

9.e.1. *The international legal process should adopt the procedural requirement of full and adequate fact pleading and proof.*

There was noted above Shabtai Rosenne's observation that the International Court of Justice isolates "the legal problem from the circumstances in which it had its immediate origin," considers "that legal problem is an objective and even abstract way," and reaches its decision "to the exclusion of all political, moral or other extra-legal considerations."[91] It is understood that some members of the court, at least, are concerned over the court's isolation from

---

[90]*Ibid.*, 350-351.
[91]Rosenne, *International Court*, 66.

the full factual background of the cases brought before it and its preoccupation with the abstract consideration of legal issues apart from fact. In any event, international law, no less that any other law, is an organic part of a social system. Its norms arise from the life of the international system. The content of its norms must be directed to making that system a viable and stable means for the realization of the demands and values of the actors participating in it. For the international legal process to cut itself off from the full realities of the world in which it is to function is to make it a sterile and ineffective instrument.

It is elementary in any judicial system that the court has the right to be fully informed of the facts. The exercise of this right is conceived to be essential to the adequate discharge of the judicial function. A court is not of age, a legal system is not matured, and the social system in which they function cannot achieve its full potentialities for the attainment of the goals of its members when the judicial process is denied the ability to require that an adequate proof of the facts of a dispute be made. In the resolution of a dispute, the court must select the rule of law which thereafter will structure social action in similar situations in an appropriate and desired manner. It must for each case find the right or ideal form of social order to which the individual shall be required to adhere. This demands the power to inquire fully into the facts and to require the litigating parties to provide full proof of the facts.

The facts in an international situation of interstate conflict, moreover, are not merely those in which the dispute "had its immediate origin." The international court is in a situation comparable to that of a national tribunal concerned with a constitutional law question in which so-called "fact brief" is often used. The international court is concerned with questions of how the international society shall be constituted, that is, how states shall adapt themselves to the international system. To answer such questions intelligently will often require a careful investigation of questions of international economics, questions of technology, and questions of history. The international court must possess the full power of factual inquiry.

This means that the international judge must be equipped to make those inquiries of fact and to evaluate and weigh those elements of fact upon which a sound decision will rest. The international law counselor of those distant days when the positivist methodology of international law was being created was preferably one seasoned in diplomatic history and in the ways of diplomacy. The realities of statecraft in those days were the niceties of negotiation and the art of international politics. Today's international lawyer, whether he be in the foreign office of the state or the foreign department of an international corporation, is concerned with law as it applies to economic and social problems, as well as to political problems. The practice of international law at the working level is vitally concerned with shaping international law into an effective and reliable instrument in the milieu in which it operates. The international judge should be equally motivated to make international law work. To that end, he should possess a training beyond that of Holmes's "black-letter man."[92] He must be the man of international economics, of history, and of the social sciences, as well as of comparative and international law.

9.e.2. *The international court should exercise a more vigilant control of the written and oral pleadings to insure that the factual and legal issues, which it considers to be germane, shall be fully and adequately developed.*

The traditional attitude of the international court toward the presentation of cases by states as litigants is one of affording them full opportunity to present their statements of fact and law in the manner they desire, so long as they adhere to the formal requirements of time of filing and the orderly presentation of proof of fact and law stipulated by the rules of procedure. The content of the pleading and proof is mostly left to the litigating states.

It is believed that this attitude is undesirable and should be changed. In his authoritative study, *Evidence Before International Tribunals,* Sandifer states: "The settlement of disputes in international law is distinctly a matter of public interest and is not simply in the nature of a private contest between parties. There appears to be no good reason for not recognizing the general public interest in the settlement of international disputes by thus endowing tribunals with power to conduct investigations necessary to in-

---

[92]Holmes, "Path of the Law."

sure that cases submitted to them are decided as nearly on the basis of the facts as is possible."[93]

In the light of the generally recognized power of international tribunals to determine their own rules of procedure, subject to any restrictions imposed by the constitutive agreement or *compromis*, the taking of such a step by an international tribunal on its own motion would involve no excess of jurisdiction or power. The proposed step is reasonable, consistent with general judicial practice, and not likely to cause any adverse repercussions.

9.e.3. *The opinion of the international court should demonstrate the functional appropriateness of the legal norm adopted by it as the basis for decision; that is, the opinion should demonstrate that the legal norm which the court selects as the basis for decision was, in the light of the proof of law made, that norm which would in the situation best promote a structuring of the international system as an effective means for the realization of commonly shared values by participants. Whenever, among the competing legal norms in an international situation of interstate conflict, the court selects as the basis of its decision a legal norm which is not the preferable norm for so integrating the international system, it should demonstrate that the proof of the law clearly required such a decision.*

The above proposal is new to the international legal process. International judicial practice rarely indicates in the written opinion the functional significance of the rule applied. The point of view adopted is simply: what is the law? While the assumption of such a point of view is concededly imperative in any judicial system, it does not exclude, in addition, the appraisal of competing legal norms from the standpoint of their functional appropriateness in the situation out of which the dispute arose. An ideal norm of law in such a situation cannot be stated without considering its operability as a matter of mechanical and value rationality.

As a matter of fact, considerations such as those set forth in the above proposal doubtless do receive attention by many international judges in the course of their reflection on a prospective decision. The provision of a viable order in the international system requires that such a course of reasoning definitely be made a part of decision making by international judges. It is by no means

---

[93]D. V. Sandifer, *Evidence Before International Tribunals,* 109 (1939).

suggested that, in so proceeding, evidence of the law shall be ignored by the international judge. It is only suggested that the *appropriateness* of the legal norm as a governing norm for the situation before the court shall, *among other things,* be considered as a part of the process of adjudication and the written opinion. When the evidence of the law directs the application of an inappropriate norm to an international situation of interstate conflict, it is proposed that the international judge should frankly say so. This is a function of the municipal law judge. When adherence to *stare decisis* leads to a bad result, the judge will deplore the fact and suggest legislation as the remedy. When the application of a rule of international law in a particular situation makes international nonsense or leads to undesirable results from the standpoint of international order, the international judge should frankly acknowledge that fact. He would then discharge his proper judicial function of stimulating action in the political sphere to remedy the defect.

With such a functional orientation of the law-declaring and law-making process in the international system, the growth of international law would be thrust into more constructive channels. International law would thereby be assured that its application and development in international situations of interstate conflict would better conform to reality. The investigation of a problem in international law is just begun when the statement and analysis of the legal doctrine is made in accordance with the shared methodology of positivism. The rule which the international judge reaches from his search of the legal materials cannot be viewed in isolation from its appropriateness as a functional rule and as an embodiment of cultural values and ethical principles. The international judge who looks only at the weight of the evidence of custom in support of competing rules for decision, apart from their suitability for promoting the viability of the international order and the opportunity of its actors to realize their important values by their participation in that order, cuts himself off from the reality of life and the ability to search for the full meaning of truth that is the spirit of our culture.

9.e.4. *The international legal process, in its decision making, should make greater use of the general principles of law recognized by civilized nations.*

9.e.4.a. *The general principles of law recognized by civilized nations provide both a valid criterion for controlling state conduct involving its participation in the international system and a valid source for the further development of international legal norms.*

Sir Hersch Lauterpacht, in his last work and out of his great experience as an international jurist and international judge, made some very discerning remarks which are pertinent to the above proposition. He began by pointing out that the performance of the judicial function constantly extends the body of the law "by means of the fiction that the enunciation of the new rule is no more than an application of an existing legal principle or an interpretation of an existing text." The international court must exercise the "caution and restraint called for by the sovereignty of States and by the voluntary and, therefore, precarious nature of the jurisdiction of international tribunals." At the same time, there is the impelling motive "to supplement and remedy the deficiencies and inconsistencies of an imperfect system of law."[94] Article 38.1.c. of the statute of the court could not be made a universal basis of decision making by the court. Resort to article 38.1.c. was permissible "only if conventional and customary rules of international law provide no solution." Even then, the "overriding rule of presumptive freedom of action of States" must be considered. However:

there is force in the view that in practice the situation is not that of simple absence or simple presence of rules of customary or conventional international law; that in practice these rules are often obscure or controversial; that, as the result, the question is not one of displacing them but interpreting them against the background or in the light of general principles of law; and that the difference between disregarding a rule of international law in deference to a general principle of law and interpreting it (possibly out of existence) in the light of a general principle of law may be but a play on words. These, inconclusive, considerations may help to draw attention to the vast potentialities of that source of the law which the Court is authorized to apply and the application of which must be tempered by the knowledge that the primary—though not the exclusive—function of the Court is the application of the existing law. On the realisation of that fact depends in the last resort the usefulness and the authority of the Court.[95]

In clarifying rules of international law, and in drawing logical

---

[94]H. Lauterpacht, *The Development of International Law by the International Court,* 155 (1958).
[95]*Ibid.,* 165-166.

inferences from and synthesizing parallel developments in different fields of international law, the resort to "general principles of law" as a basis of decision making enables "an expression of socially reliable morality."[96]

Bin Cheng, in his *General Principles of Law as Applied by International Courts and Tribunals,* finds that the Permanent Court of International Justice, the International Court of Justice, and international arbitral tribunals have many times applied such principles as an integral part of international law. He concludes:

These general principles of law fulfill three different functions. First, they constitute the source of various rules of law, which are merely the expression of these principles. Secondly, they form the guiding principles of the juridical order according to which the interpretation and application of the rules of law are oriented. Thirdly, they apply directly to the facts of the case wherever there is no formulated rule governing the matter. In a system like international law, where precisely formulated rules are few, the third function of general principles of law acquires special significance and has contributed greatly towards defining the legal relations between States.[97]

It should be clearly understood that resort to the general principles of law recognized by civilized nations, as a basis for decision making by international courts, should be gradual in its growth and development. As stated before, where there is strong value conflict in an international situation of interstate conflict, the parties in controversy may not be ready to accept a decision based on such evidence of law alone. They may demand that the decision be based on state practice as well as general principles of law. Nevertheless, a continuing awareness and appropriate application by international judges of general principles of law recognized by civilized nations as a source of law would do much to develop the body of international law. In any event, while the international judge may tend to shrink from resting his judgment solely on general principles of law recognized by civilized nations, he is still free to express his opinion on such an issue.

9.e.4.b. *State action as organizational action cannot escape evaluation, though it may escape control, in the light of cultural experience and legal and moral standards. An act which, but for the fact that the state is the performer, would be culturally irrational*

---

[96]*Ibid.,* 172.
[97]B. Cheng, *General Principles of Law as Applied by International Courts and Tribunals,* 390 (1953).

or would violate generally accepted legal or moral standards, still remains subject to evaluation on such bases.

Under the positivist methodology of international law, state action is subjected to normative evaluation on the basis of those rules for the behavior of state officials which spring from the practice of states and which are adhered to by them on the basis that they represent binding or obligatory legal rules. But state action is merely another form, and the most massive form, of organizational action. Organized action cannot escape the domains of rationality, law, and morals. It is at least to be presumed that organized man cannot do that which is reprehensible in man as an individual. Indeed, organized man is often more to be feared as the source of social harm than is man as an individual. Organized man may seek ends and resort to means for himself which the culture condemns. When he does so and strikes at deeply felt values of the culture, the culture responds and condemns.

Whether killing be effected by the mob, by organized crime syndicates, or by the state itself, such as, in the mass-extermination of Jews by Nazi Germany, the culture responds with abhorrence and revulsion, as well as by modes of legal control. Whatever may be said of the judgments of Nuremberg in terms of positivism, it must be conceded that they have validity as a cultural judgment based on profoundly felt beliefs and morals.

It is submitted that the action of man organized in the state is not above evaluation on the basis of rationality, law, and morals. The propriety of a legislative act, as the embodiment of general principles of law of civilized nations, is open to critical cultural evaluation. An act of state may have, at the moment of its occurrence, internal supremacy as the law of the state and a very considerable external authority under private international law. This fact, however, does not remove the act from evaluation on the basis of standards and traditions of the state in question, as previously developed. Nor does it remove the act from evaluation in the light of the cultural standards of the world society. Among these standards may be included the general principles of law of civilized nations.

It would seem that the strong growth of international demands for the protection of human rights is evidence of a current application of the above principle. Another area in which it should be more widely applied is that of the growing entrance by the state into affairs of commerce. Here the principle should be applied that as the state enters the sphere of the *jus gestionis*, it should not escape judgment thereunder by placing its action under the cloak of the *jus imperii*.

With the developed techniques of the comparative law jurist at hand, a case-by-case development and growth of international law through the interplay of its rules with the general principles of law recognized by civilized nations is feasible and desirable. Beyond this, broad research programs "to find and formulate a core of legal ideas which are common to all civilized legal systems" have been suggested.[98]

9.e.4.c. *Order and law in the world society are not to be perceived solely in terms of the structure of the state.*

It is at this point that the ultimate perspective is found from which world society and the problem of the provision of order and the establishment of law therein may be viewed. It is suggested that prior perceptions of order and law have found themselves *within* the compass of the state. The limits of the action of the state have been the horizon of vision. Its hypothesized, but empirically nonexistent, will has been the sole standpoint from which valid law in the world society was deemed to flow.

Action in the international system is not to be viewed solely from the confines and perspectives of separate states. International law as a science must find a world perspective outside and above the state. It must find a basis for the normative evaluation of state conduct beyond its self-created standards. The general principles of law of civilized nations provide the normative standard and source of rules to which state conduct must adhere if it is to possess validity in the light of our cultural experience.

9.e.5. *The international legal process should acknowledge the fact that international judicial and arbitral decisions are in fact today a source of international law.*

---

[98]R. B. Schlesinger, "Research on the General Principles of Law Recognized by Civilized Nations," 51 *Am. J. Int. Law* 735, 739 (1957): "If it were possible to find and formulate a core of legal ideas which are common to all legal systems, the effect might transcend the area of international law (however broadly defined) and of international organizations, and might go far beyond the goal—even though in itself it is an ambitious goal—of implementing Article 38 of the Statutes"; see C. W. Jenks, *The Common Law of Mankind*, 120ff. (1958).

Any practicing international lawyer is aware of the force and persuasiveness of judicial precedent in the argument of an international case and the broad extent of the use of judicial precedent for that purpose. Any international law scholar is aware of the extent to which the Permanent Court of International Justice and the International Court of Justice rely on their written jurisprudence in their decision making. Any reader of the current literature of international law is aware of the extent to which decisions by international courts are cited as proof of the law and with but little, if any, less weight attached to them than to the practice of states. Yet classic positivism ranks "judicial decisions" with "the teachings of the most highly qualified publicists, as subsidiary means for the determination of rules of law."[99] Judicial precedent, it is held, may be evidence of the law, but not a source of law.

This view was challenged and placed within its proper limits by Sir Hersch Lauterpacht:

Decisions of international courts are not a source of international law in that sense [that is, practice of states]. They are not direct evidence of the practice of States or of what States conceive to be the law. International tribunals, when giving a decision on a point of international law, do not necessarily choose between two conflicting views advanced by the parties. They state what the law is. Their decisions are evidence of the existing rule of law. That does not mean that they do not in fact constitute a source of international law. For the distinction between the evidence and the source of many a rule of law is more speculative and less rigid than is commonly supposed.

. . . .

It is of little import whether the pronouncements of the Court are in the nature of evidence or of a source of international law so long as it is clear that in so far as they show what are the rules of international law they are largely identical with it. For what are rules of international law for the purpose of judicial settlement? They are rules which, according to legal opinion, based—among other things—on the study of the work of the Court, the latter will apply. It is to a large extent in this practical aspect of its operation, namely, in the ability of the lawyer to attempt to predict the nature of the decision, that law is a science. This is, of course, not the assertion of the rigid positivist view. For while it must be assumed that the judge will apply existing law, the law thus applied is not the mechanical product of an effortless interpretation of clear manifestations of the will of States. For the reasons stated, previous decisions of the Court are, as a matter both of legal principle and of

---

[99]International Court of Justice, Statute, Art. 38.1.c.

actual experience, one of the enduring factors which influence its future decisions. They are evidence of what the Court considers to be the law; they are a reliable indication of the future attitude of the court; for most practical purposes they show, therefore, what international law is. In fact they are to a substantial degree identical with the sources of law enumerated in the first three paragraphs of Article 38. In form they may be merely a subsidiary means for determining what these sources are. The effect is the same.[100]

10. *The further development of international law requires that states exercise leadership in their adaptation to the international system in such a manner that the system becomes for all states, including underdeveloped nations, a valued means of goal gratification.*

Only the alienated personality of organizational man, only the rationality of the organizational view of life, could tolerate the absurdity of force as a mode of adaptation by states to their external environment. No one state possesses an energy potential which would enable it to dominate its entire external environment by force, except by resort to the anachronistic holocaust of nuclear destruction. The use of energy for domination through force is, in any event, inherently wasteful. The same energy devoted to a constructive adaptation to the external environment, in which interaction with other actors in the international system is employed to attain goals embodying commonly shared values, would vastly transform the character of many national societies. National economies of scarcity would be transformed into economies of relative abundance.

The view of the international system as something to be controlled by dominance, or authority based on power, as something to be exploited as mining exploits the mineral resources of the earth, may be the source of many of our international ills. Leadership in the economic organization has learned that, for the organization to prosper and endure, it must relate its action to the values of the members of its social base. Leadership in the modern state has yet to demonstrate dedication to the principle that a viable international system, in which the state may realize its values on an enduring basis, represents a new and enormous dimension for state growth.

The fifth and sixth principles of this chapter emphasize the

---

[100]Lauterpacht, *Development of International Law*, 20-22.

primacy of leadership and administration in a social system in the determination of the character of its order and law. An international law limited to a law of peace will not emerge until the state system can break out of its prison of organizational rationality, in which the use or threat of use of force is an ingrained element. Cultural or empirical rationality condemning the phenomenon of war is denied recognition by the rationality resulting from the structuring of action in organizations known as states. Leadership in states has its own perspective of reality in the chaos of international politics, in which planning for war becomes inevitable. The exercise of leadership to organize for war means that international law, in the predictive sense indicated by Kelsen that states will behave as they customarily have behaved, is constrained to accept the fact of war.

The opening chapters of this study emphasized the importance of a linkage by states with the economic phase of the international system, which would provide the members of a state with constantly expanding provision for the attainment of their various goals. The United States and the industrialized states of the free world, particularly Western Europe and Canada, have largely achieved such a mode of adaptation to the international system. Their linkages with each other and with the various states of the free world have brought them a space of free movement in which their peoples can find satisfaction in the attainment of the widest variety of goals. They provide for their peoples means for material and spiritual satisfactions on a scale the world has hitherto never witnessed. The integration and adaptation of their social systems have produced stable social orders. For them, a law and legal process in the international system which would provide security of transactions embodies a value of the highest order.

In the chronological present, there are states and societies which exhibit the widest spectrum of social orders and posts in cultural time. The industrially organized, democratically structured states, of which the United States and the states of Western Europe are examples, achieved their social orders over the centuries. The clan-structured tribal society was supplanted by the role-structured feudal society. This in turn was superseded by the organized nation-state and the corporate structure of social action. The loyalties to the chief and the lord were replaced by the loyalty to the impersonal entity of the state and the corporate organization. An

African state still largely at the tribal stage, a Middle Eastern state at a curiously composite state of tribal-feudal-corporate structure, a Middle American state at that point described in Chapter IV, are today all faced with the same problem. How can they achieve in decades a cultural growth which the states mentioned in the preceding paragraph took centuries to accomplish? How can planning and the intelligent use of the experience and intellectual resources provided by the maturely developed states enable underdeveloped nations to reach a similar point in cultural time tomorrow?

The free world is an economic entity. No state, not even a largely tribal-structured African state, can cut itself off from participation in the economy of the international system without grievous wound. To a considerable extent, the free world shares common values and common perspectives. There is a preference for democratically structured governments with a recognition of the interests of all classes and groups and a paramountcy of none. There is an interest in egalitarianism in the political, economic, and cultural life. There is an interest in recognizing, in a steadily increasing measure, the aspirations of all members of the society. There is a considerable sharing of a common, historically derived culture, including its traditions.

Those states which have progressed the farthest along the path described above, those states whose independence, growth, and economics depend critically upon the persistence of a free world and *of access to a free world,* have a profound interest that those states which are laggard in cultural time shall follow the same path. If the industrially organized, democratically structured states of the free world desire an international law protecting the realization of their basic values, they should exercise leadership in the international arena in a manner whereby the underdeveloped nations will also find that a realization of their values is promoted by participation in the international system. The industrially organized states of the free world should be committed to a policy of encouraging the growth of underdeveloped nations *in a pattern of evolutionary development to a social system in which there is a broad diffusion among its members of control over the direction of political authority and a widespread participation by its members in action directed toward the realization of their values.* It should be a central policy of the United States, for example, to take such action as will promote the progress of underdeveloped nations to industrially organized nations by following *the path of evolutionary development of a democratically structured state.* The United States, in addition, has a particular interest in following the above policy with respect to those nations whose mineral resources are critical to its economy and the economies of the free world.

The Massachusetts Institute of Technology Center for International Studies made a study for the Committee on Foreign Relations of the United States Senate, which should be read in full in this connection, and in which the following perceptive statement is made:

A gradual consensus appears to be developing in this country as to the American interest in the course taken by the transitional societies. It is our interest to see emerge out of the transition processes nation states which—

1. Maintain effective independence, especially of powers hostile or potentially hostile to the United States.

2. Do not resort to violence in their relations with other states. The development of modern weapons has made the outbreak of violence anywhere in the world exceedingly dangerous for all nations, especially because of the opportunities it opens for intervention by Communist or other extremist powers.

3. Maintain effective and orderly government internally without resort to totalitarian controls. The effort to impose rigid controls is likely to produce tensions within a society which cannot indefinitely be contained. If internal conflict erupts, intervention by an outside power and the consequent spread of violence become a serious threat. Our interest therefore lies in the emergence of institutions for the wielding and transfer of power by consent of major groups; this is essentially what we mean by the creation of "democratic" forms of government.

4. Are capable of progressively meeting the aspirations of all major classes of their people. This is a condition which must be met if the first three objectives are to have much chance of realization.

5. Are willing to cooperate in those measures of international economic, political, and social control necessary to the functioning of an interdependent world community.

6. Accept the principles of an open society whose members are encouraged to exchange ideas, goods, values, and experience with the rest of the world.[101]

---

[101]U.S. Senate, Committee on Foreign Relations, *Economic, Social and Political Change in the Underdeveloped Countries and Its Implications for United States Policy,* 86th Cong., 2nd Sess., Committee Print 12, March 30, 1960, 10.

As noted in Chapter IV, many underdeveloped nations are at a point in which, in their search for a larger measure of realization of their aspirations, a most uneasy political equilibrium exists. Sometimes the pressures of the submerged groups are held in momentary check by authoritarian regimes based on force and xenophobia. There is for such groups and even for many of the intellectuals a powerful attraction in the simple Communist model of revolution, expropriation, and authoritarian control in the interest of the proletariat. The harsh realities beyond the promises of the model are overlooked in view of the emptiness of the existing social and political order. As Michael Ionides says in this connection: "The idea that there is some short cut by which capital investment from outside, paid for by other people, can be injected into the economic body, causing it to spring painlessly into prosperous, productive life is nonsense. The challenge is to the people themselves."[102]

If the United States and the states of the free world wish to create an environment in which there will be evolutionary progress by underdeveloped nations to those patterns of life characteristic of the modern welfare state organized on democratic lines, certain consequences for their foreign policy seem clear. The extension to underdeveloped nations of assistance toward economic growth, or foreign aid, will have to recognize these principles:

10.a. *Foreign aid should be extended by industrialized states of the free world to an underdeveloped nation in such a manner as to contribute to the emergence of a democratically structured society.*

The United States has quite properly adopted the policy of nonintervention in the administration of its foreign aid program. Charles Bohlen succinctly stated our policy to be as follows in this respect: "while political considerations of course play a part in the allocation of our foreign aid, we have not sought to dictate to any country how it should conduct its foreign or domestic policies."[103] The principle of nonintervention is not violated, however, if the donor, in the exercise of its own judgment in the disposition of its own intellectual and physical resources, should lay down the above-stated policy as an overriding criterion for

---

[102]See M. Ionides, "Technical Aid: The Role of the West," 35 *International Affairs* 151, 156 (1959).

[103]C. E. Bohlen, "Economic Assistance in Foreign Policy," 42 Dept. of State Bulletin 495, 499 (March 28, 1960).

the extension of foreign aid. While no state should "dictate to any country how it should conduct its foreign or domestic policies," certainly the use of foreign aid pursuant to domestic policy is a matter of concern to the donor state. Unless the recipient of the aid possessed, or could find, a basis of mutual interest in the above-stated policy, aid would not be then forthcoming. When, however, donor and recipient nations possess, at least in some degree, a common interest in evolutionary progress toward a democratically structured society, they should be able to arrive at a common basis as to the manner of extension of foreign aid without a suggestion of intervention by the country extending such aid.

10.b. *The mode of foreign aid should be determined for each recipient country in the light of the above objective and should be continually reassessed as its impact affects the achievement of the above objective.*

In Chapter IV a considerable degree of similarity in the social and political structures of several underdeveloped nations was found to exist. In the Massachusetts Institute of Technology study cited above, three fairly typical stages of modernization by states were discerned: (1) the traditionalist oligarchies, (2) the modernizing oligarchies, and (3) the potentially democratic societies.[104] While such orderings of data are most useful for analytical, methodological, and administrative purposes, it must be realized that above everything else each country is a unique entity. It has its own history, traditions, symbols, culture, value system, and social structure. Its value system, while susceptible to considerable generalization, is in considerable measure a reflection or composite of the values of its various groups and classes. Its culture breaks up into subcultures of regions, groups, and classes. Hence foreign aid cannot be routinized or administered on universal patterns. It must be administered with a close awareness of the social and political realities of each particular country. Otherwise, it may set in motion or accelerate the impact of forces which could lead to Communist regimes.

10.c. *Foreign aid must be related to the realization of valued goals by all groups in the recipient country and with a particular*

---

[104]Committee on Foreign Relations, *Economic, Social and Political Change,* 35-40.

*awareness of the demands and values of large submerged groups;
that is, foreign aid must be directed to promoting stable integration
of the social system of the recipient country.*

Foreign aid by an industrially organized country typically takes
those forms which are most convenient for its structures of action
to accomplish. The determination of the content of foreign aid
at the government-to-government level and the preoccupation of
decision making with the organizational structure as a mode of
action means that the West characteristically adopts massive programs of foreign aid which leave largely untouched the social
structures of the recipient countries. Road and railway development, communication facilities, public utilities, electrical plants,
water works, harbor development, industrial plants, and similar projects take up the great bulk of foreign aid by industrially
organized states. These are also the projects which the government
and élite of an underdeveloped nation seek, as well as those which
it is convenient for the industrially organized donor to provide.
Yet their position leaves largely untouched the position of the
submerged peasant and industrial worker. Their provision leaves
unsatisfied the explosive demands of such groups for health, education, and other opportunities for realization of important values,
including political power. Unless foreign aid is related to the
integration of these groups in the social system of the recipient
state on a viable basis, there is considerable likelihood that recipient
countries will go the direction of Iraq and Cuba.

Iraq is a remarkable but tragic example of the consequences of
the misdirection of foreign aid and internal growth by an underdeveloped nation. With an unusual degree of probity in its leaders,
as compared with much of the Middle East milieu, vast sums from
its oil revenues were spent in public projects of the nature described in the preceding paragraph. Iraq was thought to be a
stable bastion of the West. The neglect of the village community,
the failure to make provision for the industrial worker in the squalid
alleys of the city, among other things, led to a social and political
revolution that has not yet found its order and equilibrium. Foreign
aid, therefore, must not leave the agricultural and industrial worker
without hope of change. It must not leave them with their outlook
unimpaired that however things change, their fate remains the
same.

In this respect, the Soviet counterpart of foreign aid is more realistic than our own. It works at all levels of society and with all appropriate means to bring underdeveloped nations to an acceptance of its philosophy. Its resort to what is termed subversion is simply the adoption of procedures which are related to the individual as the ultimate determinant of the political and social structure of a nation. The processes of subversion work to create a foundation in which the emergence of the Communist structure of leadership and administration becomes inevitable.

Michael Ionides made very pointed remarks concerning the nature of the needs of underdeveloped nations and the inappropriateness of Western ways to provide means for their satisfaction:

Western-inspired ideas of industrialization also miss some vital needs. If you go into the hut or cottage of any peasant in these countries, you will find that most of the things to be seen there are locally made "industrial" products—the hut or cottage itself, the woodwork and furniture (if any), the food, much of the clothing, leather work, etc. They are "manufactures" in the original, literal sense of the word. To the extent that the standard of living depends on these things, improvement means that they should be made better and be more plentiful. This leads straight to a whole range of "industries" which already exist and are capable of improvement. Building and building materials, food processing, animal products of all kinds, leather, weaving and dyeing, the work of the blacksmith, the tinsmith, the electrician, motor repairs, plumbing—all these are industrial processes. Only for a tiny minority can these needs be satisfied by imports from abroad. Many of them are inherently "local" in the sense that the industrial process belongs naturally to the local town or village rather than to large, centralized industrial units.

This is simply a matter of observation. It is "industrialization," or a part of it, but our thinking, governed by what our institutions of finance, commerce, and technical services are designed to do, has not so far taken this great sphere of need into account. Our system works best, in underdeveloped countries, on industrial "projects" large enough to carry the cost of technical investigation, and to be catered for by our financial institutions. The emphasis naturally goes where our system works best.

In our own more advanced countries, the system also meets the needs of small-scale industrial activities. The small man in a provincial town knows how to go about it, and can easily find out from people and agencies around him. The apparatus of finance, administration, law, technicalities, supply of plant, labour, the markets is all geared in, evolved in tune with industrialization over the generations. But in the underdeveloped countries it is not so. A local man has to be something of a pioneer; he is working beyond the boundary of what Western-style institutions are designed to do best. That is what being underdeveloped means.[105]

---

[105]Ionides, "Technical Aid," 156-157.

In short, foreign aid by the industrially organized, democratically structured states of the free world has largely been extended by organizations to organizations through organizationally structured action. It has typically eventuated in changes in the physical endowments of the recipient national society. It has changed the physical character of an underdeveloped nation by providing it with a system of roads, bridges, utilities, sanitation facilities, and the like. It has left largely untouched, and to a considerable extent intentionally so, the social and political character of the underdeveloped nation. When it ignores such matters, foreign aid will likely set in motion, or accelerate the motion of, internal forces which will be more dedicated to the destruction of the existing social and political structures than to their preservation.

The United States recently revealed an awareness of the fact that foreign aid must be related to the goals and values of neglected groups in underdeveloped nations. In the revised program for foreign aid to Latin America announced July 11, 1960, President Eisenhower spoke of the need of directing the common efforts of donor and recipient nations "to improving the opportunities of the bulk of the population to share in and contribute to an expanding national product."[106] This point of view reached fruition in the Act of Bogotá, adopted September 13, 1960, by the Special Committee of the Council of the Organization of American States to Study the Formulation of New Measures of Economic Cooperation (Committee of 21). The act looks forward to measures for social improvement and the creation of a special fund for social improvement, as well as measures for economic development. Its preamble recognizes that "the preservation and strengthening of free and democratic institutions in the American republics requires the acceleration of social and economic progress in Latin America adequate to meet the legitimate aspirations of the peoples of the Americas for a better life and to provide them the fullest opportunity to improve their status." The contemplated measures for social improvement fall in the categories of the improvement of conditions of rural living and land use, housing and communication facilities, educational systems and training facilities and public health.[107]

The administration of President Kennedy is developing the above

[106]*The New York Times*, July 12, 1960, p. 6, col. 3.
[107]Act of Bogotá, 43 Dept. of State Bulletin 537 (Oct. 3, 1960).

philosophy into an administrative reality in the concept of the Alliance for Progress and the Charter of Punta del Este.

10.d. *The above principles for the extension of foreign aid must be administered on a coordinated basis by all instruments of policy.*

This proposition is a reaffirmation of the fundamental principle that any action to be effective must be organized and coordinated. In the above-cited Massachusetts Institute of Technology study, the point is made as follows:

> Another central proposition of this study is that modernization is a dynamic process which takes place through the interaction of the economic, political, social, and psychological aspects of a society. Several important implications for policy follow from this proposition.
> First, an American policy designed to have the maximum constructive influence on the course of modernization must bring together in a coordinated way all the instruments of policy—diplomatic, economic, military, and informational. In our view, the coordination of these instruments is often wholly inadequate, both in Washington and abroad.[108]

This proposition also applies at the international level. New organizations for foreign aid are not needed as much as the coordination of existing institutions. There is, however, one direction which international cooperation can take which would be of extraordinary importance in the relations of the industrially organized states with the underdeveloped nations. Attention was called in Chapters III and IV to the emphasis in their economies upon the production of one or two basic commodities for export and sale on the international commodity markets. The inadequacy of price behavior in such markets to provide a basis for planning and growth in producer countries was also noted above. The international system does not provide, at this most crucial point in international relations, a basis upon which producer countries can establish satisfactory ways for realizing their important values. The fluctuations of price in the international commodity markets are also of concern to consumer countries.

It is accordingly most important that there shall be international study of this question and formulation of methods of dealing with it. The United States should be particularly sympathetic to the plight of producer countries, for it also has to face this problem in its internal economy.

---

[108]Committee on Foreign Relations, *Economic, Social and Political Change,* 71.

It is by exercising leadership in directions such as are suggested above that the industrially organized, democratically structured states will lay a foundation for the widespread growth among states, generally, of the value of promoting the integration and viability of the international system. The existence of such a value among the participants in the international system is a necessary condition for the growth of legal norms protecting the security of transactions in the international arena.

10.e. *The extension of technical assistance to underdeveloped nations is a necessary and proper function of international organization.*

The foregoing principles are applicable to the bilateral extension of foreign aid to underdeveloped nations by individual states in the free world. Beyond this, there is a consensus among members of the United Nations that the extension of technical assistance and financial support for the modernizing process is a proper function for the organization. An orderly and peaceful international system is dependent upon the stability of action of its members. Unless participation in the action of the United Nations by underdeveloped nations can bring to these nations, which are its members, a sense of progress toward the attainment of desired goals, including economic and social progress, the United Nations will not realize to the fullest possible extent its integrating function in the international system. There is accordingly an interest in all members of the United Nations to make contributions to funds to be used for technical assistance to underdeveloped nations. The previous principles and propositions concerning the extension of foreign aid by individual, industrially organized states of the free world should be complemented by an adherence to this principle as well.

11. *The modes of adaptation by "veneer" states to the international system will be a future important source of tension in interstate relations. Planning to meet the problems thereby created, as well as other problems which leadership in a state will encounter, should be institutionalized in a body independent from, but also linked with, the government of a state. The effectuation of policies adopted by leadership to meet such problems should be facilitated by the maximum utilization of communication.*

It is the purpose of the above proposition to indicate some of the implications of proposition 10, as well as those in Chapter IV. The remarks at this point are of highly conjectural character and are offered simply as a stimulus to further thought.

It is suggested that the problems of the West-East relationships and the North-South relationships in today's international politics are essentially phases of the same problem, that is, the problem of the modernizing state as its policies affect the international system. Such a state has been termed a "veneer" state, having a surface veneer of development which presents to the world the outward aspect of a viable, modern society. The underlying fact is, however, that such a state will typically possess a populace of which as much as 90 per cent is illiterate and 75 per cent is engaged in agriculture. It may possess a few industrialized cities, but the larger part of its people are found in primitive agricultural villages. A long period of its independence as a state is not probative of its viability.

Indeed, as one stands within the region of the United States, Canada, and the states of Western Europe, which for the sake of convenience will be called the "Atlantic Community," and looks out upon a world of Asia, Africa, and Latin America, a world of states is seen which are living today in various stages of the cultural past, but which have a common aspiration to economic growth and modernization.

The nature of the international problems of the Atlantic Community is very largely miscast when it is viewed to present problems of expanding Communist power, constituting a direct and immediate threat to the territory of the community and a source of the subversion of its peoples. Generally speaking, the states of the community are now stable and viable states. Their internal integration and modes of external adaptation have provided them with stable social systems. Their stability, however, rests upon an irreversible commitment to the international system and an increasingly important value in the security of their linkages with the international system.

Although the Soviet still remains in the modernizing stage, the Soviet system has nevertheless achieved a considerable degree of integration.

For the peoples of underdeveloped nations, however, the Communist ideology of revolution, expropriation, and authoritarian control of the means of production, as well as all other aspects of state life, has a strong attraction. It is viewed as a quick means to provide those social, economic, and political advantages which state control by a landowning oligarchy denies them. The fact that the philosophy of action in the Communist state is dedication to the goals of the Communist party is overlooked.[109]

The current debate in the United Nations concerning the question of the permanent sovereignty of peoples and nations over their natural wealth and resources represents the use of the United Nations as a forum to find bases of adjustment between competing philosophies of modernization, as well as a basis for the expounding of such philosophies.[110] The underlying patterns in such debates are found in (1) the concern of the states of the Atlantic Community for the preservation of a stable international system under law and adherence to evolutionary growth along democratic lines, (2) the concern of underdeveloped nations over problems created by the participation of foreign investment in their internal, distorted, and unstable social and political orders, and (3) the appeal to underdeveloped nations of a Communist ideology as a means for economic growth. The debate evidences the imperative need for the exercise by the states of the Atlantic Community of the political function of leadership to create a type of economic order in the international system which will be meaningful to, and valued by, underdeveloped nations as well as developed nations. Only through the exercise of such leadership to create such an order in

---

[109]"The leader [in the Soviet system] is not considered to be an executive for a people which has expressed its choice of policies after full debate invigorated by the existence of separate parties, or separate factions in those areas when history has created but a single effective party. The Soviet leader is conceived as being the enunciator to the people of policies which he and his colleagues think beneficial out of long study of Marxism and Soviet development.

"It seems likely that it is this difference in attitude toward the relationship between the leaders and their public that has set apart the Soviet system from that of the West, and not the existence of different economies. There are welfare states in the West and in Asia which consider themselves socialist, yet they maintain their faith in the people as the source of policy." J. N. Hazard, "The General Principles of Law," 52 *Am. J. Int. Law* 96 (1958).

[110]United Nations Commission on Permanent Sovereignty over Natural Resources, *Historical Summary of Discussions Relating to the Question of Permanent Sovereignty of Peoples and Nations over Their Natural Wealth and Resources,* U.N. Doc. A/AC.97/1, May 12, 1959; United Nations Commission on Permanent Sovereignty over National Resources, *The Status of Permanent Sovereignty over National Wealth and Resources, Preliminary Study by the Secretariat,* U.N. Doc. A/AC.97/5, Dec. 15, 1959.

the international system will an international law emerge which will provide the states of the Atlantic Community with the security they desire (see proposition 10 above).

Whereas yesterday the modernizing states of Western Europe faced the problem of external political domination, today the underdeveloped nations face the problem of breaking free from the captivity of an inappropriate political, social, and economic order and arriving at a more satisfactory linkage with the international system. The states of the Atlantic Community must find a means whereby adherence to evolutionary growth on democratic lines will provide the underdeveloped nations with a genuine opportunity to solve their problems and achieve the goals of their citizenry and whereby the image of that means can be clearly expressed. They must communicate that image and the possibility of its becoming a reality to the peoples of the underdeveloped nations. Unless they do so, they will find that acceptance of the Communist ideology and resort to the Communist formula for growth will become a characteristic pattern of state order for the underdeveloped nation or veneer state. They will find that outside the Atlantic Community their own pattern of political and economic order will be largely absent. Planned economies, in which the economic sphere is subjected to the control of the political institutions, will be prevalent. Where states of the community were once free to trade for needed minerals and other commodities on the international markets, they will then be compelled to use political negotiation with states of a hostile orientation to acquire such commodities. They will no longer be assured stable and inviolate foundations for their national power and welfare. Those foundations will become considerably the captive of Communist-directed or Communist-oriented national societies.

The Atlantic Community is fundamentally committed to the continuance of the international system and to achieving unity in the diversity of states. It is fundamentally committed to an international system composed of independent, democratically structured states. The preservation of the identities of its several members and of the system of interstate relations and law based thereon is, for the Community, the prime value of life. For the Communist party, however, the elimination of the autonomous state and the world-wide ascendancy of the Communist party to authority over all social action is the prime value of life.

The implications for action in the international system of this central fact of international life are the first concern of leadership in the states of the Atlantic Community. Planning to meet the conflicts and tensions which will be created by the clash of these fundamental values should, among other things, be institutionalized in some body which will possess an authority based on the respect and prestige accorded its members generally in the state. To confine the consideration of such problems in executive or administrative departments, governmental councils, committees, and commissions typically means that the view of truth which emerges is administratively and politically colored.

It is believed that planning for the exercise of the leadership function in the state must be institutionalized in some body which will make such planning its first and continuing concern. It is believed that this body must possess its own purity, integrity, and independence. Autonomy to discharge its function is as important for it as independence of the judicial organ is for the discharge of the judicial function. Its search for and statement of truth must be free. It must be empirically based. The conditions for such a body could be met in the creation of an institute or center of scholars for foreign policy studies. Such an institute should be established on a basis whereby it will have a magnitude of prestige, derived from the respect generally accorded the intellectual authority and responsibility of its members, comparable to that of the Institute for Advanced Studies at Princeton, New Jersey. The authority of its conclusions in the state would flow from its recognized competency and prestige.

Such an institute could not effectively function unless its members were accorded substantially complete access to governmental information and findings. Truth in the worlds of politics and economics cannot fully be reached without access to the special information possessed by governmental agencies and departments. Its full measure cannot be known unless there is access to governmental files and records and to discussion with policy-making and other governmental officials. Moreover, such sources of information would provide a contact with reality for policy planning which exclusive reliance on published data cannot provide. Continuing liaison with the government, but freedom from governmental control and support, must be a second characteristic of the planning and research body.

In addition to the continuing and responsible planning of policy for leadership in the state, there must also be full communication in the state of the conclusions and plans of leadership when they are formulated. The strength and purpose of the totalitarian society is considerably based on the extent to which policy is communicated by its leaders to its members. It is not suggested that the content of communication in the democratic state should become the captive of a distorted truth shaped on policy instead of fact. This study has elsewhere insisted on the importance in social action of preserving the integrity of channels of communication in a social system (Chapter V, 13.d.; Chapter VI, 8.c.). It is only suggested that, together with respect for truth in communication, there must be a far greater use of communication by those occupying leadership roles in the democratically structured state. The validity of the conclusions of leadership must be tested by their communication to the forums of free thought and expression. Only in such a manner can the foundations for great leadership be laid. Only in such a manner can sound policies be developed and effectively carried out. Only in such a manner can great leadership find that support by followers which is necessary to make its call for action a reality.

THE IMPACT OF
NATIONALIZATION UPON
CONCESSION AGREEMENTS

Note on the methodology employed in this chapter.
It was said in the introduction that consideration of the international impact of nationalization promised new bases and insights for a statement of a theory of law and organization in world society and a crucible for testing such a theory. The source of that promise lies in the fact that the impact of nationalization upon the international system creates international situations of interstate conflict characterized by a diversity of perceptions, attitudes, and values on the part of the actors. The discernment of the province of law therein, the separation of the political aspects of the situation from its legal aspects, the appraisal of the value and functional significance of the competing legal norms involved, and the consideration of the other aspects of arriving at the appropriate legal norm to control such a situation of conflict are here subjected to such stresses that the statement of theory consequent upon such a testing procedure is much more likely to be complete and accurate in its content than one not so tested. Such a statement of theory is also likely to develop principles and propositions which will escape broad empirical observation and classification. In other words, that

point has been reached in this statement of theory where its application to a concrete case or situation may bring about a restatement of previous hypotheses, or further clarification, elaboration, or unfoldment of prior principles and propositions.

Thus the chapter will contain new principles or propositions of a general character, as well as those directly concerned with the problem at hand. Those of the former category will have varying degrees of direct application to nationalization. The principles and propositions set forth below are those which come to fore as, in the light of the statement of theory made above, the concrete problem is considered of control embodied in the termination of a concession agreement effected as a consequence of an act of nationalization.

1. *An international situation of interstate conflict enters the sphere of law and the legal process only to the degree that action therein falls within the compass of a legal norm.*

It is most important to realize at the outset that, in embarking upon the legal analysis of the problem which is the topic of this chapter, an exploration is being undertaken of the problem of the statement of law in a system where consensus to values formerly manifested by states as actors in the system is now disintegrating. States as actors in the international system are no longer principally cast in the Western European mold. They represent an increasing diversity of maturity, outlook, and values. The positivist methodology of international law developed in an earlier and different world society, characterized by relatively few important states and by very considerable sharing of values relating to their interaction in the world society. It must now be amplified, as well as rendered more precise, in order that it may be appropriate to a later and vastly more complex world society, characterized by a considerably greater number of states as actors and a diversity of their values, together with actors other than states.

The principle that an international dispute falls within the sphere of law only to the degree that it is encompassed by a legal norm begins the discussion. This is indeed quite simple, almost absurdly so. Yet it must be stated, and stated with emphasis. Many persons are often too prone to approach the solution of an international dispute from the standpoint of law and the legal process, faced as we are by the fact that there is only a most germinal form of an international legislature and administration in the United Nations. To cast international disputes characteristically in terms of law and the legal process is to impose upon them burdens and responsibilities that are not properly theirs. The point might be made clearer if the above principle were rephrased in somewhat greater detail: *In an international situation of interstate conflict characterized by a diversity of perceptions, attitudes, and values of its actors, it is seen that the determination of a governing legal norm requires a clear separation of those factors in the situation which are political in nature from those that fall in the sphere of law and the legal process.*

The term political is used, as opposed to the sphere of law and the legal process, to indicate those aspects of a situation which become the concern of leadership and administration. It was previously stated that the conditions in which the international system (that is, interactions transcending state borders) functions are such as to deny it the opportunity to establish and control its own order as an independent system of action and to deny in substantial measure the opportunity of its actors to realize their important values by participation therein (Chapter VI, 8). It was also stated that the provision of order in a social system is not the function of law and the legal process alone but is also the function of leadership and administration (Chapter VI, 5). Our concern with the failure of the international system to be all that we as individuals, or states as actors, might desire it to be must not lead us to impose upon law and the legal process burdens that are properly within the political sphere or the responsibility of negotiation and agreement among states.

The definition of the term "political" may be put as follows: *As the priority of, and intensity of attachment to, competing values by actors in a conflict situation increases and the number of such actors in the society also increases, the likelihood of the categorization of the situation as one of a political, rather than a legal, nature will increase.* Stated somewhat more simply: *When conflict in a society involves competing group demands based on incompatible values held by such groups, its resolution is typically the task of the political rather than the legal process.* By way of illustration, the social conflict in the segregation problem in the United States is not one that should be left solely to the legal process and the courts. It also, and primarily, requires the energetic and thoughtful exercise of the political functions of leadership and administration, as embodied in the legislature and the executive branch of government. The variety of approaches open to the legislature and the executive, as compared with the judiciary, enables their attack upon such a social problem to deal directly and flexibly with its causes and manifestations. The judiciary, on the other hand, must solve problems of human conduct by using the simple dichotomy of obligation and privilege.

The sphere of law and the legal process is the control of social action. The resolution of conflict therein is usually restricted to two actors, the moving party and the defendant. Law and the legal process regulate deviant action toward an ideal norm of behavior (Chapter VI, 3) which embodies shared values of the members of a social system (Chapter VI, 4). The statement of the ideal norm by the judge or legal scholar is confined to the accumulated social experience represented by the body of the law. The freedom of the scholar or the judge to state a dispute in terms of a governing legal principle is limited by the necessity of a rational application of the approved legal methodology to the approved evidence of law. Fidelity to their discipline or their craft, respectively, restrict the *creative* aspects of their thought or decision making to the selection, from the evidence of law, of such rules of law as are rationally relevant according to the received principles of their methodology.

As the scholar examines the practice of states in the search for an international law norm applicable to an international dispute, he has two tasks, among others, before him. First, in the examination and weighing of the evidence of the practice of states bearing on a possible legal norm, he must exclude political influences and considerations, because he is searching for a rule which the participants in the international system will accept as an ideal norm of a *legal* nature. This is a norm which they will acknowledge, in the light of the evidence, to be an existing rule in the body of the law. It is a rule which, evidenced by the past practice of states, can fairly be considered binding upon the parties. The remarks of the International Court of Justice in the *Asylum* case are most illuminating at this point:

The facts brought to the knowledge of the Court disclose so much uncertainty and contradiction, so much fluctuation and discrepancy in the exercise of diplomatic asylum and in the official views expressed on various occasions, there has been so much inconsistency in the rapid succession of conventions on asylum, ratified by some States and rejected by others, *and the practice had been so much influenced by considerations of political expediency in the various cases, that it is not possible to discern in all this any constant and uniform usage, accepted as law,* with regard to the alleged rule of unilateral and definitive qualification of the offense.[1] (Italics supplied.)

In other words, the scholar's search for customary rules of international law must be a search for "constant and uniform usage, accepted as law," not "influenced by considerations of political expediency." The political motivations influencing state conduct must be separated from the legal in his search for rules of law based on state practice.

Second, after he has determined the content of a legal norm based on the practice of states by faithful adherence to the established methodology of positivism, he must be sure that he limits the applicability of the legal norm thus framed to those aspects of the international dispute which fall within it.

The foregoing principles of methodology frequently represent an ideal to which scholars aspire, but which is difficult to realize in practice. As Judge Lauterpacht said:

For, once we approach at close quarters practically any branch of international law, we are driven, amidst some feeling of incredulity, to the conclusion that although there is as a rule a consensus of opinion on broad principle—even though this may be an overestimate in some cases—there is no semblance of agreement in relation to specific rules and problems. . . .
The fact, which is both quieting and chastening, speaks for itself. There is, upon reflection, nothing astonishing about it. How could it be otherwise in a society in which there is no legislative activity in the accepted sense and in which custom is slow of growth and controversial in interpretation and application?[2]

Any international lawyer will testify to the lack of certainty as to a governing legal norm, from the standpoint of the logical weighing of the evidence of law and the prediction of judicial decision based thereon, in any concrete international dispute falling in the domain of international law.

---

[1]Columbian–Peruvian Asylum Case, Judgment of Nov. 20, 1950, I.C.J. Reports 1950, 266 at 277.
[2]H. Lauterpacht, "Codification and Development of International Law," 49 *Am. J. Int. Law* 16, 17-19 (1955).

Thus the formulation of a governing legal norm for an international situation of interstate conflict is a demanding task, even in terms of classic positivism, which restricts the search for general rules of law to the practice of states. It must be added that the statement of a governing legal norm for an international dispute, in the light of the current conditions in the international system and development of the methodology of international law, requires that due consideration be given to the established, as well as the proposed, bases for decision making set forth in principle 9 of Chapter VI, as well as in the principles and propositions concerning methodology outlined in this chapter.

2. *Although an international situation of interstate conflict may fall within the sphere of law and the legal process pursuant to proposition 1, it may not be susceptible to resolution through the legal process because of the strength of the value attachments of the actors involved in such a situation.*

When one moves into the domain of law and the legal process, he does not leave all questions of value behind. Quite the contrary, the law is profoundly a product of human values. The search for and statement of governing legal norms is a search for values, as embodied in legal norms, which are to be given priority in situations of interstate or individual conflict (see Chapter VI, 4). The positivist who searches for law abstractly, apart from value considerations, pursues a vain task. Law and human values are bound together in a single entity; we may close our eyes to questions of value but we can never escape them.

The international system presents a situation in the control of human behavior not found in any social system characterized by the presence of law and the legal process. It has rules of law but relatively little jurisdiction in courts to apply and enforce those rules. Only to the degree that states have agreed to accept the compulsory jurisdiction of the International Court of Justice or to arbitrate their future disputes is there any established jurisdiction over parties and subject matter by an international court. Thus, internationally, there is law without jurisdiction. Moreover, in the degree that there is an increase in intensity of attachment to the conflicting values involved in an international dispute on the part of the states in such a dispute, the likelihood of resort to the legal process for the solution of their dispute will diminish. This is particularly true when there is considerable disparity in the power position of such actors or in their attachment to the value of the orderly solution of international controversy. Such a dispute is far more likely to be handled by the process of diplomatic negotiation. Indeed, the value conflict between the parties may be so intense that the dispute cannot even enter the sphere of peaceable discussion and negotiation.

This is precisely the situation in international disputes arising out of nationalization. The injured state is typically denied recourse to force, even to establish jurisdiction in an international court to adjudicate the dispute. Iran and Egypt both successfully evaded international adjudication of the legality of their respective nationalizations. The position of the United States in the expropriation involved in the *Interhandel* case is not one to which it can point with pride, as representative of a zealous adherence to the rule of law in the solution of international conflict.[3]

The foregoing point may be illuminated by discussing the legal concept of "jurisdiction" as it is confronted with the reality of diverse values in different social systems.

Jurisdiction is derived from the Latin *jurisdictio,* meaning a saying or speaking of the law. Webster's dictionary identifies three different aspects of jurisdiction: (1) the legal power to hear a cause, that is to say, the sphere of authority of a court; (2) the sphere of authority of the sovereign as legislator; and finally, (3) the sphere of authority within which any particular power may be exercised. Beale defines jurisdiction as: "The power of a sovereign to affect the rights of persons, whether by legislation, by executive decree, or by the judgment of a court."[4] Under the Restatement of Conflicts, jurisdiction means "the power of a state to create interests . . . which will be recognized as valid by other states."[5]

Law, including jurisdiction, does not arise from physical power or coercion alone. Law is a product of consent as well as coercion. And consent, in turn, is a product of human values, for asserted rules of law constantly press upon human values of varying in-

---

[3]I.C.J. Reports 1959, 6.
[4]J. H. Beale, "The Jurisdiction of a Sovereign State," 36 *Harv. L. Rev.* 241 (1923).
[5]American Law Institute, *Restatement of the Law of Conflict of Laws,* sec. 42 (1934).

tensity. Within our own times, the problems of prohibition and segregation have brought home to us that there are limits to effective authority when legal rules clash with deeply felt values, and law must rely primarily on force to establish desired rules. Even Soviet power encountered this principle of social mechanics in Soviet policies toward Hungary, Poland, and the satellite states.

To summarize the discussion up to this point, it was said that jurisdiction, as a claim to "speak" the law with respect to individuals and to influence their behavior in desired ways, encounters human values as a force limiting the exercise of authority. There is a principle of social mechanics that, as commanded conduct conflicts with felt values, the use of force must be increased proportionately with the intensity of attachment to the values concerned.

The grasp of jurisdiction may conflict with values which are central to the survival of our culture and civilization. Such a claim of jurisdiction may even be formally legitimate under the relevant legal system. Yet, when the challenge to the culture is made, the response of the culture must be immediate and effective and must pierce the cloak of legitimacy. This is the lesson of the Nuremberg trials. Whatever else may be said of them, their recognition of crimes against humanity remains an ominous warning against attempts to remove law altogether from its mooring in the traditions of our inherited culture.

The grasp of jurisdiction may seek to bring within the sphere of national power those institutions which are international in character. The shock to the international order in the seizure of the Suez Canal Company was profound indeed. When such a grasp of jurisdiction strikes so fundamentally at the values and interests of the international society, one may well ask whether an institution which derives its very meaning and vitality from the life of the international society can, under international law, lawfully be brought within the sole compass and power of a single national will.

States are no longer—if, indeed, they ever were—pure systems of action, self-contained and free from the presence of aliens or alien interests. States are interdependent. Regional interdependence, commodity and service interdependence, financial interdependence, and institutional interdependence characterize the world today. International corporations and international transactions erode national boundaries. Systems of action are horizontally organized in a world life of trade, intercourse, and communication which transform the vertical systems of action of the state as territorially viewed.

Property, as a reflection of the ordering of a society in the use of its physical resources, is importantly a product of the life of the international society. Complementary systems of action extending through many states are the foundation of the international commodity markets. A state's exclusive sovereignty or jurisdiction over its national resources becomes virtually meaningless when it is the international use of these resources which gives them meaning and value as property.

The grasp of jurisdiction may try to encompass what a United Nations General Assembly resolution termed "natural wealth and resources,"[6] but the interests of the international society which give value to those resources through their international use cannot become the captive of a single state, for a rule which would extend the lordship of the sovereign over resources exported from his state into all lands in which they are used would fragmentize our world to the breaking point. The supplanting of the impersonal forces of the international market by the personal dictate of the sovereign, the withholding of access by all countries to mineral resources essential to the mineral-based economies of industrialized states, except on political terms agreeable to the sovereign of the source state, would create unendurable strains on the international legal system.

The grasp of jurisdiction to compel Harry Blackmer, an American citizen in France, to testify in the United States[7] is quite different from the grasp of jurisdiction which would compel a parent corporation to use its authority over a foreign subsidiary in a manner inimical to the interests of that foreign state. Canada, interested in safeguarding a local electronics industry, is alarmed when jurisdiction is asserted by the United States under the American antitrust laws over the Canadian manufacture of television sets. Such an exercise of jurisdiction is viewed simply as a weapon for the further economic penetration of Canada by American capital. "A British Columbian," said a Canadian writer, "is a man who smokes

---

[6]U.N. General Assembly Res. 626, (7), Dec. 21, 1952; Hyde, "Permanent Sovereignty over Natural Wealth and Resources."

[7]Blackmer v. United States, 284 U.S. 421 (1932).

Virginia cigarettes, drinks South American coffee, eats Ontario cheese, California oranges, Norwegian sardines," and "gets his home entertainment listening to an American imitating a Scandinavian on a machine that was made in Ontario by some outfit whose head office is in Pittsburgh."[8]

The grasp of jurisdiction to nationalize foreign-owned property against inadequate compensation and the grasp of jurisdiction to nullify an international development contract or concession agreement raise issues not only of power but also of right, and in last analysis, of self-interest. For just as property may be a product of international, rather than national, systems of action, so an international development contract is something more than a bilateral agreement under some one system of municipal law. It constitutes an international assemblage and coordination of human skills directed to the maximum world distribution and utilization of a natural resource.

When a national state exercises jurisdiction with respect to some phase of the international society, policy should never be equated with legitimacy or physical power, for answers to the formal question of legitimacy or the practical question of physical power will never provide an answer to the ultimate question of the wisdom of action. There is an interest of all peoples in the stability and growth of the international society. There is an interest of all peoples in the international economy as a means for national integration and individual welfare. When the state seeks to "speak the law" in that part of the international society which is within its jurisdiction, its policy should be directed to the promotion of the viability of the international society. At this point the interest of the state becomes identified with the interest of the international society. The relevant interest of the state is not alone one of respect for the values and interests of other states, important as that is; the relevant interest is in preserving the benefits flowing to the state from its membership in the international society.[9]

To state the fact of the coincidence of national interest with action in the international system is not to imply the fact of the acceptance of the value of action in the international system by

---

[8]B. Mather, "The British Columbian," in R. E. Watters, ed., *British Columbia: A Centennial Anthology,* 481 (1958).
[9]See Carlston, "The Grasp of Jurisdiction," 170.

states. Cognitions of action in the international system by states and their members are often more emotional than rational, and based more on prejudice than on reason.

3. *The value aspects of an international situation of interstate conflict are so important that the value premises of an international law scholar or judge, in his search for a governing legal norm for such situation, should either be made explicit or should be appreciated in appraising the significance or validity of his conclusions.*

It is said that the physical sciences are existential and outside the sphere of value, while the social sciences are normative in character and always involve questions of values. The author has elsewhere commented upon this distinction as it applied to law,[10] in addition to the discussion of value and law made previously in this volume. Classic positivism would let the formulation of the rules of law by the legal scholar or judge be guided solely by the evidence of law, apart from any value considerations. The search for and statement of law was to be made abstractly and without regard to "such misleading notions" as "justice, equity, good conscience, common sense."[11]

The substantial sharing of relevant values by the states which were the principal actors in the international system during the period of development of the rules of international law shielded the positivist in international law from the necessity of considering value issues in his formulation of rules of law. Now such issues are testing the validity of much of the content of international law and are profoundly present in attempts to define rules of law in those areas of interstate relations where conflicts of ideology and power are sharp. When the international law scholar or judge is confronted with a problem, such as nationalization, which entails highly differing and intensely felt views of the desirable by states, it is seen that his statement of the law tends to proceed from his particular set of value premises and preferred image or model of international order. He who asserts that all value considerations are irrelevant and that his search for law is simply a search for the law in the abstract, solely upon the basis of the evidence of law, is one whose model of international society is necessarily

---

[10]Carlston, *Law and Structures*, 18-28.
[11]Smith, "The English Analytical Jurists," 270, 284.

a stable system of interstate relations. With respect to the problem of nationalization, one who places a primacy upon the freedom of a sovereign state to effect social change will tend to minimize the requirement of prompt, adequate, and effective compensation as a condition of the lawfulness of expropriation. One who moves beyond this point to acceptance of the value of revolutionary change in structures of social action will tend to regard the practice of nationalization as wholly outside the domain of law. On the other hand, one who values the establishment in the international system of those conditions which will promote participation, and render secure expectations arising from participation, will tend to adhere to the view that the use of a state's internal monopoly of force to despoil others of their property acquired in the course of their participation in the international system, or to terminate contracts with impunity, does not reflect a solid and enduring basis for the growth of a viable international system.

The search for the governing value, which is implicit in the search for the governing legal norm, is a search that should be brought into the open. It should not be ignored under the mask of positivism. The search for the governing legal norm must of course adhere to the tenet of positivism that the statement of law must be faithful to the evidence of the law. Yet, as was indicated at the close of the discussion under principle 1 above, once an international dispute is found to enter the domain of international law, it will usually be found that the task of the scholar or the judge is to select a governing legal norm from competing legal norms demanding recognition. There is usually no inevitable or logically inescapable single governing legal norm and consequent value; it is a matter of choice among competing legal norms and a delicate adjustment of values in the exercise of that choice. The methodology for the international law scholar or judge which this study proposes, once the question of general value orientation is brought into the open, will be found under principle 9 of Chapter VI and in the following outline of methodological precepts.[12]

4. *If actors in the international system desire the continuance of a legal norm, as against the pressures of changing values on the*

---

[12]See G. Myrdal, *An International Economy: Problems and Prospects,* appendix, "Methodological Note on the Concepts and the Value Premises," 336-337 (1956).

part of other actors with respect to such a norm, they must exercise leadership and administration to create, as well as to preserve, those conditions in the international system conducive to maintaining the strength of the value or values implicit in such legal norm.

Once it is perceived that law does not lie in regulation alone but in regulation designed to maintain an ideal and valued norm for behavior (Chapter VI, 2-4), the fact will be apparent that the preservation of a preferred type of international order and the rules of law eventuating from it cannot rest upon a clamorous insistence upon the validity of legal rules whose foundations are in process of erosion, even though they may, at the moment, still be considerably unimpaired. To cry for the rule of law to support rules of law which are not prized by a substantial number of actors in the social system, is to reach for a means of support which may soon vanish altogether. A drowning man is little helped by a leaking air raft. The character of the law in a social system is a product of the manner of performance of its leadership and administration (Chapter VI, 6). The preservation of a preferred international law norm, in the face of forces which would destroy the foundations of that norm, demands the exercise of leadership and administration by the interested states to create and maintain those conditions in the international system which will cause the disaffected states to change their lack of value attachment with respect to such norm. At the very least, the interested states must act so that disaffected states will not increase to the point where the norm is altogether destroyed.

The international spread of nationalization and the emergence of international legal norms facilitating that spread, at the expense of the viability of the international system itself, will not be stopped by mere appeals to follow the rule of law or insistence upon the application of specific rules of law. If a state finds no value in its participation in the international system, it will find no value in rules supporting action in the system, valid and necessary as such rules may be for that purpose. If promotion of a system of law designed to secure participation in the international system is desired, then action of the nature indicated in principles 10 and 11 of Chapter VI must be taken. If we wish to lessen the nationalization of foreign property by underdeveloped veneer states having a considerable dependency upon foreign markets for selling one or a few basic commodities, including minerals, if we wish to diminish opposition by such states to any rules of law limiting their freedom to nationalize foreign property, such as the requirement of adequate, prompt, and effective compensation, then steps must be taken to stabilize international commodity markets and to promote the over-all development, along democratic lines, of such veneer states.

As the implications of the above remarks are pondered, they lead to a general principle of some importance. At the outset, it may be said that if the process of foreign investment is to endure it must bring about an important realization of values by the members of the host country as well as the source country. This fact could be generalized in the following principle: *Successful interaction between two social systems requires that such interaction shall embody value rationality from the standpoint of the members of both systems.* The same principle can be expressed in terms of adaptation: *Successful adaptation by members of one social system to those of another demands that interaction between the respective systems enables the realization of shared values.* In other words, if the process of foreign investment is to find growing protection against the menace of nationalization under an expanding body of rules of international law, it must take place in such a manner that it is *valued* by the actors involved in the process.

The only alternative to such procedures as are suggested above, with a view to establishing and supporting types of behavior in the international system which reinforce desired legal norms, is that of the external establishment of authority based on power to preserve such types of behavior. This aspect of action in the international system was discussed in Chapter VI, principle 8.h.

5. *An act of state in the international system does not escape evaluation by cultural and legal standards, even though there may be no customary rule of international law directly bearing on it.*

The above principle is an implicate of principle 9.e. of Chapter VI; namely, the fact that international law today includes sources of law in addition to the practice of states. It is a restatement of principle 9.e.4.b. of Chapter VI to the effect that the circumstance that the state is the performer of an act otherwise subject to cultural or legal evaluation does not necessarily remove such an act from such evaluation.

This study has noted a number of aspects in which the law and legal process of the international system present an extraordinarily unique situation. Principle 8 of Chapter VI adverted to the decentralized character of the international system and the fact that it largely operates subject to the control of the law and legal processes of states. The principle pointed to the conditions which precluded it from becoming an independent system of action controlling its own order. The present chapter reaffirms the interdependency of law and values. It notes the fact of jurisdiction without law in the international system. It should be added that action *does* take place in the international system, that states are irreversibly committed to participation in the international system, that if the point is ever to be reached in which such participation will embody the realization of widely shared values by the participants, there are certain minimal steps to be taken. A number of such steps were indicated in previous chapters as well as elsewhere in this chapter. At this point, it is affirmed that international law must cease to take the position that because no customary rule of international law has eventuated, indicating whether a certain act of state is right or wrong, on the basis of the practice of states, it is therefore to be adjudged as legally valid for all purposes, including that of determining the necessary minimal bases of an international order. This is not in any way to detract from principle 1 above. It is only to say that the legal quality of an act of state may be determined other than by resort solely to the practice of states as a source of law. It is, for example, to repeat the statement made in principle 9.e.4.a. of Chapter VI that the general principles of law recognized by civilized nations provide a valid criterion for controlling state conduct which involves its participation in the international system and a valid source for the further development of international law norms. This is particularly true when such principles of law concern the bases upon which any enduring social order must be established. The application of such a criterion in any one case as a basis for decision is subject to the several principles stated above, and particularly at the beginning of this chapter, concerning the role of the international judge and the growth of international law.

The application of the foregoing to the phenomenon of nationalization will be taken up in principle 10.

6. *The values of the particular actors involved in an inter-*

national situation of interstate conflict acquire significance for purposes of deciding upon a governing legal norm only when they are viewed from some larger context for normative evaluation than that embodied in the situation itself.

When nationalization is viewed in the context of a particular situation involving its use by an underdeveloped nation to achieve national growth and promote integration, when the values of such an actor are compared with those of private foreign investors thereby deprived of their property, the sympathies of many bystanders tend to lie with the nationalizing state. Such an evaluation of the situation would be strengthened if the foreign investment had taken place against a background of imperialist economic expansion. Yet, in the search of an ideal norm to govern such a situation from the standpoint of *law,* it does not follow that all the elements necessary for a value judgment are to be found in the situation itself. If the ideal and valued norm in the international system is to be found, the situation must be viewed from some larger context revealing the cultural and other factors by which the situation should be appraised. A normative criterion for such appraisal is set forth in principle 7 below. In principle 8 a still broader context for the appraisal and selection of a governing legal norm is delineated.

7.   *The appropriateness of a legal norm for promoting the viability of the international system by rendering secure participation in it, is a valid normative criterion to be considered in the selection of a governing legal norm for an international situation of interstate conflict.*

7.a.   *A basic function of law and the legal process is to establish and maintain those conditions in a social system which will render secure participation. The performance of that function has its own value importance in rendering secure a social structure which enables effective action for the realization of the values of the actors in the system.*

Political and legal philosophy from Hobbes to von Ihering searched for a perspective from which to view, describe, and evaluate social action cut loose from feudalism and moving toward an industrially organized, democratically structured society. Western society reflects a unique combination of authority based on power over the individual, as he acts in the economic sphere, and authority based on consent, as he acts in the political sphere.[13] The dominance of the state over the individual was a preoccupation of political and legal philosophy well into the nineteenth century, and a deep concern for this problem still remains with us. The circumstance that political thought has since turned to other matters has not displaced its interest in the nature and province of sovereignty. Liberal political thought of the eighteenth and nineteenth centuries insisted that the sphere of government should be restricted and that of the individual kept open. The elimination of social anarchy implicit in the decentralized possession and use of force by individuals was the postulate of social order vividly insisted upon by Hobbes in the seventeenth century. The assumption by law of the task of securing the conditions of social life and the use of law to render secure social action as a means for realizing individual values were the fundamental purposes of law in the view of von Ihering in the nineteenth century. Both may be said to support the principle that the first order of business of law should be to establish and render secure a social structure, or framework, which would enable action directed toward achieving the goals and realizing the values of individuals.

Law as social control may be said to have two aspects. The first of these is the establishment and maintenance of the minimal necessary bases for any social order. The second of these is the establishment and maintenance of those ideal and institutionalized norms of behavior which embody shared values of the members of a social system (Chapter VI, 2 and 4). As a social system is coming into being, the first of these tasks is seen to be paramount.

The tasks of international law in the control of the international system includes those of law, as viewed by Hobbes centuries ago and by von Ihering less than a century ago. War still remains a form of action in the international system. Its menace to civilization today and concern for its control is, if anything, more profound than that of Hobbes. The minimal bases of protection of a social order, as found in the international system, are still lacking in international law and are largely to be found in the laws and legal processes of the several states (Chapter VI, 9). Property used

---

[13]See Carlston, *Law and Structures,* chap. 8, and "International Administrative Law," 329, and postulate 13, 373-377.

in international patterns, contracts of an international character, and corporations whose business extends over several states find their protection more under national than under international law.

The questions asked here concern the adequacy of the rules of international law to perform the essential tasks of law in any social system: First, do the rules protect participation in the system as a means of attaining goals and realizing values of the actors or do they tend to frustrate or render precarious such participation? Second, do the rules, individually or generally, reveal a preference for an international system so designed as to maximize the absolute freedom of states as actors or do they reveal a preference for limiting the exercise of sovereignty by individual states when it will enhance the ability of all states to attain their goals and realize their values by participation in the system? Third, are the rules functionally appropriate in the particular situations to which they apply, that is to say, do they enable a realization of the shared values of the actors in the system, as such values are found in such situations?

7.b.   *The value of promoting the viability of the international system through rendering secure participation in it is a valid basis for appraising competing legal norms in the selection of a governing legal norm in an international situation of interstate conflict.*

The above principle was previously discussed in Chapter VI, 9.e. and 9.e.3. The principle is one which can never be subjected to the degree of proof or demonstration available to substantiate or validate an existential fact. Its validity essentially has a pragmatic base. Our world is an interdependent one; if we are to make it a better one, we will have to accept that fact, along with its consequences and implications. We will have to render secure that phase of our life which involves action in the international system if we wish to make the most of such action as a means of realizing our values.

The normative criterion set forth in this principle is not an exclusive one. Its appropriate sphere is indicated here and in the succeeding principle. The necessity of its consideration arises from the fact that usually the evidence of law bearing on the situation of interstate conflict does not overwhelmingly lead to only one conclusion. As the advocates of the states in dispute present their competing rules for adoption by the international court, or as the legal scholar is faced with the necessity of making a choice among competing rules in affirming the governing legal norm, that rule should be preferred which best promotes the viability of the international system. The rule should contribute to that end by protection of the basic expectations of the actors in the system arising from their participation and provision of the opportunity to realize their important values by such participation. The actors in question are not only the parties to the situation of conflict; they are all the actors in the system. The rule of law to be selected is one which typifies or generally reflects their perception of the situation, their attitude toward it, and the values which they find important in it.

The normative criterion advanced here has its structural aspect of promoting the establishment of a system of law which will render secure participation in the international system as a means of realizing shared values. It also has what may be termed its situational or functional aspect, that is to say, the preference for a governing legal rule, among competing legal rules, which will embody mechanical and value rationality as applied to the particular situation.

8. *The appraisal of action with a view to its control under law is not to be limited to the application of any one legal norm, but is subject to a number of considerations.*

8.a. *The appraisal of action as a phase of the control of action must be appreciated in the light of the full range of a theory of action.*

The theory of action developed in the preceding chapters needs to be briefly restated and further developed as a prelude to the more intense development of the theory of the control of action. In terms of philosophy, action has three phases of idea, substance or objective reality, and reflection. In behavioral terms, action has the creative or exploratory phase, the performance phase, and the control phase. It must be clearly understood that from the standpoint of individual behavior, as manifested in the interplay of inner neural and chemical responses, or reactions, and objective physical behavior, there is no neat dividing line between the three phases. Thought and action are a continuum in the individual. In this continuum, the control of past action takes place simultaneously with decision making as to future action. The relevant dichotomy is between the inner or subjective aspect of behavior and its outer or objective aspect. As an individual acts, he also explores or mentally rehearses future action while he appraises and evaluates past action.

Appraisal of action with a view to its control has a number of aspects. There is the matter of verifying the attainment of the goal, in which the question is asked whether the desired state of affairs to which action was initially directed was reached. There is the matter of weighing the contentment following the achievement of the goal or the frustration and disappointment incident to disfunction or failure of goal attainment. There is also, most importantly, the matter of relating action to the characteristic values of the culture itself. Appraisal of action is not merely hedonistic; it takes place in a context in which the individual views himself as a member of his culture and as sharing its values and value priorities. The individual may even at times indulge in a certain amount of appraisal of the validity of the values of his culture. He will do this both as they relate to his personality and value system and as they involve the ethical worth of his culture. For example, as the scale of mass consumption reached in the United States is enjoyed, the validity some of the directions a market-structured economy takes may be questioned. Institutionally, religion is found to be both the custodian of the moral quality of a society and the agent for leading it to new moral perceptions and attitudes. It is also found that a society has writers and speakers who communicate to its members the facts about the environment in which the society finds itself. These include persons who point to emerging, existing, and declining social values and who appraise the validity of the resultant value system of the society. Thus, from the standpoint of both the individual and the institutions in society, there is a constant appraisal of action with a view to its control.

8.b. *The appraisal of action with a view to its control under law requires the exercise of leadership within the area of freedom open to the actor performing such control function. This includes consideration of the degree of attachment by the actors in the system to the values embodied in the situation, possible future changes in such value attachment, including the emergence of new values, and the cultural validity of the values finally decided upon to be controlling, as embodied in the governing legal norm.*

The appraisal phase of the control function in an organized social system may be said partly to duplicate within its particular sphere the exercise of the leadership function in the organized social system as a whole. The standpoint or perspective from which the actor concerned with the control of action views action is that of an overview of past action as a part of decision making as to *future* action. Such an overview of action is typically that of leadership. When, however, the actor's sphere of action is marked out by the necessity of adhering to the received or legitimate methodology of the legal system, he may exercise the leadership function within his particular area of free movement only to the extent permitted by the approved methodology of law.

An actor entrusted with the role of decision making as to the control of action within the legal system of a society has freedom to act in any one situation of conflict to the extent that the application of the received methodology of the law provides him with rational possibilities of choice among competing legal norms. In the performance of his role, he must know the degree to which the values in the situation before him, as embodied in rules of law, are shared by the actors in the society, and the degree of their intensity of attachment to such values. Such information is necessary if he is to decide upon the appropriateness of the governing legal norm finally selected from the standpoint of (1) the degree to which it embodies widely shared values in the society, as found in the situation, and (2) the degree to which it is likely to encounter disfavor or resistance when it fails to embody widely shared values. He must also be aware of changing value attachments and the emergence of new values in the society if he is to make the best value judgment in affirming a governing legal norm.

A decision maker exercising the leadership function must, however, be more than a mere litmus paper of public opinion or thermometer of the degree of value attachment. In the performance of his role, he must reflect upon the character and destiny of his culture as it is embodied in the situation before him. The grand design of social action which is the culture is a mosaic of great intricacy and minuteness of parts. It is subject to rapid erosion and change. If its massive configurations are to be governed at all, they can only be governed by a constant preoccupation of decision making in all its parts as to the appropriateness and enduring quality of its action. It is at this point that the full meaning and the full performance of the control of action in a society is reached.

A decision maker concerned with the control of action must relate himself to the culture in which he finds himself. He must appraise that culture as it comes before him in the situation demanding decision for control. Should he be merely the pragmatist who finds any want or claim to be intrinsically valid, then the drift and swirl of human action will be without ultimate direction. If the grand design of our culture is to embody both the dynamism and balance of, say, the design of an Oriental rug, that design must be created through our will, that is, our decisions and resultant action.

9.   *The statement of the governing private and public international law norms for an act of nationalization prematurely terminating a concession agreement requires a clear and precise analytical definition of the legal issues involved in each such system of law and a careful articulation of such norms.*

9.a.   *Private international law will regulate an act of nationalization prematurely terminating a concession agreement insofar as conflicting claims of persons, whose interests are thereby affected, may be resolved by adjectival rules, in a national system of law, concerned with the choice of one state system of law as against another. A decision maker in the sphere of private international law will be considerably influenced by the perspective and values of the forum in selecting a governing legal norm.*

Private international law would subject a contract between a state and an alien to the proper law of some one state. The designation of what that proper law shall be is the subject matter of the rules of private international law. The foregoing is in substance the purport of the classic remark of the Permanent Court of International Justice: "Any contract which is not a contract between States in their capacity as subjects of international law is based on the municipal law of some country. The question as to which this law is forms the subject of that branch of law which is at the present day usually described as private international law or the doctrine of the conflict of laws."[14]

It is considered that an agreement becomes a contract only because the municipal law of some one country makes it so. Thus

---

[14]Case of Serbian and Brazilian Loans, P.C.I.J., ser. A, nos. 20/21, 41 (1929).

Judge Learned Hand said: "But an agreement is not a contract, except as the law says it shall be, and to try to make it one is to pull on one's bootstraps. Some law must impose the obligation."[15] Private international law, as a part of the law of the forum, will indicate the law of the state which shall be the governing law of the contract.[16] It will do so on the basis of general doctrines, such as the express or implied intention of the parties determines the proper law.

Private international law, in general, determines the legal norm finally applicable to a particular situation by following a series of steps, which include the classification of the cause of action, for example, contract or tort, the selection of the *lex causae,* and the application of the *lex causae.* Each of these bristles with conceptual and analytical difficulties.[17] When the applicable norm is reached, however, that ends the matter, unless some established ground for exception can be found.

Parties to an international contract may reduce the risk of its subjection to the law of a state likely to be hostile to the process of foreign investment, including nationalization, by selecting the law of some more friendly state as the governing law of the contract. Under the subjective intent theory for determining the proper law of a contract, the law governing a contract is to be ascertained from the express or presumed intention of the parties. The objective theory for determining the proper law of a contract, however, would impose a governing law on the basis of general principles. The subjective intent theory seems to be the one most generally recognized.

English private international law, which has a most liberal view of the autonomy of the parties to select a governing law, is said to have developed in a context of precedent in which the law selected by the parties in fact had some connection with the contract.[18] The divergence between the above two theories has been said to be largely academic.[19] In any event, the choice of law must

---

[15]E. Gerli and Co., Inc. *v.* Cunard S.S. Co. Ltd., 48 F.2d 115, 117 (2nd Cir., 1931).

[16]See generally Chapter VI, 9.b.

[17]Cheshire, *Private International Law,* chap. 3.

[18]*Ibid.,* 206-207.

[19]Nussbaum, *Principles of Private International Law,* 161; F. A. Mann, "The Proper Law of Contract," 3 *Int. L. Q.* 60 (1950).

be made by the parties in good faith and for a lawful purpose.[20] They cannot select a law which would be opposed to the public policy of the forum or would render as valid a contract otherwise invalid. They cannot choose "a system which they have freely invented."[21] The prevailing continental doctrine is said to prohibit the parties from adopting "as the proper law of the contract a system of law with which the contract has no connexion."[22]

American cases have often recognized the intention of the parties theory, subject to the principles that choice must be exercised in good faith and not violate any public policy of the forum and that the law selected must have a substantial connection with the contract. On the other hand, many cases would limit choice by the parties to the law of the place of performance. There is also a strong authority which would deny altogether the ability of the parties to select the law of their contract.[23]

In discussing the autonomy of the parties to select their own governing law, Donnedieu de Vabres notes that French jurisprudence has developed a general theory of the international contract. He states that it is the nature of its economic operation which confers upon a contract its international character, and that certain operations by their nature fall within the internal economic life of a state, while others, by contrast, fall within the international economic life. He concludes that the jurisprudence demonstrates that there is "an international economic activity escaping the sovereignty of individual legislative bodies and cloaked by its own juridical regulation, incapable of being reduced to the simple confines of internal laws in conflict."[24]

---

[20]Vita Food Products, Inc. *v.* Unus Shipping Co., Ltd., [1939] A. C. 277; E. Rabel, 2, *The Conflict of Laws: A Comparative Study,* 401-402 (1947); Schmitthoff, *A Textbook of the English Conflict of Laws,* 100.

[21]M. Wolff, *Private International Law,* 416 (2nd ed., 1950); see also Cheshire, *Private International Law,* 216-218.

[22]*Ibid.,* 417; see also D. S. Stern, "The Conflict of Laws in Commercial Arbitration," 17 *Law and Contemp. Prob.* 566 at 569 (1952).

[23]Beale, 2, *A Treatise on the Conflict of Laws,* 1174; Cheshire, *Private International Law,* 200; (note), "Choice of Law by Contractual Stipulation," 16 *U. Chi. L. Rev.* 157 at 158-159 (1948); American Law Institute, *Restatement . . . of Conflict of Laws,* secs. 332, 346, 348; O'Toole *v.* Meysenburg and others, 251 Fed. 191 (8th Cir., 1918); Louis-Dreyfus and others *v.* Paterson Steamships, Ltd., 43 F.2d 824, 827 (2nd Cir., 1930); E. Gerli and Co., Inc. *v.* Cunard S.S. Co., Ltd., 48 F.2d 117 (2nd Cir., 1931).

[24]J. Donnedieu de Vabres, *L'Évolution de la Jurisprudence Francaise en Matière de Conflit de Lois,* 553-561, quotation at 561 (1938), trans. by author.

Niboyet takes up the analogous situation of a business concern (*fonds du commerce*) which in its functioning comprehends several states, and concludes: "By virtue of the phenomenon of frontiers which come between home offices and various branch offices, each state may provide a different set of rules for the branches which are on its territory and subject to its control. The universality of the business concern cannot be realized unless all of its parts are in the same country (which is the case in a national business concern), otherwise there results a veritable juridical splitting-up."[25]

When, however, the law governing the contract is finally determined and the state in question has prematurely terminated a concession agreement through an act of nationalization, a question which private international law would raise is whether such an act is to be regarded as an expropriation or a confiscation. In the view of Professor van Hecke:

. . . By confiscation is meant the taking of property without adequate compensation, by whatever method it may be carried out or cloaked. Expropriation on the other hand is the taking or use of property by public authority with adequate compensation; for example, the compulsory purchase of land and the requisitioning of property. Nationalization, a word commonly used in recent years with regard to industrial undertakings, may be either confiscation or expropriation according as compensation is or is not given.[26]

J. E. S. Fawcett states:

Confiscation, then, is the taking of private property by the state without payment or compensation to the divested owner; where, however, payment or compensation is given, the taking may be called ex-

---

In the memorial of Switzerland in the Losinger and Co. case, it was contended: "In a wide sense, the notion of international obligations or engagements covers not only those existing directly between states, but also those existing between States and private individuals protected by their governments, when such engagements produce international repercussions and when, by their origin or their effects, they extend in reality to several countries." P.C.I.J., ser. C, no. 78, 128-219 (1936).

[25]J. P. Niboyet, 4, *Traité de Droit International Privé*, 630-633, quotation at 632-633 (1947), trans. by author. "There is no reason why a municipal court which may thus consider international law incidentally, should not also apply it directly so as to secure the submission of a single and indivisible instrument under a single legal system." F. A. Mann, "The Law Governing State Contracts," 21 *British Yearbook of International Law* 11, 22 (1944).

[26]G. A. van Hecke, "Confiscation, Expropriation and the Conflict of Laws," 4 *Int. L. Q.* 345-346 (1951).

propriation. In either case the property may after the taking be vested in the state or an agency of the state, that is to say, nationalized.[27]

Now that necessary concepts are defined, the methodology of private international law and the results of the application of that methodology, when it is confronted with the task of deciding a private dispute arising out of a foreign act of nationalization, can be indicated.

Private international law is applied in the course of the administration or carrying out of a system of law of a state. Admittedly, the policies and interests of the forum are a force in the formulation and application of rules of private international law in any given case. Yet any international situation involving interpersonal conflict inherently raises issues concerning the policies and interests of the international society. The basic assumption of private international law is that national laws are in conflict in such an international situation. This makes it necessary to relate the *international* situation to the law of some *one* state because of the appropriateness of that law from the *domestic* instead of the *international* standpoint, and tends to prevent private international law from realizing its function of establishing those conditions in the international system which would enable it to become an effective means for the realization of shared values by the participants. Until the various policy criteria which should be considered in the formulation and application of private international law are brought to light and become formally acknowledged in the content of its rules of law for the classification and disposition of international situations involving disputes of a private character, private international law can never reach full maturity in performing its necessary function.

Since the important interests and policies of states vary to a considerable degree when they are concerned with a foreign act of nationalization, there is a corresponding lack of uniformity in the application of the rules of private international law relating to such an act. The existent consensus in the decisions may in part be attributable to the degree to which the fact situations with which they deal are localized in a particular jurisdiction and are thus easily classified as subject to the law of such jurisdiction. Primarily, however, the consensus which does exist flows from the

---

[27]Fawcett, "Some Foreign Effects of Nationalization," 355.

coincidence of common interests among states, either from the standpoint of their national policies or of their shared interest in supporting the international society. The inconsistencies in the application of the rules of private international law to essentially similar fact situations will perhaps be lessened when the practices of courts in dealing with foreign acts of nationalization are classified not according to the formal rules which they proclaim, but instead on the basis of the interests and policies which they seek to safeguard, and which in fact motivate their decisions. If such a system of classification is to be useful, it must permit a more complex, sophisticated analysis and classification of cases on a factual basis than is possible under the present rude categories of broad doctrine, in which the law of the situs of the property is said to prevail, subject to the exception of public order or public policy.

Applying the somewhat broad generalizations made above, the principle may be stated that when a state nationalizes the property of its own national located within its own territory and a claim to the possession of such property later arises in another jurisdiction, ordinarily there will be slight policy interests of the forum in disturbing the legal relations established under the foreign law. On the other hand, if the property be that of a national of the forum, there may be strong policy considerations against the application of the foreign law, particularly in instances of confiscation. Thus policy interests of the forum would dictate two different results in law. The foreign law will be applied in the first case, but not in the second.

From the standpoint of the methodology of private international law, however, only one result seems possible. The *lex rei sitae* must rationally or logically be applied in both situations because of the high degree of localization of the facts. If, however, the act of nationalization should be of a confiscatory nature, private international law will, in general, provide only two avenues for escape from its application. It may be viewed as falling within the domain of political, penal, and revenue laws, to which the principle of the territoriality of laws applies, or it may be viewed as not entitled to recognition because it is violative of public policy. In the former case, the foreign law is viewed to have only territorial application within the foreign state and the *situs* of the property becomes critical. In the latter case, *situs* is immaterial;

no third party may ever acquire a valid title in the view of the forum.[28]

The area of freedom of a judge applying private international law to a confiscatory act of nationalization is indicated in the following categories of fact situations and rules of law.[29] Comment will be included on the value or policy aspects of such situations.

1. When the situation concerns a confiscatory foreign act of nationalization, the effects of which when promulgated are limited to a tangible *res* physically located in the nationalizing state and to the interests of nationals of such state, legal effect to such act of nationalization will be given by private international law, and claims of foreign nationals asserted against the *res* will be rejected on the basis of the application of the *lex rei sitae*. While nominally the foreign court will in such a situation affirm the applicability of the *lex rei sitae*, any interest of the forum opposed to confiscatory measures will in fact be minimal, as against its interest in stability, security of transactions, and preservation of the received system of private international law. Thus, no later circumstances or conflicting claims will cause it to disturb the *status quo*. When the *res* is in the possession of the nationalizing state, such rejection of foreign claims is often additionally influenced by the principle of immunity of state property under international law.

2. When the situation described in the paragraph above is altered by the circumstance that a national of the state of the forum has an interest in the situation, arising from a claim against a national of the nationalizing state or in the nationalized property, then the court of the forum may be influenced to protect such interest. The court may in such a case subtly shift the significant

---

[28]van Hecke, "Confiscation, Expropriation and the Conflict of Laws."

[29]For a most illuminating examination of the theory of private international law in its application to foreign confiscatory acts, see L. A. E. Hjerner, "The General Approach to Foreign Confiscations," 2 *Scandinavian Studies in Law* 177 (1958). See generally van Hecke, "Confiscation, Expropriation and the Conflict of Laws"; Fawcett, "Some Foreign Effects of Nationalization"; I. Seidl-Hohenveldern, "Extraterritorial Effects of Confiscations and Expropriations," 49 *Mich. L. Rev.* 851 (1951) and "Probleme des internationalen Konfiskations und Enteignungrechtes," 83 *Journal de Droit International (Clunet)* 380 (1956), answering W. Lewald, "Das internationale Enteignungsrecht in Lichte neuen Schrifttums," 21 *Rabel's Zeitschrift für ausländisches und internationales Privatrecht* 119 (1956); R. Sarraute and P. Tager, "Hier et aujourd'hui. Les effects en France des nationalisations étrangères," 79 *Journal de Droit International (Clunet)* 1138, 1148 (1952).

situs to that of the forum by categorizing the significant property not to be in the tangible property but in the intangible claim and by giving to the latter an external situs. It then becomes easy to declare that a confiscatory foreign act of nationalization need not be given extraterritorial effect.

3. When the situation described in paragraph 1 is altered by the circumstance that possession of the confiscated *res* is claimed by a person whose asserted right to it is based on the act of nationalization, whether the forum court will disturb the *de facto* possession of the *res* will depend on the policy of the forum state toward the confiscatory element of the act of nationalization.

There is now a situation in which a consequence of any decision giving effect within the system of law of the forum to the foreign act of nationalization will be to disturb, instead of to secure, possession and to upset the *status quo*. When the nationalizing state, or a person basing his claim on the foreign act of nationalization, seeks delivery of the confiscated *res,* whether the court of the forum will use the force of its legal system in aid of the policy interests of the nationalizing state will depend on the degree to which the confiscatory nature of the act of nationalization becomes significant to the court from the standpoint of the interests of the forum. If the legal system of the forum be of a stable, conservative character, or if there be a strong interest in protecting foreign investment from confiscation, then the policy significance of the fact of confiscation looms larger and the court may formally reject the *lex rei sitae* on the exception of public order, or it may distinguish the application of the *lex rei sitae* by the verbal formula that the court is being required to "enforce" instead of merely to "recognize" the foreign act of nationalization. If, however, there should be opposing policy interests in the forum, such as establishing protection for an act of nationalization of the forum as a precedent in the system of private international law generally, then the court will affirm the applicability of the *lex rei sitae*.

4. When the situation concerns a confiscatory foreign act of nationalization as applied to a tangible *res* which is at the time located *outside* the nationalizing state, only very strong policy considerations of the forum will cause the court to give legal effect in its system of law to the foreign act of nationalization.

5. The assimilation of intangibles to the law of some state other than that of the nationalizing state may be more readily manipu-

lated in the judicial art, and hence property interests of such a character may more facilely escape the application of the *lex rei sitae* and fall under the principle stated in paragraph 4.

6. In the degree that the situation may be viewed by the forum court as a matter of local concern within the nationalizing state and as not affecting the international society, the *lex rei sitae* will likely become applicable under private international law. Conversely, in the degree that the situation may be viewed by the forum as not localized in the nationalizing state but as a phase of the international society—and if it is at the same time subject to effective control by a court of the forum—the court will likely recognize the interests of the international society in its decision. Thus, the forum court may apply the rule that a violation by a state of its obligations under public international law cannot become the source of private rights in the international system.[30]

In a series of cases growing out of the attempts by the Anglo-Iranian Oil Company, Limited, to recover its nationalized oil in tankers at various world ports, examination was made of the proposition set forth in the preceding sentence. Judge Lauterpacht examined such cases and reached the conclusion that they either support, or are not inconsistent with, the stated proposition.[31] A critical analysis of the cases also appears in a study by D. P. O'Connell.[32]

In the *Rose Mary* case, recovery of the claimed oil was granted on the theory that inasmuch as the expropriatory legislation was confiscatory, "following international law as incorporated in the domestic law of Aden, this court must refuse validity to the Persian Oil Nationalization Law in so far as it related to nationalized

---

[30]Lauterpacht, *Recognition in International Law,* 420; Oppenheim, 1, *International Law,* 270; Morgenstern, "Recognition and Enforcement," 326, 329; B. A. Wortley, "Expropriation in International Law," 25, 30, 31; Wolff *v.* Oxholm, [1817] 6 M. & S. 92; *In re* Fried Krupp A/G, [1917] 2 Ch. 188; Confiscation of Property of Sudeten Germans Case, Dec. 7, 1948, 1948 *Annual Digest and Reports of Public International Law Cases,* Case no. 12, 24-25 (1953); Anglo-Czechoslovak and Prague Credit Bank *v.* Janssen, [1943] V.L.R. 185; N. V. de Bataafsche Petroleum Maatschappij and Ors. *v.* The War Damage Commission, Singapore Court of Appeal, April 13, 1956, 22 *Malayan L. J.* 155 (1956), and also 51 *Am. J. Int. Law* 802 (1957).

[31]Oppenheim, 1, *International Law,* 269, note.

[32]D. P. O'Connell, "A Critique of Iranian Oil Litigation," 4 *Int. and Comp. Law Q.* 267 (1955); see, however, R. Delson, "Nationalization of the Suez Canal Company: Issues of Public and Private International Law," 52 *Colum. L. Rev.* 755, 776-778 (1957).

property of the plaintiff which may come within its territorial jurisdiction."[33]

In a decision of an Italian court, it was held that the Iranian law could be examined to determine whether it was confiscatory, and it was held that *prima facie* a procedure for compensation existed.[34] A Tokyo court, however, felt itself unable to enter into the difficulties of determining whether the legislation in question was compensatory.[35]

In two cases growing out of the Indonesian nationalization of property of Netherlands subjects, conflicting conclusions were reached as to the principle of whether private rights arising out of foreign acts of state, violative of international law, would be recognized as valid. A Netherlands court ruled that the nationalization in question violated fundamental principles of international law in that it was discriminatory, since it was directed solely against Netherlands enterprises, failed to provide for effective compensation, and was used as an instrument of national policy to exert pressure on the Netherlands in the dispute concerning sovereignty over West New Guinea (Irian Barat).[36]

A German court, the Court of Appeals at Bremen, reached different conclusions.[37] It ruled that it had not been proved that there was "a new rule of international law which binds the national

---

[33]Anglo-Iranian Oil Co., Ltd. *v.* Jaffrate, [1953] 1 *Weekly L. R.* 246, 259, and also 1953 *Int. Law Rep.* 316. In a later decision commenting on the Rose Mary case, the court stated that it did not "challenge the correctness of the decision . . . upon the facts" but that it did not wish to go so far as to say that "confiscation without adequate compensation is per se a ground for refusing recognition to foreign legislation." *In re* Claim by Helbert Wagg and Co. Ltd., [1956] 2 *Weekly L. R.* 183, 195-197, [1956] 1 Ch. 323, 346-349.

[34]Anglo-Iranian Oil Co. *v.* Societa Unione Petrolifera Orientale di Roma, 67 *Il Gazzetino*, no. 61, 4, abstracted in O'Connell, "A Critique of Iranian Oil Litigation," 283-284.

[35]Anglo-Iranian Oil Co., Ltd. *v.* Idemitsu Kosan Co. (YO) 2, 942 (1953), 1953 *Int. Law Rep.* 305; abstracted in O'Connell, "A Critique of Iranian Oil Litigation," 280-283.

[36]Senembah Maatschappij N. V. *v.* Republik Indonesie Bank Indonesia and De Twentsche Bank N. V., Appellate Court of Amsterdam, 1959, abstracted in M. Domke, "Indonesian Nationalization Measures Before Foreign Courts," 54 *Am. J. Int. Law* 305 (1960).

[37]N. V. Verenigde Deli—Maatschappijen and N. V. Senembah—Maatschappij *v.* Deutsch—Indonesische Tabak—Handelgesellschaft m.b.h., Court of Appeals at Bremen, 1959, in Domke, "Indonesian Nationalization Measures." A copy of the English translation of chapters 3 and 4 of the opinion were furnished the writer through the courtesy of Ondernemersraad voor Indonesie.

courts in pursuance of international law to treat an act of sovereignty contrary to international law as null and void from the start." In any event, it was far from clear that a violation of international law of severe character had taken place. This case involved the territorial application of the Indonesian law of nationalization, which was quite a different issue from that of applying it extraterritorially to property located outside Indonesia. The charge that the expropriation violated international law on the ground that it discriminated against Netherlands nationals was rejected. The court ruled that the case was instead one involving the dissimilar treatment of parties who were not in an equal position in view of the former colonial role of the Netherlands in the territory.

A thoughtful treatment of the legal issues involved in the nationalization by Lord McNair, Professor Henri Rolin, and Professor Alfred Verdross will be found in the literature.[38] A much more intensive reporting and analysis of the relevant precedents under international law is presented there, as compared with the opinion of the German court. It will be observed that the latter was largely influenced by private international law principles and that its consideration of international law was from the standpoint of whether such law *obliged* it to deny validity to the Indonesian act of state and not whether it was privileged by international law to do so.

The validity of the act of state doctrine of private international law, which would preclude the forum court even from inquiring into the question of whether a foreign act of state was violative of international law, is discussed in Chapter VI.[39] It is a most unfortunate extension of a doctrine initially concerned with the question of whether the forum court should inquire into the validity, from the standpoint of the constitutional law, of a legislative act of a foreign state taking effect in the territory of such state. If the basic concern of private international law is to protect action in the international system, it would seem an unfortunate extension

---

[38]Lord McNair, "The Seizure of Property and Enterprises in Indonesia," 6 *Nederlands Tidschrift voor Internationaal Recht* 218 (July, 1959); H. Rolin, "Opinion," *ibid.* 260; A. Verdross, "Dir Nationalisierung Niederländischer Unternehmengen in Indonesien im Lichte des Völkerrechts," *ibid.* 278.

[39]An important United States court decision rejecting the act of state doctrine when the act of the foreign state violates international law, viz., foreign expropriation of a confiscatory nature, rendered since the above was written, is Banco Nacional de Cuba *v.* Sabbatino, 193 F. Supp. 375 (S.D.N.Y., 1961).

of this principle to place completely beyond the scope of inquiry by the forum the validity of foreign acts of state violative of international law.

It is believed that the act of state doctrine, in holding sacrosanct foreign legislative acts even though they may violate international law, has by no means reached widespread acceptance as a rule of private international law. Failure to apply it does not violate any international duty owed another state. It is open to any court of first impression to reach its own decision of whether to accept the doctrine as a part of the private international law of the forum. The fact that the rule has gained considerable acceptance in the United States and Great Britain reveals the extent to which the methodology of private international law insulates itself from the consideration of value issues, as they are raised by specific legal norms applied to specific fact situations, a point discussed in some length in principle 9.b. of Chapter VI. The very states which would appear to be most concerned with the value of insuring respect to the principles of international law by other actors in the international system are found to be those which affirm a legal norm, in private international law, which prevents the realization of that value. Assuredly logic here prevails over experience, to paraphrase inversely Justice Holmes's famous phrase.

It is now necessary to integrate the above findings with the general theory or approach of this study.

First, the set of rules of private international law bearing on the legal effect to be attributed by the law of the forum to a foreign act of nationalization provides a considerable area of freedom to a decision maker acting thereunder. While there are a number of constraints upon him, (a) the flexibility of the system or methodology of private international law, as it proceeds through its several steps of classification, and (b) the possibilities for escape from the legal norm finally resulting therefrom, when such a norm is found to be incompatible with the values of the decision maker and the social system in which he is acting, provide the decision maker with considerable freedom of choice as to a governing legal norm.

Second, the exercise of that choice on the basis of a consideration of the appropriateness of the values embodied in the competing legal choice is not made in open manner. Although the value aspects of the problem are concealed by the methodology, they in fact considerably influence the decision maker. There is a tendency to emphasize the values which are important in the value system of the national society of the forum. This, however, remains a tendency. There is no invariable correlation between decision making and the preferred values of the social system. The highly conceptual character of private international methodology, in which the governing law is viewed remotely from the concrete human values embodied in the case, leads to anomalous results from the standpoint of values in many situations, whether they be the values of the forum or the widespread value of promoting the viability of the international system.

By way of illustration, it would appear that the rule that an act of state which violates international law cannot become the source of private rights in the international system is a rule of private international law which demands recognition and application, if private international law is to be effectively articulated with international law as the law of the international system. It is a rule strongly conducive to the viability of the international system and designed to protect the expectations of the participants in the international system. It is a rule which goes to the very foundation of a stable international system in which it will be possible for the actors to realize their shared values. International law would not deny internal validity and effect to such an act of state within the territory of the state. Neither would private international law. International law would not command adherence to the rule of private international law here affirmed; it would privilege its adoption by the forum. In such a context, it would seem that private international law should, at the minimum, support a common value in insuring respect for international law in the international system. Such a rule would affect only that part of the total commerce of the world which would be represented by goods exported to states adhering to the rule.[40] The courts of states supporting the rule would consider that their interest in supporting the viability of the international society required adherence to the rule. Consideration of such a question of policy or value is entirely appropriate in the light of the inconclusive state of the relevant law.

---

[40]Compare with N. V. Verenigde Deli—Maatschappijen and N. V. Senembah —Maatschappij v. Deutsch—Indonesische Tabak—Handelsgesellschaft m.b.h., in Domke, "Indonesian Nationalization Measures": "such a sanction would adversely affect world trade."

9.b. *A clear demarcation of the systems of private and public international law, as they bear upon an international situation of interstate or interpersonal conflict, is an essential part of the decision-making process.*

In a recent study in private and public international law concerning state contracts, the author speaks of "a fundamental error which would not have arisen if public international lawyers had had due regard to the character and teachings of private international law."[41] The study in question avers that when a contract by a state with an alien is subjected to the law of the contracting state, legislative measures of that state, which are of a general character involving the regulation of property and are put into effect for the benefit of the community at large, do not constitute an unlawful taking of property, even though they may bring about a breach of such contract. United States decisions are principally cited in support of this thesis.[42] The author is, however, of the opinion that "measures specifically designed to terminate or interfere with the particular contract in issue" entrain international responsibility.[43]

The principle under discussion, namely, that a clear demarcation of the systems of private and public international law is required in the decision of international disputes, is one with which the author in question appears to be in agreement. The point at issue is only that of where the demarcation line shall be drawn. This inquiry will be the subject matter of the remaining portion of this chapter. For the present, the following thoughts seem relevant.

International law treats legislative and executive acts of a state as objective facts. The circumstance that legislation is of a general character, as distinguished from a specific character, is of relevance only to the degree that the practice of states and other sources of international law have found the distinction to be significant in determining the content of international law norms. Whether a state's law of nationalization which prematurely terminates its contractual obligation is a violation of international law

---

[41] F. A. Mann, "State Contracts and State Responsibility," 54 *Am. J. Int. Law* 573, 580-581 (1960).
[42] *Ibid.*, 584.
[43] *Ibid.*, 575.

is precisely the legal issue before us for determination. It is not determined under international law when it is relegated to the sphere of private international law, and a consequent determination is made that the law of the state engaged in nationalization is the governing law of the contract. The question at this point is how public international law would characterize the legal consequences of such an act of state, namely, an act of nationalization prematurely terminating an international contract. For this purpose, international law treats the law of the state in question as an objective fact to which the appropriate rule of international law is applied. The received methodology of international law determines what that rule may be. It is not found by asserting that the matter falls in the domain of private international law, true as that fact may be as an independent proposition in the body of private international law.

9.c. *International law will regulate an act of nationalization prematurely terminating a concession agreement insofar as claims of states, whose interests are thereby affected, may be resolved by the accepted methodology of international law.*

9.c.1. *The first step in the legal analysis of an act of nationalization under international law is the determination of what facts are, as a matter of law, relevant to a decision as to the legality of such an act.*

The first step in the legal analysis of a problem is the determination of what facts are operative, under the law, to establish legal relations of a defined content. To know what is in life a duty, what behavior involves performance of a duty, on the one hand, or a violation of a duty, on the other hand, must be known. A legal norm is always related to specific, concrete, describable human behavior. The norm attributes meaning to the behavior pursuant to the operation of the legal system.

Statements of such an elementary character are made at this point because nationalization initially raises the fundamental question of what acts raise what legal issues for the purpose of deciding on the governing legal norm. The literature on nationalization reveals some rather baffling examples of analytical definition of the legal issues, as raised by facts. Thus F. V. Garcia Amador, of the International Law Commission, states: "According to a generally accepted principle, an expropriation is not necessarily 'unlawful' even when the action imputable to the State is contrary to international law . . . an expropriation can only be termed 'unlawful' in cases where the State is expressly forbidden to take such action under a treaty or international convention."[44]

It is apparent that Amador has adopted a referent for the term "unlawful" which is of a rather restricted, if not unusual, character. Elsewhere he seems to be of the view that "expropriation is intrinsically lawful" under international law and becomes "unlawful" only when it violates an international agreement. He states that "responsibility, if any, in the case of (lawful) expropriation will depend, in so far as indemnification is concerned, solely on the amount, promptness and form of the compensation paid. Responsibility would in fact arise from the 'arbitrary' act of the compensation."

Other writers have affirmed the lawfulness, or legitimacy, of an act of nationalization, even when adequate compensation is not paid. This proposition is said to be sustained by the views of writers and the *Chorzow Factory* case.[45]

Examination of the above references to other writers reveals that generally they do not categorically affirm that nationalization may be lawfully accomplished under international law, without compensation. From the standpoint of international law, one of them, Doman, correctly states the rule: "The predominant view in international law today seems to recognize the sovereign right of a state to embark upon social experiments provided it grants adequate and fair compensation to foreign owners of property.[46]

De Visscher also recognizes that international law does not preclude a state from establishing within its own territory its own internal economy and government, but, in the event of nationalization, does "make adequate indemnification the international obligation, and make refusal to indemnify the basis of a responsibility

---

[44]F. V. Garcia Amador, *Fourth Report on International Responsibility*, International Law Commission, U.N. Doc. A/CN.4/119, Feb. 26, 1959.

[45]Delson, "Nationalization of the Suez Canal Company," 755, 762, 764; Foighel, *Nationalization*, 41, 71; N. R. Doman, "Postwar Nationalization of Foreign Property in Europe," 48 *Colum. L. Rev.* 1125, 1127 (1948); J. H. Herz, "Expropriation of Foreign Property," 35 *Am. J. Int. Law* 243, 253 (1941); Case of the Chorzow Factory, P.C.I.J., Judgment 13, ser. A, no. 17, 47 (1928).

[46]Doman, "Postwar Nationalization."

which is generally delictual, but becomes contractual if nationalization is decreed in violation of an international undertaking."[47]

Herz distinguishes between an act of expropriation creating the duty to pay compensation for the property taken, which he classifies as "ordinary, lawful expropriation," and an act of expropriation which is "legal or tortious," as in violation of a treaty. The latter type of act is said to be of significance in creating the duty to make *restitutio in integrum;* whereas the former creates the duty to pay cash compensation for direct losses.[48] The dichotomy arises from the *Chorzow Factory* case, discussed later, and is significant in the matter of measurement of damages; it is not to be viewed as implying that expropriation without compensation is a lawful act under international law.

The power of a state to nationalize property in its own territory and under its own municipal law is to be distinguished from the consequences of the exercise of that power under international law. When such an exercise of power takes place in violation of the conditions imposed by international law, a violation of international law occurs. More precisely, a right of the injured state is violated and a duty owed it fails to be performed by the nationalizing state. The circumstance that the act of nationalization may be internally of force and effect under the municipal law of the nationalizing state does not lead to the consequence that it is "lawful" or valid under international law, nor does it prevent the creation of the rights granted by international law to a state whose interests have been injured by an act of nationalization failing to meet the standards imposed by international law.

Foighel affirms that the nationalization of foreign property is "a legitimate expression of the jurisdiction of a state" from the standpoint of international law.[49] It would seem from his discussion of the topic of legality in Part II of his text, as well as from the context of the statement itself, that he is asserting that international law does not bar nationalization within the territorial jurisdiction of a state. He states that "the liability to pay compensation is not a pre-condition for the lawfulness of the said act, but a result of the same."[50] Elsewhere he strongly affirms the rule

[47]C. de Visscher, *Theory and Reality in International Law,* 193 (1957).
[48]Herz, "Expropriation of Foreign Property," 253.
[49]Foighel, *Nationalization,* 71.
[50]*Ibid.,* 41.

that compensation must be adequate, promptly paid, and effective.[51] It is highly significant that he does so after a full examination of postwar treaty practice in the matter of settlement of claims for losses occasioned by nationalization. His conclusion on this point should be carefully borne in mind when we later take up the legal significance of the nationalization settlements: "the traditional principles of international law concerning the determination of compensation have not been set aside in the treaties so far concluded, although the discretionary element—which as a matter of fact is inherent in most calculations of compensation—as a result of the nature of the nationalized property and its extent, plays a predominant part."[52]

The *Chorzow Factory* case has been cited for the proposition that a state may lawfully nationalize foreign-owned property within its jurisdiction, unless prohibited by treaty.[53] There is no question that the Permanent Court of International Justice held that expropriation in violation of a treaty was an internationally unlawful act, requiring restitution of its equivalent in damages. It did so, however, pursuant to a broader rule, which is clearly enunciated, that the duty to make such reparation arose because the violation of a treaty was "an act contrary to international law."[54] Any other internationally illegal act would equally entail the duty to make such reparation. The lawfulness of expropriation without adequate compensation was not recognized. On the contrary, the court took pains to make it clear that expropriation without fair compensation was unlawful under international law, and, as such, equally subject to the duty to make restitution in kind or, if not possible, its equivalent in damages. The court stated that "the principle of respect for vested rights . . . forms part of generally accepted international law, which, as regards this point, amongst others, constitutes the basis of the Geneva Convention."[55]

It now becomes appropriate to examine the *Chorzow Factory* case, which is typically cited to support the asserted lawfulness of

---

[51]*Ibid.*, 115-126.

[52]*Ibid.*, 119.

[53]Delson, "Nationalization of the Suez Canal Company," 764.

[54]"Such are the principles which should serve to determine the amount of compensation due for an act contrary to international law." P.C.I.J., ser. A, no. 17, 47.

[55]*Ibid.*, 42.

expropriation of foreign interests in property, except where prohibited by treaty. The usual citation is to the judgment on the
claim for indemnity on the merits, being Judgment 13 of the
Permanent Court of International Justice.[56] This judgment was
preceded, among others, by Judgments 7 and 9, dealing in part
with the same matter and entitled, respectively, *Case Concerning
Certain German Interests in Polish Upper Silesia (The Merits)*
and *Case Concerning the Factory at Chorzow (Claim for Indemnity) (Jurisdiction).*[57] All three must be considered in determining
the general propositions of law for which the jurisprudence of the
court stands in this matter.

The *Chorzow Factory* case arose between Germany and Poland
out of the expropriation by the latter of a nitrate factory at
Chorzow in Upper Silesia pursuant to a Polish law of July 14,
1920. The ownership of the land and factory had originally been
in Germany. By a contract of March 5, 1915, Germany had given
the Bayerische company the right to operate the factory until
1941. On December 24, 1919, the ownership of the property was
transferred by Germany to the Oberschlesische company, but the
operation of the factory still remained in the Bayerische company.

In July, 1922, as the territory of Upper Silesia had come under
the control of Poland, pursuant to the law of July 14, 1920, Poland
extinguished all property interests of the Oberschlesische company,
substituted for it the Polish treasury, and caused a delegate of the
state to take over the management of the factory. Germany contested the legality of these acts in a suit before the court, contend-
ing *inter alia* that they violated the Geneva Convention.

It now becomes necessary to examine rather closely the content
and scope of the decisions of the Permanent Court of International
Justice and the exact meaning of the language used by it in its
judgments.

The precise holding of the court in the decretal part of its
judgment was that the application of the Polish law of July 14,
1920, in Polish Upper Silesia was contrary to article 6 and the following articles of the Geneva Convention, insofar as it affected
German nationals or companies controlled by German nationals.
The court specifically ruled that the attitude of the Polish govern-

---

[56]*Ibid.*
[57]*Ibid.*, no. 7 (1926) and no. 9 (1927).

ment in regard to the Oberschlesische and Bayerische companies was not in conformity with said articles of the convention. It expressly did not enter into any ruling upon what conduct on the part of Poland would have been in conformity with such articles.[58]

The court so ruled in response to the first submission of the German government, as amended, and the second submission, to the effect that any application of the law of July 14, 1920, not authorized by said articles of the Geneva Convention, was "illicit" and, specifically, that such application to the Oberschlesische and Bayerische companies was not in conformity with said articles.

Article 6 of the Geneva Convention provided that: "Poland may expropriate in Polish Upper Silesia, in conformity with the provisions of Articles 7 to 23, undertakings belonging to the category of major industries including mineral deposits and rural estates. *Except as provided in these clauses,* the property, rights and interests of German nationals or of companies controlled by German nationals *may not be liquidated* in Polish Upper Silesia." (Italics supplied in this and subsequent quotations from this case to assist reader in grasping the court's reasoning.)

The court construed article 6 "to convey the meaning that, *subject to the provisions authorizing expropriation,* the treatment accorded to German private property, rights and interests in Polish Upper Silesia *is to be the treatment recognized by the generally accepted principles of international law.*" In any event, it was said to be certain that expropriation was only lawful to the extent authorized by article 7 and the following articles.[59]

The relevant principles of international law were laid down in the next page of the judgment:

Further, *there can be no doubt that the expropriation allowed* under Head III of the Convention *is a derogation from the rules generally applied in regard to the treatment of foreigners and principle of respect for vested rights.* As this derogation is itself strictly in the nature of an exception, it is permissible to conclude that no further derogation is allowed. Any measure affecting the property, rights and interests of German subjects covered by Head III of the Convention, *and which oversteps the limits set by the generally accepted principles of international law,* is therefore incompatible with the régime established by the Convention.[60]

---

[58]*Ibid.*, no. 7, 81.
[59]*Ibid.*, 21.
[60]*Ibid.*, 22.

Some pages later the court said that it clearly emerged from Head III of the Geneva Convention "that *expropriation, in the cases and under the conditions mentioned therein,* is the *only* measure not allowed by generally accepted international law *which may be taken in regard to German private property in Upper Silesia.*"[61]

The court was careful to reaffirm that "the principle of respect for vested rights . . . *forms part of generally accepted international law*" and "amongst others, *constitutes the basis of the Geneva Convention.*"[62]

The exact scope of its holding in Judgment 7 was laid down by the court as follows in a reference to it in Judgment 9:

> In Judgment No. 7 it held that, as the expropriation allowed under Head III of the Geneva Convention, *is a derogation from the rules generally applied as regards the treatment of foreigners and from the principles of respect for vested rights,* and this derogation is itself of a strictly exceptional character, any other measure affecting the property, rights and interests of German nationals contemplated in Head III and not supported by some special authority having precedence over the Convention, *and which oversteps the limits of generally accepted international law,* is incompatible with the régime established by the Convention. The *seizure* of the property, rights and interests belonging to the Oberschlesische and Bayerische *was precisely a measure of this kind.*[63]

Consequently, when the court came to consider the German government's claim for reparation or indemnity in Judgment 13, it was careful to define the exact scope of the case before it: "The present application is explicitly and exclusively based on Judgment No. 7 which declared that the attitude of the Polish Government in respect of the two Companies, the Oberschlesische and the Bayerische, was not in conformity with Article 6 and the following articles of the said Convention."[64]

The first question which the court took up concerned the extent of reparation to be made to Oberschlesische, *as the owner of the factory.* The court said that "the damage caused by an *unlawful* act," insofar as the "damage suffered by the Oberschlesiche in respect of the Chorzow undertaking" is concerned, was "equiva-

---

[61]*Ibid.,* 32.
[62]*Ibid.,* 42.
[63]*Ibid.,* no. 9, 27.
[64]*Ibid.,* no. 17, 26.

lent to the total value—but to that total only—of the *property rights and interests* of this company in that undertaking, without deducting liabilities."[65]

The court then proceeded to consider the question of the extent of reparation for the seizure of the property, rights, and interest of the Bayerische company, *as the operator of the undertaking or enterprise.* It will be recalled that the court had ruled in Judgment 7 that the expropriation under the Polish law of July 14, 1920, was unlawful as contrary to the Geneva Convention "insofar as it affects German nationals or companies controlled by German nationals." It will be further recalled that article 6 of that convention had permitted Poland to "expropriate" certain types of property in Polish Upper Silesia, but otherwise had expressly prohibited any German private property from being "liquidated." Concerning the operative language of article 6 of the Convention, the court had said in Judgment 7:

It is only in the second part of this article that the word "liquidated" occurs: as has already been stated, the section is headed "Expropriation," and in all the articles the words "expropriate" and "expropriation" are used. Having regard to the context, it seems reasonable to suppose that the intention was, *bearing in mind the régime of liquidation instituted by the peace treaties of 1919,* to convey the meaning that, subject to the provisions authorizing expropriation, the treatment accorded to German private property, rights and interests in Polish Upper Silesia is *to be the treatment recognized by the generally accepted principles of international law.*[66]

Article 7 of the Convention, in authorizing the expropriation of major industries, had required that such expropriation conform to articles 92 and 297 of the Versailles Peace Treaty, which regulated the liquidation of German property. Article 92 required that the proceeds of liquidation be paid directly to the German owner, and safeguarded, through arbitration, any claim of such owner that the amount of payment was inadequate.[67]

With respect to the meaning to be attached to the word "expropriation" in its Judgment 7, the court had said that it would use that term *to denote the measures referred to in Head III of the Geneva Convention.*[68]

---

[65]*Ibid.,* 31.
[66]*Ibid.,* 21.
[67]*Ibid.,* ser. C, no. 9-I, 323, 327.
[68]*Ibid.,* ser. A, no. 7, 22.

It is now necessary to consider the critical language of Judgment 13, cited as supporting the proposition that nationalization is lawful under international law, apart from the issue of compensation.[69] It seems quite clear that with this language in its context the court is contrasting *lawful expropriation under or consistent with the convention with unlawful dispossession in violation of its terms,* and is doing so against the background of its previously stated view that international law protects vested rights from spoliation. The full language of the court on this point is as follows:

> The action of Poland which the Court has judged to be contrary to the Geneva Convention is not an expropriation—to render which lawful only the payment of fair compensation would have been wanting; it is a seizure of property, rights and interests which could not be expropriated even against compensation, save under the exceptional conditions fixed by Article 7 of the said Convention. As the Court has expressly declared in Judgment No. 8, reparation is in this case the consequence, not of the application of Articles 6 to 22 of the Geneva Convention, but of acts contrary to those articles.[70]

In short, if the term "lawful" in the above-quoted critical phrase, "to render which [expropriation] lawful only the payment of fair compensation would have been wanting," be taken to refer to lawful in the sense of international law, the court is clearly saying that expropriation *without* fair compensation is *unlawful* under international law. If, however, the court is using the term "lawful" in the sense of whether a violation of a treaty was involved, it had very clearly elsewhere negated any implication that the expropriation of foreign private property without compensation was in its view lawful under international law. Such an act was instead unlawful as a violation of the principle of respect for vested or acquired rights. The "expropriation allowed under the Convention . . . is a derogation from the rules generally applied in regard to the treatment of foreigners and principle of respect for vested rights."

The term "expropriation" in the critical quotation in the second paragraph above, which has been used as a foundation for the reasoning that expropriation, in and of itself, is lawful under international law, can only be appreciated and validly used in the light of the meaning which the court itself attributed to the term. There

---

[69] *Ibid.,* no. 17.
[70] *Ibid.,* 46.

appear to be three situations with which the court considered itself to be concerned:

First, the "liquidation" by a state of the property of foreigners, apart from the Versailles Peace Treaty and the Geneva Convention. The court was of the view that such a liquidation departed from the generally accepted principles of international law, including the principle of respect for vested or acquired rights.

Second, the "liquidation" of German private property by the Allied and Associated Powers pursuant to article 297 of the Versailles Peace Treaty.

Third, the "expropriation" of specific categories of German private property by Poland pursuant to the Geneva Convention. Here the ruling of the court was that, except to the extent that "expropriation" was permitted under the Geneva Convention, any liquidation must be in conformity with international law as stated in the first situation above.

The above-quoted language, once it is understood in the context of the entire situation before the court and its judicial reasoning concerning that situation, becomes quite clear. The action of Poland was not "expropriation" pursuant to the Geneva Convention; it was action *outside* the Convention and *not in conformity with the generally recognized principles of international law*, namely, the principle of respect for vested or acquired rights. The action was, therefore, unlawful, and its unlawfulness could not now be cured by "the payment of fair compensation," as stipulated by the Convention. Thus the opinion is precisely to the contrary of the meaning attributed to it by the writers named above.

To state that expropriation or nationalization by itself is "lawful" or "unlawful" under international law is lacking in precision in that it does not point to (1) whether international law does or does not altogether deny to a state the power to nationalize property in its territory, insofar as the legal effects thereof under its *own* system of law are concerned; and (2) whether such an act is to be accepted as a juridical or operative fact leading to certain legal consequences in international law, and whether, if so, such legal consequences under international law involve the exercise of a privilege by the nationalizing state or the violation of a duty owed another state. If the latter, it does not indicate whether such other state is privileged under international law to deny legal effects under its own municipal system of law, to reparation or other appropriate relief for the injury sustained, or to use measures of coercion short of war when the violation of the duty is not remedied by the delictual state.

9.c.2. *The statement of the applicable legal norms, in international law as well as any other system of law, is a statement of facts comprising a situation and the legal consequences of such facts.*

The rules of international law bearing on nationalization of a property by a state will briefly be summarized at this point; the demonstration of the evidence of law in support of these will be made later. It is necessary to state, as precisely and briefly as possible, the pertinent facts and the legal consequences of such facts as they are embodied in the relevant international law norms.

First, when a state nationalizes a tangible *res* physically located within its territory and no national of any other state has any claim to it, the situation falls outside the scope of international law.

Second, when a state nationalizes on a nondiscriminatory basis and for a public purpose a tangible *res* located within its territory and a national of another state has a claim to it, but adequate (that is, full and effective) compensation is promptly paid for it, ordinarily no consequences under international law follow.

An exception to the foregoing may be property strongly impressed with an international character. The Suez Canal, physically located within the territory of Egypt, would in this view be immune from nationalization by Egypt, even if adequate compensation were promptly paid. The United States, France, and the United Kingdom took this position.[71] Such a position rests on the international character of the canal, which was recognized in the international character of the Universal Company of the Suez Maritime Canal in its constitutive acts, the membership of its board of directors, its staffing, its concession agreement with Egypt, its protection under treaty, and the ramifications of the effect of its operation upon international trade and the economies and military strength of other states.

Despite the nationalization of the Suez Canal established by Egypt, the canal still possesses an international character. The

---

[71]Tripartite Statement, Aug. 2, 1956, U.S. Dept. of State, *The Suez Canal Problem,* July 26–Sept. 22, 1956, 34 (1956).

inconsistency of national control of an institution of an international character will be a continuing source of tension in international affairs.

Third, the nationalization by a state of property in which a national of another state then has an interest will involve the following consequences under international law:

a. If such property should be located in the territory of the nationalizing state but adequate compensation for it is not paid or its payment is unduly withheld, such other state is under no duty to the nationalizing state to give legal effect within its territory to the act of nationalization and is privileged to deny such legal effect, either legislatively or judicially, to the extent necessary to protect its interests, including the interest of its national. The exercise of such a privilege may occur when the property so nationalized later becomes subject to the territorial jurisdiction of such other state.

b. If such property should be located in the territory of the nationalizing state, and without regard to whether adequate compensation is paid by the nationalizing state, the rule of the paragraph above applies when such nationalization is violative of a treaty, is not in the exercise of a public purpose, or is discriminatory against nationals of the other state.

c. If at the time of the act of nationalization such property should be located in the territory of another state, whether or not adequate compensation is paid by the nationalizing state, the state of the situs and other foreign states are under no duty to the nationalizing state to give legal effect to the act of nationalization.

d. In the situations described in paragraphs a and b above, the injured state may use such means of coercion short of war, such as sequestration of assets, as may be reasonably calculated to protect its interests and the interests of its national.

e. In the situations described in paragraphs a and b, the nationalizing state violates a duty owed under international law to the other state and the latter may recover in any international court possessing jurisdiction adequate reparation or other appropriate relief for any loss or injury resulting therefrom.

10. *The international law norm governing a premature termination by a state of a concession agreement with an alien effected*

*by an act of nationalization is that such action will entail interna-
tional responsibility to the state of which the alien is a national
to make prompt, adequate, and effective compensation.*

10.a. *The above legal norm represents an ideal and valued
norm of behavior by virtue of the fact that it embodies an acceptable composite or adjustment of the values involved in the
situations to which the norm is applicable.*

A rule of law represents a composite or adjustment of values.
The reaching of a value consensus with respect to a rule of law
is not a process of drawing a graph in which lines representing
values, as found in different norms of behavior, finally intersect. It
is a matter of arriving at a statement of conduct in the situation
which, taking into account the various aspects of mechanical and
value rationality implicit in the situation, will become an authoritative statement of an ideal and valued norm. The term "authoritative," as used in the preceding sentence, means that it is a
statement which the relevant actors in the society will accept as a
basis for their conduct and for determining the point at which measures of social control shall become applicable to deviant conduct.
There will be many elements leading to such an acceptance, including the degree to which it is perceived to be an appropriate
means for attaining valued goals, its congruence with the cultural
outlook of the actors, the formal and substantive legitimacy surrounding the enunciation of the rules, and the like. When the decision maker proclaims the governing legal norm for the situation
before him, he brings to the surface the ideal image of action
implicit in the situation and congeals the attitude of actors in the
society with respect to the situation.

A situation of interpersonal conflict is not appropriate for decision by the legal process when the intensity of attachment of the
actors in the society to the conflicting values embodied in the situation is so great that the principle of third-party adjudication is
incapable of resolving that conflict (see principle 3 in this chapter).
In such a situation, the appropriate means for structuring social
action is the political process and institutions rather than the legal
process. It will be recalled that the term "political" was defined
in principle 1: As the intensity of attachment of the actors in a
situation of conflict to the opposing values involved increases and

the number of actors in such value conflict increases, the situation approaches the political sphere. When conflict in a society involves competing group demands based on incompatible values held by such groups, its resolution is typically the task of the political process and institutions, rather than the legal process. On the other hand, when the typical attitude of actors in the society to the value conflict involved in a situation of interpersonal conflict is one which tolerates its resolution by third-party adjudication *and the conflict is statable in competing legal norms,* then the judge may resolve the conflict within the framework of the legal process. In such a situation, his decision and his reasoned opinion, together with the formal and substantive legitimacy of the legal system, as embodied in the performance of his role, will congeal the attitude of actors in the society so that they will accept his statement of ideal behavior in the selected governing legal norm. For example, in 1946 the author made a study of the instances in which international arbitral awards had been attacked for nullity. It was found that charges of nullity were often made with respect to decisions in boundary controversies. Even though such disputes were statable in terms of competing legal norms, the value conflict of the litigating states created such tensions as to impose great stress upon adherence to the principle of third-party adjudication.[72]

In principle 3 of this chapter, the need to appraise the findings of the international law scholar or judge in the light of his value premises was emphasized. The writer's perspective toward the province and function of law in the international system has been made abundantly clear by this time. It is that law in the international system, as in any social system, should secure the conditions necessary for effective interaction in the system with a view to realizing commonly shared values by the actors, as well as adherence to ideal and valued norms of behavior.

It is now necessary to demonstrate, to the extent possible, that the above norm possesses value rationality from the standpoint of

---

[72]"The sensitiveness of States in boundary controversies, touching, as they do, a vital source of state power, renders exceedingly difficult the task of an arbitrator in such a controversy. It is believed that this factor of sensitiveness is in large part the cause of the recurrence of boundary arbitrations in the several instances in which the validity of an award has been attacked." K. S. Carlston, *The Process of International Arbitration,* 207 (1946).

actors in the international system to the degree that it can be said to be an ideal and valued norm. The standard or ideal norm of conduct upon which the law applicable to disputes is based is to be found in the day-to-day life of the international system. Search for it is not to be limited to the pathology of international conduct involved in disputes.

Moreover, the search for legal norms in the international system binding those actors which are states is not to be limited to the practice of states. The general principles of law recognized by civilized nations and international judicial and arbitral decisions may today be regarded as valid sources of international law (Chapter VI, 9.e.4. and 9.e.5.).

Principle 11.e. of Chapter V affirmed that resort to the agreement rather than resort to authority is the principal means for coordinating action in the international system. Where actors find that they share a value attachment to certain goals which can be attained by complementary patterns of action, the agreement embodies a definition of such goals and the processes of interaction to which the actors will commit themselves to attain them. Since the actors involved are organizations, that is, both states and international corporations, the agreement makes possible the joint use of the *internal* authority of such actors to mesh their organizational action in a combined, single structure of action, as defined in the agreement. Inasmuch as actors in the international system only minimally acknowledge a superior authority as a means of coordinating their action, adherence to the principle of *pacta sunt servanda* is of prime importance. International law has correspondingly adopted as one of its basic principles *pacta sunt servanda*.[73]

While treaties or agreements between states are binding, in the sense that a violation thereof by one party is a violation of a duty under international law to the other party to respect the terms of the treaty, the rules by which respect for international contracts between a state and an alien is secured are not quite so simple and direct. The relevant legal norms will be briefly described at this point in order to make clear their value implications.

When a state makes a contract with an alien, it may be said to leave the public sphere and its corresponding *jus imperii,* and to enter the private sphere of commerce and its corresponding *jus*

---

[73]H. Wehberg, "Pacta Sunt Servanda," 53 *Am. J. Int. Law* 775 (1959).

gestionis. As long as the state confines its conduct to that which is appropriate for any private contracting party, no issue in international law arises. The contract is considered to be governed by some system of municipal law, as determined by private international law. A breach of a contract by a state, arising as a consequence of claimed contractual power, is one regulated by the proper law of the contract and subject to remedy in the courts of the forum possessing jurisdiction. For this purpose, such courts will be those of the contracting state. Jurisdiction elsewhere would, in any event, be most difficult to establish under the principle of sovereign immunity. If nonperformance by the state of its contractual obligation owed the alien results in an injury to such alien and the local remedies are exhausted without adequate redress, the state is responsible under international law and owes a duty to the alien's state to make adequate reparation.

The foregoing statement of law is based on the findings of the Harvard Draft Convention on Responsibility of States of 1929,[74] as well as the evidence of law to be cited later. A later study by Professors Sohn and Baxter of Harvard University, bearing the title "Convention on the International Responsibility of States for Injuries to Aliens, Preliminary Draft with Explanatory Notes, Harvard Law School, May 1, 1959," lists a number of types of state action with respect to a contract or concession agreement by a state with an alien which entail international responsibility. In the explanatory note, it is stated that "doctrine and jurisprudence" limit "State responsibility for a violation of a concession or contract to those cases in which there has been a 'denial of justice' in litigation in the courts of the respondent State respecting an alleged breach of the contract; to cases in which the breach of the contract or concession has been 'tortious'; or to cases in which there has been

---

[74] "(a) A state is responsible if an injury to an alien results from its non-performance of a contractual obligation which it owes to the alien, if local remedies have been exhausted without adequate redress. (b) A state is not responsible if an injury results from the non-performance of a contractual obligation which its political subdivision owes to an alien, apart from responsibility because of a denial of justice." It should be noted that the comment following this statement distinguished cases in which "the arbitrary annulment of a contract by the Executive without appeal to the courts was held to justify diplomatic interposition and to render the state responsible." Harvard Research in International Law, "Draft Convention on Responsibility of States," 23 *Am. J. Int. Law* (spec. supp.) 167, 170-171 (1929).

an 'abusive' use of the executive powers of the State in order to avoid obligations under the agreement."[75]

The reciprocal character of an international contract was deemed in one international case to render unlawful its termination by the act of a state.[76] Certainly here is one of the most basic of human expectations, namely, the expectation that a solemn promise of another, upon which future action of both promisee and promisor is to be based, will be kept. This is an expectation which any system of law must protect. Its protection is indeed a general principle of law universally recognized by civilized states. Yet international law can hardly make its articulation with municipal law by so crude a means as making its own norm precisely coextensive with the municipal law norm that substantially any breach of a contractual expectation is unlawful. On the other hand, it cannot adopt a rule which would fail to reflect the general principle of protection of contract, if the economic interdependency of states is to be preserved.

It becomes apparent that the circumstances in which a state terminates its contract with an alien are critical. Clearly, a termination by a state in claimed exercise of a contractual power should not engage international responsibility when the courts of the contracting state are available to resolve the controversy on a basis of uniform justice. On the other hand, an arbitrary or tortious termination of the contract will engage international responsibility.

Officials concerned with the contract will typically view it from the perspective of their own national society and its value system (Chapter VI, 8.b.). The appropriate means for control of questions arising with respect to the contract will be considered by them to be the law and legal process of the contracting state (Chapter VI, 9.a.). The reasonableness of such a viewpoint will be conceded by the alien and the state of which he is a national, at least when any disputes that may arise are limited to the sphere of contract action. Accordingly, when conduct by the state with respect to its contract with the alien is confined to that of any private person in a contractual situation, when termination of a

---

[75]Harvard Law School, *Convention on the International Responsibility of States*, 75 at 77.

[76]Cedroni (Italy) *v.* Guatemala, Award of Oct. 12, 1898. H. La Fontaine, *Pasicrisie International: Histoire Documentaire des Arbitrages Internationaux,* 606 (1902).

contract is pursuant to a claimed contractual power, instead of an exercise of sovereign power, and access by the alien to the courts remains open to secure an adequate remedy, then the matter remains outside the concern of international law. The expectations of individuals contracting with a foreign state or international system are then still protected by the legal system of such foreign state. However, those expectations cease to be so protected and the basis for the rule vanishes when there is no adequate local remedy, when the foreign state so exercises its sovereignty as to make impossible, or unreasonably delay, resort to local remedies to obtain justice.

In the *El Triunfo* case, the relevant value was put as follows: "It is abhorrent to the sense of justice to say that one party to a contract, whether such a party be a private individual, a monarch, or a government of any kind, may arbitrarily, without hearing and without impartial procedure of any sort, arrogate the right to condemn the other party to the contract, to pass judgment upon him and his acts, and to impose upon him the extreme penalty of forfeiture of all his rights under it, including his property and his investment of capital made on the faith of that contract."[77]

In the *Rudloff* case, Commissioner Bainbridge said: "It is contrary to every principle of natural justice that one party to a contract may pass judgment on the other and this is no less true when the former is a government and the latter is a foreign citizen. Public law regards the parties to a contract as of equal dignity, equally entitled to the hearing of an impartial and disinterested tribunal."[78]

In the *Trujillo and Salaverry Railroad* case, the United States Department of State took the following position with respect to the action of Peru in seizing an investment made under concessions:

These investments have been made under concessions from the government of Peru which no subsequent revolutions in that state can invalidate, and which can only be cancelled by judicial action sustainable on the principles of international law applicable to such cases. Not only, however, has there been no such judicial action but such action can not, I

---

[77]El Triunfo Company, Ltd. (U.S.) *v.* Salvador, Award of May 8, 1902, 1902 *For. Rel. U.S.* 859, 862 at 871.

[78]Rudloff (U.S.) *v.* Venezuela, American-Venezuelan Claims Commission, Ralston's Report, Venezuelan Arbitrations of 1903, Sen. Doc. 316, 58th Cong., 2nd Sess., 182, 187 (1904). This document is hereafter referred to as Ralston's Report.

am advised, be obtained, there being no tribunal in Peru invested with the functions of determining as to the validity of legislative acts. And even were there such a tribunal, its decrees, validating in defiance of international law such confiscations, could not bind the citizens of foreign states thereby despoiled. The function of vindicating the rights. so impaired belongs in such cases to the sovereign of the parties despoiled. It becomes, therefore, the function of the government of the United States, acting on the basis of the facts stated, to intervene to protect under such circumstances the persons and property of its citizens in Peru. It will be your duty to protest in the most serious terms against the enforcement of the edicts of spoilation [sic] of which the memoralists complain.[79]

Thus the rational and value basis is laid for the norm that *when a state terminates its contract with an alien in the exercise of a sovereign power, instead of claimed contractual right, such as an act of nationalization, international responsibility to the state of which such alien is a national will directly and immediately arise.* The foregoing norm becomes an ideal and valued norm because it embodies an acceptable composite or adjustment of values.

The above principle becomes applicable with particular force and appropriateness when there is an arbitration clause in the concession agreement which the state has violated in nationalizing the enterprise and property constituted by the agreement. There is a growing rule that the legality of questioned state action may be made to depend upon the issue of whether the state involved is willing to submit such a question to judicial determination. One of the earliest examples is the provision of article 1 of the Hague Convention (No. 2) respecting the "Limitation of the Employment of Force for the Recovery of Contract Debts." This article embodies the so-called Porter Proposition and provides that a state may not use force to recover contract debts owed its nationals by another state unless "the debtor State refuses or neglects to reply to an offer of arbitration, or, after the arbitration, fails to submit to the award."[80] Under article 33 of the Charter of the United Nations, the parties to a dispute are required, first of all, to seek a solution thereof by peaceful means, including arbitration and judicial settle-

---

[79]Instructions from Secretary of State Thomas F. Bayard to Mr. Buck, Jan. 19, 1888, J. B. Moore, 6, *Digest of International Law*, 253, 254 (1906); see also J. H. Ralston, *Law and Procedure of International Tribunals*, 83 (rev. ed., 1926).

[80]J. B. Scott, *The Hague Conventions and Declarations of 1899 and 1907*, 489 (1915).

ment. The failure or refusal by a state to submit to arbitration the validity of its termination of the concession agreement, in violation of an arbitration clause contained therein, creates international responsibility to the state of the concessionaire.[81]

The availability of the arbitral process is of peculiar significance in the resolution of disputes which must inevitably arise in the long-term arrangements usually provided for in a concession agreement. The agreement typically contains a clause requiring resort to arbitration as a means for settling such disputes. Provision is thereby made for dealing in a regularized and impartial manner with the problems of changed conditions arising in the course of the term of the contract.

As stated in one international arbitration between a private corporation and a state, the fact that the state has not realized its expectations of profit cannot be considered sufficient reason for releasing the state from its obligations as signatory of the concession agreement.[82] Nevertheless, with the passing of the years, new and unanticipated conditions may arise creating unexpected hardships upon one of the parties. It is at this point that the presence of arbitration clauses in concession agreements becomes of critical importance. The right to rely upon arbitration as a means for the solution of difficulties arising out of the contractual relationships of the parties has, among other forces, led to the creation of a type of "living law" of the contract that the parties will, first of all, negotiate in good faith in an effort to resolve their disputes.

When such negotiation fails, then there is always available the arbitral process, and usually under the contract it becomes the duty of the parties to resort to arbitration to settle their difference. In appreciating the suitability of the arbitral tribunal for this purpose, it must be remembered that, unless otherwise restricted in

---

[81]North and South American Construction Co. (U.S.) *v.* Chile, J. B. Moore, 3, *History and Digest of the International Arbitrations to Which the United States Has Been a Party*, 2318 (1898); de Visscher, *Theory and Reality*, 194; A. Verdross, "Die Sicherung von ausländischen Privatrechten aus Abkommen zur wirtschaftlichen Entwicklung mit Schiedklauseln," 18 *Zeitschrift für ausländisches öffentliches Recht und Völkerrecht* 635 (1958), translated under the title of "The Status of Foreign Private Interests Stemming from Economic Development Agreements with Arbitration Clauses," 9 *Osterr. Zeitschrift für öffentliches Recht* 449 (1959).

[82]Czechoslovakia *v.* Radio Corporation of America, Award of April 1, 1932, 30 *Am. J. Int. Law* 523, 534 (1936).

the arbitration clause, it does not sit exclusively as a court of law, applying the law of the contract under the law of the state, but also as a tribunal of justice and equity.

There are additional fundamental values embodied in the above international law norm. First of all, the situation under consideration is one which, in reliance not only upon the system of laws of the capital-importing country in the matter of the protection of property but also upon the covenants of that state as expressed in an international concession agreement, a foreign investor establishes in such country an enterprise which becomes a part of the functioning of the international system. It is posited that this enterprise is a source of mutual advantage. In these circumstances, it is submitted that to expropriate the enterprise constituted by the concession agreement through the unilateral exercise of sovereign power and thereby to deprive the foreign state, in the person of its national, of the wealth represented by the enterprise and to cause it to become the exclusive property of the expropriating or nationalizing state without adequate compensation, is to result in an unjust enrichment. Here are actors in the person of states. They are equal before the law, that is, international law. One of those actors has used its internal monopoly of force to deprive another actor of part of its resources. No municipal system of law, including socialist law, recognizes as lawful and just a forceful taking by one subject of the law of the property of another subject having equal standing before the law, particularly when the loser is left without compensating advantage. International law has recognized and applied this general principle of law to state conduct in the past. It must continue to apply it in the future. The present-day interdependency of states reinforces the conclusion that no state shall take advantage of the fact that the resources of another state have entered into its territorial sphere and enrich itself with such resources at the expense of its neighbor.

The principle of unjust enrichment (*enrichissement sans cause*) is one of the general principles of law recognized by civilized nations.[83] This principle is based on the fact that there are circumstances in which the acquisition by one person of property interests of another will generally be conceded, in all justice, to require restitution in kind or in value. The existence of this prin-

---

[83]See the brilliant comparative law study of J. P. Dawson, *Unjust Enrichment, a Comparative Analysis* (1951).

ciple and the necessity of its application was recognized in the *Landreau* case involving a guano concession.[84]

O'Connell states, in connection with the obligation of a successor state to recognize a concession granted by its predecessor, that: "The expropriation of a concession, however, is only justified when accompanied by a recognition of the equities involved. . . . For the successor State to ignore this expenditure of capital and labour, and to appropriate to itself the benefits accruing therefrom, is unjustifiably to enrich itself. The concessionaire's equitable interest is an acquired right constituted by his activity, and international law imposes on the successor State a correlative duty to make restitution to the extent of its enrichment."[85]

It should be clearly understood, however, that the international liability of a nationalizing state in the circumstances of this inquiry does not arise *solely* from the aspect of unjust enrichment. That liability is a result of the circumstance of unjust enrichment, but it is also a product of the application to its act of the other principles or propositions set forth herein. It is most important to realize this fact, since it is of critical analytical importance in determining the legal consequences of the act of nationalization.

The precedents reveal the dichotomy upon which the international legal process will operate. If the act of termination be in the bona fide exercise of a claimed contractual right, it is to be deemed an act *jure gestionis*, and the rule of exhaustion of local remedies and the requirement of a denial of justice therein applies. On the other hand, if the act of termination be in the exercise of sovereign power independently of contractual right, so as to preclude effective resort by the alien to local remedies to obtain adequate redress, it is an act *jure imperii*, of which international law may directly take cognizance and which may be held to be a violation of a right of the state of the concessionaire.

In either event, the interests of the international society are protected. If the termination be in the exercise of a claimed contractual right, it may be said that the normal and usual expectation of the contracting parties would be that any dispute resulting therefrom would be adjusted by resort to the local courts. There is in such case no impairment of the security of the transaction,

---

[84]Landreau (U.S.) *v.* Peru, Award of Oct. 26, 1922, United Nations, 1, *Reports of International Arbitral Awards*, 352, 364.

[85]O'Connell, *The Law of State Succession*, 131-132.

if such resort be required as an antecedent to establishing international responsibility. If the termination be in the exercise of sovereign power, in the circumstances stated above, then the security of the transaction is directly protected by international law, the termination being deemed a violation of a duty owed to the state of the concessionaire.

There are two aspects of the term unjust enrichment: that of enrichment and that of the justice or injustice of the enrichment. The first is a matter of empirical or existential fact; the second is in the normative realm. When, through an act of nationalization, a state terminates a concession agreement with a foreign investor and expropriates for its own use and control the enterprise and property of the foreign investor constituted by the agreement, there is clearly an enrichment of the nationalizing state. Property, whose control, use, and benefit formerly inured to the foreign investor and the state of which he was a national, now inures to the nationalizing state. The corpus of the state of which the foreign investor is a national is correspondingly diminished. The benefits of participation in the international system by the medium of the enterprise in question, through its ability to control, tax, and otherwise derive advantage from the enterprise as the sovereign of the investor, are now lost to such state.

Actors in the international system early appraised such a taking, from the standpoint of values, as an unjust enrichment because it did violence to basic expectations of such actors. The foreign investor was viewed as making a contribution to the local society when he brought to it his skills and capital. His entrance into, and participation in, the local society enriched it in a measure not possible when it was constrained to rely on its own resources for growth. To expel the foreign investor from further participation in the local society, to take over his enterprise and property, and to fail to grant him prompt, adequate, and effective compensation was considered to be unjust enrichment and a violation of the principle of acquired or vested rights. (This last principle will be discussed later in this study.) It was considered that no social system could endure and prosper in which basic expectations were frustrated and basic rights obliterated. International law, it was believed, lost its contact with reality if it enabled one member unilaterally to determine its content, to enrich itself at the expense of another, to pervert to its exclusive advantage property which should serve an international function, or to interfere with or frustrate with impunity those expectations upon which any system of coordinated activity depends.

When the property of the citizens of a state is nationalized against less than full compensation, it has been said that no unjust enrichment may result "because in such a case, each individual affected, as a member of the same community, is enriched, at the same time, by the sacrifices of others. . . . This explains the diminishing scale of compensation as the circle of individuals affected widens."[86] Internationally, however, any such justification fails. As stated by Judge Carneiro in his dissenting opinion in the *Anglo-Iranian Oil Company* case, "such a justification cannot be put forward as applying to foreigners who, by the very fact of nationalization, have been cast from the national community in whose favour nationalization has been carried out."[87]

The straitened circumstances of the nationalizing state do not by themselves afford any basis for the international validation of its act. A state may not rely on its own law with a view to evading its international obligations.[88] Justice Holmes once remarked: "In general, it is not plain that a man's misfortunes or necessities will justify shifting the damages to his neighbor's shoulders."[89]

The protection of concession agreements has been justified by the view that the "rights of exploitation emanating from concessions which are also embodied in an undertaking, a plan or a definite object" are a vested or subjective right entitled to legal protection in the international sphere.[90] The Permanent Court of International Justice has held that the property interests involved in a concession are subject to protection under international law in the sense that the "principle of respect for vested rights . . . forms part of generally accepted international law." The court stated that the expropriation of the property of aliens permitted under Head III of the Geneva Convention is of an exceptional character in that it "is a derogation from the rules generally applied as regards the

---

[86]B. Cheng, "Expropriation in International Law," 21 *The Solicitor* 98, 100 (1954).

[87]Anglo-Iranian Oil Co. (Jurisdiction), I.C.J. Reports 1952, 151 at 162.

[88]Case of the Free Zones of Upper Savoy and the District of Gex (second phase), Order of Dec. 6, 1930, P.C.I.J., ser. A, no. 24, 12; Treatment of Polish Nationals in Danzig, Advisory Opinion of Feb. 4, 1932, P.C.I.J., ser. A/B, no. 44, 24.

[89]Pennsylvania Coal Co. *v.* Mahon, 260 U.S. 393, 416 (1922).

[90]Jablonsky *v.* German Reich, June 24, 1936, 1935-37 *Annual Digest and Reports of International Law Cases,* Case no. 42, 138, 140 (1941).

treatment of foreigners and from the principle of respect for vested rights."[91]

While the theory of acquired or vested rights as a basis for decision making in the field of private international law was strongly criticized in the preceding chapter,[92] the term is used in public international law to categorize numerous precedents into a fundamental rule of law.

One aspect of the value question now under consideration is how expropriation of property by states is typically regarded by actors in the international system. Certainly those actors which are international corporations will not regard such action to be a valued norm of behavior. However, it will quickly be said that the critical actors whose values are controlling in the creation of law norms are states. If so, one cannot say that the nationalizing states alone, such as Mexico, Rumania, Poland, Iran, Egypt, Indonesia, and Cuba, which have created international controversy through their acts of nationalization, are to be regarded as those actors whose values should be controlling in creating the law of nations.

The American and Panamanian General Claims Commission flatly stated that: "It is axiomatic that acts of a government in depriving an alien of his property without compensation impose international responsibility."[93] This result, it held, should apply even in a case where the state was in the process of working out a system of land administration.

Similarly, in the *Norwegian Shipowners' Claim,* involving the requisitioning by the United States of contracts for the building of ships, "just compensation" was held to entail an obligation for "a complete restitution of the *status quo ante,* based, not upon the future gains of the United States or other powers, but upon the loss of profits of the Norwegian owners as compared with other owners of similar property."[94]

---

[91]Case Concerning Certain German Interests in Polish Upper Silesia (The Merits), May 25, 1926, P.C.I.J., ser. A, no. 7, 42, see also 22; Case Concerning the Factory of Chorzow, July 26, 1927, *ibid.,* no. 9, 27.

[92]See Chapter VI, 182-183.

[93]Marguerite de Joly de Sabla (U.S.) *v.* Panama, U.S.–Panama General Claims Commission, Award of June 20, 1933, *Report of Bert L. Hunt,* U.S. Dept. of State, Arb. Ser. 6, 1934, 432 (1934); Walter Fletcher Smith (U.S.) *v.* Cuba, Award of May 2, 1929, 24 *Am. J. Int. Law* 384 (1930).

[94]Award of Oct. 13, 1922, United Nations, 1, *Reports of International Arbitral Awards,* 309, 338.

298

territory. This is illustrated in the negotiations between Hungary and Yugoslavia, in which each claimed compensation for the nationalization of the property of its nationals in the other state. The Soviet successfully demanded that its property in Bulgaria and Rumania be exempted from the nationalization laws of such countries.[96]

Alfred Drucker examined several compensation treaties between Communist states made to settle property and financial questions. These dealt with measures of compensation for property of persons of one state which had been acquired by another state as a result of nationalization legislation or otherwise. The author reaches the conclusion that ". . . Communist states vis-a-vis each other recognize that their nationalization legislation has no extraterritorial effect and that their measures of dispossession give rise to legal obligations towards those who have been dispossessed."[97] These examples are cited to illustrate the universality of the point of view that, when actors are regarded to be on a parity of position within a society, no law would validate a property taking by one from another simply through the use of force. This is the point of view which becomes the typical reference point for characterizing the forceful dispossession of property by one actor of another in the international system.

The explanation of the dichotomy of the Communist attitude toward appropriation of capitalist-owned property and Communist-owned property in the Communist sphere is not found solely in the dialectic of the class struggle. It is a product of the realities of the process of foreign investment behind and across the Iron Curtain. The revolutionary expropriation of property owned by both foreign and domestic capitalists not only excludes existing foreign investors but also precludes further foreign investment in the Communist state. Communist states are not capital-exporting states, nor are they the recipients of foreign capital investment from the free world. Thus, no reciprocal basis exists on the part of a Communist state for support of a universal rule protecting foreign-owned property from confiscation. It has already appropriated foreign-owned property in its territory and it has little of its own located abroad about which to be concerned. In any event, its

---

[96]Foighel, *Nationalization*, 30, 87.
[97]A. Drucker, "On Compensation Treaties Between Communist States," 229 *Law Times* 279 at 293 (1960).

ownership of property in the capitalist states beyond the Iron Curtain is protected under the laws of those states. Behind the Iron Curtain and in its own world, it demands protection and compensation against foreign expropriation of its property.

The writers on international law in the Communist sphere have looked upon the nationalization of foreign property as both an instrument of the universal class struggle and as a means of liberation of modernizing states from imperialist, colonial control of the past. It must be said that their writings have had an important influence in the development of legal theories justifying naturalization. These in turn have hastened and spread the process of nationalization in modernizing states.

Another category of actors in the world society whose relevant values must be considered is that of the modernizing state, particularly the modernizing state in its early stage of development. These include states such as the veneer state, described in Chapter IV, and other states whose members are experiencing the so-called revolution of rising expectations. The members of such states perceive that they are denied the realization of such base values as sustenance, shelter, health, and education. They further hold the conviction that it is possible for them to eliminate these conditions and to have a better life.

Their problems are essentially political in character and are to be solved in the political sphere. This fact, together with the inappropriateness of the reaction of xenophobia and resort to nationalization of foreign property as a solution for their problems, was discussed in Chapters IV and VI. It is imperative that the industrialized states of the West convince the modernizing states that they are vitally concerned with their growth and development. More than this, it is essential that the industrialized states demonstrate that participation in the international system will enable members of the modernizing states to realize their base values of wealth, enlightenment, health, and respect. This involves a new dedication by all states to the principle of the international division of labor and the creation of stable and growing international commodity markets, among other things.

The aspirations of undeveloped nations to succeed in their revolution of rising expectations and to raise the level of well being of their peoples will be laggardly realized, if they are confined to their own resources for growth. The import of foreign capital in the form of both physical facilities and skilled personnel is essential, if they are to achieve a rapid economic growth. Agreements with industrialized states and their nationals must be made. Transactions with them must be had. Participation in the international system cannot be effective, unless cooperation is viewed as a matter of mutual interest and unless agreements are respected. Whether transactions be had by the modernizing states with the Western states or those in the Communist sphere, both Western and Communist states will have an interest in, and will demand security of, those transactions. Insofar as the modernizing states are concerned, they have already had considerable experience in the failure of their expectations based on the promises made to them by Communist states with a view to their economic growth and trade.

One of the central facts to be faced in the next decade, and indeed in the decades thereafter, is the impact of the modernizing states on world society. Inevitably their participation in the international system, both with the West and the East, will increase. That participation will be promoted in the degree to which the value of the security of transactions is respected. It will be retarded in the degree to which respect both for promises to foreigners and property of foreigners is lessened. This is true whether the foreigners in question take the form of the Communist state or trading agency, or the Western state or private corporation. It is imperative for the modernizing state to accept the inherited social experience represented by international law, including the general principles of law recognized by civilized nations. Without that acceptance, it will inevitably be turned back to its own resources as a base for its economic growth.

Consideration of the general question raised above, namely, the extent of attachment by actors in the international system to the basic values and expectations discussed earlier, including the values of promoting the viability of the international system and securing the conditions of social order therein, cannot be dropped at this point. The issue is much too profound and too important to be dismissed.

The third paragraph from the conclusion of the foreword to this volume may be recalled at this point. That paragraph ended with the proposition that the centripetal economic forces of the world are increasingly in conflict with its political forces.

The formal legal norms must be consistent with the perceptions, attitudes, and values of the actors in the social system, if they are to govern the action of those actors. Will international law meet this test if its methodology is to look *exclusively* to the action of states, or more precisely, the relevant officials of states making decisions in the international system, as the primary, if not exclusive, source for arriving at its formal legal norms? The massiveness of the currents of international trade, communication, and travel, the vital importance of the flow of persons and ideas across international borders, in the international system of today, raise the question of whether the values, as well as the legal norms, of the international system can as a matter of scientific, empirical fact be ascertained by looking solely to states as the only actors in the system.

In other words, international law, as a scientific method for discerning legal norms and the values embodied therein, must rise to the vantage point which any science must have with respect to its subject matter. That is to say, it must stand outside its subject matter and view its data as an entirety. This implies that the international system is not to be viewed solely as a constellation of structures of social action identified as states. It is to be viewed more broadly as a composite of action in which the *relative significance* of states as actors in the system is considered, as well as the relative significance of other actors.

One way to make our point clearer, as a matter of imagery, is to refer to the image of society and law held by Jeremy Bentham. In his view, each individual counted as one unit and no more than one unit in the social order. The goal of the political order, to be achieved through law and legislation, was a mathematical maximization of pleasures and minimization of pains of individuals considered as units, whose pleasures and pains were capable of quantification. Instead it is affirmed that just as a national society cannot be reduced to such an atomistic, deterministic structure, so world society cannot be quantified on the basis of units of states acting therein. In other words, the totality of action in the international system will not be accurately perceived if it is viewed in terms of states as individual units, each counting for one and no more than one. If we wish to view action in the international system through the interactions of those organizations called states, then the necessary implications of such a viewpoint must be accepted. State action in the international system must be viewed from the standpoint, among other things, of the significance or the quantity and character of participation by the various states.

Moreover, the action of states in the international system acquires meaning and value as it is viewed in the light of the inherited culture of the world. The action of states in world society is not to be seen through the eyes and in the light of the values of discrete national societies. States exhibit a very wide range indeed of size, cultural growth, maturity, stability, integration, and opportunities for their members to achieve dignity, respect, and development of their personalities. They exhibit a wide degree of attachment to and participation in the international system.

Proposition 9.e. of Chapter VI indicated a number of steps which international law has taken and should take in its evolutionary growth as a scientific discipline. This discussion closes with the statement that action, merely because it becomes organized in the state, does not escape normative evaluation in the light of our culture. The general principles of law recognized by civilized nations thus become an important normative criterion for evaluating state conduct in the international sphere.

10.b. *The above norm represents an international law norm established by the relevant evidence of law.*

Some of the evidence of law supporting the norm has been noted. It now remains to complete the proof that it is an established norm in the light of the evidence of the law.

In the well-known *Delagoa Bay* case, the disputing states themselves acknowledged a liability for the termination by Portugal of a railway concession and seizure of the concessionaire's property, in that the arbitration was limited to a determination of the amount of reparation due.[98] In rendering its award of May 30, 1900, holding that reparations should be made on the basis of *dommages et intérêts,* that is, for damage sustained and profit lost, the tribunal stated:

Whether one would, indeed, brand the action of the Government as an arbitrary and dispoiling measure or as a sovereign act prompted by reason of State which always prevails over any railway concession, or even if the present case should be regarded as one of legal expropriation,

---

[98]Delagoa Bay and East African Railway Company (U.S.) *v.* Portugal, La Fontaine, *Pasicrisie International,* 398; M. M. Whiteman, 3, *Damages in International Law,* 1694-1703 (1943).

the fact remains that the effect was to dispossess private persons from their rights and privileges of a private nature conferred upon them by the concession, and that in the absence of legal provisions to the contrary—none of which has been alleged to exist in this case—the State, which is the author of such dispossession is bound to make full reparation for the injuries done by it.[99]

In the *Company General of the Orinoco* case before the French-Venezuelan Mixed Claims Commission of 1902, the Venezuelan government had unilaterally terminated in 1890 two concession agreements on the ground that the current holder of the concession was a British company and relations between Great Britain and Venezuela were at that time very tense. The termination of the concessions was held to give rise to an international liability to Great Britain. The tribunal reasoned that the exercise of the power of cancellation by the government was a sovereign act violating the rights of the concessionaire and giving rise to a claim for damage in the amount of the value of the concession at the time. It stated expressly that the judgment rested on the principles of "international law, equity and good conscience."[100]

In the *May* case between the United States and Guatemala involving a claim based on the taking over of a railway concession by the Guatemalan government, the arbitrator was charged with the duty to "render an award in favor of the party entitled thereto." Compensation was awarded for losses and other sums, including lost profits. In so doing, the arbitrator stated: "If, for imperative reasons of state, the railroad had been withdrawn from May before he had completed the term fixed by his contract, he would have been entitled to all the profit to be derived from the railroad until the completion of the term."[101]

In the *El Triunfo* case, in which an award was made for the cancellation by El Salvador of a concession agreement, the tribunal quoted with approval the language of Secretary of State Lewis Cass to the effect that: "The case is widely different when the foreign government becomes itself a party to important con-

---

[99]La Fontaine, *Pasicrisie International*, 402; Whiteman, 3, *Damages in International Law*, 1698.

[100]Company General of the Orinoco (France) *v.* Venezuela, Opinion of Umpire Plumley, July 31, 1905, Ralston's Report, French-Venezuelan Mixed Claims Commission of 1902, 244 at 322, 360, 365, 367 (1906).

[101]Robert H. May (U.S.) *v.* Guatemala, Award of Nov. 16, 1900, 1900 *For. Rel. U.S.* 659, 672.

tracts, and then not only fails to fulfill them, but capriciously annuls them, to the great loss of those who have invested their time, labor, and capital in their reliance upon its good faith and justice."[102]

In the dissenting opinion of Commissioner Nielsen in the *International Fisheries Company* case, "an arbitrary cancellation of a concession" was considered to involve a "confiscation of valuable contractual rights" and resulting international liability. The majority opinion is not inconsistent with this position in that it stated that it could find no "arbitrary act" or "international delinquency" on the part of Mexico in canceling the concession by virtue of the exercise of a contractual right to cease performance where the other party had failed in his obligations.[103]

In the *Shufeldt* case, the tribunal ruled that the Guatemalan decree of May 22, 1928, canceling Shufeldt's concession was subject to review by an international court, and held that he was entitled to pecuniary indemnification. The tribunal so ruled, even though it appeared to view the issues involved as contractual.[104]

In the case of the *Anglo-Iranian Oil Company (Jurisdiction)*, the International Court of Justice could not come to grips with the present problem, since the court ultimately held itself to be without jurisdiction to consider the merits of the case.[105] Jurisdiction was claimed by Great Britain on the basis of a declaration of acceptance of the so-called optional clause of the statute of the court (article 36, paragraph 2) by Iran to the effect that the obligatory jurisdiction of the court was accepted with respect to "the application of treaties or conventions accepted by Persia and subsequent to the ratification of this declaration." Since the concessionary contract before it could not be categorized as a treaty, the court held that it was unable to exercise jurisdiction. Judge Carneiro, in his dissenting opinion, stated that an invocation of the interests of the nationalizing state would not justify internationally a payment of less than full compensation to a foreigner who was "by the very fact of nationalization . . . cast from the national

---

[102]El Triunfo Company, Ltd. (U.S.) *v.* Salvador, Award of May 8, 1902, 1902 *ibid.* 859, 862 at 871.

[103]International Fisheries Co. (U.S.) *v.* Mexico, General Claims Commission, U.S.–Mexico, United Nations, 4, *Reports of International Arbitral Awards*, 691, 700, 714-715.

[104]P. W. Shufeldt (U.S.) *v.* Guatemala, Award of July 24, 1930, U.S. Dept. of State, Arb. Ser. 3, 849, 876-877 (1932).

[105]Judgment of July 22, 1952, I.C.J. Reports 1952, 93.

community in whose favour nationalization has been carried out." Judge Carneiro further stated that a refusal by Iran to set up the arbitral tribunal provided for in the concession agreement "constitutes a denial of justice on the part of the Iranian Government."[106]

In addition to the international cases previously cited, awards or payments have been made for the termination by a government of a concession agreement, or governmental interference with such agreements in numerous other instances.[107]

In the *Lena Goldfields, Limited* arbitration with the Soviet Union, the arbitral tribunal granted £12,965,000 representing "a fair purchase price for a going concern" by virtue of the loss of a concession agreement through governmental interference, including the secret police. The tribunal reasoned that except for performance inside Russia, the contract contemplated the application of international, rather than national, principles of law.[108] With respect to a provision in the contract that it should only be prematurely terminated by a decision of the arbitration court provided for therein, Dr. Nussbaum said in an article concerning this arbi-

---

[106]*Ibid.*, 151 at 162, 166.

[107]H. Milligan (U.S.) *v.* Peru, U.S.–Peruvian Claims Commission Under Convention of Dec. 4, 1868, Moore, 2, *International Arbitrations*, 1643-44; George L. Hammeken (U.S.) *v.* Mexico, Mexican Claims Commission Under Convention of July 4, 1868, 4, *ibid.*, 3470-72 (injury to rights and immunities of concessionaire by governmental authorities); Central and South American Telegraph Co. *v.* Chile, U.S.—Chilean Claims Commission Under Convention of Aug. 7, 1892, Whiteman, 3, *Damages in International Law*, 1679 (interference by government authorities); Dr. Marion A. Cheek (U.S.) *v.* Siam, Award of March 21, 1898, Moore, 5, *International Arbitrations*, 5069 at 5071; Punchard, McTaggart, Lowther and Company (Great Britain) *v.* Colombia, Award of Oct. 17, 1899, La Fontaine, *Pasicrisie International*, 544; Martini and Co. (Italy) *v.* Venezuela, Ralston's Report, 819 (1904); Aboilard (France) *v.* Haiti, Award of July 26, 1905, 12 *Rev. Gén. de Droit Int. Public*, docs. 12-17 (1905); The Mavromattis Jerusalem Concessions, Judgment of March 26, 1925, P.C.I.J., ser. A, no. 5 (governmental action interfering with exclusivity of a concession; admission by respondent government of lack of power under treaty to effect expropriation).

Diplomatic settlement: Henry W. Thurston (U.S.) *v.* Dominican Republic, Award of May 20, 1898 (limited to determination of value of property of concession), 1898 *For. Rel. U.S.* 274-291; George D. Emery Co. (U.S.) *v.* Nicaragua, 1909 *ibid.* 460, 463, Whiteman, 3, *Damages in International Law*, 1643-45; United States and Venezuela Co. (U.S.) *v.* Venezuela, 1909 *For. Rel. U.S.* 624; Turnbull, Manoa Company, Ltd., and Orinoco Company, Ltd. (U.S.) *v.* Venezuela, *ibid.* 626-628, see also Ralston's Report, 201; Charles J. Harrah (U.S.) *v.* Cuba (1903), Whiteman, 3, *Damages in International Law*, 1718-20.

[108]Lena Goldfields, Ltd. *v.* U.S.S.R., Award of Sept. 3, 1930, 36 *Cornell Law Q.* 42, 50 (1950).

tration that the provision "imposes an obligation *exclusively on the Government*, namely, the obligation not to use its sovereign power of revoking the concession during the contract period, earlier termination of the concession being reserved to the tribunal."[109]

The duty to respect concession agreements has been recognized in cases of state succession. D. P. O'Connell states in his exhaustive study that "The generally consistent practice which has just been analyzed is clearly based on the principle that the acquired rights of a concessionaire must be respected by a successor state."[110]

The Harvard Research in International Law on the Responsibility of States stated that there were numerous cases "where the arbitrary annulment of a contract by the Executive without appeal to the courts was held to justify diplomatic interposition and to render the state responsible."[111]

It will be recalled that the League of Nations addressed itself to the question of whether the fact that the rights of a concessionaire under his contract were impaired by legislation, rather than through executive action, would entail international responsibility. The conclusion was reached that if such legislation directly impaired contractual rights, international responsibility would be incurred for damage thereby sustained by the foreigner, but that the circumstances of the particular case must be examined when the legislation was of a general character. Judge Lauterpacht has said that "There may be little difference between a Government breaking unlawfully a contract with an alien and a Government causing legislation to be enacted which makes it impossible for it to comply with the contract."[112]

The circumstance that the termination of the concession agreement is effected through legislation, which will render clear the finality of the state act, points rather conclusively to the conclu-

---

[109]A. Nussbaum, "The Arbitration Between the Lena Goldfields, Ltd. and the Soviet Government," *ibid.* 30, 38-39 (1950); see also Czechoslovakia *v.* Radio Corporation of America, Award of April 1, 1932, 30 *Am. J. Int. Law* 523, 531 (1936) (rule *pacta sunt servanda* applies to public law agreements).

[110]O'Connell, *Law of State Succession,* 129, 131-132.

[111]23 *Am. J. Int. Law* (spec. supp.) 171 (1929); see also C. Eagleton, *The Responsibility of States in International Law,* 165 (1928); C. C. Hyde, 2, *International Law Chiefly as Interpreted and Applied by the United States,* 990-991 (2nd rev. ed., 1945); Borchard, *Diplomatic Protection,* 292-294, 336; C. Rousseau, *Droit International Public,* 370-371 (1953) (state becomes responsible upon enactment of legislation violating its international obligations).

[112]League of Nations, *Conference for the Codification of International Law, Bases of Discussion,* vol. 3, C. 75. M. 69.1929.V. at 30, 33.

sion that the termination was in the exercise of sovereign power rather than contractual right, and usually will render resort to the courts fruitless. If the courts of the state are precluded from any inquiry into the validity in international law of such an act, then a violation of a right of the state of the concessionaire arises.[113]

The general question of the responsibility of a state under international law for the expropriation of the property of aliens will now be examined. The rule has been affirmed by a number of authorities that a violation of international law occurs on the taking by a state of foreign property against inadequate compensation.[114] The question has been most extensively investigated in the literature.[115] The precedents previously considered in this study, insofar as they involve issues of property, are pertinent to this issue. At least independent of the nationalization precedents of the period from World War I to the present, it was fairly settled that the property of aliens is not to be expropriated except against adequate, effective, and prompt compensation.

On November 23, 1936, an expropriation law was enacted by Mexico. On March 18, 1938, the properties of seventeen oil companies were expropriated by decree. The Mexican government had also for some time been engaged in the nationalization of foreign-owned land in a program of agrarian reform. American-owned landholdings, chiefly farms of moderate size valued over $10 million, had been expropriated by 1938.[116]

A settlement was reached in 1941 whereby American oil proper-

---

[113]Individual Opinion in Case of Certain Norwegian Loans, Judgment of July 6, 1957, I.C.J. Reports 1957, 9, 37.

[114]Sibert, 1, *Traité de Droit International Public*, 515; Hyde, 1, *International Law Interpreted*, 710-711; Rousseau, *Droit International Public*, 372; G. Scelle, 2, *Précis de Droit des Gens*, 113 (1934); Herz, "Expropriation of Foreign Property," 243; C. C. Hyde, "Confiscatory Expropriation," 32 *Am. J. Int. Law* 758, 760-761 (1938), and "Compensation for Expropriations," 33 *ibid.* 108, 112 (1939) (questions legality of power to expropriate if adequate compensation cannot be given aliens); P. Guggenheim, 1, *Traité de Droit International Public*, 336 (1953) (right to exercise diplomatic protection).

[115]See bibliographies in Friedman, *Expropriation in International Law*, and M. Domke, "American Protection Against Foreign Expropriation in the Light of the Suez Canal Crisis," 105 *U. Pa. Law Rev.* 1033, 1041, n.51 (1957). For other studies of the problem of nationalization, see books cited in the bibliography by I. Foighel, B. A. Wortley, G. Viénot, and C. Rousseau; and articles by C. J. Olmstead, N. R. Doman, A. Drucker ("Compensation for Nationalized Property"), E. D. Re, and S. J. Rubin.

[116]J. L. Kunz, "The Mexican Expropriations," 17 *N.Y.U. Law Q. Rev.* 327 (1940).

ties were to be appraised by two experts to be appointed by the two governments, respectively. Their joint report was to be made the basis of compensation. Mexico agreed to pay $9 million (U.S.) as an initial deposit. The two governments accepted the report of the two experts, made on April 17, 1942. The United States government stated that "This report placed an evaluation of $23,995,991 on the losses sustained by American nationals, including all elements of tangible *and intangible value,* and provided for interest at three percent per annum from March 18, 1938 to the date of final settlement on all balances due; in conformity with the basic agreement, the evaluation was final" (italics supplied). The sum thus found to be due, less the deposit of $9 million, was to be paid in five annual installments beginning in 1943.[117] By the Claims Convention of November 19, 1941, Mexico agreed to pay the United States $40 million at the rate of $2,500,000 a year.[118] The United Kingdom effected a settlement for the expropriation of its oil properties in Mexico, whereby two experts were to be appointed by the two countries to value the expropriated properties, after which Mexico was to reach an agreement for payment with the Mexican Eagle Company and its associated companies. The sum of $81,250,000 was finally agreed upon to be paid the Mexican Eagle Company in fifteen annual installments, under an agreement of August 29, 1947.[119]

The Iranian oil expropriation of 1951 was couched in general terms as a nationalization of "the oil industry throughout all parts of the country, without exception." In practical effect it was directed to the expropriation of the properties of the Anglo-Iranian Oil Company, Limited, and the consequent termination of its concession agreement of April 29, 1933.[120]

---

[117]"Compensation for Petroleum Properties Expropriated in Mexico," 9 Dept. of State Bulletin 230 (1943).

[118]Exchange of notes of Nov. 19, 1941, respecting expropriation of petroleum properties, 55 Stat. 1554 (1941-42); Claims Convention of Nov. 19, 1941, 56 Stat. 1347 (1942); L. H. Woolsey, "The United States–Mexican Settlement, 36 *Am. J. Int. Law* 117 (1942); H. W. Briggs, "The Settlement of Mexican Claims Act of 1942," 37 *ibid.* 222 (1943).

[119]Great Britain, *Agreement Between His Majesty's Government in the United Kingdom and the Government of Mexico* . . . , Command 6768/1946, and *Correspondence Incorporating the Texts of the Agreement* . . . , Command 7275/1947.

[120]A. W. Ford, *The Anglo-Iranian Oil Dispute of 1951-1952,* 233 (1954); I.C.J., Anglo-Iranian Oil Co. Case, Pleadings, Oral Arguments, Documents, 20.

The International Court of Justice ruled that it lacked jurisdiction to hear the resulting dispute between Great Britain and Iran.[121] Among other things, it held that the concession agreement was not an international convention within the terms of the Iranian declaration accepting the compulsory jurisdiction of the court. Negotiations thereafter took place between the Iranian government and a consortium of eight international oil companies, including the Anglo-Iranian Oil Company, Limited. These resulted in the establishment of a new concession agreement of September 19, 1954, with such companies for a minimum period of twenty-five years, subject to extension. There was a settlement of claims and counterclaims between Iran and the Anglo-Iranian Oil Company, Limited, resulting in a net sum of £25 million, or about $70 million, which Iran agreed to pay the company in ten annual installments.[122] The new concession agreement appears to have been regarded in part as a reaffirmation and sharing of the rights and privileges of the earlier concession, since on October 29, 1954, it was announced that the seven other oil company parties had agreed to pay the Anglo-Iranian Oil Company, Limited, a sum which would amount to more than $600 million for its share in the concession.[123]

The legality of expropriation of foreign property in the course of the agrarian reforms of the Eastern European states following World War I was most vigorously and exhaustively debated in connection with the so-called *Hungarian Optants* case.[124] The position of Hungary that expropriation without compensation was prohibited by international law and by articles 232 and 250 of the Treaty of Trianon appears to have prevailed in the discussions in the League of Nations in 1928,[125] and in the reasoning of the Permanent Court of International Justice in the *Chorzow Factory*

---

[121]Anglo-Iranian Oil Co. (Jurisdiction), I.C.J. Reports 1952, 151.

[122]Hearings Before the Antitrust Subcommittee (Subcommittee 5) of the Committee on the Judiciary, House of Representatives, 84th Cong., 1st Sess., May 23–June 6, 1953, ser. 3, pt. 2, 1563, 1644.

[123]*The New York Times*, Oct. 30, 1954, p. 6, col. 3.

[124]A brief history and analysis of some of the legal issues involved in the dispute will be found in Carlston, *The Process of International Arbitration*, 116-126, 176-184; see F. Déak, *The Hungarian-Rumanian Land Dispute* (1928); *Some Opinions, Articles and Reports Bearing upon the Treaty of Trianon and the Claims of the Hungarian Nationals with Regard to Their Lands in Transylvania* (2 vols., 1929).

[125]See Carlston, *Process of International Arbitration*, 181.

case.[126] A special agrarian fund was created for the payment of claims arising out of the agrarian legislation of Rumania, Czechoslovakia, and Yugoslavia.[127]

The Russian expropriations following the Revolution of 1917 and the establishment of the Soviet state were all-embracing in their inclusion of means of production and capital, whether or not foreign-owned. The courts of Western states uniformly refused to recognize the extraterritorial effects of acts of confiscation, and varied in their approaches to the problem of the recognition of their internal effects upon property within the territory of Russia.[128] In the diplomatic sphere, the problems raised were massive and were insoluble upon any other basis than a political one. In the economic sphere, a consequence was to preclude further foreign investment in Russia and to bring to an end investment by Russia abroad. The reciprocal basis for an interest by the Soviet in a rule of international law protecting foreign investment was thereby destroyed.

The nationalization by Egypt of the Universal Suez Maritime Canal Company on July 26, 1956, ended in an agreement of July 13, 1958, between the government of Egypt and the company under its new corporate regime. In that manner, Egypt obtained protection against possible claims of individual stockholders, since the act of the company on signing the agreement became binding on all its members. The agreement was another negotiated settlement, with varying claims and positions being taken on both sides. It is of relatively little weight as an international law precedent, in that it took place in the private instead of the public sphere and that the company did not abdicate its legal position on the governing principles of international law by entering into the agreement.

Under the settlement, the company retained the ownership and control of its foreign assets, the estimate value of which was £56 million sterling. On the other hand, it assumed responsibility for all liabilities and debts outside Egypt, of which the most important item was pensions, amounting to £13 million sterling. Egypt agreed to pay the company £28,300,000 (Egyptian). The company had in hand £5,300,000 (Egyptian) of this sum, representing canal dues

---

[126]See note 96 of this chapter.
[127]Agreements Concluded at the Hague Conference, Jan., 1930, 373.
[128]See footnote 29 of this chapter and note 62 of Chapter VI.

paid in London and Paris after the date of the seizure. The balance was payable in five annual installments, without interest.[129]

The recent Indonesian nationalization of the property of Netherlands subjects and the Cuban nationalization of the property of United States subjects raise a number of issues in international law. For present purposes it may be noted that when an act of nationalization takes place in such a manner as to involve an abuse of power and not a proper exercise of the power of sovereignty, as when it is not for a public purpose or is of a discriminatory character, it escapes the shield of sovereignty, and for such reason alone becomes a wrong under international law when it entails an injury to an alien.[130]

The International Court of Justice in the *Chorzow Factory* judgments declared that "respect for private rights . . . forms part of generally accepted international law," that liquidation is "a derogation from generally accepted international law," and that the expropriation of private property without fair compensation is "unlawful," and "a derogation from the rules generally applied in regard to the treatment of foreigners and the principle of respect for vested rights."[131] There can be no doubt that the court characterized expropriation without compensation to be an unlawful act under international law.

The court's principal judgments in the *Chorzow Factory* case were rendered from 1926 to 1928. By this time the Mexican, Russian, and Rumanian nationalizations were accomplished facts. Hence, the statement in the *Chorzow Factory* case of the rules of international law concerning nationalization or expropriation is of very considerable weight and authority today. Only the practice of nationalization during and since World War II is available to lead to any different conclusion.

The global or lump-sum settlements of international disputes arising from such practice do not detract from the validity of the general rules laid down in this study because they involve situa-

---

[129]Agreement of April 29, 1958, *The New York Times*, April 30, 1958, p. 8, cols. 4-8; E. Lauterpacht, ed., *The Suez Canal Settlement*, 47ff. (1960).

[130]See the evidence of law on this point collected by Lord McNair, "The Seizure of Property and Enterprises in Indonesia," 219 at 243-250 (1959), and H. Rolin, "Opinion," 260 at 269-270.

[131]See note 91 of this chapter.

tions essentially of a political character. On the one hand, the state is free to establish within its own territory and system of law such legal relations as it may elect. Such relationships are immune under international law from alteration by any other state, even though they may in operation violate a duty owed or infringe a correlative right held by another state under international law. On the other hand, the foreign state may under public international law deny legal consequences within its system of law, legislatively or judicially, to any such act injuring its said right, and may take appropriate affirmative measures to secure respect for and to enforce such right. The polarity of the two legal principles necessarily leads to the operation of the political process to secure a fair adjustment or compromise between the opposing principles.

There is strong reason to believe that the postwar global settlements have proceeded against the background set forth above. Injured states were not likely to concede that nationalizing states were entitled by legal right to pay less than adequate compensation. If such were the rule of law, then reparation would be measured by convenience of the wrongdoer instead of injury to the victim. Those subjects of the law who were unable to respond in damages would be excused from legal responsibility for their wrong. The duty to pay reparation in case of spoliation of property would be measured by the economic position of the spoliator, apart from his enrichment by the property unlawfully taken. Confiscation, which would admittedly be illegal when practiced on a small scale, would become in effect legal when practiced on a mass basis. As the alien victims of confiscation multiplied, they would be denied legal rights otherwise available to them. There must be clear evidence indeed to indicate that such a reversal of fundamental rules of law has taken place. On the contrary, the World War II global settlements appear to have been dictated by political and practical realities.

As pointed out by Viénot, the formula of a global settlement should be viewed only as a useful procedure, enabling, in practice, a concrete agreement to be reached between two states of a different juridical character for the purpose of settling their differences. For the nationalizing state, it permits a general liquidation to be made of the private interests of the subjects of the other. Both the nationalizing and the investing states are thereby freed from all differences interfering with the development of their mutual relations.[132]

No clear affirmation of a rule of international law appears to have been involved in the determination of the global settlements. They were primarily a product of the political rather than the legal process. They were no more productive of a rule of law permitting payment to be suited to the expropriator's circumstances and convenience than the forgiveness by a creditor of a debt implies that there was no antecedent obligation to pay it. Moreover, the issues in the negotiation of such settlements were regarded as primarily property issues, and no questions of the status of any foreign concession agreements appear to have been involved. Friedman, in his study of *Expropriation in International Law,* in which he vigorously supports the power of a state to nationalize property, goes so far as to say that "the expropriation may apply to all movable and immovable property rights, *with the exception of contractual rights*" (italics supplied). The latter he regards as being outside the sphere of law relating to denial of justice, though he does not admit the principle of confiscatory breach.[133] Professor de La Pradelle, as Rapporteur at the 1950 meeting of the Institut de Droit International, affirmed that: "Nationalization, as a unilateral act of sovereignty, shall respect validly concluded agreements, whether by treaty, or by contract."[134] The evidence of the law must be examined and weighed in its entirety. The validity of a unilateral termination by a state of a concession agreement through nationalization cannot be determined solely in terms of the nationalization precedents and in property concepts.

The recent nationalization precedents may, therefore, be regarded essentially as presenting a legal situation in which, in the words of the International Court of Justice, "the practice has been so much influenced by considerations of political expediency in the various cases, that it is not possible to discern in all this any constant and uniform usage, accepted as law, with regard to the alleged rule."[135]

---

[132]G. Viénot, *Nationalisations Étrangères et Intérêts Francais,* 273 (1953).

[133]Friedman, *Expropriation in International Law,* 157, 220-221.

[134]43 *Annuaire de l'Institut de Droit International* 67 (1950, pt. 1). No final decision was taken by the Institute on this matter, action being postponed to a later date, 44 *ibid.* 324 (1952, pt. 2).

[135]Colombian-Peruvian Asylum Case, Judgment of Nov. 20, 1950, I.C.J. Reports 1950, 266, 277.

There remain certain additional questions to be considered in weighing the evidence of law bearing on the above legal norm. It perhaps may be objected that much of the evidence of law is of an earlier and different era. It perhaps may be said that some of the precedents are somewhat remote from the international situations of the magnitude now being considered.

It is true that the precedents range from the individual employment contract in the *Cedroni* case[136] to the international contract creating an organic part of the international system involved in the *Anglo-Iranian Oil Company* case.[137] The various international precedents noted herein involve situations in which a state resorted to the international system to bring to the local society the requisite capital, management, and technological expertise to develop public utilities and local industries. They also involve situations in which there was not only such a tie with the international system, but also there was an international market for the local production. It seems clear that an international law norm which has come to the fore in such a variety of precedents, a norm which in part developed in cases in which the linkage with the international system was not strong, is clearly applicable to the typical international concession agreement of today, and to situations in which there is an overwhelming and irreversible commitment to the international system. The international concession agreement for the development and sale of mineral resources profoundly possesses an international character, as seen in Chapters II and III.

The above international law norm found its genesis in a somewhat more simple and less developed world society than now exists. In today's highly interdependent, sensitive world society, the norm possesses even greater imperativeness. The norm was early held to be applicable to an international contract of a considerable degree of localization in one state, such as a concession to establish a railroad or other public utility. The norm possesses even greater justification and necessity for today's international contract, with its widespread international ramifications and operation.

---

[136]Cedroni (Italy) *v.* Guatemala, Award of Oct. 12, 1898, La Fontaine, *Pasicrisie International.*

[137]Anglo-Iranian Oil Co. (Jurisdiction), I.C.J. Reports 1952, 151.

CONCLUSION: JUSTICE AS THE REALIZATION OF VALUES UNDER LAW

The failure of authority in the Greek city-states to create an enduring order of trade and security in the Mediterranean world was the cultural setting in which the Stoic and Aristotelian ideal image of an order of natural law emerged. The failure of Roman authority to bring order and the good life to the peasants and populace of the Roman world was the setting in which Cicero expressed his ideal image of an order of natural law. The failure of the authority of the Italian city-states, of the Capetian authority in France, and of the Hapsburg authority in Austria to achieve an internal order of peace, as against competing papal claims of authority, led successively to Marsilius' ideal image of the supremacy and unity of the authority of the state in an order of peace and to Bodin's ideal image of supremacy of sovereign power in the state.

When princely authority in the state became supreme and was reinforced, instead of opposed, by spiritual authority, when the restraints of natural law precepts upon the exercise of princely authority were removed, then the ideal image emerged of the individual as the end of public order. The way to the good life was no longer viewed to be one of achieving order under authority but instead to be one of securing individual liberty as against the excess and abuse of political authority. The goal of achieving order under the authority of the state had been reached. Now the problem was the threat to the good life which was posed by the exercise of political authority based on coercive power. Hence the emergence in the seventeenth and eighteenth centuries of the ideal image of political authority based on social contract, instead of inherent or divine right, and of securing the good life of individual liberty through the Kantian imperative directed to the exercise of the individual will.

An order of the state, in which the good life is to be found to the maximum extent, can be achieved through the exercise of the individual will, as expressed in consent or contract, on the one hand, or through political authority, on the other hand. These ways to social order in the state are not exclusive of one another but are complementary. Individuals act in unison both through consent and agreement and through acceptance of authority. Stated otherwise, authority rests on consent, as well as on legitimacy and power or force. Stated in behavioral terms, if the energy potential of group action is to be achieved to the maximum extent, a group must move through both agreement and authority to reach important group goals.

Justice, viewed simply as an optimum condition in the social life of individuals, has two basic aspects or characteristics. Justice may be viewed from the perspective of form, structure, and static state, on the one hand, or it may be viewed in terms of idea, content, and dynamic state, on the other hand. It may be viewed as a static equilibrium of forces or as a moving equilibrium of forces. The Kantian notion of the good life as a condition of human affairs, in which there is the greatest area of freedom for the exercise of the individual will, subject to the constraint of the Kantian imperative, tends to reflect a view of justice which is one of form, structure, and constraint of action in a static order. The pragmatic conception of the good life tends to reflect a view of justice which emphasizes the substance and content of action in a dynamic order. A Kantian view of the good life, appropriate to a culture which had solved the problem of the creation, but not the abuse, of authority, ceased to be adequate for an industrially organized, democratically structured society concerned with the use of authority to attain goals embodying widely shared values. The structure of society in which the good life was to be preserved still remained an important question, but now the principal question with which the culture was confronted was the content of the good life, that is, how authority was to be used to attain the good life. The state no longer carried an alien image of dominance through the exercise of authority based on power. The state was now held to be a subservient instrument for the achievement of human welfare and social goals.

Justice is, among other things, ancillary to the concept of authority. It refers to a situation of human affairs in which authority is used to achieve the optimum of human happiness. "Happiness" is here used to refer to the maximization of value realization by the members of a politically organized society. Until the twentieth century, the fundamental task of authority in achieving justice was held to be primarily one of securing individual freedom as against the exercise of authority by the state. Today, in the latter half of the twentieth century, the impact upon individual freedom of the exercise of authority by the giant corporation is a subject of deep concern. Another profound problem in the world today lies in the exercise by the totalitarian state of authority based on the possession of power and force, both internally and in its relations with other states. The structure of authority and the particularistic quality of its exercise are, however, no longer the primary obstacles to the attainment of justice in the industrially organized, democratically structured state, which has reached a relatively mature state of development. For such a state, the content of the good life and its attainment through authority, which is responsive to cultural values and accepts control by majority decision, have instead become the central problem in attaining justice.

The problem of attaining justice under law is basically one of how to maximize value realization by individuals through the making and the enforcement of law in a society and a culture. There are four variables or concepts to be defined in this proposition and their relation to one another indicated: (1) value realization, (2) maximization of value realization, (3) making of law, and (4) enforcement of law. This task will be undertaken below in the course of a formulation of an operational statement of how justice is to be achieved to the utmost extent, in the sense of promoting and protecting the realization of human values in social action through the exercise of authority by the state.

1. An individual achieves meaning as he expresses himself in action—and action includes contemplation and reflection as well as movement—and adapts to his environment. The setting in which this takes place in modern society is the setting of the organization, more precisely, the exercise of authority in organizations. The area in which the individual is free from organizational authority is steadily diminishing. Authority exists in the relations of individuals when a person typically accepts the command or direction of another as a basis for action, without awaiting reasoned persuasion as a basis for action. Organization exists in the relations of individuals where, in typical situations, authority appears and is exercised by persons occupying fixed roles or posts. Organizations of a permanent character are composed of members who, in repeated and predictable situations, accept the command or direction of persons occupying authoritative roles or posts.

2. The character and direction of action in a society is in large measure a product of decision making by persons exercising authority in organizations. The character and direction of such decision making in organizations is in turn determined by the appropriativeness and adequacy of action in the organization as a means for the realization of values by those who take part in its action. Values reflect the priority of wants or needs in an actor as he organizes his action. They are the factors which influence the exercise of choice among available courses of action.

3. The appearance and maintenance of an organization in a society depends upon its effectiveness as a means of value realization for those taking part in its system of action. These participants comprise two categories of actors: first, its members who accept its authority as a basis for action in predictable situations, and second, those who interact with its members in such situations. The latter category of actors may be termed participants, instead of members, since their action is not determined by authority but instead by their own volition or as a consequence of their acceptance of authority in some other organization of which, at the time in question, they are acting as members. Participation in the action of an organization by persons who are not its members is principally structured in the form of the transaction or agreement and occasionally in the form of ceremony, ritual, and the like.

4. An organization achieves permanence in a society when (1) the goals of its system of action embody values of its members

and its participants and have sufficient priority or importance to induce participation in its system of action to attain such goals and (2) the psychic cost involved in the attainment of such goals and the contentment following such attainment (that is, goal gratification) result in a surplus of satisfaction on the part of actors in the system, which outranks competing opportunities for action. In the degree that the above condition is established in an organization, the realization of values is maximized on the part of those participating in its system of action.

5. The state is an organization which is subject to the foregoing principles and propositions but which is also possessed of the monopoly of the use of force in a society as an inducing factor to create and maintain authority. The authority of a state extends principally over citizens and aliens within its territorial jurisdiction and, to a lesser degree, over citizens abroad and even over aliens abroad in limited circumstances. This last statement is asserted as an empirically demonstrable statement as well as a proposition of legal theory.

6. The state, as that form of organization which embraces the largest number of actors and the widest variety of values and degree of value priorities on the part of such actors in the world today, is confronted with the most massive of problems in creating and maintaining authority. To the extent that the total potential energy of a society of a state is channeled to the use of force to support the exercise of authority directed to the realization of values of relatively low priority or a small amount of attachment on the part of members of the society, and to the extent that this energy is diverted from the realization of values of higher priority and wider extent of attachment by such members, the energy utilized for the realization of more important and more widely held values among the members of the state will diminish. The consequence will eventually be a breakdown of the authority system itself, as the government and law of such state is perceived to be no longer a government and law uniquely characteristic of the members of the society in question and expressive of its value system. Such an attitude toward the government and law is frequently found in emerging nations, the government of which is controlled by a thin veneer of élite which utilizes such control to realize its particularistic values, and notably familial values, instead of the values of the citizenry generally.

7. The establishment and preservation of justice in a state are determined by the degree to which decision making in the state is faithful to universal, empirically based principles of organizational action, as the government and courts of the state perform those tasks of group and individual coordination of action and resolution of conflict characteristic of the political and legal process. Such principles of organizational action are mainly derived from a temporal view of action as it relates to value realization.

8. The phrase "temporal view of action as it relates to value realization," as used in the preceding paragraph, entails three perspectives of action as it is directed by the exercise of authority in an organization. These three perspectives of organizational action find their counterpart in the state in the spheres of legislation, administration, and adjudication, although in no one sphere is there a pure and unmixed perspective of action unique to that sphere alone. The two dimensions in which the action of an individual is to be viewed are action as form or substance, that is, a physical event in time and space, and action as an instrument for the realization of values.

The three perspectives from which action is to be viewed are temporal. There is, first, the perspective of action as occurring in the spectrum of the future which is beyond that contemplated by such terms as "immediate" and "present." There is, second, the perspective of action as occurring "immediately" and "in the present." There is, third, the perspective of action as a past event.

In the dimension of action as form or substance, first, the actor imagines, mentally rehearses, and reshapes images to create a final idea of action, second, performs the idea, and third, reshapes future performance of the idea in the light of experience, all from the standpoint of the physical shape and design of action and its fidelity to idea. In the dimension of action as a realization of values, the actor relates action as form or substance to his system of values. First, he considers such action in terms of his value priorities, that is, the varying degrees of importance of his values to him over the long perspective of time and the manner in which he shall allocate his energy in a global way to value realization. Second, he selects a particular mode of action for immediate performance as a means for value realization. Third, he appraises the contentment or satisfaction following performance of the selected mode of action for the purpose of planning his future action.

9. If value realization in organizational action is to be maximized, decision making by those exercising authority must view and direct action in the long-run perspective of the future and in terms of broad goals and the use of relatively large segments of human energy to attain such goals over a substantial period of time. Foresight must be exercised to anticipate and meet changes in the environment in which the organization acts. Future changes in the value systems of actors participating in the organization must be foreseen and action planned to meet such changes. Decision making directed to the making and adoption of plans for organizational action over several years reflects the exercise of the leadership function in an organization. Such decision making influences the nature of the charter, that is, the unique character of mission, or the organization. It determines the grand design of the organization's action as a means for value realization.

The performance of the leadership function in the state is shared in varying degrees by its legislative, executive, and judicial organs. The legislature, notably in the exercise of its taxing power but also in its power to create binding norms of conduct of general application, is the governmental organ which is most productive of authoritative decision making in the exercise of the leadership function. The exercise of the leadership function by the legislature is more than the mere computation of group pressures and group demands and the estimation and selection of that course of action which will resolve them with the minimum of friction. It is a creative process, as are also administration and adjudication. It involves the discernment of new modes of action which will make possible an enhancement of value realization by groups and a lessening of group conflict which existing courses of action fail to achieve. It involves such imaginative planning in the internal economy as the Tennessee Valley Authority and in the international economy as the European Common Market.

The leadership function, as exercised by the legislature, entails the resolution of group conflict in the society, as well as the establishment of new group goals. In a society with a scarcity of resources in the light of competing demands for their use, planning over the long term for the allocation and use of such resources necessarily entails consideration and resolution of group claims for such allocation and use. If decisions adopting plans for the allocation and use of such resources are to be authoritative in the society, resolution of such conflicting group claims in a manner acceptable to the groups in question must be achieved. The legislative process and the acceptance of the principle of majority rule by the members of a society enables such group conflict to be resolved. Legislation, in brief, establishes the bold contours of action in a society as it allocates its resources in a global manner and otherwise directs action over large segments of time to the attainment of the important goals of the society.

10. If value realization in organizational action is to be maximized, decision making by those exercising authority must view and direct action in the immediate perspective of concrete action. Administration of the conduct of members of an organization as they employ its physical resources is necessary, if value realization is to occur in human affairs. The making and carrying out of plans for such administration are as necessary as they are in the exercise of the leadership function. In both situations, authoritative decisions coordinating future action of members of the organization are made. In administration, they are directed to the production of those tangibles and the provision of those services whereby the realization of values of members and participants will in fact take place.

11. If value realization in organizational action is to be maximized, decision making by those exercising authority must appraise and evaluate past action and insure the direction of future action to maintain certain standards of performance. This is the function of control in an organization. Control insures that both leadership and administration adhere to fixed standards of performance. Such standards may develop as a consequence of competitive necessities, of cultural norms, of individual attitudes and values, and of the experience of the organization itself.

Control may involve simply the feedback of information when organizational action has departed from authoritative direction and the imposition of measures designed to restore such action to stipulated patterns of behavior. Or, more fundamentally, it may involve reflection upon past action of the organization, and weighing, appraising, and evaluating such action from the standpoint of its mechanical efficiency as means to ends or its psychic or value adequacy as a means for value realization by actors in the system of action of the organization. Both of these types of control are exerted over leadership and administrative action. Sometimes

The crucial question, in the relation of rules of law to the space of free movement of an individual, is whether they are perceived to be barriers to the realization of values or as means to attain particular values or to protect attainment of such values. Do they restrict the boundaries of the space of free movement or do they expand those boundaries by providing and safeguarding new avenues for meaningful and valued participation in the life of the society?

The individual is not ideally to be left in a blissful nirvana of suspense, inaction, and contemplation, if justice under law in the culture of the twentieth century is to be achieved. Government and law must constantly raise the individual's level of appreciation. It must, on the one hand, insure that he is educated and trained in the inherited culture of the civilization, so that the potentialities for the expression of his personality will become increasingly meaningful to him. It must, on the other hand, insure that he is provided in constantly expanding measure with opportunities to express his personality and realize his self in concrete action. His space of freedom must become characterized by a constantly increasing ability to participate in the good life afforded by a maturing culture and growing economy. Justice includes participation in constantly expanding measure in the good life, as well as liberty to pursue the good life.

20. The legislative, administrative, and judicial processes establish in varying degree, each according to its own nature and function, a body of legal norms of general application which unite the society and express and preserve its ideal and valued order.

21. Justice in the Communist state assumes an ideal image of order which is much more remote from the values of the day than in the democratically structured state. Justice is embodied in a prescribed or preordained ideal image of societal structure and world order, the attainment of which demands the immediate realization of important values to be foregone in considerable measure. The centrally directed, bureaucratically controlled economy is selected in preference to the market directed, privately controlled economy. Only through such an instrumentality may action be directed to the planned goals. The leadership function looms larger in the functioning of the social order, as action is globally directed to distant ends. Control supported by force, together with other means, such as a state monopoly of communica-

tion, is required to sanction and sustain the extreme exercise of the leadership function.

The performance of the leadership, administrative, and control functions in the Communist state is not closely responsive to cultural values, as they in fact exist in society. Values which ought to exist in man, as he is perceived by an ideology, instead of values which *in fact* exist in man, perceived as a sentient individual and a product of his culture, determine the content of justice. It is the Soviet man, the presumed man of materialism and of dedication to prescribed ideal forms of action in the party, the bureaucracy, the school, and the home, whose values influence decision making in the all pervasive realm of officialdom. Although there is now a fluctuating pattern of relinquishment of the exercise of stern measures of control in the Soviet society, the bold configurations of the above design of social action in the Soviet state still remain.

22. Justice in the democratic state assumes an ideal image of order which is placed in the immediate present and is much more directly related to the values of the day than in the Communist state. Leadership, administration, and control in the democratic state function in a moving equilibrium of value realization in a societal order which requires a minimum of force to support the exercise of authority.

23. In its most universal terms, the degree to which justice is manifest in the state is a product of the extent to which the action of the state, as determined by the legislature, the administration, and the judiciary, enables the realization of values found in the society and the culture in which it functions.

24. The society and the culture in which the state functions is increasingly becoming world-wide in scope. State action expands beyond state borders and its character is increasingly influenced by its external relations. Decision making in the state in the spheres of legislation, administration, and adjudication, however, still continues to function in large measure subject to the constraints imposed by the particularistic attitudes and values of the members of the society of that state. Such constraints affect the exercise of authority over that part of the international society which is found within the state's territorial jurisdiction, or is otherwise subject to its influence or power. The attainment of justice by action in the international sphere is often frustrated as diverse, particularistic value

systems of the internal orders of many states come to bear on decision making affecting action in the international sphere.

The state departs from basic principles of effective organizational action when its internal order reflects value realization of the few instead of the many. It departs from an ideal image of international order when its interaction with other states does not enhance the value realization of all or when it assumes an image of menace to other states instead of a way to important goal attainment. The state will not express the full potentialities of an organization as a way of life until it secures permanence and growth on the basis that its action is directed to value realization of its members and others participating in its system of action.

Authority, as a means for coordinating conduct among states to attain common goals embodying shared values, is largely lacking. It still finds its most significant manifestation in joint state action when it is used to protect the values of survival and dominance through the use of armed force. Agreement, instead of authority, is the primary means for establishing justice in a world of diverse social orders, perspectives, and value systems.

On the other hand, authority based on power and force is used by states not to attain common goals embodying shared values but instead to realize the particularistic values of a single state. In the bipolar power struggle between East and West, power politics clash with power politics, with no ascendancy of the authority of one sphere over another. An extraordinary amount of energy is used not to create an expanded sphere of justice throughout the world but instead to preserve, through the possession of power and force, the division of the world into two spheres and to prevent the absorption or obliteration of one by the other.

Under these conditions, the problem of attaining justice under law in the world society is one of searching for agreement in those areas of interstate activity which will utilize authority to coordinate action to attain goals embodying important and shared values. Agreement then becomes constitutive in nature; it establishes authority to plan and direct action. Instead of being rigidly fixed by the terms of agreement, action of numerous actors now flows, through the exercise of authority, in flexible and changing patterns responsive to environmental change. When such agreement indicates successive stages which expand the area of authority to attain goals of an increasingly significant character, as in the European Common Market, international organization of a viable nature will supplant national systems of authority.

BIBLIOGRAPHY

Adams, R. N., and others. *Social Change in Latin America Today: Its Implications for United States Policy.* New York, 1960.

Amador, F. V. Garcia. *Fourth Report on International Responsibility.* International Law Commission. U.N. Doc. A/CN. 4/119, Feb. 26, 1959.

American Law Institute. *Restatement of the Law of Conflict of Laws.* St. Paul, Minn., 1934.

Anderson, H. H. (ed.). *Creativity and Its Cultivation.* New York, 1959.

Annuaire de l'Institut de Droit International. Brussels, 1877——.

Annual Digest and Reports of International Law Cases. London, 1919-49.

Banfield, E. C. *The Moral Basis of a Backward Society.* Glencoe, Ill., 1958.

Barlow, E. R., and I. T. Wender. *Foreign Investment and Taxation.* Englewood Cliffs, N.J., 1955.

Battifol, H. *Aspects Philosophiques de Droit International Privé.* Paris, 1956.

Beale, J. H. *A Treatise on the Conflict of Laws.* New York, 1935. 3 vols.

Bentham, J. *Principles of Morals and Legislation.* Oxford, 1823.

Berle, A. A., Jr. *Power Without Property.* New York, 1959.

Beutel, F. K. *Some Potentialities of Experimental Jurisprudence as a New Branch of Social Science.* Lincoln, Neb., 1957.

Bidwell, P. W. *Raw Materials: A Study of American Policy.* New York, 1958.

Bodin, J. *The Six Books of the Commonwealth.* Oxford, n.d.

Borchard, E. M. *Diplomatic Protection of Citizens Abroad.* New York, 1915.

Boulding, K. *The Image.* Ann Arbor, Mich., 1956.

de Bracton, H. *De Legibus et Consuetudinibus Angliae.* Woodbine ed. New Haven, Conn., 1922.

Brewster, K., Jr. *Antitrust and American Business Abroad.* New York, 1958.
Brierly, J. L. *The Basis of Obligation in International Law.* Oxford, 1958.
_____. *The Law of Nations, an Introduction to the International Law of Peace.* 5th ed. Oxford, 1955.
_____.*The Outlook for International Law.* Oxford, 1955.
Cardozo, B. N. *Paradoxes of Legal Science.* New York, 1928.
Carlston, K. S. *Law and Structures of Social Action.* London and New York, 1956.
_____. *The Process of International Arbitration.* New York, 1946.
Cheng, B. *General Principles of Law as Applied by International Courts and Tribunals.* London, 1953.
Cheshire, G. C. *Private International Law.* 5th ed. Oxford, 1957.
Cook, W. W. *The Logical and Legal Bases of the Conflict of Laws.* Cambridge, Mass., 1942.
Corbett, P. E. *Law and Diplomacy in the Relations of States.* Princeton, N.J., 1951.
_____. *Law in Diplomacy.* Princeton, N.J., 1959.
_____. *Morals, Law, and Power in International Relations.* Los Angeles, 1956.
Cottrell, F. *Energy and Society: The Relation Between Energy, Social Change and Economic Development.* New York, 1956.
Dawson, J. P. *Unjust Enrichment, a Comparative Analysis.* Boston, 1951.
Déak, F. *The Hungarian-Rumanian Land Dispute.* New York, 1928.
Develle, P. *La Concession en Droit International Public.* Paris, 1936.
Dimock, M. E. *A Philosophy of Administration Toward Creative Growth.* New York, 1958.
Duguit, L. *Law in the Modern State.* New York, 1919.
Dunlop, J. T. *Industrial Relations Systems.* New York, 1958.
Eagleton, C. *The Responsibility of States in International Law.* New York, 1928.
Eells, R. *The Meaning of Modern Business.* New York, 1960.
Ehrenzweig, A. A. *Conflict of Laws.* Vol. 1. St. Paul, Minn., 1959.
Einaudi, M., M. Bye, and E. Rossi. *Nationalization in France and Italy.* Ithaca, N.Y., 1955.
Foighel, I. *Nationalization: A Study in the Protection of Alien Property in International Law.* London, 1957.
Ford, A. W. *The Anglo-Iranian Oil Dispute of 1951-1952.* Berkeley, Calif., 1954.
Fordham, J. B. *A Larger Concept of Community.* Baton Rouge, La., 1956.
Friedman, S. *Expropriation in International Law.* London, 1953.
Friedmann, W. *Law in a Changing Society.* London, 1959.
Friedrich, C. J. (ed.). *Authority.* Cambridge, Mass., 1958.
Fromm, E. *The Sane Society.* New York, 1955.
Fugate, W. L. *Foreign Commerce and the Antitrust Laws.* Boston, 1958.
Gewirth, A. *Marsilius of Padua: The Defender of Peace.* New York, 1957. 2 vols.

Gibb, H. A. R. *Modern Trends in Islam*. Chicago, 1947.

Gould, W. L. *An Introduction to International Law*. New York, 1957.

Great Britain. *Agreement Between His Majesty's Government in the United Kingdom and the Government of Mexico Regarding Compensation in Respect of Expropriated Petroleum Industrial Properties*. Command 6768/1946.

_____. *Correspondence Incorporating the Texts of the Agreement Between the Government of Mexico and the Mexican Eagle Oil Company Regarding Compensation to be Paid in Respect of Expropriated Petroleum Industrial Properties*. Command 7275/1947.

Grotii, H. *De Jure Belli ac Pacis Libri Tres*. 1646 ed. Washington, D.C., 1913.

Grotius, H. *De Jure Belli ac Pacis Libri Tres*. F. W. Kelsey, trans. London, 1925.

Guggenheim, P. *Traité de Droit International Public*. Geneva, 1953.

Haas, E. B., and A. S. Whiting. *Dynamics of International Relations*. New York, 1956.

Haas, W. S. *Iran*. New York, 1946.

Haire, M. (ed.). *Modern Organization Theory*. New York, 1959.

Hanson, S. G. *Economic Development in Latin America*. Washington, D.C., 1951.

Harvard Law School. *Convention on the International Responsibility of States for Injuries to Aliens, Preliminary Draft with Explanatory Notes*. May 1, 1959.

Hirschman, A. O. *The Strategy of Economic Development*. New Haven, Conn., 1958.

Hoffmann, S. H. *Contemporary Theory in International Relations*. Englewood Cliffs, N.J., 1960.

Hyde, C. C. *International Law Chiefly as Interpreted and Applied by the United States*. 2nd rev. ed. Boston, 1945.

International Law Reports. London, 1950____.

Issawi, C. C. *Egypt: An Economic and Social Analysis*. London and New York, 1947.

Jacobini, H. B. *A Study of the Philosophy of International Law as Seen in Works of Latin American Writers*. The Hague, 1954.

Jenks, C. W. *The Common Law of Mankind*. New York, 1958.

Jessup, P. C. *A Modern Law of Nations*. New York, 1948.

_____. *Transnational Law*. New Haven, Conn., 1956.

_____. *The Use of International Law*. Ann Arbor, Mich., 1959.

de Jouvenel, B. *Sovereignty: An Inquiry into the Political Good*. Chicago, 1957.

Kaplan, M. A. *System and Process in International Politics*. New York, 1957.

Katzarov, K. *Théorie de la Nationalisation*. Neuchâtel, Switzerland, 1960.

Kelsen, H. *General Theory of Law and State*. Cambridge, Mass., 1945.

_____. *Principles of International Law*. New York, 1952.

Kuhn, A. K. *Comparative Commentaries on Private International Law*. New York, 1937.

La Fontaine, H. *Pasicrisie International: Histoire Documentaire des Arbitrages Internationaux.* Berne, 1902.

La Pradelle, A., and N. Politis. *Recueil des Arbitrages Internationaux. 1856-1872.* Paris, 1932.

Lauterpacht, E. (ed.). *The Suez Canal Settlement.* London and New York, 1960.

Lauterpacht, H. *The Development of International Law by the International Court.* London, 1958.

_____. *The Function of Law in the International Community.* Oxford, 1933.

_____. *Private Law Sources and Analogies of International Law.* London and New York, 1927.

_____. *Recognition in International Law.* Cambridge, 1947.

League of Nations. *Conference for the Codification of International Law, Bases of Discussion.* Vol. 3, C. 75. M. 69.1929.V.

_____. *The Network of World Trade.* Publications, II, Economic and Financial, 1942, II, A3.

Lee, R. W. *An Introduction to Roman-Dutch Law.* 5th ed. Oxford, 1953.

Lenczowski, G. *The Middle East in World Affairs.* 2nd ed. Ithaca, N.Y., 1956.

_____. *Oil and State in the Middle East.* Ithaca, N.Y., 1960.

Lewin, K. *Resolving Social Conflicts.* New York, 1948.

Lewis, O. *Life in a Mexican Village.* Urbana, Ill., 1951.

Linton, R. (ed.). *The Science of Man in the World Crisis.* New York, 1945.

Maier, N. R. F. *Principles of Human Relations.* New York, 1952.

Maine, H. S. *Ancient Law.* London, Toronto, and New York, 1917.

March, J. G., and H. A. Simon. *Organizations.* New York, 1958.

Mason, E. S. (ed.). *The Corporation in Modern Society.* Cambridge, Mass., 1960.

McDougal, M. S., and others. *Studies in World Public Order.* New Haven, Conn., 1960.

Milliot, L. *Introduction a l'Étude du Droit Musulman.* Paris, 1953.

Moore, J. B. *Digest of International Law.* Washington, D.C., 1906. 7 vols.

_____. *History and Digest of the International Arbitrations to Which the United States Has Been a Party.* Washington, D.C., 1898. 6 vols.

Myrdal, G. *An International Economy: Problems and Prospects.* New York, 1956.

Nadel, S. F. *The Theory of Social Structure.* Glencoe, Ill., 1957.

Nail al-Awtar. Cairo, 1938.

National Bureau of Economic Research. *Capital Formation and Economic Growth.* Princeton, N.J., 1955.

New York University. *Law: A Century of Progress 1835-1935.* Vol. 3. New York, 1937.

Niboyet, J. P. *Traité de Droit International Privé.* Paris, 1947. Vol. 4.

Niemeyer, G. *Law Without Force.* London, England, and Princeton, N.J., 1941.

Northrop, F. S. C. *Philosophical Anthropology and Practical Politics.* New York, 1960.

Nussbaum, A. *A Concise History of the Law of Nations.* 2nd ed. New York, 1954.

———. *Principles of Private International Law.* London, 1943.

Nys, E. *Les Origines du Droit International.* Brussels, 1894.

O'Connell, D. P. *The Law of State Succession.* Cambridge, 1956.

Oppenheim, L. *International Law.* H. Lauterpacht, ed. Vol. 1. 8th ed. London, New York, and Toronto, 1955.

Organski, A. F. K. *World Politics.* New York, 1958.

Parsons, T., R. F. Bales, and E. A. Shils. *Working Papers in the Theory of Action.* Glencoe, Ill., 1953.

———, and E. A. Shils. *Toward a General Theory of Action.* Cambridge, Mass., 1951.

———, and N. J. Smelser. *Economy and Society: A Study in the Integration of Economic and Social Theory.* Glencoe, Ill., 1956.

Peaslee, A. J. *Constitutions of Nations.* 2nd ed. The Hague, 1956.

Plucknett, T. F. T. *A Concise History of the Common Law.* Rochester, N.Y., 1929.

Poincaré, J. H. *The Foundations of Science.* New York, 1913.

Polya, G. *Mathematics and Plausible Reasoning.* Princeton, N.J., 1954. Vol. 1.

Rabel, E. *The Conflict of Laws: A Comparative Study.* Ann Arbor, Mich., 1947. 4 vols.

Ralston, J. H. *Law and Procedure of International Tribunals.* Palo Alto, Calif., 1926.

———. *Venezuelan Arbitrations of 1902.* Sen. Doc. 316, 58th Cong., 2nd Sess. Washington, D.C., 1904.

Reuber, G. L. *The Growth and the Changing Composition of Trade Between Canada and the United States.* Canada, 1960.

Reuter, P. *International Institutions.* J. M. Chapman, trans. London, 1958.

Reynolds, B. *Proponents of Limited Monarchy in Sixteenth Century France: Francis Hotman and Jean Bodin.* New York, 1931.

Rippy, J. F. *British Investment in Latin America, 1822-1949.* Minneapolis, Minn., 1949.

Rose, A. M. *The Institutions of Advanced Societies.* Minneapolis, Minn., 1958.

Rosenne, S. *The International Court of Justice.* Leyden, 1957.

Rousseau, C. *Droit International Public.* Paris, 1953.

Royal Commission on Canada's Economic Prospects. *Preliminary Report.* Ottawa, Dec., 1956.

Royal Institute of International Affairs. *The Middle East: A Political and Economic Survey.* London, 1958.

Rubin, S. J. *Private Foreign Investment.* Baltimore, Md., 1956.

Sandifer, D. V. *Evidence Before International Tribunals.* Chicago, 1939.

Sauer, E. *Grundlehre des Völkerrechts.* 3rd ed. Cologne, 1956.

———. *Souveränitat und Solidarität.* Göttingen, Germany, 1954.

Sauer, W. *System des Völkerrechts—Eine lehrbuch mässige Darstellung.*
Bonn, 1950.
von Savigny, F. C. *A Treatise on the Conflict of Laws.* W. Guthrie, trans.
Edinburgh, Scotland, 1869.
Scelle, G. *Droit International Public: Manuel Élémentaire.* Paris, 1944.
_____. *Précis de Droit des Gens.* Paris, 1934.
Schmitthoff, C. M. *A Textbook of the English Conflict of Laws.* 3rd ed.
London, 1954.
Scott, J. B. *The Hague Conventions and Declarations of 1899 and 1907.*
Oxford, 1915.
Selznick, P. *Leadership in Administration: A Sociological Interpretation.*
Evanston, Ill., and White Plains, N.Y., 1957.
Shannon, L. W. (ed.). *Underdeveloped Areas.* New York, 1957.
Sibert, M. *Traité de Droit International Public.* Paris, 1951.
Sinnott, E. W. *Biology of the Spirit.* New York, 1955.
*Some Opinions, Articles and Reports Bearing upon the Treaty of Trianon
and the Claims of the Hungarian Nationals with Regard to Their
Lands in Transylvania.* London, 1959. 2 vols.
Stein, M. I., and S. J. Heinze. *Creativity and the Individual.* Glencoe,
Ill., 1960.
Tax, S. *Heritage of Conquest.* Glencoe, Ill., 1952.
Tead, O. *Administration: Its Purpose and Performance.* New York, 1959.
_____. *The Importance of Administration in International Action.* Car-
negie Endowment for International Peace, International Conciliation,
no. 407, Jan., 1945.
Teichert, P. C. M. *Economic Policy Revolution and Industrialization in
Latin America.* Oxford, Miss., 1959.
J. Walter Thompson Co. *The Latin American Markets.* New York, 1956.
United Nations Commission on Permanent Sovereignty over Natural Re-
sources. *Historical Summary of Discussions Relating to the Question
of Permanent Sovereignty of Peoples and Nations over Their Natural
Wealth and Resources.* U.N. Doc. A/AC.97/1, May 12, 1959.
_____. *The Status of Permanent Sovereignty over National Wealth and
Resources, Preliminary Study by the Secretariat.* U.N. Doc. A/AC.97/
5, Dec. 15, 1959.
United Nations. *Economic Development of Underdeveloped Countries,
the International Flow of Private Capital, 1957.* U.N. Doc. E/3128,
June 4, 1958.
_____. *The International Flow of Private Capital, 1946-1952.* U.N. Doc.
E/2531 ST/ECA/22, 1954.
_____. Security Council. *Official Records.* 11th year. Oct. 13, 1956.
_____. Security Council. *Official Records.* 11th year. Supp. for Oct., Nov.,
and Dec. U.N. Doc. S/3675, 1956.
_____. *World Economic Survey, 1955.* U.N. Doc. E/2864 ST/ECA/38,
April 27, 1956.
_____. *World Economic Survey, 1958.* U.N. Doc. E/3244 ST/ECA/60,
1959.

United States. *Economic Report of the President.* 86th Cong., 2nd Sess., H.R. Doc. 286. Washington, D.C., 1959.

_____. *Papers Relating to the Foreign Relations of the United States.* Washington, D.C.

_____. Dept. of Commerce. *Investment in Cuba.* Washington, D.C., 1956.

_____. Dept of Commerce, Office of Business Economics. *Foreign Investments of the United States.* Washington, D.C., 1953.

_____. Dept. of Interior, Bureau of Mines. *Mineral Facts and Problems.* Bulletin 556. Washington, D.C., 1956.

_____. Dept. of State. *Report of Bert L. Hunt.* Arb. Ser. 6. Washington, D.C., 1934.

_____. Dept. of State. *The Suez Canal Problem.* July 26–Sept. 22, 1956. Washington, D.C., 1956.

_____. Federal Trade Commission. *A List of 1,000 Large Manufacturing Companies, Their Subsidiaries and Affiliates, 1948.* Washington, D.C., 1951.

_____. Federal Trade Commission. *Report on the Concentration of Productive Facilities, 1947, Total Manufacturing and 26 Selected Industries.* Washington, D.C., 1949.

_____. Senate Committee on Foreign Relations. *Economic, Social and Political Change in the Underdeveloped Countries and Its Implications for United States Policy.* 86th Cong., 2nd Sess., Committee Print 12, March 30, 1960. Washington, D.C.

_____. Senate Committee on Foreign Relations, Sub-Committee on American Republics Affairs. *Problems of Latin American Economic Development.* 86th Cong., 2nd Sess., Committee Print 6, Feb. 11, 1960. Washington, D.C.

_____. Senate Committee on Foreign Relations. *Worldwide and Domestic Economic Problems and Their Impact on the Foreign Policy of the United States.* 86th Cong., 1st Sess., Aug., 1959. Washington, D.C.

_____. Hearings Before the Antitrust Subcommittee (Subcommittee 5) of the House Committee on the Judiciary, House of Representatives. 84th Cong., 1st Sess., May 23–June 6, 1953, ser. 3, pt. 2. Washington, D.C., 1955.

_____. President's Material Policy Commision. *Resources for Freedom.* Washington, D.C., 1952. Vols. 1, 5.

Urwick, L. F. *The Pattern of Management.* Minneapolis, Minn., 1956.

de Vabres, J. Donnedieu. *L'Évolution de la Jurisprudence Francaise en Matière de Conflit de Lois.* Paris, 1938.

Viénot, G. *Nationalisations Étrangères et Intérêts Francais.* Paris, 1953.

de Visscher, C. *Theory and Reality in Public International Law.* P. E. Corbett, trans. Princeton, N.J., 1957. Originally published as *Théories et Réalitiés en Droit International Public.* Paris, 1953.

Voet, J. *Commentarius ad Pandectas.* The Hague and Leyden, 1698 and 1704.

Voskuil, W. *Minerals in World Industry.* New York, 1955.

Wallas, G. *The Art of Thought.* New York, 1926.

Weber, M. *The Theory of Social and Economic Organization*. A. M. Henderson and T. Parsons, trans. New York, 1947.
Weiss, R. S. *Processes of Organization*. Ann Arbor, Mich., 1956.
White, G. M. *Nationalization of Foreign Property*. London, 1961.
Whiteman, M. M. *Damages in International Law*. Vol. 3. Washington, D.C., 1943.
Whyte, W. H., Jr. *The Organization Man*. New York, 1956.
Wilber, D. N. *Iran: Past and Present*. Princeton, N.J., 1955.
Wolff, M. *Private International Law*. 2nd ed. Oxford, 1950.
Wortley, B. A. *Expropriation in Public International Law*. Cambridge, 1959.
Wright, Q. *The Study of International Relations*. New York, 1955.
Young, R. (ed.). *Approaches to the Study of Politics*. Evanston, Ill., 1958.
Zouche, R. *Juris et Judicii Fecialis sive Juris inter Gentes, et Questionum de Eodem Explicatio*. J. L. Brierly, trans. Washington, D.C., 1911.

ARTICLES

Adelman, M. A. "The Measurement of Industrial Concentration," 33 *Review of Economics and Statistics* 269 (1951).
Ago, R. "Positive Law and International Law," 51 *Am. J. Int. Law* 691 (1957).
———. "Science Juridique et Droit International," Académie de Droit International, 90 *Recueil des Cours* 857 (1956, pt. 2).
Association of the Bar of the City of New York, Committee on International Law. "A Reconsideration of the Acts of State Doctrine in United States Courts" (1959).
Beale, J. H. "The Jurisdiction of a Sovereign State," 36 *Harv. L. Rev.* 241 (1923).
Beals, R. L. "Social Stratification in Latin America," 58 *American Journal of Sociology* 327 (1953).
Beauvois, J. J. "Internationalism: A New Concept for U.S. Business," 2 *California Management Review* 28 (Winter, 1960).
Bohlen, C. E. "Economic Assistance in Foreign Policy," 42 Dept. of State Bulletin 495 (March 28, 1960).
Brierly, J. L. "Le Fondement du Charactère Obligatoire du Droit International," Académie de Droit International, 23 *Recueil des Cours* 549 (1928, pt. 3).
Briggs, H. W. "The Settlement of Mexican Claims Act of 1942," 37 *Am. J. Int. Law* 222 (1943).
Cámara, F. "Religious and Political Organization," in S. Tax, *Heritage of Conquest*, 142.
Campbell, N. J., Jr. "Principles of Mineral Ownership in the Civil Law and the Common Law Systems," 31 *Tulane L. Rev.* 303 (1957).
Carlston, K. S. "Antitrust Policy Abroad," 49 *Northwestern U. L. Rev.* 569 (1954).
———. "The Grasp of Jurisdiction," *Proceedings of the American Society of International Law* 170 (1959).

_____. "International Administrative Law: A Venture in Legal Theory," 8 *Journal of Public Law* 321 (1959).

_____. "Nationalization: An Analytical Approach," 54 *Northwestern U. L. Rev.* 405 (1959).

Cavers, D. F. "A Critique of the Choice-of-Law Problem," 47 *Harv. L. Rev.* 173 (1933).

Cheatham, E. E., and W. L. M. Reese. "Choice of the Applicable Law," 52 *Colum. L. Rev.* 959 (1952).

Cheng, B. "Expropriation in International Law," 21 *The Solicitor* 98 (1954).

"Choice of Law by Contractual Stipulation," 16 *U. Chi. L. Rev.* (note) 157 (1948).

"Compensation for Petroleum Properties Expropriated in Mexico." 9 Dept. of State Bulletin 230 (1943).

Currie, B. "The Constitution and the Choice of Law; Governmental Interests and the Judicial Function," 26 *U. Chi. L. Rev.* 9 (1958).

_____. "On the Displacement of the Law of the Forum," 58 *Colum. L. Rev.* 964 (1958).

Davies, D. J. Llewellyn. "The Influence of Huber's *De Conflictu Legum* on English Private International Law," 18 *British Yearbook of International Law* 49 (1937).

Delsen, R. "Nationalization of the Suez Canal Company: Issues of Public and Private International Law," 57 *Colum. L. Rev.* 755 (1957).

Dennis, W. C. "Compromise—The Great Defect of Arbitration," 11 *Colum. L. Rev.* 493 (1911).

Doman, N. R. "Postwar Nationalization of Foreign Property in Europe," 48 *Colum. L. Rev.* 1125 (1948).

Domke, M. "American Protection Against Foreign Expropriation in the Light of the Suez Canal Crisis," 105 *U. Pa. Law Rev.* 1033 (1957).

_____. "Indonesian Nationalization Measures Before Foreign Courts," 54 *Am. J. Int. Law* 305 (1960).

Dorsey, G. L. "Chinese Recognition: Law and Policy in Perspective," 23 *U. Pitt. L. Rev.* 17 (1961).

Drucker, A. "Compensation for Nationalized Property: The British Practice," 49 *Am. J. Int. Law* 477 (1955).

_____. "On Compensation Treaties Between Communist States," 229 *Law Times* 279 (1960).

Ehrenzweig, A. A. "The *Lex Fori*—Basic Rule in the Conflict of Laws," 58 *Mich. L. Rev.* 637 (1960).

Farmanfarma, A. "The Oil Agreement Between Iran and the International Oil Consortium: The Law Controlling," 34 *Texas L. Rev.* 259 (1955).

Fawcett, J. E. S. "Some Foreign Effects of Nationalization of Property," 27 *British Yearbook of International Law* 355 (1950).

de la Fuente, J. "Ethnic and Communal Relations," in S. Tax, *Heritage of Conquest,* 76.

Gardot, A. "Jean Bodin: Sa Place parmi les Fondateurs de Droit International," Académie de Droit International, 50 *Recueil des Cours* 545 (1934, pt. 4).

Ghosh, S. K. "The Anglo-Iranian Oil Dispute." Doctoral thesis, Urbana, Ill., 1956.

Gidynski, J. C. "Duguit's Approach to the Bases of International Law," 31 *Iowa L. Rev.* 599 (1946).

Gillin, J. "Ethos and Cultural Aspects of Personality," in S. Tax, *Heritage of Conquest,* 193.

Guldberg, T. "International Concessions, a Problem of International Economic Law," 15 *Acta Scandinavica Juris Gentium* 47 (1944).

———. "International Concessions, a Problem of International Economic Law," 25 *Acta Scandinavica Juris Gentium* 18 (1955).

Gutzwiler, M. "Le Développement Historique de Droit International Privé," Académie de Droit International, 29 *Recueil des Cours* 291 (1929, pt. 4).

Harvard Research in International Law. "Draft Convention on Responsibility of States," 23 *Am. J. Int. Law* (spec. supp.) 133 (1929).

Hazard, J. N. "The General Principles of Law," 52 *Am. J. Int. Law* 96 (1958).

Herz, J. H. "Expropriation of Foreign Property," 35 *Am. J. Int. Law* 243 (1941).

Hjerner, L. A. E. "The General Approach to Foreign Confiscations," 2 *Scandinavian Studies in Law* 177 (1958).

Holmes, O. W., Jr. "The Path of Law," 10 *Harv. L. Rev.* 457 (1897).

Huang, T. T. F. "Some International and Legal Aspects of the Suez Canal Question," 51 *Am. J. Int. Law* 277 (1957).

Huber, M. "Die Soziologischen Gründlagen des Völkerrechts," 2 *Internationalrechtliche Abhandlungen* (Berlin-Grunewald, 1928).

Hyde, C. C. "Compensation for Expropriations," 33 *Am. J. Int. Law* 108 (1939).

———. "Confiscatory Expropriation," 32 *Am. J. Int. Law* 758 (1938).

Hyde, J. N. "Permanent Sovereignty over Natural Wealth and Resources," 50 *Am. J. Int. Law* 854 (1956).

Ionides, M. "Technical Aid: The Role of the West," 35 *International Affairs* 151 (1959).

Johns, R. W. "Observations on Law in the Americas Relating to Hard Minerals," paper delivered before Conference on Natural Resources, Inter-American Bar Assoc. April 18, 1956.

Katzarov, K. "The Validity of the Act of Nationalisation in International Law," 22 *Mod. L. Rev.* 639 (1959).

de B. Katzenbach, N. "Conflicts on an Unruly Horse: Reciprocal Claims and Tolerances in Interstate and International Law," 65 *Yale L. J.* 1087 (1956).

Kluckhohn, C., and W. H. Kelly. "The Concept of Culture," in R. Linton, ed., *The Science of Man in the World Crisis.*

———, and others. "Values and Value-Orientations in the Theory of Action," in T. Parsons and E. A. Shils, *Toward a General Theory of Action.*

Kosters, J. "Les Fondements du Droit des Gens," 4 *Bibliotheca Visseriana* 1 (1925).

Kunz, J. L. "The Mexican Expropriations," 17 *N. Y. U. Law Q. Rev.* 327 (1940).

Landheer, B. "Les Theories de la Sociologie Contemporaine et le Droit International," Académie de Droit International, 92 *Recueil des Cours* 525 (1957, pt. 2).

———. "Contemporary Sociological Theories and International Law," Académie de Droit International, 91 *Recueil des Cours* 7 (1957, pt. 1).

Lauterpacht, H. "Codification and Development of International Law," 49 *Am. J. Int. Law* 16 (1955).

Levy, M. J., Jr. "Some Social Obstacles to Capital Formation in 'Underdeveloped Areas,'" in National Bureau of Economic Research, *Capital Formation and Economic Growth*. Princeton, N.J., 1955.

Levy, W. J. "Issues in International Oil Policy," 35 *Foreign Affairs* 454 (1957).

Lind, J. H. "Strategic Materials We Must Depend Upon from Outside Sources," 103 *Magazine of Wall Street* 237 (1958).

Mann, F. A. "The Sacrosanctity of the Foreign Act of State" (pts. 1, 2), 59 *L. Q. Rev.* 42, 155 (1943).

———. "State Contracts and State Responsibility," 54 *Am. J. Int. Law* 573 (1960).

———. "The Law Governing State Contracts," 21 *British Yearbook of International Law* 11 (1944).

———. "The Proper Law of Contract," 3 *Int. L. Q.* 60 (1950).

Masterson, W. D., Jr. "A Comparative Study of Laws Affecting the Production and Development of Oil and Gas in the Americas," paper delivered before the Inter-American Bar Assoc., April, 1956.

Mathers, B. "The British Columbian," in R. E. Watters, ed., *British Columbia: A Centennial Anthology*, 481. Vancouver, B.C., 1958.

McDougal, M. S., and H. D. Lasswell. "The Identification and Appraisal of Diverse Systems of Public Order," 53 *Am. J. Int. Law* 1 (1959).

———. "International Law, Power and Policy: A Contemporary Conception," Académie de Droit International, 82 *Recueil des Cours* 137 (1953, pt. 1).

McNair, Lord. "The Seizure of Property and Enterprises in Indonesia," 6 *Nederlands Tidschrift voor Internationaal Recht* 219 (1959).

Meijers, E. M. "L'Histoire des Principes Fondamentaux de Droit International Privé a Partir du Moyen Age," Académie de Droit International, 49 *Recueil des Cours* 547 (1934, pt. 3).

Morgenstern, F. "Recognition and Enforcement of Foreign Legislative, Administrative and Judicial Acts Which Are Contrary to International Law," 4 *Int. L. Q.* 326 (1951).

Murdock, G. P. "The Common Denominator of Cultures," in R. Linton, ed., *The Science of Man in the World Crisis*, 123. New York, 1945.

Northrop, F. S. C. "Underhill Moore's Legal Science: Its Nature and Significance," 59 *Yale L. J.* 196 (1950).

Nussbaum, A. "The Arbitration Between the Lena Goldfields, Ltd. and the Soviet Government," 36 *Cornell Law Q.* 31 (1950).

_____. "Rise and Decline of the Law-of-Nations Doctrine in the Conflict of Laws," 42 *Colum. L. Rev.* 189 (1942).

O'Connell, D. P. "A Critique of Iranian Oil Litigation," 4 *Int. and Comp. Law Q.* 267 (1955).

_____. "The Relationship Between International Law and Municipal Law," 48 *Georgetown L. J.* 431 (1960).

Olmstead, C. J. "Nationalization of Foreign Property Interests, Particularly Those Subject to Agreements with the State," 32 *N.Y.U. Law Rev.* 1122 (1956).

Parsons, T. "Suggestions for a Sociological Approach to a Theory of Organizations," 1 *Administrative Science Quarterly* 63 (1956).

Pizer, S., and F. Cutler, "Capital Flow to Foreign Countries Slackens," U.S. Dept. of Commerce, *Survey of Current Business* 25, Aug., 1959.

Pound, R. "Philosophical Theory and International Law," 1 *Bibliotheca Visseriana* 73 (Leyden, 1923).

Re, E. D. "Nationalization of Foreign Owned Property," 36 *Minn. L. Rev.* 323 (1952).

Rheinstein, M. Book review, 28 *Ind. L. J.* 443 (1953).

Rolin, H. "Opinion," 6 *Nederlands Tidschrift voor Internationaal Recht* 260 (1959).

Rubin, S. J. "Nationalization and Compensation: A Comparative Approach," 17 *U. Chi. L. Rev.* 458 (1950).

Sack, A. N. "Conflicts of Laws in the History of the English Law," in New York University, *Law: A Century of Progress 1835-1935.* Vol. 3, p. 342.

Samore, W. "The New International Law of Alejandro Alvarez," 52 *Am. J. Int. Law* 41 (1958).

Sarraute, R., and P. Tager. "Hier et aujourd'hui. Les effects en France des nationalisations étrangères," 79 *Journal de Droit International (Clunet)* 1138 (1952).

Sayres, W. C. "Disorientation and Status Change," 12 *Southwestern Journal of Anthropology* 79 (1956).

Schindler, D. "Contribution a l'Étude des Facteurs Sociologiques du Droit International," Académie de Droit International, 46 *Receuil des Cours* 233 (1933, pt. 4).

Schlesinger, R. B. "Research on the General Principles of Law Recognized by Civilized Nations," 51 *Am. J. Int. Law* 735 (1957).

Seidl-Hohenveldern, I. "Communist Theories on Confiscation and Expropriation, Critical Comments," 7 *Am. J. Comp. Law* 541 (1958).

_____. "Extraterritorial Effects of Confiscations and Expropriations," 49 *Mich. L. Rev.* 851 (1951).

_____. "Probleme des internationalen Konfiskations und Enteignungsrechtes," 83 *Journal de Droit International (Clunet)* 380 (1956).

Silberman, C. E., and L. A. Mayer, "The Migration of U.S. Capital," 57 *Fortune* 125 (Jan., 1958).

Simons, W. "La Conception du Droit International Privé d'après la Doctrine et la Pratique en Allemagne," Académie du Droit International, 15 *Recueil des Cours* 437 (1926, pt. 5).

Smith, G. H. "The English Analytical Jurists," 21 *Am. L. Rev.* 270 (1887).

Stern, D. S. "The Conflict of Laws in Commercial Arbitration," 17 *Law and Contemp. Prob.* 566 (1952).

Stevenson, J. R. "The Relationship of Private International Law to Public International Law," 52 *Colum. L. Rev.* 561 (1952).

Stone, J. "Problems Confronting Sociological Enquiries Concerning International Law," Académie de Droit International, 89 *Recueil des Cours* 66 (1956, pt. 1).

———. "On the Vocation of the International Law Commission," 57 *Colum. L. Rev.* 16 (1957).

Tax, S. "Economy and Ethnology," in S. Tax, *Heritage of Conquest,* 43.

van Hecke, G. A. "Confiscation, Expropriation and the Conflict of Laws," 4 *Int. L. Q.* 345 (1951).

Verdross, A. "Die Sicherung von ausländischen Privatrechten aus Abkommen zur wirtschaftlichen Entwicklung mit Schiedklauseln," 18 *Zeitschrift für ausländisches öffentliches Recht und Völkerrecht* 635 (1958), translated under the title of "The Status of Foreign Private Interests Stemming from Economic Development Agreements with Arbitration Clauses," 9 *Österr. Zeitschrift für öffentliches Recht* 449 (1959).

Voskuil, W. "The Strategic Position of Iron Ore in the Economy of the Atlantic Basin Nations," *Illinois Engineer* (Nov., 1956).

Wagley, C., and M. Harris. "A Typology of Latin American Subcultures," 57 *American Anthropologist* 428 (1955).

Wehberg, H. "Pacta Sunt Servanda," 53 *Am. J. Int. Law* 775 (1959).

Wolf, E. R. "Types of Latin American Peasantry: A Preliminary Discussion," 57 *American Anthropologist* 452 (1955).

Woolsey, L. H. "The United States–Mexican Settlement," 36 *Am. J. Int. Law* 117 (1942).

Wortley, B. A. "Expropriation in International Law," 33 *Grotius Society Transactions* 25 (1947).

———. "The Interaction of Public and Private International Law Today," Académie de Droit International, 85 *Recueil des Cours* 245 (1954, pt. 1).

Wright, Q. "The Teaching of International Law in the Post-War World," *Proceedings of the Eighth Conference of Teachers of International Law and Related Subjects.* Washington, D.C., 1946.

Yntema, H. E. "The Historic Bases of Private International Law," 2 *Am. J. Comp. Law* 297 (1953).

decision making in the exercise of such control functions is vested in persons directly concerned with the exercise of the leadership function or the administrative function. Sometimes it is vested in persons occupying roles or posts outside the spheres of such functions. In the latter case, such persons are typically found in the accounting or legal departments of private business organizations.

12. The function of control in the state is primarily performed by the judicial process. The "enforcement of law" is a function carried out by the judicial process. Control is also exercised in the performance of the legislative and administrative processes in order to insure that goals are reached according to plan and also in order to reshape future action in the light of experience.

13. The performance of the function of control by the judicial process in the state is unique in organizational action in the degree to which it operates as a means for solving interpersonal conflict as well as a means for norm creation and norm enforcement. To appreciate the place of the judicial process in the organizational functioning of the state, it is necessary to understand the meaning of legal norms in terms of values.

14. In its most universal terms, law is a statement of the patterns to which action must adhere in order to express an idea. Action which is disorganized, random, fleeting, and erratic has no meaning. It must adhere to the patterns of action embodied in an idea if that idea is to be expressed in action.

15. A legal norm is a statement of an ideal pattern of action which is socially valued to the degree that departure from such pattern of action may be expected to lead to measures of control designed to restore the deviant action to the ideal pattern of action. In both primitive societies and advanced societies there are ideal norms of conduct which are so highly prized and which bear such importance to the members of the society that group measures of control in the primitive society, or institutionalized measures of control in the advanced society, will be resorted to in order to control deviations. The expectation of the members of the society that such measures of control will be applied to deviant conduct operates to inhibit the occurrence of such conduct, as well as to restore future conduct to adherence to the established norm.

16. The judicial process operates to maximize value realization by the members of the society in part through resolving value conflict arising from conflicting individual or group demands, which

are statable in terms of the applicability of legal norms to a situation of interpersonal conflict. Acceptance by the members of the society of the principle of third-party decision or adjudication by a judicial body, as a means of conflict solving, is a necessary condition for the appearance and maintenance of the judicial process.

The friction and tension arising from the denial of important expectations and the frustration of the realization of values, when an actor departs from the ideal and valued norm of behavior which is a legal norm, must be alleviated and the appearance of aggressive responses to such stimuli must be controlled, if value realization by the members of a society is to be maximized. Stated otherwise, cases of trouble, which reflect value deprivation and are a potential source of agression in the society and arise out of deviance from valued norms of behavior, must be handled if the society is to go its way with a minimum of friction and value impairment. This task of control in society is performed by the judicial process. The judicial process operates to control future action and to restore it to the performance of ideal and valued norms, when there has been a departure therefrom, in considerable measure through the imposition of the obligation of a reparation upon the violator of a legal norm. Reparation has a number of functions. Reparation by the deviant performer creates a new equilibrium or substitute *status quo ante* by repairing the denial of an expectation of the injured party that performance of the norm would be forthcoming and the advantage, benefit, or value realization of such performance would be experienced. The disturbed balance in the relations of the parties to the litigation is largely restored and there is a feeling by the aggrieved party, as well as by others in the society who view the situation, that "justice has been done." Such a payment also operates to create a greater likelihood that the deviant performer and others in the society at large will thereafter adhere to the legal norm. It has been tested and its continuing validity has been affirmed by a court.

17. The judicial process operates to maximize value realization by the members of a society in part through the creation of legal norms in its decision making. Such norm creation activity must take place consistently with the approved method of rational and gradual extension of the existing body of legal norms known as *stare decisis*, or adherence to precedent.

Situations of interpersonal conflict are brought to the courts because conflict exists between the litigants as to the applicability of different legal norms. In the resolution of that conflict, and faithful to the principle of *stare decisis,* the courts will from time to time discern in the situation before them elements which require a refashioning or extension of a prior legal norm. The consequence will be a decision creatively stating a new ideal form of action which, as a new legal norm, becomes an authoritative and sanctioned statement of the patterns to which action thereafter shall adhere in similar situations arising in the life of the society.

18. Justice viewed in terms of the content of action in a world of change entails a view of the individual as not being a mechanistic structure or creature of predictable responses to stimuli. It involves a view of man, in the existentialist perspective, as open to the world about him, open to his culture, and open to his future. It looks upon man as a creative person, influenced by values and aware of time as he acts. It assumes that experience, as a guide to the content of the good life, is constantly modified and enlarged, as man learns more and more about himself and the world in which he *moves*—and not solely *exists.*

If law is to be consonant with justice, it must always be open to change and respond to change in man and his culture. It must be faithful to man's view of himself and the world about him—a view which is constantly changing as a consequence of experience and cultural change.

While the legislative process is uniquely concerned with solving the problem of justice in the perspective of the maximization of values in the largest dimension of future time, the executive and judicial processes must also in their own spheres similarly be aware of and respond to changing perspectives, attitudes, and values in the culture. The executive of the mid-twentieth century learns that participation in the decision-making process by workers reflects value realization which enhances the effective exercise of authority. The judge of the mid-twentieth century is aware that blind, logical, mechanistic adherence to prior precedent creates a rigid legal system which departs farther and farther from the ideal image of law which is in fact held by the members of society. The judge in the mid-twentieth century is aware that his function of control must be creatively exercised and that he must upon occasion overrule, as well as distinguish, prior precedent.

In the course of history, the judicial process has relied upon legal fictions and equity, as well as norm creation subject to the precepts of *stare decisis,* to mold law so that it will continually reflect justice in a world of change. Criminal law, for example, ceases to be primarily a law of retribution for and deterrence of criminal action and moves toward an administration of criminal justice which is aware of the problems of the individual personality of the criminal and has the objective of rehabilitation as well as punishment.

The operation of the judicial process, as a means of preserving, on the one hand, and constantly reviewing and revising, on the other hand, the rules of conduct which best express the society's current ideal image of its order, is subject to the following basic postulates:

1. The function of the judicial process, as a norm-enforcing and norm-creating process, is to resolve situations of interpersonal conflict which are capable of being characterized in terms of the applicability thereto of legal norms.

2. The judge's area of freedom, in the exercise of such function, is limited to alternative choices in the selection of rules and interpretation of facts marked out in the course of the adversary process and otherwise rationally available to him, consistent with the precepts and standards of judicial reasoning in the legal system.

3. The judge must be faithful to postulate 2 in selecting or creating those norms which will best express the society's ideal image of its order.

19. The problem of achieving justice under law is no longer a problem statable solely in terms of liberty or freedom. It is a problem of an order in which liberty or freedom has two dimensions. One of these is the traditional dimension of securing the maximum space of free movement for individuals in a society. The other dimension is the creation and maintenance of goals to the attainment of which individual action may be directed in order to realize values.

The space of free movement becomes meaningful to an individual not merely because its boundaries are remote and it is characterized by a minimum of restraint and a maximum of freedom or liberty. Its importance is enhanced when an individual's ability to act, to enjoy, and to appreciate is enhanced, and when the opportunity to realize an enlarging set of meaningful, individual values is constantly increased.